THE JOAN ROBINSON LEGACY

THE JOAN ROBINSON LEGACY

Ingrid H. Rima, editor

M. E. Sharpe, Inc.
Armonk, New York · London, England

Available in the United Kingdom and Europe from M. E. Sharpe, Publishers, 3 Henrietta Street, London WC2E 8LU.

Library of Congress Cataloging-in-Publication Data

The Joan Robinson legacy / edited by Ingrid H. Rima.
p. cm.
Includes bibliographical references and index.
ISBN 0-87332-611-3
1. Robinson, Joan, 1903– . 2. Economists—Great Britain
I. Rima, Ingrid Hahne, 1925– .
HB103.R63J65 1991
330.1'092—dc20 90-28932
CIP

Printed in the United States of America

MV 10 9 8 7 6 5 4 3 2 1

Remembering
Sid Weintraub and Al Eichner
who were too soon taken from us

JR

CONTENTS

JR

PREFACE

This collection has had, as is no doubt typically the case, a longer gestation period than was anticipated when the project was conceived. Along the way I have reaped a bountiful intellectual harvest from my fellow authors, who were undaunted by the voluminous correspondence that emerged as we undertook to clarify our respective ideas. I thank them not only for the enthusiasm with which they responded to my invitation to participate, but also for their generosity in sharing their ideas with me and one another. A special word of thanks is surely due to Geoff Harcourt who, while he is not a contributor to this volume, helped in numerous ways to "get me settled in" during my first Cambridge visit. It was he who directed me to Dr. Michael Halls, curator of the King's College Archives, whom I thank for so graciously accommodating my greatly time-constrained schedule for studying the Robinson papers. The usual caveat, of course, applies. Their assistance absolves them from responsibility for whatever shortcomings may become apparent in the final product.

While an anthology such as this does not generally seek distinction for its bibliography, the present collection is an exception. I am particularly pleased to be able to include a bibliography that is the product of several years of research by Maria Cristina Marcuzzo. Marcuzzo's Joan Robinson bibliography had already been circulating informally among Robinson scholars, who had called my attention to it when I was beginning the present collection. Because it was not yet complete, she initially hesitated to make it available for publication. However, good fortune later brought Marcuzzo from Italy to Harvard University, where she was able to complete her mammoth cataloging effort. Robinson scholars everywhere will profit from her painstaking work.

I am also pleased to acknowledge the assistance of American Friends of Joan Robinson for providing the dust jacket photo.

Ingrid H. Rima
February 1991

JR

CONTRIBUTORS

Krishna Bharadwaj, School of Sciences, Jawaharlal Nehru University, New Delhi, India

Meyer Burstein, York University, Downsview, Ontario, Canada

Phyllis Deane, Professor Emeritus, Newnham College, Cambridge University, Cambridge, England

Harvey Gram, Queens College, City University of New York, Flushing, New York

Omar F. Hamouda, Glendon College, York University, Canada

Geoffrey M. Hodgson, Newcastle upon Tyne Polytechnic, Newcastle upon Tyne, England

Hans E. Jensen, Professor Emeritus, University of Tennessee, Knoxville, Tennessee

J. A. Kregel, University of Bologna, Bologna Center, Italy

Chidem Kurdas, Fitchburg State College, Fitchburg, Massachusetts

David Laibman, Brooklyn College, Brooklyn, New York

Larry Levine, University of New Brunswick, Fredericton, New Brunswick, Canada

Brian J. Loasby, Professor Emeritus, University of Sterling, Sterling, Scotland

Maria Cristina Marcuzzo, Universita Degli Studi Di Modena, Italy

J. S. Metcalfe, University of Manchester, Manchester, England

Edward M. Miller, University of New Orleans, New Orleans, Louisiana

Edward J. Nell, New School for Social Research, New York, New York

Ingrid H. Rima, Temple University, Philadelphia, Pennsylvania

Ian Steedman, University of Manchester, Manchester, England

Marjorie S. Turner, Professor Emeritus, San Diego State University, San Diego, California

THE JOAN ROBINSON LEGACY

JR

CHAPTER ONE

Introduction

INGRID H. RIMA

A second and more substantial wave of Joan Robinson tributes is now crowding upon the earlier and, understandably, briefer expressions of intellectual admiration and personal affection that marked her death the summer before her 80th birthday.[1] These undertakings are testimony to the professional legacy Robinson left behind.[2] Most economists know at least something of her work and the folklore that has come to surround it: her irreverence for established theory, her seemingly unquenchable zest for intellectual argument, doggedly pursued on the conviction that she was at least *morally* right, the sharpness of her wit (and often her tongue), along with her occasionally unconventional mode of dress and her enjoyment of nature. These are the aspects of the Robinson *persona* that made her something of a legend in her own time. Less well known is the depth of the despair she felt toward the end of her days and her disillusionment about the economics profession and her fellow economists. The source of her acute negativism was that despite her best efforts to give direction to the profession's perception of "What are the questions?" the majority (an important segment of which she lambasted as "bastard Keynesians") not only resisted her persuasions regarding the essentials of Keynes's revolution but, on many an occasion, responded in kind to the tone of her adversarial style.

Yet, less than a decade after her death the magnitude of the intellectual legacy she left is becoming more clearly defined even though it is not manifesting itself either in firm agreement about "What are the questions?" or in "coherence" in the thinking of those dissenting from the mainstream.[3]

The discord between Robinson and the mainstream mounted as the neoclassical synthesis swept over the profession during the 1960s. Especially after she vacated her Chair in Economics in the Faculty of Economics and Politics of the University of Cambridge in 1971 at age sixty-eight, much of her time and energy was given over to trying to stem its tide. Reflecting back on the decade of the 1950s at Cambridge, when the Keynesian revolution was being consolidated and expanded, her agenda for the 1970s became what she saw as the ongoing challenge to reeducate those whom she held responsible for returning economics to its pre-Keynes status because they perpetuated neoclassical approaches to economic theory. The invitation of the American Economic Association in 1971 to give the Richard T. Ely Lecture, during the presidency of John Kenneth Galbraith, provided a unique and undoubtedly sweet opportunity to reiterate her message that economics was in the throes of a "second crisis." Equally sweet must have been the delivery, in the same year, of the Presidential address to Section F (Economic Studies) of the British Association for the Advancement of Science. There were other honors: the University of Manchester Special Lectures in Economics in 1974; the delivery of the commencement address at the University of Maine entitled "Morality and Economics" when she was seventy-one; her lecture at the Scarborough Campus of the University of Toronto in 1978, her honorary Doctor of Laws degree from Harvard in 1980, followed in the same year by her Notre Dame lecture on "Inflation and the Economic Crisis"; in 1981, the Tanner Lecture on Human Values at the University of Utah; and on her final American visit in 1982, her fellowship at Williams College. The honors were many. Yet they failed to assuage the bitter disappointment that the Keynesian message she distilled and refined over the years was bearing such limited fruit, especially at MIT and Harvard.

But she was not without champions, apostles, and kindred spirits, not all of whom were Keynesians. Besides Richard Kahn, Michal Kalecki, and Nicholas Kaldor, these were chiefly drawn from among their former pupils (which included a handful of Americans, Canadians, and Italians). Among the Americans, Sidney Weintraub, in particular, and later his students, eventually became the vanguard of the American post-Keynesian tradition. This group has taken on (with differences, of course) Robinson's intellectual mantle. They have not only reiterated the Robinsonian critique of the mainstream (as have followers of Michal Kalecki and Piero Sraffa, though with important differences), but more importantly, they have developed an alternative paradigm to which Robinson was in large measure eventually willing to subscribe.[4] Thus, toward the end of her life she was also accorded extraordinary respect, admiration, and even affection from that segment of the economics profession, much of it American, that sought her out.

This seems not to have been enough. Robinson became increasingly agitated that the majority of the profession subscribed to the neo-Walrasian paradigm, and that she had not made converts at the power seats of MIT and Harvard, for that was the task she seemed to have assigned herself. That she departed this life without the great intellectual victory she sought is sad, though there was surely hubris in the role into which she cast herself. Yet, the present "second wave" of Robinson tributes less than ten years after her death is testimony to the magnitude of her post-Keynesian legacy. Her intellectual message has, indeed, gotten through, even if it has not been with the thunder-roll she so badly wanted. The present collection of essays celebrates Robinson's great intellectual legacy, not only in laying the foundation for the post-Keynesian paradigm, but as a harbinger of the "other half" of Keynes's revolution.

Unlike other current appreciations, which include tributes from the great and the near great of our profession, the present collection has a relatively narrow focus. It is neither an intellectual biography nor does it undertake to reexamine, from her Cambridge days forward, the details of Robinson's long career. It remembers Joan far less on the basis of the close intellectual contact that was possible for Cambridge colleagues of the same generation or even one removed from it. Rather, it remembers Joan on the basis of the permanent legacy of her substantial literary output, enlivened, of course, by an oral tradition of remembrances but only a few personal contacts with Mrs. Robinson herself. The authors of the present collection came to intellectual maturity long after the famous "struggle to escape" from Marshall and Pigou of the Robinson-Keynes generation. They are, so to speak, "second-generation" and even "third-generation" post-Keynesians. If they also endured a struggle to escape, it was from the neo-Walrasian synthesis that dominated (and still dominates) the profession. But most of the authors who have contributed to this volume imbibed the orthodox critique early on, having studied either with Robinson herself before she retired in 1971 or with someone whose thinking Robinson substantially influenced, in particular, Lorie Tarshis or Sidney Weintraub. They thus take as their starting point the view that Walrasian equilibrium models cannot provide a viable microeconomic foundation for Keynes's macroeconomics.[5] Indeed, it is a common thread of the present collection of essays that their authors implicitly eschew the contemporary micro/macro dichotomy as a matter of principle. Though most recognize that the assumption of perfect competition underlies the *General Theory*, the need for microfoundations that are realistic in the sense of incorporating increasing returns and imperfect competition is recognized as basic. For this, Robinson taught them they could draw on the work of Michal Kalecki (though Weintraub documents his independent development of the mark-up equation) and on recent research by industrial organization economists.[6] Their chief concern is thus to understand the economic problems of the real world as it moves ahead into the 1990s.

The contemporary monetary economies the present group of authors perceive are highly oligopolized and confront a future that is uncertain in the Keynes-Shackle sense. Thus, the pure competition, perfect-foresight, neutral-money models of the mainstream are thought to contribute little to our understanding, especially with respect to the phenomenon of economic growth that must be understood in an historical context as an ongoing process of erratic change. Markets—especially labor markets—do not automatically clear, so that unemployment may not only persist but is likely to become exacerbated by conventional "tight money" efforts to control inflation. Moreover, the problem of inflation emerges essentially as a struggle over relative income shares. Post-Keynesians of all persuasions generally agree that mass unemployment is neither the result of rational preferences to "consume" leisure, nor the painful price that must be paid if a sick economy is to "recover." There is, of course, much disagreement among Keynesians about policy, especially as it relates to coping with inflation and unemployment.

Given the common threads articulated above, these essays have allowed each author to develop a refinement, extension or clarification of some aspect of their view of the Robinsonian message. The authors were given wide latitude. The editor dictated neither the specific topic to be explored nor that the treatment of the chosen topic conform to a preconceived standard of "Robinsonian economics." Thus, all of the variants of alternative post-Keynesian formulations—American post-Keynesian, post-Kalecki, post-Sraffa, post-Marx, post-Shackle, and post-Institutionalist—have gained admission as also building on Robinson's legacy.[7] There is a clearly discernible body of concepts and principles that reflects Robinson's intellectual concerns especially over the last twenty years of her lifetime, which coincides with the intellectual maturation of the second- and third-generation post-Keynesian scholars who contributed to this volume.

The first chapter is, quite fittingly, an autobiographical appreciation written by Phyllis Deane at the time of Robinson's death in 1983. Apart from their Cambridge association, Robinson and Deane served, along with Gautam Mathur, as editors of the Modern Cambridge Economics Series. Professor Deane's memoir is the only direct link that this collection has to one of Robinson's own colleagues. But it is an important link, for it was Professor Deane who encouraged the present undertaking during a 1984 sabbatical semester I spent at Cambridge. In particular, she invited me to tea to meet Sir Austin Robinson, who gave the project his blessing to the extent of saying, "Joan would have appreciated an American post-Keynesian tribute." It was also an occasion for meeting Professor Chakravarty who later sent a copy of his own "Appreciation" of her life and work.

Among the points Sir Austin particularly wanted to recall that afternoon was Joan's great concern with the social, moral, and political questions that are so frequently lost sight of in the abstract arguments of contemporary theorists. His explicitness on this point suggests that, without an understanding of Robinson's values, one can have only a less than comprehensive appreciation of: (1) why she asked the questions she posed; (2) why she constructed or selected (as the case may be) the analytic tools she employed to try to answer these questions; and (3) why she formulated the particular answers that she developed. It is on this basis that Hans Jensen has chosen to focus on seeking out the *foundations* of Robinson's theories and models rather than on theories and models *per se*. His chapter, "The Role of Values in the Economics of Joan Robinson," interprets Robinson's values under two headings, specifically *ultimate* values and *instrumental* values. "Ultimate values" shaped her vision of how society ought to be organized to function in the future—a vision that, when she was still very young, induced her to become an economist, and that, as a mature scholar, she believed to be realizable. "Instrumental values" are reflected not only in her description of an economic reality plagued by multiple dilemmas, but also in her assessment and critique of the neoclassical school and her discussion of policy options. Jensen's search for the "prescientific" foundations on which Robinson erected her "scientific" edifices thus provides a philosophical and epistemic perspective to the more technical papers that follow.

Brian Loasby's chapter, "Joan Robinson's 'Wrong Turning,' " also provides perspective, albeit from a methodological standpoint. It proceeds from Robinson's well-known declaration that she "took the wrong turning" when she "worked out *The Economics of Imperfect Competition* on static assumptions." His reexamination of Robinson's reflective comment leads him to explore the evolution of Robinson's research program from its Marshallian origins, through Pigou and Sraffa, and eventually to her famous 1969 recantation. Of particular interest is Loasby's highlighting of the difficulties, not only for Robinson but for all economists, of approaching the subject matter of economics as a study of forces that cause change and movement. This was Marshall's real objective, yet he also perfected the static method. Thus, the method Robinson later came to see as a "wrong turning" was taken, Loasby maintains, at least partly because "Marshall had striven so hard to convince everyone that there was a single broad highway." As a result, in her first major book, Robinson became a pioneer in the axiomatic method, complete with warnings that theoretical analysis could not readily generate policy prescriptions. It is this methodological limitation that later provoked her to write her "shameless fudge" preface to the second edition of *Imperfect Competition* (1969).

For Loasby, writing with a deep understanding and appreciation of George Shackle's insight into the nature and meaning of uncertainty as the impossibility of foreknowledge, Robinson's "tangency solution" was, perhaps, a more grievous sin, at least from a methodological perspective, than Robinson's "fudge admission" records. She was, of course, soon to recognize the importance of uncertainty—not in connection with the value problem, but in her critique of general equilibrium theory.

Robinson was making her "wrong turning" in 1933 when her mind and heart had already become attracted to Keynes's aggregate demand theory. The attraction was fatal in the sense that she had taken on the self-set task of "generalizing the general theory." Especially important in this connection is her equilibrium versus history perspective, which she clearly did not have when she undertook *Imperfect Competition.* Given this "starting point," Larry Levine's chapter, "Joan Robinson: Journeys into Heterodoxy," provides fresh perspective about the ambivalence of her intellectual kinship with Marshall, which also led her to destinations removed from the neoclassical tradition. In particular, her intellectual journeys brought her into close touch with Sraffa and von Neumann via the notion of a supply-side determined set of relative commodity prices. Also linking her to Sraffa is her rejection of the neoclassical production function and the marginal productivity approach to the theory of factor pricing and income distribution. Finally, Levine wishes to emphasize that while her chief concern became the behavior of the economy in conditions of uncertainty, she also saw that "it is equally necessary to apply it to so-called micro-economics, and the behavior of markets." The latter concern, as has already been noted, reiterates Loasby's "missed opportunity" view concerning the profession's research program.

The central question of "time" in economics is explored further by Meyer Burstein, whose critical point is that the equilibrium theory Robinson undermines is that of Walras, Hicks, the neoclassical synthesis implicit in "IS/LM," and prospectively, new classical macroeconomics, but *not* that of Marshall, Wicksell, or Hayek. Nevertheless, he would have us remember Joan Robinson for having been the first writer fully to understand that because the time concept inherent in *tâtonnement* is "logical" time, "rigorous" general equilibrium models cannot be related to a real world that moves forward in calendar time.

Bearing in mind Robinson's concerns about history, time, and uncertainty, which are shared by post-Keynesians generally, J. S. Metcalfe and Ian Steedman draw attention to the issue of stock-flow (in-)consistencies that arise in IS/LM analysis. They thus offer the notion of "coherent equilibrium," suggesting that this concept is free from stock-flow inconsistencies, although it remains vulnerable to unfulfilled expectations. While some economists may take the position that no IS or LM schedule can have a determinate position because of the volatility of expectations, Metcalfe and Steedman maintain that the general state of expectations is not typically in a state of turmoil. Thus they propose that their notion of "coherent equilibrium" offers a way of understanding many actual economic situations, even though they agree that there may well be periods of expectations changing so rapidly and with such confusion that they will not be amenable to *any* formal method of analysis.

Krishna Bharadwaj, whose theme is also history versus equilibrium but whose roots are in the Sraffian tradition, proceeds from a fundamentally different perspective. Unlike Levine and Burstein, she maintains that the fault of neoclassical theory lies deeper than method; it lies in "the basic limitations of the theory's approach and framework." While most post-Keynesians subscribe to the fundamentals on which she criticizes neoclassical equilibrium theory, some will part company with her concerning the superiority of adopting Sraffa's view (1960) of circular production as contrasted with the one-way avenue of the neoclassicals. Like Bharadwaj, they are likely to be in fundamental agreement with Robinson's criticism of conventional equilibrium analysis for envisioning demand and supply forces as capable of producing equilibrium. Yet not everyone is prepared to embrace the classical theory of value and distribution as the alternative choice for reasons of its greater "openness" to accommodate historical changes. How to capture the infinite variety of historical change within the framework of deductive analysis remains, in Bharadwaj's view, a major unresolved methodological problem, for "even in the simplest case of certainty and fulfilled expectations, neoclassical theory has no ground left to stand upon." Bharadwaj is deeply appreciative that Joan Robinson not only understood this, but also that she was fully cognizant of the need to study the dynamics of irreversible processes working through time. Yet, she finds fault with Robinson's "solution" of "leaving equilibrium analysis behind" so that the problem may be approached as a historical process of "lurching from one out-of-equilibrium position to another." What is needed, Bharadwaj insists, is an analytical structure that, like that of the classical authors, keeps open the possibility of incorporating the whole spectrum of forces that shape not only production, exchange, and distribution activities, but also the social relations through which their participants are linked.

The relationship between the history versus equilibrium question and the capital controversy—especially the "unimportance of reswitching" view to which Robinson was eventually led—is reviewed from a different perspective by Jan Kregel, a former Robinson student. Among other points, Kregel especially underscores that much of Robinson's positive contribution to exploring the relationship between growth and technical progress has been obscured by the controversy stirred up by her debate with neoclassical growth theorists. He also finds it "unfortunate" that Robinson's criticisms of neoclassical theory have become "linked so closely" to Sraffa's critique, when the two are, in fact, entirely independent.

The significance of the passage of time is addressed from still another perspective by Harvey Gram, whose chapter, "Value and Capital, Robinson Style," finds that the key to understanding the capital theory controversy lies in recognizing a distinction between two theories of relative prices—the Walrasian or pure exchange model of supply and demand, and the alternative "normal price" model of Marx, Marshall, Sraffa, and von Neumann. The former does not admit a concept of capital and so does not allow us to ask what determines the distribution of income between work and property. As soon as the Keynesian theory of the short period is extended to encompass accumulation, the meaning of capital needs to be considered. The "measurement controversy" was an unfortunate detour that drew attention away from the critical question that relates to the meaning of capital. Capital cannot be treated analogously with labor and land, as it is in neoclassical theory. Robinson's key point is that to vary the amount of capital is tantamount to altering the entire production process, and it is not at all clear what the effect on the rate of profit will be. The neoclassical theory of scarcity and substitution cannot be pressed into service to grapple with the forces behind accumulation, for neoclassical theory misconstrues not only capital but also the income that derives from its ownership, as distinct from the income derived from labor.

While Robinson eventually concluded that it is the "meaning" of capital that should concern us, the question of measurement continues to command attention. Thus, Edward M. Miller revisits the measurement controversy and poses the question, in what units is capital to be measured? The question has on-going relevance, for it is implicit in empirical growth accounting and productivity estimates.

Returning to Professor Solow's exchange with Robinson, which proposed a simple formula for calculating the output growth attributable to the growth of capital inputs per capita, Miller notes that the specific unit in which capital is to be measured is not identified, presumably in order to side-step disputes about measurement. Yet Miller suggests that weighting different vintages by marginal product or rent can make Solow's growth-accounting formula workable. Those engaged in growth accounting, among them Denison and the Department of Labor, have not understood that the concept of capital services required for growth accounting cannot be used for studies of factor inputs, including investment studies. While capital can be defined to preserve strict quasi-concavity, this is not suitable for many other purposes, such as growth accounting. A fundamental criticism of neoclassical economics follows since all of its results cannot hold if one is consistent in the definition of capital. This difficulty arises precisely because capital is not malleable (i.e., there are no "leets"). Quality differences among capital outputs, as well as other factors, imply that analogous problems arise with respect to predicting what are the inputs that a cost-minimizing firm will use.

Robinson's emphasis that it is the *meaning* rather than the measurement of capital that is her essential concern is part and parcel of the critical distinction she makes between income from property and income from work. This distinction has become the basis for an analogous distinction between exchange and production activities. Thus, Geoffrey M. Hodgson takes as his starting point the conventional view that these distinctions are quite trivial. It is the inappropriateness of scuttling the distinction between exchange and production and between income from work and income from property that Hodgson wishes to challenge in his "Marx after Robinson" chapter. Drawing on two burgeoning bodies of contemporary literature—specifically, information and uncertainty theory and contract and organizational theory—Hodgson argues that they reflect "a modernization of some of the key themes of the economics of Marx, with the introduction of uncertainty in the sense of Knight or Keynes." These developments, Hodgson argues, sustain Robinson's "constant reminders of the stature and complementarity of Keynes and Marx as economists."

Omar F. Hamouda's study of "Joan Robinson's Post-Keynesianism" undertakes the exploration of multiple intellectual bridges that link the work of contemporary post-Keynesians to one another and to Robinson. Whether their component parts can ever become integrated into what Hamouda terms a "fully coherent synthetic way of thinking in economics" of course remains for future determination. A clear source of difficulty, as Robinson was well aware, is "the competing influences that derive from two such apparently incompatible sources as Piero Sraffa's interpretation of Ricardo and Michal Kalecki's interpretation of the theory of employment." This competition did not, in Robinson's view, inevitably preclude a possible synthesis of ideas. It is precisely because the development of economic theory is an ongoing process that it appropriately draws on the work of writers of different periods to address particular issues. Thus, Hamouda credits Robinson with her efforts to bring (albeit with only limited success) three strands of thinking—specifically, the Marshall-Keynes strand, the Marx-Ricardo-Sraffa strand and the Marx-Kalecki strand—"under the umbrella of post-Keynesian economics."

The phenomenon of inflation has sparked a very large post-Keynesian literature, much of it centering on the causes of inflation and the mark-up equation as an alternative to the quantity equation. In order to reexamine this longstanding controversy, Edward Nell's chapter, "The Quantity Theory and the Mark-up Equation," returns to Robinson's pithy observation that "the archetypal quantity theory formula MV = PY, like any identity, must have its terms defined in such a way as to make it hold." Thus, Nell argues that if it is valid to interpret the money supply as being generated endogenously by business demands for funds to cover working capital needs, principally for the wage bill, it can be demonstrated that the quantity equation is simply another way of writing the mark-up equation. That is, given an endogenous money supply, the quantity equation is simply a reflection of the forces that determine the mark-up. More to the point with respect to understanding causality, in Nell's view, is that "money doesn't drive anything, it adjusts. . . . What drives the system is the ratio between the speed of production and the speed with which money is spent."

Robinson anticipated that the next major theoretical issue to confront economists will revolve about the income share question. The issues that are likely to be raised will be of such magnitude as to constitute a "second revolution," which is likely to meet with even greater resistance than Keynes's first revolution for, in contrast to the relatively benign marginal productivity view of income distribution, there are political implications inherent in the distributional aspects of the wage-cost mark-up hypothesis. Robinson has made important contributions towards catalyzing this still-to-be-realized revolution, as Ingrid H. Rima's chapter, "Robinson and the 'Other Half' of the Keynesian Revolution," undertakes to articulate. While the "high theory" revolution which Shackle so brilliantly interpreted was essentially intellectual, "the other half of Keynes's revolution" cannot be in the realm of pure theory alone for it will also involve politics and ideology. Thus, the signposts with which Robinson marked the way for those who would follow led her in the direction of the classical or surplus view of distribution. To this she added the Kaleckian interpretation that the wage share varies inversely with the "degree of monopoly," and that wages rather than profits are the residual category of income. This is clearly a model intended to be useful for examining a variety of politically related questions that Robinson chided the profession for evading.

As is well known, the generalization of the *General Theory* to incorporate a foreign trade sector was among Robinson's contributions to the first half of Keynes's revolution. Later, the distinction between capital as equipment and materials and as "command over finance" was seen also to be relevant to foreign investment. Thus, Robinson noted that while the historical function of exports was to acquire imports, the objective of contemporary neomercantilism is to cultivate exports to acquire "sterile money." This is an objective that has still-to-be-examined implications. Building on Robinson's earlier insights, Rima concludes that the aspirations of the more recently industrialized countries to pursue export-led growth is likely to exacerbate the conflict between receivers of labor and nonlabor income in import surplus economies, in much the same way as inflation. But beyond this, it may also predispose import surplus economies to underemployment in the long run, as well as in the short run. If this becomes the case, as Rima's joining of the Robinson-Kaldor-Keynes insights to neomercantilistic practices suggests, large and sustained import surpluses may prove a vehicle that leads, in terms of Robinson's growth-age taxonomy, to a "leaden age" as the likely long-run counterpart to Keynes's short-run underemployment equilibrium.

The next two papers address aspects of Robinson's seminal contribution to growth theory. The first, "Investment in Post-Keynesian Growth Theory" by Chidem Kurdas, tackles the question of the time period implications that are inherent in post-Keynesian growth theory in consequence of the process of capital formation and their relationship to the income shares. Given the "stylized fact" of the secular stability between labor and property incomes, post-Keynesian growth theories, among them Robinson's, link these shares to the accumulation rate that derives from investment driven by "animal spirits," which generates cyclical rather than secular phenomena. Kurdas thus views Robinson's analysis of investment as inconsistent with her conception of the secular growth process and the long-term stability of the income shares. What appears to be needed, Kurdas urges, is a more systematic study of the factors underlying investment spending. We cannot, she argues, proceed further without entering into the "dark room" of capital formation.

The phenomenon of capital accumulation necessarily also raises questions about the choice of technique and how it is related to the rate of profit. Robinson's concern about the effects of technical progress was that it might generate structural imbalances that compromise the steady rate of profit that is a prerequisite to a steady rate of accumulation. Marxian theorists have suggested analogous scenarios predicated on the possibility of capital-intensifying, labor-saving technical change. They have not, as yet, developed models that undertake to link their technical change analyses to choices being made at the microlevel. This omission prompts David Laibman to develop a micro rational choice model that is both Robinsonian, in that it reflects a response to endogenous economic forces, and Marxian, in that it is consistent with technical changes biased in the Marxian direction, i.e., it is labor-saving. While his aggregative one-good model is admittedly austere, he is able to show that under parameter values likely to be realistic, technical changes can lead to a deteriorating trade-off between the wage share in output and the rate of profit. This generalization is thus very much in the

Robinsonian tradition of undertaking to grapple with possible sources of structural imbalance that predispose capitalist economies to instability and long-term crisis.

Finally, we ask what has so often been asked: Why was Joan Robinson, who was many times over nominated for a Nobel Prize in Economics, never the recipient of that coveted honor? Marjorie S. Turner provides us with a retrospective about the process by which Nobel laureates are selected in the economics field. She also speculates what might have been the relevance of Robinson's gender, her politics, her lack of interest in general equilibrium and welfare theory, her preference for literary rather than mathematical forms of communication, and perhaps most of all, her constant barrage of criticism against mainstream theory in depriving her of that singular honor.

Was this criticism so voluminous or its fury so intense that it overwhelmed everything else? While it is for her critiques of the mainstream (and, of course, *The Economics of Imperfect Competition*) that Robinson is best known, her legacy is by no means only, or even chiefly, one of destruction. That Robinson *did* provide "shoulders" on which other scholars are now standing is attested to by the papers in this volume, which reflect the positive aspects of her work: helping to build an alternative to the neoclassical paradigm.

Notes

1. Chakravarty, 1983; Gram and Walsh, 1983; Asimakopulos, 1984; Harcourt, 1979; Deane, 1984.
2. Feiwell, 1989a, 1989b; Turner, 1989; Marcuzzo, 1985.
3. Hamouda and Harcourt, 1988, pp. 1–33.
4. Turner, 1989, p. 193.
5. It it perhaps relevant that others besides post-Keynesians agree on this matter, among them Frank Hahn, Robert Solow, and Paul Samuelson.
6. Sidney Weintraub, 1981, p. 12, n. 2.
7. Brian Loasby, noting that there is some common ground between Keynes and the Austrians, suggested in our correspondence that there are, no doubt, also Austrian insights in Robinson's work. That none of the papers in this volume reflects this is, perhaps, still another manifestation of the fragmentation among those who dissent from the mainstream on whatever grounds.

References

Asimakopulos, A. (1984) "Joan Robinson and Economic Theory." *Banca Nazionale del Lavoro–Quarterly Review*, 151 (December).

Chakravarty, Sukhamoy. (1983) "Joan Robinson: An Appreciation." *Economic and Political Weekly* (October 1).

Deane, Phyllis. (1984) Biographical Memoir, American Philosophical Society Memoir.

Feiwel, George R., ed. (1989a) *Joan Robinson and Modern Economics*. New York: New York University Press.

———. (1989b) *The Economics of Imperfect Competition and Beyond*. New York: New York University Press.

Gram, Harvey and Vivian Walsh. (1983) "Joan Robinson's Economics in Retrospect." *Journal of Economic Literature*, 21 (June): 518–50.

Hamouda, O. F. and G. C. Harcourt. (1988) "Post-Keynesianism: From Criticisms to Coherence?" *Bulletin of Economic Research*, 40(1):1–33. Reprinted in John Pheby, ed., *New Directories in Post-Keynesian Economics*. Hants, U.K.: Edward Elgar.

Harcourt, Geoffrey C. (1979) "Joan Robinson." Biographical Supplement, *International Encyclopedia of Social Science*, pp. 663–71. New York: Free Press.

Marcuzzo, Maria Cristina. (1985) "Joan Violet Robinson, 1903–1983." Materiali di Discussione, Departimento di Economia Politica, Modena.

Robinson, Joan V. (1933) *The Economics of Imperfect Competition*, 2d ed. 1969. London: Macmillan.

Sraffa, Piero. (1960) *Production of Commodities by Means of Commodities*. Cambridge: Cambridge University Press.

Turner, Marjorie S. (1989) *Joan Robinson and the Americans*. Armonk, NY: M. E. Sharpe.

Weintraub, Sidney. (1981) "An Eclectic Theory of Income Shares." *Journal of Post-Keynesian Economics*, 4, 1(Fall):10–24.

JR

CHAPTER TWO

Joan Robinson (1903–1983)

A Biographical Memoir

PHYLLIS DEANE

Joan Robinson was the daughter of a famous major-general, Sir Frederick Maurice, and the descendant of two distinguished Cambridge scholars. Her great-grandfather was F. D. Maurice, the Christian socialist who was a formidable intellectual influence on English nineteenth-century academics, and her grandfather Frederick Marsh was professor of surgery and Master of Downing College, Cambridge. She went from St. Paul's, the leading London girls' public school, to Girton College in 1922 to read for the Economics Tripos at a time when the Cambridge School, inspired by Alfred Marshall, was enjoying an unsurpassed international reputation. As a woman, she was not a full member of the University and was not admitted until 1948 to the degree she had earned in 1925. This quaint circumstance in no way impeded her rapid acceptance as an equal into an outstanding economic community that by the later 1920s included among its stars J. M. Keynes, A. C. Pigou, D. H. Robertson, E. A. G. Robinson (whom she married in 1926), and P. Sraffa, and that was already attracting a dazzling stream of talented visitors from the world's leading universities. She became assistant lecturer in economics in 1931, lecturer in 1937, reader in 1949, and professor in 1965. From the early 1950s up to the illness that led to her death in 1983 she was the Cambridge School's most charismatic teacher of students (especially keen graduate students) and its most devastating critic of economic orthodoxy in all its forms—whether neoclassical or Marxist or "bastard Keynesian" (to use her own term for those who reconstructed the Keynesian revolution in the post–World War II era).

Joan Robinson's path-breaking contributions to modern economics were primarily in the area of economic theory. Assessing them is made more difficult by her own readiness to diminish the novelty of her own ideas (she always began her most innovative monographs with generous tributes to those who had pointed

Reprinted courtesy of American Philosophical Society Yearbook 1984.

her in new directions) and then to dismiss her past writings as "wrongheaded" as soon as she had moved on in the unremitting search for economic truth. Fierce though she was in her determination to slip the shackles of economic dogma, she always worked within a discipline, as a member of an economic community, the rules of whose game she recognized and respected. It was one of the special strengths of her own analyses, and one of the most important lessons she passed on to her students, that she punctiliously spelled out the assumptions and defined the concepts on which her theories hinged.

Her first major work, *The Economics of Imperfect Competition* (1933), was designed as a formal contribution to the Marshallian theory of value. It followed a seminal article by Piero Sraffa (*Economic Journal* 1926), which revealed the logical flaws associated with the conventional assumption of perfect competition, and using the familiar Marshallian techniques of partial equilibrium analysis, Mrs. Robinson showed that it was possible to dispense with that unrealistic assumption (moving it to the innocuous situation of a special case) by focusing not on the conditions of equilibrium of an industry but on those of the firm. Unlike E. H. Chamberlin (whose *Theory of Monopolistic Competition* was independently conceived and also published in 1933), Mrs. Robinson did not present her response to the debate as a revolutionary new paradigm, but as a contribution to an ongoing research program. Indeed, her solution (which was basically similar in form and implications to that of Chamberlin) did not seem as revolutionary to her British colleagues as Chamberlin's did to American economists. Her *Economic Journal* reviewer, Gerald Shove, for example, himself an active participant in the program to reconstruct the Marshallian theory of value, was less impressed by her theoretical results than by her distinctively rigorous technique of analysis. With hindsight one can see that this is where she blazed the trail for a powerful new system of economic theorizing, the model-building approach. Generations of students since 1933 have read *The Economics of Imperfect Competition,* with its systematically specified assumptions and concepts and its magical geometrical illustrations of the behavior patterns of the model firm, as their blueprint for building their own engines of economic thought. Characteristically, however, having done exactly what she set out to do, viz., "to demonstrate that the output and price of a single commodity can be conducted by a technique based upon individual decisions," she ended with the kind of disclaimer that relatively few subsequent model builders have been candid enough to make explicit:

> The reader who is interested in results immediately applicable to the real world has every right to complain that these tools are of little use to him. The knives are of bone and the hammers of wood, only capable of cutting paper and driving pins into cardboard. But the analytical economist who is prepared to work stage by stage towards the still far-distant ideal of constructing an analysis which will be capable of solving the problems presented by the real world may perhaps find in this toolbox some implements which will serve his turn.

By the early 1930s, then, Joan Robinson was an active member of the small group of high theorists (mainly in Cambridge but also in Oxford and London) who were deeply concerned by the inadequacy for current policy problems of the orthodox system of Marshallian theory in which they had all been educated. They were committed to the goal of reconstructing it along more useful lines. When J. M. Keynes embarked on his "long struggle of escape from habitual modes of thought and expression" in a bid to "largely revolutionize . . . the way the world thinks about economic problems," it was this group, sometimes called the "Cambridge circus," that actively encouraged and criticized his efforts. In time he submitted to them the proofs of his *General Theory of Employment, Interest and Money* (1936) before releasing it to the world at large. They were young enough to stomach the economic heresies he proposed and self-confident enough to shoot down arguments that seemed untenable. Along with the other members of the "circus" (the nucleus of which included Roy Harrod, Richard Kahn, James Meade, Austin Robinson, and Piero Sraffa), Joan Robinson played a constructive role in the Keynesian Revolution.

She played an even more significant role in its acceptance, largely by virtue of her special talent for expressing unfamiliar or complex arguments in lively, lucid, and unpretentious prose. For the *General Theory*, the bible of the "new economics" that came out of the Keynesian Revolution, was not an easy book for the profession to digest. It actually proved easier for students, who were in Keynes's words "not properly brought up," to swallow than it did for their teachers. In essence, Joan Robinson's *Introduction to the Theory of Employment* (1937) was the first and easily the most perceptive of the numerous texts that set out to distill the essence of the Keynesian theoretical framework. Nor was this merely an exercise in popularization, for she went on to identify some of the critical implications for orthodox economic theory of the new approach.

A few years later, having spent some time mastering Marx's convoluted economics, Joan Robinson set out to expound the essentials of his theory from a Keynesian perspective. To this end she published in 1942 her *Essay on Marxian Economics.* The problem she encountered here was a wall of prejudice, for neither the professionals, nor those they advised, nor indeed modern Marxists, were yet ready to dissociate Marx's pure economic theory from his political doctrines. So although she found a receptive audience among the students who were still doctrinally fancy-free, the majority of her readers enjoyed the limpid prose and missed the serious message. In effect, while the leading economic theorists were endeavoring to reconcile a Keynesian system designed to analyze the short-term problems of an economy suffering from persistent unemployment, with a classical system that assumed a persistent tendency towards long-term equilibrium (a self-regulating economy), Mrs. Robinson was searching for ways of escaping altogether from the unrealistic assumptions of equilibrium theory and of dynamizing the Keynesian model. "For me," she was to write later, "the main message of Marx was the need to think in terms of history, not of equilibrium."

Through the 1940s and 1950s the main theme of Joan Robinson's self-imposed research program was the creation of a theory appropriate to the analysis of a dynamic economic system. In the preface to *The Rate of Interest and Other Essays* (1952, republished in 1979 as *The Generalisation of the General Theory and other Essays*), she defined her terms of reference thus: "The characteristic of dynamic analysis in the sense intended here, is that it cannot explain how an economy behaves in given conditions without reference to past history." The message she was concerned above all to get across was that "the concept of equilibrium is incompatible with history. It is a metaphor based on movements in space applied to processes taking place in time. In space it is possible to go to and fro and to remedy misdirections, but in time, every day, the past is irrevocable and the future unknown." Four years later, in 1956, she broke new ground in dynamic theory with *The Accumulation of Capital*. Again her *tour de force* was an impeccable example of the model-building approach to economic theorizing. What she did was model the internal relationships of a capitalist economy in a state of steady growth (a golden age) and use that as the framework against which to explore the consequences of departures from steady growth. By 1956 macroeconomic model building was high fashion for economic theorists and their students, Keynesian economics was the current orthodoxy for macroeconomic analysis, and the commitment of government policy makers to promoting economic growth had caused an upsurge of academic interest in growth theory. The new orthodoxy, however, was based on a synthesis of Keynesian macroeconomics and neoclassical microeconomics ("bastard Keynesianism," which had moved a long way from Keynes's *General Theory*). Most model builders were more interested in devising predictive econometric models than in "engines of thought." The production function models that were all the rage were unequivocally based on traditional neoclassical assumptions and concepts.

The result was that modern growth theory developed along two disparate lines. One deployed Keynesian national income techniques within a mathematically sophisticated equilibrium framework of analysis, while the other worked on causal models designed to apply to a world where the rules governing human behavior change through time and differ as between social groups. In the methodological and doctrinal disputes between protagonists of the two approaches, Joan Robinson was an uncompromising advocate for the Keynesianism that rejected the notion that the economy was inherently self-regulating. She repudiated her own *Economics of Imperfect Competition* in the preface to the 1969 edition of what had become an economic classic. She contributed brilliantly to a succession of rousing debates on pure theory with the exponents of the new orthodoxy. A long string of collected essays and articles was thereby added to the student reading lists. Leading economists who were justifiably irritated by her persistent propensity to attribute economic fallacies to her opponents on inadequate grounds, were nevertheless forced by her theoretical insights and incisive arguments to engage in running debates with her in the learned journals.

Apart from her works on pure theory, which have set Joan Robinson among the giants of economic thought, she wrote (to an increasing extent in her later years) on many subjects of direct interest to a wider audience, e.g., on philosophical or moral aspects of economics, on economic management in modern China, and on problems of less-developed countries generally. She also collaborated with John Eatwell on an *Introduction to Modern Economics* (1979). Younger colleagues in Cambridge and elsewhere who followed Keynes's example in giving her their *magna opera* to read, found that her forthright and constructive criticisms immensely improved the logic and lucidity of the final product.

Despite her analytical qualities, however, her ability to expound abstract economic theory in sparkling prose, and her prolific pen, it was through her direct personal contact with generations of students, particularly research students, that Joan Robinson's influence on twentieth-century economic thought has probably been most profound and extensive. In the heady, booming, economics faculties of the 1950s and 1960s her reputation as a rebel against orthodox economic doctrine of all kinds spread worldwide. She listened to and argued with newcomers to the discipline as though they were her intellectual peers, a daunting experience for some, but exhilarating for those who were as dedicated as she to finding new and effective ways of thinking about urgent policy problems. Always approachable, if rarely ingratiating, she charmed students and academics from developing countries by her passionate concern with problems of inequality within and between nations and by her eagerness to learn about, and put her mind to, their distinctive regional problems. Joan Robinson never founded anything so rigid as a school of economic thought, but few of the many young professionals who had come to sit at her feet in Cambridge, or who took the opportunity to spar with her on her frequent visits to other universities, failed to respond to a mind that refused to be confined by conventional techniques of economic analysis.

JR

CHAPTER THREE

The Role of Values in the Economics of Joan Robinson

HANS E. JENSEN

In her *Economic Philosophy*, Joan Robinson observed that "it is not possible to describe [a particular economic] system without moral judgments creeping in."[1] Thus being in agreement with John Maynard Keynes that "economics is essentially a moral science . . . [that] employs . . . judgments of value,"[2] Robinson admonished her fellow economists "to combat, not foster, the ideology which pretends that values which can be measured in terms of money are the only ones that ought to count."[3]

Values enter at two different levels in Robinson's work: in her *vision* and in her *conceptualized reality*. Because these two mental constructs constitute the motivational element for her studies and the universe into which she inquired, respectively, an investigation of the place and role of values in the two compartments provides some clues as to (1) why Robinson asked the questions she posed, (2) why she pursued her economic analyses in the way she did, and (3) why she arrived at certain of her answers.[4]

Because of their centrality, I begin with a brief discussion of the meaning I attach to the terms value, vision, ideology, and conceptualized reality.

Values, Vision, Ideology, and Reality

As used in this paper, the term "value," or "values," relates to the concept of "value judgments" in the sense of "arguments of what ought to be." Following Schumpeter, value judgments are interpreted to involve "moral or cultural appraisals of institutions."[5] In other words, a value is the result of a process of assessment in the course of which a "judgment [is made] on the goodness or otherwise" of a particular object, proposition, act, or outcome of an act.[6] Thus, values pertain to evaluationally established "ends-in-view,"[7] *as well as* to the judgmentally selected instruments or " 'means' of achieving these [final] goals."[8] The "final and instrumental values" are formulated on a "temporal continuum of activities," however, "in which each successive stage is equally end and means.'' It is an ''end in so far as it is temporarily and relatively a close; a means, in so far as it provides a condition to be taken into account in further activity.''[9]

Values are closely associated with the vision an economist formulates of the potentially good society. Hence I use the term ''vision'' in Alfred Marshall's sense of a ''hopeful view of the possibilities of human progress'' in the *future*,[10] rather than in the Schumpeterian sense of ''vision of economic reality'' as it exists *today*.[11] A vision is a blend of two closely related components. It includes a set of ''wish-images''[12] that specifies how the socioeconomic order ought to be shaped, organized, and functioning in the future. It also encapsulates a historically conditioned view of society as an organism that contains the prerequisites for a realization of the ''ideal [future] conditions of social life.''[13] As this phraseology indicates, a vision is ''ideological almost by definition.''[14]

But what is meant by ''ideology?'' This is a term that has been ''thoroughly muddied''[15] by the ''wide range of definitions to which the concept is commonly subjected.''[16] A conception of ideology that seems useful in connection with Robinson's work is that values are the substance of ideology. Simply put, ideology is a *cluster of values*.[17] These values are of two kinds. One consists of *ultimate values* (à la John Dewey's ''final'' values)[18] that specify how an ideal social system ought to be structured and functioning. The ultimate values of a reform-oriented economist, which Robinson certainly was, are absorbed chiefly from the intellectual and socioeconomic environment that prevailed during the intellectually formative years of such a person. The values in the second group are *instrumental values* (à la Dewey's version)[19] in the sense that their realization serves as a means to the achievement of the ultimate values. Most instrumental values are formed judgmentally by the economist in question.

It would seem, therefore, that ''[i]deologies are pervaded with values''[20] and that visions are permeated with value-laden ideologies. Values and ideologies are not restricted to an economist's vision, however. They are also present in those apparent aspects of the world that a particular economist chooses to study. That is so because the socioeconomic actuality in which such an economist lives cannot ''be 'known' in the same way as natural objects get to be 'known.' ''[21] To analyze economic phenomena, an economist is therefore forced to substitute something knowable for the essentially unknowable actuality. This knowable entelechy, which constitutes the ''prescientific'' foundation[22] of a reform-oriented economist's analytic work, may be called a ''conceptualized reality.''[23] By reality, therefore, I understand an economist's mentally formulated approximation to, or her/his image of, the actual socioeconomic order and thus a proxy for that order.

Robinson was the first one to admit that her economics was based on ''ideological proposition[s]'' that she equated with ''[m]etaphysical propositions.'' However, her ''metaphysical statements are not without contents. They express a point of view and . . . provide a quarry from which hypotheses can be drawn.

They do not belong to the realm of science and yet they are necessary to it. Without them we would not know what it is that we want to know.''[24] What Robinson wanted to know is reflected in those ultimate values that constitute the mortar that binds together the bricks of which her vision is built.

Ultimate Values in Robinson's Vision

What Robinson wished ultimately is a society in which, after ``the worst poverty'' has been ``overcome,'' we ``could set about making a country where all can be comfortable, cheerful and free to follow their fancies.'' She admitted that ``this is a selfish ideal'' because its realization would not contribute directly to an improvement of the conditions in the poor countries. ``Compared to these [conditions], our problems are trivial, but until we have settled these little problems [of ours] we are powerless to use any influence at all to contribute to [the solution] of the great ones.''[25] Thus, Robinson's vision had a global dimension. But inasmuch as ``the arms race is continuing at an accelerating rate and the spread of commercialism is destroying human values everywhere, it is not easy to take an optimistic view of the situation in the Third World today.''[26]

The ideology of laissez-faire was therefore anathema to Robinson. Its ``cult of self-interest and competition has created the lonely crowd of other-directed status-seekers'' that she found ``far from satisfactory.''[27] Consequently, whatever ``may be the difficulties and confusion of partial laisser faire, it is greatly to be preferred to total laisser faire.''[28] That is to say, the modern welfare state is preferable because it has ``very much softened the harshness of raw capitalism,'' but it is far from ideal because the ``democratic welfare state in the rich countries of the Western world is essentially, by its very nature, protectionist and nationalistic.'' Worst of all, the ``requirements of the warfare state and the welfare state meet in the export of armaments, which keep industry in ex-imperialist countries prosperous and permit enmities in the ex-colonial countries, which were frozen at the level of bows and arrows and flintlocks, to break out with bombs and tanks.''[29]

In spite of the fact that her hopes for ``a decent house . . . a reliable health service and the best possible education'' for everybody were ``still a long way from fulfilment,'' Robinson was not despairing because anyone ``who writes a book, however gloomy its message may be, is necessarily an optimist.''[30] Her optimism was stimulated by the young ``generation now in rebellion'' against the establishment. The ``task of . . . [this] generation . . . is to reassert the authority of morality over technology.'' And, added Robinson, it is ``the business of social scientists . . . to help them see both how necessary and how difficult that task is going to be.''[31]

What were the sources of that bundle of ultimate values that undergirded, tinted, and conditioned Robinson's vision of the good society of the future in which ``the great productive power'' of the economy would be ``used to abolish poverty and create conditions in which we would 'prefer to devote our further energies to non-economic purposes' "?[32] Her answer was: "The ethical system implanted in each of us by our upbringing . . . [was] handed to us" by mentors, teachers, and creative fellow scholars.[33] And in Robinson's case, those who influenced her when she formulated her ultimate values were Marshall,[34] Keynes, Michal Kalecki, Piero Sraffa, and through the latter two, Karl Marx, as well as Lord Kahn and Gunnar Myrdal.[35] Thus, Robinson described herself as "the archetypal left-wing Keynesian" who "was drawing pinkish rather than bluish conclusions from the *General Theory* long before it was published." And she added: "I understand Marx far and away better than" do the Marxists. "I have Marx in my bones" and they have him in their "mouth."[36]

It was in order to identify the means for achieving her ultimate values, concretized in her goal of a massive improvement of "human welfare,"[37] that Robinson forged those instrumental values that she implanted in her conceptualized reality.

Instrumental Values in Robinson's Reality

The instrumental values of Robinson's reality are interspersed with formal analysis in nearly everything she wrote, though they appear in many different contexts and guises. Thus, they are to be found in her view of the apparent "dilemma of modern capitalism,"[38] in her assessment of standard economic theory, and in her critique of the "neoclassical school" as "based on a revival of Walrasian supply and demand" that is "rapidly infecting the profession all over the world,"[39] and above all in her willingness to fight "tenaciously for the causes she believed in."[40]

For society to realize the Robinsonian ultimate goal of a decent and comfortable level of living for all, it is absolutely essential that the "human misery" inherent in unemployment be eliminated through the achievement of "continuous prosperity with full employment." Closely associated with the employment problem, but looked at from the longer term, there is the problem of "distribution."[41] The "large fortunes built up in the process of [past] accumulation . . . as well as those inherited from feudalism, have left a permanent legacy of great inequality of property" and incomes. "Inequality in post-tax income and capital gains gives rise to inequalities in consumption." Families "with high incomes cannot be prevented from spending them on what they most need, and so the two-tier system of health and education services is perpetuated, and contributes to perpetuating inequality."[42] In Robinson's opinion, the maldistribution of income is part of a series of interconnected and interlinked dilemmas. These she described thus:

> [O]ne dilemma of modern capitalism . . . is that no policy has been found to solve the *financial* problem of rising prices without making the *real* problem of unemployment worse. Behind this lies a further dilemma. Employment . . .

> can be maintained only when investment is profitable. To maintain investment requires continuous growth of output and industrial growth involves continuous consumption of exhaustible natural resources. . . . Behind this again, lies . . . [still another] dilemma. To maintain "growth" capitalist governments have to foster investment; investment beneficial to their populations is a concession to socialism so that investment in armament is preferred. But to justify armament, it is necessary to have enemies. We cannot blame the Cold War *only* on commercial motives, but they certainly play a *part* in preventing it from being called off. . . . "Growth" is [also] advertised to the public as a means of overcoming poverty. This is evidently a deception. Obviously a far greater contribution to human welfare could be made by reducing inequality in the distribution of household incomes, overcoming misery at the bottom of the scale and the need to cater to conspicuous consumption at the top.[43]

The employment problem is closely associated with the fact that technical "progress is continually raising output per man hour in industry, and the labour force is continuously increasing." Consequently, in order to "preserve near-enough full employment, market demand must be expanded as fast as potential output."[44] The industrialized nations have failed to achieve this goal. Hence they are "gradually drifting into the situation of an underdeveloped economy" in that the "system fails to offer jobs to all available workers, not through a temporary fall of demand, but for lack of a sufficient increase in the stock of means of production to employ them." The "shortening of working hours . . . demanded by Trade Unions as a defence against redundancy . . . is [only] a palliative, not a cure."[45]

The problems of unemployment and slow growth are not the only blemishes of the system. There is also the problem of latent and open inflation. "To combine . . . full employment with the traditional wage system of liberal capitalism must be expected to lead to a . . . 'vicious spiral.' "[46] Robinson accepted the Kaleckian and Keynesian "view that inflation is essentially a political problem" because it is rooted in "the relationship between the formation of prices and the share of wages in the proceeds of industry."[47] That is to say, inflation is closely related to what she viewed as the two principal functions of unemployment in capitalist society. The "first function of unemployment . . . is that it maintains the authority of master over man." The second function is that of "preserving the value of money" because whenever full employment breaks out, there is "a constant upward pressure upon money wage-rates" and prices.[48] Some of the "most respectable and conservative people" are therefore convinced "that full employment with a stable value of money is unattainable, and that the only possible policy is to keep a sufficient margin of unemployment to discipline the unions."[49] It is also "sometimes said that the trouble [of inflation] arises from monopoly." But, said Robinson, the "trouble does not lie in monopoly but in the class war—workers must struggle to keep their share in the product of industry and corporations must struggle to prevent them from increasing it." There "is not only a class war between employers and workers as a whole. There is an internal struggle of each group to maintain its relative position.''[50] In the 1960s, Robinson summed up her impressions of modern capitalism in the following manner:

> It has not been proved that recessions can be avoided, except by armament expenditures, and, since to justify armaments, international tension has to be kept up, it appears that the cure is a good deal worse than the disease. It has not been proved that continuous prosperity is compatible with stable prices. It has not been proved that a tolerable system of trading relations can be developed between nations each pursuing its own economic policy. Above all, it has not been found possible to maintain the pace of development without which the system is continually in danger of falling below its stalling speed. . . . All this concerns the performance of latter-day capitalism on its own terms. A deeper doubt is raised by the question whether capitalism, even when prosperous, can provide us with what we really want. . . . The services to meet basic human needs . . . are not an easy field for making profits. . . . Consequently they must be largely provided through taxation. To supply goods is a source of profit, but to supply services is a ''burden upon industry.'' It is for this reason that when, as a nation, ''we have never had it so good'' we find that we ''cannot afford'' just what we most need.[51]

Robinson concluded, therefore, that the ''hopes which accompanied the Keynesian revolution, of reforming capitalism so as to ensure continuous prosperity with full employment, are now all but extinguished.'' Instead of enjoying prosperity, capitalist economies suffer from a high ''general level of unemployment and recurrent crises, involving massive waste of resources and considerable human misery.''[52] The ''dismal poverty'' that is associated with this situation ''is a disgrace'' because it occurs ''in the richest nations the world has ever seen.''[53] In short, the ''modern economies have failed to develop the political and social institutions, at either domestic or international level, that are needed to make permanent full employment compatible with capitalism.''[54] Further, the ''costs of . . . pollution and destruction of amenities are reaching a critical level.''[55] The ''prevalence of pollution is admitted'' by business leaders and their defenders among orthodox economists, ''but it must not be allowed to affect the general presumption in favour of laisser faire.''[56] If you ''are arguing in favour of maximizing profits,'' however, ''you must be in favour of allowing the industry to make cheap newsprint—so that you can have very thick newspapers at the expense of poisoning the rivers of Canada and allowing the Indian population to be killed (or worse, to remain half-alive).''[57] And then there is ''the whole question of the Third World, where hunger and misery are growing as development fails to keep up with the growth of numbers,'' a train of events that ''begins to overshadow the success of modern capitalism and [to] threaten it [sic] self-satisfaction.''[58] In India, for example, the economic ''problem is so formidable that the mind boggles at it.''[59] Hence Robinson asked: ''What should be done?''[60] It is at this point that her discussion shades over into a value-laden investigation of economic policies and reforms.

An appreciation of Robinson's value-based critique of the way in which orthodox economists deal with the problems of modern capitalism is an essential beginning for considering her approach to the formulation of policies and reforms, for she viewed human beings as both creators and beneficiaries of those improvements in human welfare that economic activities are supposed to foster. To understand the dual role of the human factor in the economic drama, however, we must descend ''from the neoclassical cloud-cuckoo-land'' with its ''given physical means of production already in existence—labour, machines, stocks of cement and copper, and so forth.''[61] Although the neoclassical theory may illuminate the ''account of prisoners of war swapping the contents of their Red Cross parcels'' or, ''with some modifications,'' the operations of an ''economy of artisans and small traders,'' orthodox theory ''cannot be applied to capitalist production.''[62] That is so largely because this kind of production takes place in ''historical time,'' in contradistinction to the ''logical time'' in which the neoclassical ''model moves.''[63] In particular, the neoclassical concept of capital is ''designed to present capital as a 'factor of production,' on a par with land and labour, and interest (rather than profits) as its just reward.'' In order to ''present interest as the reward of a factor of production,'' however, it was necessary to treat productivity as ''inhering in 'capital goods.' '' But as ''Thorstein Veblen observed'' long ago, ''productive power . . . does not reside in'' tools and machines. The ''very concept of productivity inherent in a machine is quite wrong-headed.''[64] How and ''why is it possible to get interest,'' then? Not because of ''waiting,'' but because ''businessmen make profit and are willing to borrow.''[65] Hence Robinson pointed out, à la Veblen, that ''the 'capital' which receives interest is rentier wealth that can be lent to business . . . while the 'capital' that contributes to the product of industry is the technology embodied in equipment and stocks that permits labour to produce output.'' But in spite of the distinction that Keynes likewise ''had drawn between interest—the price of loans, and profit—the return on investment,'' orthodox economists continue to take the ''rate of interest to measure the productivity of this imaginary [and allegedly homogeneous, divisible, and measurable] substance'' dubbed capital.[66]

It is thus manifestly clear from this critique that Robinson's instrumental values were at odds with those held by mainstream economists and their allies in the world of affairs. She was therefore moved to fire the following value-laden salvo in a lecture she delivered at Barnard College in 1976:

> The bastard Keynesian theory[67] never even pretended to discuss the use of resources. It fell back upon the old defense of laissez-faire: what is profitable is right. The most remarkable application of this doctrine is now to the problem of pollution. The argument is that antipollution rules are hampering invest-

> ment and reducing profits. . . . Amenities and health have to be sacrificed to profits, because if we hinder the freedom of the corporations to employ the resources of the nation as they choose, they will not be able to employ them at all. . . . In the sectors which are left to private enterprise, the great corporations, pursuing hoped-for profits, choose what lines to develop, and how the population is to be employed. A community grows up around the site where some corporation has found it convenient to install a plant, and is devastated when the corporation finds it convenient to shut the plant down. . . . Similarly with the problem of exhaustible resources. The great corporations must be allowed to go on chewing up the planet, else they will not be able to make profits and provide employment. Now we are stuck with it. We must keep the show going. . . . There is no point in thinking of what we really want, such as abolishing poverty and restoring peace. All we can ask for is what they choose to give us. We must keep the show going or else, we fear, they won't give us anything at all.[68]

Robinson concluded, therefore, that contemporary economic theory acquiesces in, and actually promotes, the "oldest element of inherent vice in the private enterprise system," namely the "anarchy of unplanned growth." Thus she asked: "*Where do we go from here?*"[69]

She answered her own rhetorical question thus: "I could only answer with the quip about the motorist who asked the way to Oklahoma. The man by the roadside answered: if I wanted to go to Oklahoma I should never start here."[70] This remark reveals a good deal about Robinson's dissatisfaction with the present economic system. But, said she, "as long as our economy [sic] system continues to survive, a clearsighted examination of it is more likely to favour radical views than to support the defenders of the status quo."[71] The principal reason for this is that the economic "problem has developed far beyond the point where it makes sense to discuss any simple remedies."[72] Robinson seldom spelled out what actually should be done, however. Rather, her opinions have to be inferred from value declarations. When she referred to the "superficial success of the full employment policy based on the arms race,"[73] her value judgments are eminently clear, as they are in the following questions and comments:

> What do we want our resources for? . . . Why do we worry about growth? . . . [W]hat is it that should grow? What is national wealth? The real national product that appears in the [national income statistics in the] blue books is the volume of sales of goods and services corrected for changes in prices. It is what is sold that counts. "Productive" investment is investment that creates capacity to increase sales. Cleaning up slums, improving health and education, preserving wild country are not counted as "productive" activities. The issue is not between what is useful to society and what is not. . . . [The attitude is this:] Create a full employment economy, where profits are easy to make, and you have a productive economy. No need to ask what is produced or who gets the benefit.[74]

> Private enterprise is wonderfully flexible in jumping from one profitable market to another, but it is very rigid in resistance to *social control*. Now that the authorities want employment to revive, they can only push industry further down the grooves that it has worn for itself.[75]

"But," said Robinson, "we cannot really escape from having to think what should be done with our resources" and what should be done to "the distribution of products between people."[76] Thus, there is no doubt that Robinson believed that "public ownership of the means of production is a necessary condition" for "control of [the] distribution of income from property."[77] Writing in 1943, Robinson had this to say about the values she placed upon public ownership:

> There are a number of spheres of activity in which operation through public corporations, on a non-profit basis, can be justified on its own merits, quite apart from the employment problem. If these were taken out of the hands of private enterprise, long vistas of useful investment would be opened up. A national medical service . . . would require a large volume of investment, not only in the bricks and mortar of health centres and sanatoria, but in training medical and nursing staff on a scheme of State bursaries. Housebuilding is . . . a proper sphere for public investment, and this opens up a huge field. Public operation of transport opens another, fuel and power a third. If such large spheres of investment were under control the whole setting of public-works policy would be altered. . . . [O]perating within the framework of a general plan, the . . . investment considered on general grounds the most advantageous would take precedence, and investment in private industry would be rationed under a system of priorities.[78]

There is no reason to believe that Robinson's values changed between the early 1940s and the late 1970s. Thus, in 1972, she referred to the desirability of being concerned with the "content of employment," and not just with the "level of employment."[79] Analogously, she argued that it would be advantageous to have "social control" of investment in order to direct "new investment into the lines that best provide for the needs and desires of society as a whole."[80]

She was fully aware, of course, that a successful "policy to achieve and maintain full employment" of a properly allocated labor force "might destroy the mechanism for restraining prices."[81] Hence she was in favor of some form of "incomes policy" which, in her opinion, would be "the only real remedy" for inflation.[82] She emphasized, however, that incomes policy has nothing to do with "social justice." Its only purpose is to slow "down the rise of costs" of production. Unfortunately, it does so in a "rough" and frequently "unfair" manner.[83] Hence, incomes policies should never be used as a means to "freeze for ever, the pattern of distribution between income from earnings and income from property," which at present "seems to correspond very ill with our notions of justice and morality."[84] She sadly conceded that "the political setting" in which incomes policies "might have been introduced has long since dissolved,"[85] which seems also to preclude for the foreseeable future any realignment of "the overall distribution of income between work and property."[86]

Thus, as far as a realization of her cherished values for her own country was concerned, Robinson was not optimistic:

> It seems to me that people of this country are not in the mood for radical change. They prefer a loose-jointed, ramshackle economic system to one streamlined for efficiency and speed. They are willing to accept much that is irrational and unjust for the sake of preserving the continuity of our political institutions and the glorious flummery of Church and State.[87]

Nor are prospects for change better in the United States, about which she asked:

> What characteristic of the private enterprise system is it that condemns the wealthiest nation the world has ever seen to keeping an appreciable proportion of its population in perpetual ignorance and misery? The professional economists keep up a smoke-screen of "theorems" and "laws" and "pay-offs" that prevents questions such as that from being asked. This situation is, I think, inevitable. In every country, educational institutions in general, and universities in particular, are supported directly or indirectly by the established authorities and whether in Chicago or in Moscow, their first duty is to save their pupils from contact with dangerous thoughts.[88]

Robinson once wrote that anyone "who writes a book, however gloomy its message may be, is necessarily an optimist."[89] She seems, however, to have ended her own career not only on a note of pessimism but in "near despair, feeling that she had been discussing economic theory for over fifty years and that it had come to pieces in her hands." This was a "depressing and nearly nihilistic conclusion to which to come."[90]

Notes

An earlier version of this paper was presented at the annual meetings of the History of Economics Society at Toronto, June 1988. The author wishes to thank Mark Lavoie and Donald A. Walker for critical comments and to express his appreciation to the editor of this volume for helpful suggestions. The usual caveats apply, of course.

1. Robinson, 1964a, p. 14.
2. Keynes, 1938, p. 297.
3. Robinson, 1964a, p. 148.
4. Thus, the focus of my inquiry is upon the "prescientific" foundations (Schumpeter, 1949, p. 350) of Robinson's analyses and conclusions, rather than upon these analyses and conclusions *per se*. In other words, I leave to others a discussion of Robinson's "hypotheses," "model" building, and analyses by means of "economic theory" (Robinson, 1977, pp. 1318, 1319, 1323).
5. Schumpeter, 1954, pp. 541, 540, 102.
6. Collini, 1985, p. 33.

7. Dewey, 1939, p. 52.

8. Myrdal, 1964, p. 1062.

9. Dewey, 1949, p. 71; 1939, p. 49.

10. Marshall, 1961, p. 48.

11. Schumpeter, 1949, p. 352. Schumpeter's concept of vision corresponds closely to what I prefer to call the "conceptualized reality" of a particular economist.

12. Mannheim, 1955, p. 193.

13. Marshall, 1961, p. 48.

14. Schumpeter, 1954, p. 42.

15. Converse, 1964, p. 207.

16. Minar, 1961, p. 320.

17. This definition may be viewed as an amendment of Schumpeter's "amended version of the Marxist definition" of ideology. According to Schumpeter, "ideologies are superstructures erected on, and produced by, the realities of the objective social structure below them; and . . . they tend to reflect these realities in a characteristically biased manner. . . . But it cannot be emphasized too strongly," said Schumpeter, that "ideologies are not lies." On the contrary, ideologies "are truthful statements about what a man *thinks* he sees" (1954, pp. 37 and 36; 1949, p. 349; emphasis added). For Karl Marx's and Friedrich Engels's views of ideology, see Marx, 1978, p. 154, and Engels, 1977, p. 30.

18. Dewey, 1949, p. 71.

19. Ibid.

20. Roucek, 1944, p. 480.

21. Kecskemeti, 1952, p. 31.

22. Schumpeter, 1949, p. 350.

23. Jensen, 1976, p. 262.

24. Robinson, 1964a, pp. 2, 3.

25. Robinson, 1967, p. 64.

26. Robinson, 1979b, p. 143.

27. Robinson, 1970, pp. 116–17.

28. Robinson, 1967, p. 37.

29. Robinson, 1970, pp. 90, 92, 93.

30. Robinson, 1965, p. 124; 1970, p. 123

31. Ibid., p. 124.

32. Ibid., p. 123. This quotation by Robinson is from Keynes's essay on the "Economic Possibilities for our Grandchildren" (Keynes, 1930, p. 365), in which Keynes argued that "the economic problem may be solved, or be at least within sight of solution within a hundred years," i.e., by 2030 A.D. (p. 366). Although Robinson was less optimistic than Keynes, as indicated in her observation that his "hopes are still a long way from fulfilment" (1970, p. 123), Keynes's ideals were also Robinson's. It was her vision of an approximation to such Keynesian conditions that led her to undertake her economic inquiries.

33. Robinson, 1964a, p. 12.

34. Robinson observed in 1953: "The more I learn about economics the more I admire Marshall's intellect and the less I like his character" (1953, p. 14). Robinson was not referring to Marshall's socioeconomic values, which she accepted, but to what she called "an unresolved conflict" in Marshall's Principles: "The hard core of [its] logical analysis . . . is purely static—it applies to an economy in which accumulation has come to an end—while all the problems that he discusses are connected with an economy in which wealth is growing as time goes by" (1955, p. 2).

35. Robinson, 1979a, pp. 115–34; 1986, pp. vi–viii; 1980a, p. 97.

36. Robinson, 1953, pp. 19, 20.

37. Robinson, 1964a, p. 140.
38. Robinson, 1980a, p. 201.
39. Robinson, 1980b, p. 63.
40. Harcourt, 1984, p. 468.
41. Robinson, 1980c, pp. 207, 206, 35.
42. Robinson, 1967, pp. 60, 61.
43. Robinson, 1980a, pp. 201–2; emphasis added.
44. Robinson, 1978, pp. 232–33.
45. Ibid., pp. 233–34.
46. Ibid., p. 234.
47. Robinson, 1980c, p. 18.
48. Robinson, 1951, pp. 84, 85.
49. Robinson, 1964b, p. 278.
50. Robinson, 1976, pp. 5–6.
51. Robinson, 1978, p. 239.
52. Robinson, 1980c, pp. 206–7.
53. Robinson, 1980b, p. 128.
54. Robinson, 1980c, p. 208.
55. Robinson, 1980b, p. 128.
56. Robinson, 1980a, p. 118.
57. Robinson, 1980c, p. 45.
58. Robinson, 1980b, p. 128.
59. Robinson, 1980c, p. 221.
60. Robinson, 1967, p. 63.
61. Robinson, 1980b, pp. 63, 62.
62. Robinson, 1980c, p. 24.
63. Robinson, 1963, p. 24.
64. Robinson, 1980a, pp. 115, 116, and 115.
65. Robinson, 1964b, p. 25; 1980c, p. 36.
66. Ibid., pp. 94–95.
67. By this term, Robinson meant the "vulgarised version of Keynes's theory" (1975, p. 127) that was developed "in North America" and spread "from there over the world." Robinson emphasized that she did not use the term "bastard Keynesian doctrine . . . just as abuse. It has a definite meaning. The old orthodoxy against which the Keynesian revolution was raised, was based on Say's law. . . . According to the bastard Keynesian doctrine, it is possible to calculate the rate of saving that households collectively desire to achieve, and then governments, by fiscal and monetary policy, can organize the investment of this amount of saving. Thus Say's law is artificially restored, and under its shelter all the old doctrines creep back again, even the doctrine that any given stock of capital will provide employment for any amount of labor at the appropriate equilibrium real-wage rate. The unemployment occurs only because wages are being held above the equilibrium level" (1976, p. 5).
68. Ibid., p. 9.
69. Ibid., pp. 8, 7.
70. Ibid., p. 7.
71. Robinson, 1980c, p. 119.
72. Robinson, 1976, p. 7.
73. Robinson, 1965, p. 109.
74. Ibid., pp. 109–12.
75. Robinson, 1976, p. 9; emphasis added.
76. Robinson, 1965, p. 112; 1972, p. 8.

77. Gram and Walsh, 1983, pp. 547, 546–47.
78. Robinson, 1951, pp. 83–84.
79. Robinson, 1972, p. 6.
80. Robinson, 1976, pp. 8, 9.
81. Robinson, 1964b, p. 272.
82. Robinson, 1967, p. 12; 1980c, p. 220.
83. Robinson, 1967, p. 15.
84. Robinson, 1965, p. 120; 1967, p. 15.
85. Robinson, 1980c, p. 220.
86. Robinson, 1967, pp. 14–15.
87. Ibid., p. 63.
88. Robinson, 1980c, p. 98.
89. Robinson, 1970, p. 124.
90. Harcourt, 1986, pp. 93, 105.

References

Collini, Stefan. (1985) "The Idea of 'Character' in Victorian Political Thought." *Transactions of the Royal Historical Society*, 5th S., 35:29–50.

Converse, Philip E. (1964) "The Nature of Belief Systems in Mass Publics." In David E. Apter, ed., *Ideology and Discontent*, pp. 206–61. Glencoe: The Free Press of Glencoe.

Dewey, John. (1939) *Theory of Valuation*. Chicago: University of Chicago Press.

———. (1949) "The Field of Value." In Ray Lepley, ed., *Value: A Cooperative Inquiry*, pp. 64–77. New York: Columbia University Press.

Engels, Friedrich. (1977) "Letter to F. Meering of 14 July, 1893." In Martin Seliger, *The Marxist Conception of Ideology: A Critical Essay*, p. 30. Cambridge: Cambridge University Press.

Gram, Harvey and Vivian Walsh. (1983) "Joan Robinson's Economics in Retrospect." *Journal of Economic Literature*, 21 (June):518–50.

Harcourt, G. C. (1984) "The End of an Era: Joan Robinson (1903–1983) and Piero Sraffa (1898–1983)." *Journal of Post Keynesian Economics*, 6 (Spring):466–69.

———. (1986) "On the Contributions of Joan Robinson and Piero Sraffa to Economic Theory." In O. F. Hamouda, ed., *Controversies in Political Economy: Selected Essays of G. C. Harcourt*, pp. 90–110. Brighton, Sussex: Wheatsheaf Books.

Jensen, Hans E. (1976) "Sources and Contours of Adam Smith's Conceptualized Reality in the *Wealth of Nations*." *Review of Social Economy*, 34 (December):259–74.

Kecskemeti, Paul. (1952) "Introduction." In Karl Mannheim, *Essays on the Sociology of Knowledge*, Paul Kecskemeti, ed., pp. 1–32. London: Routledge and Kegan Paul.

Keynes, John Maynard. (1930) "Economic Possibilities for our Grandchildren." In John Maynard Keynes, *Essays in Persuasion*, pp. 358–73. New York: W. W. Norton, 1963.

———. (1938) "Letter to R. F. Harrod." In Donald Moggridge, ed., *The General Theory and After, Part II: Defence and Development*, pp. 295–97. *The Collected Writings of John Maynard Keynes*, vol. 14. London: Macmillan, 1973.

Mannheim, Karl. (1955) *Ideology and Utopia*. New York: Harcourt, Brace and World.

Marshall, Alfred. (1961) *Principles of Economics*, vol. 1, Text. 9th (variorum) ed. London: Macmillan.

Marx, Karl. (1978) "The German Ideology: Part I." In Robert C. Tucker, ed., *The Marx-Engels Reader*, 2d ed., pp. 146–200. New York: W. W. Norton.

Minar, David W. (1961) "Ideology and Political Behavior." *Midwest Journal of Political Science*, 5 (November):317–31.

Myrdal, Gunnar. (1964) *The Negro Social Structure. An American Dilemma*, vol. 2. New York: McGraw-Hill.

Robinson, Joan. (1951) *Collected Economic Papers*, vol. 1. New York: Augustus M. Kelley.

———. (1953) *On Re-reading Marx*. Cambridge: Students' Bookshops.

———. (1955) *Marx, Marshall and Keynes*. Delhi: The Delhi School of Economics of the University of Delhi.

———. (1963) *Essays in the Theory of Economic Growth*. London: Macmillan.

———. (1964a) *Economic Philosophy*. Garden City, N.Y.: Doubleday.

———. (1964b) *Collected Economic Papers*, vol. 2. Oxford: Basil Blackwell.

———. (1965) *Collected Economic Papers*, vol. 3. Oxford: Basil Blackwell.

———. (1967) *Economics: An Awkward Corner*. New York: Pantheon of Random House.

———. (1970) *Freedom and Necessity: An Introduction to the Study of Society*. New York: Pantheon of Random House.

———. (1972) "The Second Crisis of Economic Theory." *American Economic Review: Papers and Proceedings*, 62 (May):1–10.

———. (1975) "What Has Become of the Keynesian Revolution?" In Milo Keynes, ed., *Essays on John Maynard Keynes*, pp. 123–31. Cambridge: Cambridge University Press.

———. (1976) "The Age of Growth." *Challenge*, 19 (May/June):4–9.

———. (1977) "What Are the Questions?" *Journal of Economic Literature*, 15 (December):1318–39.

———. (1978) *Contributions to Modern Economics*. New York: Academic Press.

———. (1979a) *The Generalisation of the General Theory and Other Essays*. London: Macmillan.

———. (1979b) *Aspects of Development and Underdevelopment*. Cambridge: Cambridge University Press.

———. (1980a) *Further Contributions to Modern Economics*. Oxford: Basil Blackwell.

———. (1980b) *Collected Economic Papers*, vol. 4. Cambridge, Mass.: The MIT Press.

———. (1980c) *Collected Economic Papers*, vol. 5. Cambridge, Mass.: The MIT Press.

———. (1986) *The Accumulation of Capital*, 3d ed. London: Macmillan.

Roucek, Joseph. (1944) "A History of the Concept of Ideology." *Journal of the History of Ideas*, 5 (October):479–88.

Schumpeter, Joseph A. (1949) "Science and Ideology." *American Economic Review*, 39 (March):345–59.

———. (1954) *History of Economic Analysis*. New York: Oxford University Press.

JR

CHAPTER FOUR

Joan Robinson's "Wrong Turning"

BRIAN J. LOASBY

In the introduction to the first volume of her *Collected Economic Papers* Joan Robinson declared that when she "worked out *The Economics of Imperfect Competition* on static assumptions," she "took the wrong turning"; the correct path would have entailed "abandoning the static analysis and trying to come to terms with Marshall's theory of development."[1] This chapter is intended to suggest how Robinson came to take what later appeared to be the wrong path, and to indicate some of the consequences of this error (if an error it was). To do so it is necessary to examine the path for some little distance before the turning, and the features of the landscape and the guidebooks that made the wrong path appear so obviously right. We must therefore pay particular, if selective, attention to Marshall, Pigou, and Sraffa.

Marshall

As John Whitaker[2] has emphasized, Joan Robinson's first book is a product of Cambridge economics, and Cambridge economics was dominated by Alfred Marshall, both directly and in reaction to his work. We therefore begin by considering the aspects of Marshall's thought that influenced the sequence we are attempting to explain. Three aspects appear to have been of particular importance: his views of economics as a science, of the purposes of economic study, and of the dominant characteristics of the economic system that he sought to analyze.

Pigou observed of Marshall's *Principles* that on a first reading "one is very apt to think that it is all perfectly obvious. The second time one has glimpses of the fact that one does not understand it at all."[3] Keynes made a similar judgment: "It needs much study and independent thought on the reader's own part before he can know the half of what is contained in the concealed crevices of that rounded globe of knowledge."[4] This is not accidental; for the "rounded globe" was deliberately constructed as a contribution to the establishment of economics as a science, which was a prime objective of Marshall's career, and especially of his tenure of the Cambridge chair. The relabeling of the subject from political economy and its extraction from the Moral Sciences tripos were also contributions to this objective.

Now science, in those days when Newtonian physics was believed to be definitive, appeared to be a body of well-established knowledge, founded upon an agreed and systematically developed theoretical structure. There might be disagreement about the ways in which that structure should be extended for the analysis of problems currently unresolved, but its soundness and coherence should not be in question. Marshall was therefore concerned to present his subject in a way that emphasized the solidity of its foundations, the continuity of its development, and the universality of its principles. This was especially important if economic ideas were to be widely used by nonexperts, as Marshall desired. He appears to have had a personal aversion to controversy; he certainly had a professional aversion to controversy on fundamental issues, because such controversy seemed a threat to scientific status. As is well known, he was displeased by Jevons's attack on Ricardo, arguing that it was only by reason of carelessness or infelicity in expression that Ricardo may have inadvertently given the impression of not regarding demand as a major determinant of value. He likewise tended to play down inconsistencies and analytical difficulties in favor of an assured presentation of a complex body of knowledge.

It is not easy to convict Marshall of error (and, as we shall see, Sraffa did not in fact do so), but his very careful presentation was sometimes so skillful that it concealed the need for care by those who wished to make use of his ideas. There were indeed a number of very explicit warnings, especially of the dangers of following the logic of static equilibrium analysis too far, but the dangers were not explored and explained; and so, although Joan Robinson's wrong turning was quite clearly signposted by Marshall as "not a through road," it was as if the sign had been written in invisible ink.

The problem of presentation was made particularly acute by Marshall's motivation for the study of economics—his desire to foster an improvement in the condition of the people. The improvements that he wished for could not be secured merely by a redistribution of income, although his (characteristically cautious) use of the concepts of cardinal utility and consumers' surplus was, in part, intended to facilitate an analytical consideration of redistribution. As with many other reformers of the time, Marshall was greatly concerned with the ways in which some of the poorer people spent their money, and wished to see improvements in the quality of their demands. This was partly a matter of education and advocacy (the moralizing passages in the *Principles* no doubt reflect Marshall's evangelical background and early clerical ambitions); it was also partly a matter of environment, at work and at home—thus, he believed that small firms, by offering more opportunities for working men to exercise their talents, would also tend to improve their preferences, and that suburban living, which could be promoted by the railway companies through an appropriate fares policy, was better than urban living. Although demand curves at any one time reflect given preferences, consumers' wants change over time—and these changes are not independent of the economic system. This denial of the exogeneity of demand was to become a characteristic—though not especially Marshallian—theme in Joan Robinson's work.

The influence of activities on wants provided one reason for Marshall's agreement with Ricardo that supply required more elaborate attention than demand, as is evidenced by the relative lengths of Books 3 and 4 of the *Principles*, as well as by the bulk of *Industry and Trade* (1919).[5] But that was not the only reason: Marshall believed that there were great possibilities of increasing the productivity of the economy, not so much by efficient allocation (although that was not to be neglected), as by the discovery of better ways of doing things, as well as better things to do, under the stimulus of competition. It was important to Marshall that firms should not be identical, though they might be similar, for it was the continuing experimentation in both product and process that led to steady improvement in the range, quality, and affordability of goods and services. These fairly small differences between firms played a role equivalent to that of genetic variation in Darwinian theory, which was a great influence during Marshall's formative years as an economist.[6]

Progress was likely to be fastest in those industries where demand was expanding, and Marshall defined his law of increasing returns in terms of the improvements in organization that normally follow upon an increase in demand and thereby lead to more efficient use of both capital and labor.[7] Such increasing returns differ from modern concepts in two ways: they are not strictly returns to scale, and they have to be worked for. Marshall's generalization that "while the part which nature plays in production shows a tendency to diminishing return, the part which man plays shows a tendency to increasing return," embodied a theory of development in which man continually strives to find new ways of loosening or evading natural constraints. In terms of theoretical structures, it implied a clear distinction between a static analysis in which costs rise with output and a historical view in which costs fall over time, as a consequence of human efforts and human ingenuity, which are stimulated by an expansion of the market and by the threats and opportunities of competition. This insistence on development, and on competition as an agent of progress—as fundamental as it was with Schumpeter, but handled very differently from Schumpeter's theme of creative destruction[8]—is the third aspect of his thought to be noticed; it was the importance of this aspect that Joan Robinson belatedly recognized.

Marshallian increasing returns do not imply a schedule of falling costs in long-run static equilibrium; the costs fall through real time. But Marshall's concern to present his economic world as a rounded globe, and to do so in a way that carried conviction, led him to incorporate increasing returns in a long-period analysis that also made cautious use of the methods of static equilibrium. Although the long period in economic analysis makes no reference to calendar time, but is simply a code-phrase for full adjustment, nevertheless the nonexpert reader, whom Marshall was keen to reach, would naturally tend to think in terms of calendar time; and indeed, it is a natural question to ask of any long-run adjustment theory, how long the process of adjustment may be expected to take. Although Marshall distinguished between the cost-quantity relationships appropriate to a formal static analysis and the effects on costs of new methods that were likely to be worked out under the influence of expanding markets, he clearly expected the latter to be important in most examples of sustained growth; since the static long-run analysis by itself would therefore be an inadequate guide to the consequences of increased demand, he did not wish to present it on its own.[9] That would not be true knowledge. A strictly coherent static model might be adequate for the short run (although Marshall did not care to produce what would now be termed a strictly coherent model—he did not assume anonymous competition), but it clearly would not be adequate for the long run, and therefore was not offered. But although he gave warnings of the danger of pushing static analysis too far, he never gave a precise explanation of what he was doing or why. Much of the argument was inserted into concealed crevices. He thereby laid up a great deal of trouble.

Marshall came to economics because he was anxious to do good; indeed, J. M. Keynes thought that he was too anxious, and that he therefore gave insufficient attention to the refinement of analysis in ways that had no apparent practical application.[10] As has been seen, Marshall was primarily concerned to foster improvements within the system, by voluntary action, but he also had a vision of an increasing role for government, which was expressed in a remarkable fashion in "The Social Possibilities of Economic Chivalry" (published in 1907) by reconstruing laissez-faire as "let the state be up and doing."[11] Yet in his concern to promote the scientific status of economics he became increasingly conscious of the limitations of economic analysis (limitations that were to be much more tightly drawn by the development of the logic of welfare economics in the 1930s), and correspondingly cautious of specific pronouncements on policy. He thus established an activist tradition in Cambridge that was almost bound to create greater expectations than he was himself prepared to fulfill.

Pigou

That, in Cambridge, the subject matter of economics was accepted to be economic welfare is clear from the testimony of Sir Dennis Robertson.[12] It was therefore necessary to pay some attention to the effects of what has come to be called "market failure" and to the (apparently) corresponding scope for government intervention. This became a major concern of Marshall's successor, A. C. Pigou, whose *Wealth and Welfare* (later developed into *The Economics of Welfare*) appeared in 1912. But with Pigou came an important shift of emphasis: historical development and the working of the competitive process faded into the background and formal analysis became more prominent. Pigou's most influential contribution was the distinction between private and social costs, which was clearly capable of being used to produce a wide-ranging indictment of capitalism—although Pigou himself was usually reluctant to claim that obviously superior arrangements were always readily attainable.

Among the divergencies between private and social costs to which Pigou drew attention, we should particularly note those that arose from the absence of constant returns. He argued that industries subject to diminishing returns would become larger than was socially desirable, while those subject to increasing returns would remain too small; government intervention by taxation and subsidy (or even government operation) would therefore be capable, in principle, of improving on private enterprise. If, like Clapham, one believes that constant returns must always remain a mathematical point, at which the balance of forces changes,[13] then this critique of capitalist efficiency is all-embracing, as J. A. Hobson was quick to notice.[14] It is true that Pigou's arguments (which were developed from Marshallian origins) were effectively criticized by Young, Robertson, and Knight,[15] and had to be drastically amended, but the amendments did not appear at all quickly in a revised version of *The Economics of Welfare*, and were never as extensive as they should have been.[16]

Marshall's own objections, recorded in his copy of *Wealth and Welfare*, are of particular significance. He correctly observed that the apparent inefficiency of diminishing-returns industries resulted from Pigou's confusion of real costs and transfer payments within static equilibrium; but it was Pigou's strict adherence to static analysis in his treatment of increasing-returns industries that caused Marshall to object: "I think he overrates the possibilities of the statical method." Though resolving to keep quiet for the present, Marshall continues: "When he translates W and W into realism, then I may perhaps raise a question."[17]

It was Pigou's concern for improving the formal rigor of economic argument that exposed the contradictions between long-run falling costs and perfect competition, which Marshall well understood; and it was Pigou, who was assumed—not quite correctly, as we have just seen—to be the authorized interpreter of Marshall's thought, who translated Marshall's long-period analysis into the language of static perfect competition. He did so with much less qualification than F. H. Knight, who, in his own formalization of perfectly competitive static equilibrium, drew attention to its limitations for the analysis of growth and change.[18] In the process, Pigou redefined Marshall's representative firm as an equilibrium firm—though it remained an analytical device with no necessary real-world counterpart—and the equilibrium as perfectly competitive.[19] He then identified the position of equilibrium with the minimum point on the equilibrium firm's U-shaped cost curve, thus throwing the whole burden of increasing returns onto external economies.

If any single action led to the overthrow of the Marshallian system, it was Pigou's establishment of the equilibrium firm as the central instrument of analysis; it was now a simple step (although not one taken by Pigou) to define an industry in equilibrium as a collection of equilibrium firms,[20] and this exaltation of the equilibrium firm was the work not of a critic, but of a "loyal but faithless Marshallian."[21] The phrase is D. H. Robertson's, but it has to be admitted that Robertson himself was also faithless. In his criticism of Pigou's analysis of the welfare gains supposedly attainable by subsidizing industries that were subject to increasing returns, he had insisted that these returns were the results of time and the progress of organization; yet in the symposium that followed the publication of Sraffa's (1926) article,[22] he accepted Pigou's definition of perfect competition as a correct (if uncomfortable) interpretation of Marshall's competition.[23] Joan Robinson would therefore have been entitled to claim that, if she took the wrong turning, the diversion signs were erected by Marshallians.

Sraffa

Although clearly intended as a criticism of Marshall, and so regarded by supporters and opponents alike, Sraffa's famous article, "The Laws of Return under Competitive Conditions," had nothing to say about economic development; it was an exercise in the logic of long-run static equilibrium, and therefore not applicable to Marshall's system. If one reads it now without reference to its context, it appears to be a somewhat schizophrenic exercise, reflecting its origin as an amalgamation of two papers: its criticism of contemporary value theory is directed primarily at the use of a partial equilibrium framework, while its principal proposals are clearly conceived within that very framework.

Sraffa argued that the use of partial equilibrium methods was premised on the negligibility of interactions between the part of the economy (typically a single industry) under consideration and the remainder; interdependency of costs was therefore not acceptable. Yet, only if diminishing returns were attributable to a factor employed solely in the sector being analyzed would the consequent increase in costs fail to be experienced simultaneously by other sectors. Any increasing returns that resulted from external economies were similarly inadmissible if they conferred any benefits outside the sector under study. On the other hand, economies internal to a single firm were clearly incompatible with perfect competition. So for perfectly competitive partial equilibrium, one was left only with economies that were external to a single firm but internal to the industry, and these, Sraffa claimed, were the least likely to be found. The conclusion to this part of Sraffa's argument is that "the cost of production of commodities produced competitively . . . must be regarded as constant in respect of small variations in the quantity produced."[24] But instead of developing a competitive analysis based on constant costs, which might appear the natural sequel, Sraffa took a very different line: his response was "to abandon the path of free competition and turn . . . towards monopoly."[25]

There are two odd features of this proposal: the first is the apparent assumption that only perfect competition can be free; the second is that it follows a paragraph in which the illegitimacy of partial equilibrium analysis is restated. It would appear therefore that Sraffa's recommendations apply only to industries in which any departure from constant costs is attributable to causes peculiar to that industry. Analysis of single-industry monopoly has no obvious advantages over single-industry competition in handling, or evading, problems of interdependence between industries.

Moreover, despite Sraffa's claim, the path of monopoly does not allow one to make any simple use of a "well-defined theory" when each industry is populated by a number of rival producers. Sraffa's proposals for the modification of the familiar monopoly demand curve simply ignored the problems of interdependence between firms, in a manner not entirely dissimilar from the ways in which he claimed that interdependence was ignored in partial equilibrium models when costs are not constant. These problems were carried over into the economics of imperfect competition, where they were no better handled.

Joan Robinson's Research Program

As the great-granddaughter of the Christian socialist F. D. Maurice and the daughter of a general who sacrificed his military career for what he thought was his duty to bear witness to the truth, Joan Robinson comfortably assimilated the Cambridge objective of improving the condition of the people, and in particular Pigou's program of identifying deficiencies in the existing system which might be amenable to governmental remedies. As we have seen, Pigou's treatment of increasing and diminishing returns appeared to reveal such deficiencies in almost every industry; and, although that analysis had to be modified, Sraffa's criticism seemed to reinforce the conclusion that increasing returns would be associated with prices that were too high and outputs that were too low in comparison with the welfare ideal. In this sense, what Joan Robinson offered, as both O'Brien and Whitaker have pointed out,[26] was a substantial supplement to *The Economics of Welfare*. (By contrast, Chamberlin's *Theory of Monopolistic Competition* [1933], as O'Brien has also pointed out, was not intended as a contribution to welfare economics—though it was often so misused.) The debt to Pigou is both general—the theme of market failure—and particular—the explanation of industry equilibrium through the specification of the conditions of equilibrium for the individual firm.

Joan Robinson also followed Pigou in choosing to develop formal models. As is often the way with eager and forceful newcomers, she went well beyond him. She was very explicit about her research program: indeed, the contrast with Marshall is as striking in the clarity of her methodological manifesto as it is in her method of analysis. Where Marshall had sought to make his analysis its own justification, and that justification the provision of useful knowledge for those who were not specialist economists, Joan Robinson began with a clear warning. In words that embody a stronger statement of Keynes's editorial introduction to the Cambridge Economic Handbooks, she presented her book as "a box of tools . . . [that] can make only an indirect contribution to our knowledge of the actual world."[27] Moreover, it was presented to the analytical economist; there was nothing in it for the practical man. "It is natural enough for the practical man to complain that he asks for bread and the economist gives him a stone. . . . The practical man must be asked to have patience," and may have to wait a long time; meanwhile, the economist has a duty to make clear that the questions that can be answered are not the questions that the practical man would like to ask.[28] It is a remarkably austere vision, especially for someone committed to the view that the task of economic analysis is to improve human welfare.

Later in the book the research program was outlined.[29] The first stage was to analyze the industry supply curve as "the most abstract problem, in which there is neither time nor market imperfection." It is not clear whether she accepted Sraffa's argument that such a supply curve must be horizontal. The second stage, represented by her book, was to allow market imperfection but insist on the full equilibrium of every firm; whether the failure to derive a uniquely determinate supply curve under her assumptions was to be regarded (in 1933) as unfinished business is not clear, although later, when the rest of the research program had been abandoned—or perhaps transferred elsewhere—the failure was used as a proof of its nonexistence. Time was to be introduced at the next stage, and lastly, "factors connected with ignorance, inertia and the 'human element' generally would have to be fitted into the scheme." All this reads nowadays rather like an adumbration of the general equilibrium research program; and it can hardly be denied that Joan Robinson's first book gave a powerful impulse toward the development of formalism which has been so characteristic of the last fifty years, and which she came to regard with such dismay. That is not to say that any other course of action by her would have stopped or diverted that development; indeed, the eclipse of economic growth by the theory of value may have been an inevitable consequence of the rise of neoclassical economics. It was certainly not by Marshall's desire or design.

Monopoly and Competition

Joan Robinson's analysis of monopoly was conventional; it differed from Marshall's, as she noted, only in its use of marginal conditions in place of the (formally equivalent) maximization of the area that represents profit.[30] It was, however, developed much further, notably by applying the theory to factor markets in order to undermine the marginal productivity theory of wages—which, according to the preface to the second edition,[31] was for her the main point, as it appears to have been in the capital switching controversy. (Partial equilibrium analysis is, of course, not a satisfactory basis for a general treatment of income distribution.) As Whitaker emphasizes,[32] this elaboration of monopoly theory, including a comparison with perfect competition, and a general concern (as with

Pigou) for welfare implications occupies most of the book. Sraffa had released the analysis of monopoly from its uncomfortable pen, and it had immediately swallowed up the analysis of competition.[33] What Joan Robinson had done was to exploit the Sraffian emancipation of monopoly to extend the Pigovian program of welfare economics—disregarding, along the way, Sraffa's objections to partial equilibrium analysis.

One thing is missing from this view of Joan Robinson's book, and that is precisely the analysis that is nowadays known as the theory of imperfect competition—in a phrase, the tangency solution. Here, with the help of Kahn, she took the ideas of group equilibrium that were somewhat insecurely developed in the last part of Sraffa's article, and removed Sraffa's simplifying assumption that the number of firms (and, by implication, the set of products) was fixed. By so doing, she produced an analysis that was apparently more rigorous than Sraffa's, but was actually even less secure.

The problem lies in the demand curve. Marshall considered a statutory monopoly, in which a single firm was granted control over an industry: the demand curve for the industry therefore became the demand curve facing the monopolist. Sraffa's monopolists, however, clearly have no such privileged access to an industry demand curve; as he observed, a rise in price by one firm will cause some of its customers to switch to the products of another industry, but some to rival producers within the same industry.[34] Not surprisingly, his treatment of the demand curve facing the individual firm was less than satisfactory.

Joan Robinson stated the difficulty very clearly—and defined it away, as Triffin observed.[35] "The demand curve for the individual firm may be conceived to show the full effect upon the sales of that firm which results from any change in the price which it charges, whether it causes a change in the prices charged by the others or not. It is not to our purpose to consider this question in detail."[36] She recognized that this procedure entailed discounting the consequential patterns of future revenues—a "distressingly vague" conception; but the difficulties must be ignored so that the analysis may proceed.[37] The stratagem of dealing with the problems of interdependency by assuming them to have been solved is still a favorite ploy. Indeed, it appears to be an essential element in any "solution" of the oligopoly problem; and one of the paradoxical consequences of the search for formal rigor that was being pursued by Pigou and Sraffa in their various ways (and by many others, some of them much better equipped with the mathematical expertise that came to be necessary) is that, far from unifying theory, as Joan Robinson claimed, it caused its disintegration. The pursuit of clarity and rigor led to confusion. How the leading economists of the interwar years brought about the collapse of the Great Theory, most of them with no such intention, is the theme of Shackle's masterly survey of this period.[38]

Sraffa's assumption of a fixed set of firms, buttressed by some references to barriers to entry, gave at least some cover to his use of demand curves appropriate to protected monopoly;[39] and he realized well enough that the less elastic the demand for each of the firms, the more plausible was his equilibrium story. However, unlike Sraffa, Joan Robinson had learnt economics at Cambridge, and, in Cambridge, long-run equilibrium had to accommodate changes in the number of firms. This is how she achieved the most striking welfare proposition in the book: that the absence of monopoly profits does not signify the attainment of the desirable equality of marginal cost and price. Looking back in 1969, Joan Robinson selected as the first strong point of her analysis its effective undermining of "the complex of ideas erected on the slogan of 'price equals marginal cost.' "[40] In 1933 it provided a new argument to extend Pigou's proposition, which was based on the shapes of cost curves alone, that competition in a capitalist economy would quite generally fail to achieve the maximization of welfare (in later language, that it would normally be Pareto-inefficient). With falling long-run costs, no firm could secure normal profits without setting price above marginal cost, whatever the demand conditions it faced; if, as Joan Robinson claimed, competition was generally imperfect, then the discrepancy, and the welfare loss, was so much the greater.

It may just be worth speculating (one cannot do more) about the influence of Marshall on Joan Robinson's treatment of imperfect competition. Marshall's distinction between the general market and the firm's special market, and the need in some instances to couple the firm's supply curve with its own demand curve, which might be very steep, are perhaps sufficiently familiar to need no elaboration, and were presumably known, even if their significance was not always understood, in the 1920s.[41] (Marshall's discussion contains no hint of a long-run equilibrium of the firm.) What is less familiar—and nowadays quite unacceptable—is that, as was observed earlier, Marshall treated human wants as malleable, by education and advocacy, and by the economic process itself. The malleability of wants is clearly an assumption that Joan Robinson found congenial, although she was inclined to redirect the emphasis toward deliberate attempts by firms to mold preferences for their own benefit. Such activity does not appear incompatible with Marshall's treatment, which made no claims of optimality. It is perhaps possible that this Marshallian approach may help to account for the absence of any explicit consideration of the determinants of demand (apart from the demand for factors) and, in particular, for the unanalyzed assumption that demand curves would both shift and change shape between short-run and long-run equilibrium. But Marshall himself would surely have wished for some explicit treatment of product differentiation, which received no mention in *The Economics of Imperfect Competition.*

The formal analysis of demand in this book consisted of nothing more than a definition of each producer as a monopolist of his own output,[42] facing a demand curve that was determined by the availability of substitutes; this demand curve was normally falling but as a special case might be perfectly elastic.[43] Joan Robinson clearly had in mind a situation in which preferences are defined over producers; but she neither considered what preferences are consistent with an economy of optimizing agents—the "assumption which makes the analysis of value possible"[44]—nor recognized (as Chamberlin did from the first) that such preferences undermined the strong welfare implications of her analysis.

The analysis itself was weakened, rather than strengthened, by her insistence on developing a long-run equilibrium. For she gave no sufficient reason why any single firm should be able to sell a product, however differentiated—and remember that product differentiation was not explicitly considered in her book—at a price higher than that acceptable to any other firm; and all firms were assumed to have access to the same technology and the same costs. This conclusion is not invalidated by increasing returns, which we had better call economies of scale, since Marshallian increasing returns are the result of a historical process. If these extend over a sufficient range of output, there may indeed be only one firm, but that firm will be making nothing but normal profits, since those are the only terms on which it can obtain the business. In modern phraseology, even if economies of scale exclude competition in the market, there will still be competition for the market. With fully rational producers and consumers, it is impossible for any monopoly advantage to be permanently exploited. Exploitation is incompatible with equilibrium. That conclusion was reached by Andrews and by Schumpeter.[45]

This argument does not demonstrate that welfare losses through imperfections of competition are no problem (although both Andrews and Schumpeter, for their different reasons, thought that they did not call for much action); what it does demonstrate is that the first two stages of Joan Robinson's research program are not adequate to establish the case. Only by examining processes can one hope to demonstrate that the sloping demand curves for individual firms will be preserved. But by examining processes, one also brings in many more considerations, not least the changes in technique and costs that are produced by continuing competition and inquiring minds; one therefore loses the simplicity that is attainable by abstract models. It was to obtain this simplicity that the Marshallian program was gradually (and not always consciously) abandoned.

Analysis and Policy

The change in style between Marshall and Joan Robinson could hardly be more marked. The sociological and psychological arguments disappear (in contrast to Keynes's work) and we are left with an abstract presentation that clearly points the way to the axiomatic method. As we have seen, Joan Robinson emphasized that her analysis leaves us some way from any clear policy conclusions, although, since she appears to have been somewhat disappointed by the apparent policy ineffectiveness of Marshall's more direct approach, she maintained (at that time) her faith in the superiority of roundabout methods of theory development for generating policy prescriptions. Her warnings were repeated at the end of the book, and most—though not all—of her suggestions were fairly cautious; in effect, she argued that her analysis allows one to identify the elements about which more information is required, those that require further analysis, and those that depend on political or social judgment.

The program is clearly indicated, but it was not followed. There was not even any attempt to examine the evidence on demand and competition, absolute reliance being placed on the "well-known fact" that firms would be only too happy to increase sales at their present prices, if such sales were to be available. That Marshall had offered a rather different explanation for such phenomena, in terms of growth and change, seemed to demonstrate that Marshall's explanation was inadequate. Such evidence as did appear, notably from the Oxford Economists Research Group,[46] was met (primarily by Joan Robinson's allies) with the argument that it was inconsistent, not just with the particular analysis of imperfect competition, but with the notion of rational behavior, which was fundamental to all economic theory. That it might suggest the need to proceed to a later stage in the research program outlined in 1933 seems never to have been considered. Of course, it should not be forgotten that by the time the results of the Oxford inquiries became known Joan Robinson, along with other economists, had switched her principal attention to Keynes's theory of unemployment, and although she occasionally commented on imperfect competition, she never attempted any significant further development or revision of the theory.

In those later comments she did not always heed her own warnings. Her methodological prescription of 1933 appears to have been seen increasingly as a serious impediment to her desire to build a better society; it was unreasonable to ask the practical man to have patience for the length of time that might be necessary. Having, in her own phrase, given a stone when asked for bread, she was inclined to invoke a miracle and command that the stone be made into bread, basing policy prescription directly on the abstract theory. But it was not Joan Robinson who offered the most detailed blueprint; that distinction goes to James Meade who, in a volume of confident proposals over a wide range of economic issues,[47] explained how easy it would be to restructure industry in a way that, even allowing for some unfavorable incentive effects, could not fail to produce substantial improvements in economic welfare.

As we have seen more recently in other contexts—notably in monetary and macroeconomics—the rhetoric of the formal model is extremely powerful; other models no further from the beginning of their research program than Joan Robinson's imperfect competition have had greater influence on policy than hers. The desire to do good does not always have beneficial results. The Marshallian balance was lost. Yet Marshall is perhaps not without responsibility; despite his great respect for many businessmen, he had concluded his inaugural lecture with his hopes of increasing "the numbers of those, whom Cambridge, the great mother of strong men, sends out into the world with cool heads but warm hearts" to change that world for the better.[48] That governments advised by Cambridge economists could substantially improve economic welfare is a belief Joan Robinson shared with Keynes; it is a belief that seems to be part of the

Marshallian tradition. It is not extinct in Cambridge today—although there seems to be some disagreement about which Cambridge economists can be trusted to give the advice.

Conclusion

Marshall's desire to present economics as a body of established and agreed knowledge led him to be cautious in his claims; his desire to make his work generally accessible led him to banish mathematics from his text and to allow no more than geometry in his footnotes. Although he took proper note of unresolved issues, he did not place them firmly on the research agenda in the manner of Hicks: in building a coalition, one normally gives little attention to those differences between the parties that cannot easily be accommodated. What made this attitude particularly important was his third objective, which was to present the subject matter of economics as a study of the forces that cause change and movement. By 1890, the analytical methods of economics were developing in a way that was making this more difficult. Marshall valued these methods highly, and had made his own contribution to them. But there was simply no way in which equilibrium analysis and economic development (which implied changes in the data from which equilibria could be derived) could be combined in a single consistent body of theory. Nevertheless, in order to promote his first two objectives, he wished to present it as a single body, which was not obviously inconsistent: hence what Richardson called his "characteristically . . . careful imprecision,"[49] with the difficulties, in Joan Robinson's perfect phrase, hidden in plain sight.

His motto, "the many in the one, the one in the many"—an old favorite by the time it was inscribed in *Industry and Trade*—was intended simultaneously to warn of the need for care in the application of economic doctrine to problems that are necessarily complex and to insist nevertheless on the fundamental unity of the discipline. Yet his very success in presenting his "rounded globe of knowledge," with its crevices so deftly concealed, was a source of danger. It is an interesting question whether Marshall would have contributed more effectively to the development of economics if his caution in drawing conclusions had been matched by candor in explaining the formidable obstacles to the development of economic analysis. If Joan Robinson took a wrong turning, it was at least partly because Marshall had striven so hard to convince everyone that there was a single broad highway.

Notes

1. Robinson, 1951, pp. vii–viii. While this chapter was written for this volume, it has also been published, with minor differences, in Loasby, 1989. I would like to acknowledge helpful comments and suggestions from Geoff Harcourt, Denis O'Brien, and John Whitaker; none of them, however, has any responsibility for the parts of this paper with which they do not agree.
2. Whitaker, 1989.
3. Pigou, 1925, p. 86.

4. Keynes, 1972, p. 212.
5. Marshall, 1961, p. 85; and 1919.
6. See Loasby, 1989, for a more extensive treatment of Marshall's economics of progress.
7. Marshall, 1961, p. 318.
8. Schumpeter, 1943.
9. Marshall, p. 460.
10. Keynes, 1972, p. 200.
11. Pigou, 1925, p. 336.
12. Robertson, 1952, p. 14.
13. Clapham, 1922.
14. Hobson, 1914, p. 174.
15. Young, 1913; Robertson, 1924; Knight, 1924.
16. Cf. Ellis and Fellner, 1943.
17. Bharadwaj, 1972, p. 53.
18. Knight, 1921.
19. Pigou, 1928, p. 239.
20. Moss, 1984, p. 66.
21. Robertson, 1952, p. 73.
22. Sraffa, 1926.
23. Robertson, 1930.
24. Sraffa, 1926, pp. 540–41.
25. Ibid., p. 542.
26. O'Brien, 1984; Whitaker, 1989.
27. Robinson, 1933, p. 1.
28. Ibid., p. 2.
29. Ibid., p. 91.
30. Ibid., p. 54.
31. Ibid., p. xii.
32. Whitaker, 1989, p. 187.
33. Robinson, 1933, p. 4.
34. Sraffa, 1926, p. 547.
35. Triffin, 1940.
36. Robinson, 1933, p. 21.
37. Ibid., p. 23.
38. Shackle, 1967, which is appraised in Loasby, 1989.
39. Sraffa, 1926, p. 549.
40. Robinson, 1933, 1969 (2d edition), p. xi.
41. Marshall, 1961, pp. 458–59.
42. Robinson, 1933, p. 5.
43. Ibid., pp. 50–51.
44. Ibid., p. 6.
45. Andrews, 1964; Schumpeter, 1943.
46. Hall and Hitch, 1939.
47. Meade, 1936.
48. Pigou, 1925, p. 174.
49. Richardson, 1960, p. 23.

References

Andrews, P. W. S. (1964) *On Competition in Economic Theory*. London: Macmillan.

Bharadwaj, K. (1972) "Marshall on Pigou's *Wealth and Welfare*." *Economica* (N.S.), 39:32–46.

Chamberlin, E. H. (1933) *The Theory of Monopolistic Competition.* Cambridge, Mass.: Harvard University Press.
Clapham, J. H. (1922) "Of Empty Economic Boxes." *Economic Journal,* 32:305–14.
Ellis, H. S. and W. Fellner. (1943) "External Economies and Diseconomies." *American Economic Review,* 33:493–511.
Hall, R. L. and C. J. Hitch. (1939) "Price Theory and Business Behaviour." *Oxford Economic Papers,* 2:12–45.
Hobson, J. A. (1914) *Work and Wealth: A Human Valuation.* London: Macmillan.
Kaldor, N. (1934) "A Classificatory Note on the Determinateness of Equilibrium." *Review of Economic Studies,* 1:122–36.
Keynes, J. M. (1972) *Collected Writings,* ed. D. E. Moggridge, vol. 10. *Essays in Biography.* London: Macmillan.
Knight, F. H. (1921) *Risk, Uncertainty and Profit.* Boston: Houghton Mifflin.
———. (1924) "Some Fallacies in the Interpretation of Social Cost." *Quarterly Journal of Economics,* 38:582–606.
Loasby, B. J. (1989) *The Mind and Method of the Economist.* Aldershot, U.K.: Edward Elgar.
Marshall, A. (1919) *Industry and Trade.* London: Macmillan.
———. (1961) *Principles of Economics,* 9th ed. London: Macmillan.
Meade, J. E. (1936) *An Introduction to Economic Analysis and Policy.* Oxford: Oxford University Press.
Moss, S. (1984) "O'Brien's 'The Evolution of the Theory of the Firm,' A Discussion." In F. H. Stephen, ed., *Firms, Organization and Labour.* London: Macmillan.
O'Brien, D. P. (1984) "Research Programmes in Competitive Structure." *Journal of Economic Studies,* 10:29–51.
Pigou, A. C. (1912) *Wealth and Welfare.* London: Macmillan.
———. (1920, 1924, 1929) *The Economics of Welfare.* London: Macmillan.
———, ed. (1925) *Memorials of Alfred Marshall.* London: Macmillan.
———. (1928) "An Analysis of Supply." *Economic Journal,* 38:238–57.
Richardson, G. B. (1960) *Information and Investment.* Oxford: Oxford University Press.
Robertson, D. H. (1924) "Those Empty Boxes." *Economic Journal,* 34:16–31.
———. (1930) "Symposium on Increasing Returns and the Representative Firm. The Trees of the Forest." *Economic Journal,* 40:80–92.
———. (1952) *Utility and All That and Other Essays.* London: Allen and Unwin.
Robinson, J. V. (1933, 1969) *The Economics of Imperfect Competition,* 1st and 2d eds. London: Macmillan.
———. (1951) *Collected Economic Papers,* vol. 1, Oxford: Basil Blackwell.
Schumpeter, J. A. (1943) *Capitalism, Socialism and Democracy.* London: Allen and Unwin.
Shackle, G. L. S. (1967) *The Years of High Theory.* Cambridge: Cambridge University Press.
Sraffa, P. (1926) "The Laws of Returns under Competitive Conditions." *Economic Journal,* 36:535–50.
Triffin, R. (1940) *Monopolistic Competition and General Equilibrium Theory.* Cambridge, Mass.: Harvard University Press.
Whitaker, J. K. (1989) "The Cambridge Background to Imperfect Competition." In George R. Feiwel, ed., *The Economics of Imperfect Competition and Employment.* London: Macmillan.
Young, A. (1913) "Pigou's Wealth and Welfare." *Quarterly Journal of Economics,* 27:672–86.

JR

CHAPTER FIVE

History versus Equilibrium

Joan Robinson and Time in Economics

MEYER BURSTEIN

> Time is a device to prevent everything from happening at once.
>
> —Henri Bergson*

Joan Robinson's Contributions to "Time in Economic Theory"

Joan Robinson supplied me with an offprint of her 1974 monograph, *History versus Equilibrium*, in lieu of specific comments on a draft of Burstein (1975/1988): "You will see by this," she wrote, "where we agree and where we disagree." This essay tardily completes the exchange.

Joan Robinson may have been the first writer to understand the full implications of the fact that the *time* of *tâtonnement* is ontologically distinct from time in its ordinary sense. She explained that the former is a *logical* time, pertaining to a different (mathematical) space than *calendar* time, so that "rigorous" general equilibrium theory cannot be properly related to observable phenomena, and can be supplied only with a pseudo-dynamics. Agreed!

She also believed that her work undermines that of such "neoclassical" writers as Marshall, Pigou, Robertson, Knight, and Hayek, and claimed that Keynes's immunity from her strictures explains his putative destruction of neoclassical targets. I disagree. After limning Joan Robinson's seminal work and placing her contributions within a structure accommodating writers as disparate as Paul Samuelson and Richard Feynman, I shall explain my dissent in detail, after this preliminary conspectus of my argument.

In my view, Joan Robinson confuses the cautiously optimistic consensus of leading members of the English, Austrian, and American neoclassical schools, circa 1870–1936, about the secular prospects of private-ownership economies (surely relative to "planned" alternatives) with a *methodological*

*This is the epigraph of Joan Robinson's *Essays in the Theory of Economic Growth.*

bias leading to expectation of uninterrupted market clearance in an economy modeled by a Walrasian equation system. But Marshall, Hayek, Knight, et al. do not deploy models of this sort. For them economics is a set of studies in historical time.

Joan Robinson does have real enemies: the Walrasian school; proponents of the Hicksian neoclassical synthesis (IS/LM is meaningless in historical time); and the new classical macroeconomists. But I maintain that her argument vindicates Marshall and Pigou, as well as Keynes—while eschewing the new classical economics that followed her. She did not properly sort out her enemies, which cannot surprise her friends: she disdained Oscar Wilde's maxim that one cannot be too careful about choosing one's enemies.

Joan Robinson's contributions to time-in-economic-theory are incisively stated in her *Essays in the Theory of Economic Growth* (1962). Consider the following excerpts from these *Essays*:

> [A simultaneous equations model] may determine a path through time. . . . But the time through which such a model moves is, so to speak, logical time, not historical time.[1]

> A model applicable to actual history has to be capable of getting out of equilibrium; indeed, it must normally not be in it. . . . The initial position [in historical time] contains, as well as physical data, the state of expectations of the characters concerned (whether based on past experience or traditional beliefs). The system may be going to work itself out so as to fulfill them or as to disappoint them.[2]

The second passage is enhanced by plastic interpretation. The proper subject is not so much disequilibrium as the ontological impropriety of the idea of equilibrium. Note especially that disequilibrium is not an intrinsic quality of a set of data; it can be properly defined only relative to a model.

> To have a clear understanding of a physical concept like matter is not at all equivalent to the assumption that there is a "real" world behind our sense perceptions which is responsible for the existence of matter. . . . There is scarcely any use in believing in a real material world . . . unless it is a permanent, unchanging affair toward the knowledge of which we progress with slow but certain steps. But our knowledge of it is based naturally on the prevailing physical theories.[3]

So our ability to observe a "fact" like a disequilibrium state depends on the sort of theory we hold; "facts" depend on theories. Hopi Indians, clinging to a brutally simplistic faith, might conduct econometric studies estimating parameters of their gods' preferences, and conclude that prolonged drought reflects divine yearning for fresh slaughters of maidens. It would not occur to the Hopis to abandon their hypothesis, just as it does not occur to us to test it. Value structures affect scientific theorizing. The data spaces of economic theory are objects of economists' choices, a point Joan Robinson makes in connection with the theory of index-number construction.[4]

Alfred Marshall would find the following Robinsonian observations congenial:

> At any moment in logical time, the past is determined just as much as the future. In an historical model . . . today is a break in a time between an unknown future and an irrevocable past. What happens next will result from interactions of the behavior of human beings within the economy. Movement can only be forward.[5]

Even physical systems are historical.[6] But we agree and disagree. The following passage by Robinson capsulates the dispute:

> How to match up these simple postulated entities (the money-wage rate, the price level, the rate of interest, etc.) with complex reality is an insoluble problem. But this is only to be expected, for the entities were not derived in the first place from contemplating reality; they were hastily summoned out of their setting in a closed model to try to capture for equilibrium theory the position that Keynes demolished.[7]

To repeat, I shall try to show that Robinson's argument vindicates Marshall and Pigou as well as Keynes; none of their work is "ahistorical."

Turning to *The Accumulation of Capital* (1956/1965/1969), especially the third edition, we see that Robinson shows that applications of the "metaphor of equilibrium" to economic affairs are problematical.[8] Her discussion centers on how interdependent individual expectations drive key variables, like bond prices, so that the properties of any momentary economic stasis cannot be extracted from an objective reduced form, as is possible in the mechanical examples she cites. Had she made another characteristic point—specifically that agents making markets are biological organisms, some dying over any interval, to be replaced by newcomers, and always in flux—she would have further enhanced her position. And a proper economic stasis in historical time must concern *aggregations* (like consumption and exports) that may behave highly regularly; equilibrium ideas tenable for proper economic analysis in historical time must be imprecisely macroscopic, as Robinson makes very clear in describing states of tranquility, lucidity, and harmony.

Robinson's *state of tranquility* describes a *historical* interval in which expectations are largely fulfilled. Tranquility is consistent with oligopoly, or monopoly, settings in which price-quoters obtain roughly the results they thought they would. It describes the solution of a proper Keynesian problem and is what Tobin has in mind when he describes "rational expectations without market clearing."[9] It is also congenial to Marshallian economics.

A *state of lucidity* is not consistent with history: everyone commands all relevant facts and "understands the technical properties of all commodities." Lucidity presages Rational Expectations, just as harmony anticipates the Core: "the rules of the game are fully understood . . . [n]o one tries to alter his share of the proceeds of the economy, and all combine to increase the total to be shared."[10]

The following remarks from chapter 6 of *The Accumulation of Capital* encapsulate its dénouement:

> It is only necessary to describe these conditions to see how remote they are from the states in which actual economies dwell. . . . The rules of the game have been developed precisely to make accumulation and technical progress possible in conditions of uncertainty and imperfect knowledge. Yet too much disturbance, deception and conflict would break an economy to pieces. The persistence of capitalism till today is evidence that certain principles of coherence are imbedded in its confusion.[11]

These lines, properly hostile to what Hayek calls Cartesian pseudo-liberalism, could have been written by Hayek (1960), consciously relying on Burke and J. S. Mill's middle period for his liberal credo. Hayek and liberal economists of his genre deny the rationalist precepts of the French Enlightenment, along with "design theories" in general. Instead, they see liberal order emerging from "adaptive evolution."

The distinctive contribution of Hayek, Mises, and other "Austrian" writers to the study of the informational content of price signals (going back to Hayek, 1945) flows from their rejection of the commanding importance of equilibrium properties of prices in private-ownership economies. Hayek's (1945) "tin" example pivots, after all, on the unexpected disappearance of a source of supply. Thomsen (1987), influenced by Kirzner (who emphasizes the informational role of prices in disequilibrium, promoting discovery of initially unknown facts),[12] argues that the limit point of the Hayek/Mises theory is the conclusion that

> the exclusive emphasis on prices as transmitters of information begs, rather than solves, the economic problem posed by dispersed knowledge and by the ignorance of market participants . . . [who will make exchanges] without awareness of alternatives that they would have preferred had they known about them. These prices provide profit opportunities, rather than "all the relevant information," and these opportunities attract [entrepreneurial attention].[13]

For the "Austrians," exploitation of profit opportunities latent in "disequilibrium" prices is the motor of "capitalistic" adaptation. Instead of refuting economists of Hayek's stripe, Robinson demolishes the scientific plausibility of general equilibrium ideas that Hayek skirmished against in his contributions to the socialist-calculation debate with Lange and others, a debate notable for Lange's commitment to general equilibrium paradigms. Patinkin (1981) reports, *comme* student, that the architectonic beauties of general equilibrium theory gripped Lange, but not Knight, Simons, or Viner. This is not surprising: planning paradigms rely on information that Marshallian writers say can be extracted from price signals, but that agents do not initially possess.

The following remarks in many ways climax Robinson's study of time in economics; they vividly smash Cartesian paradigms of Walrasian and/or new-classical-macroeconomic theory, and are congenial to the economics of Marshall, Hayek, Knight, et al.:

> Some theorists, even among those who reject general equilibrium as useless, praise its logical elegance and completeness. A system of simultaneous equations need not specify any date nor does its solution involve history. But if any proposition drawn from it is applied to an economy inhabited by human beings, it immediately becomes self-contradictory. Human life does not exist outside history and no one has correct foresight of his own future behavior, let alone the behavior of all the other individuals impinging upon his. I do not think it is right to praise the logical elegance of a system which becomes self-contradictory when it is applied to the question it was designed to answer.[14]

An Extended Theoretical Setting

Samuelson explicitly distinguishes historical from nonhistorical, or causal, systems.

> A truly dynamical system may be completely non-historical, or causal, in the sense that its behavior depends only upon its initial conditions and the time which has elapsed the calendar date not entering into the process.[15]

He rather tentatively adds that:

> Given a small shock (measles, etc.), [a] child's weight will deviate from "normal" growth, but afterwards will catch up. . . . Similarly, an economy recovers from . . . a war. . . . But the population . . . is forever different in absolute numbers after a shock . . . even though its relative age distribution and other features may again approach stable form.[16]

Samuelson's examples are consistent with an ahistorical approach to economic theory. Measles or a state of war qualify as initial conditions; and Samuelson properly cites entities like relative-age distributions, proportions of females between the ages of thirty-five and forty owning IBM shares, etc., as proper variables for macroeconomic formulation. But I should go further and say that the idea of equilibrium is incompatible with that of history. The gist of my position is this: an uneasy truce is possible if structures are assumed to be parametrically rigid. Then we may ask if the influence of initial conditions persists. If it does, the system's evolution is (in a nonstochastic environment) definitively determined historically. But historical processes evolve in ways that cannot be forecast. Thus, a key "evolutionary" element concerns interactions of biological agents, together with individual aging. Robinson (1974) reminds us that "I today am not I tomorrow"; or, in Proust's locution, that one's *self* over one's life is but a *suite de moi*. An economy moving in real time is in ceaseless structural evolution; in the quite amorphous upshot, the initial constellation of parameters and structural coefficients is no more than a historical reference point; "equilibria" succeed each other kaleidoscopically.

One reason why the evolution of historical processes cannot be captured by equilibrium models is based on consequences of dependence of agents' actions on their expectations of others' expectations. Frydman and Phelps interestingly develop this point:

> Unless the actors in the economy have always lived in an epistemological garden of Eden, where the economist's model of endogenous variables has been the one and only relevant model and where each actor has never embraced another model, has never embraced the hypotheses that others have, and has never entertained the possibility that others might forecast the exogenous factors differently, the estimation of the model is bound to be contaminated by misestimations of the real-life actors. . . . Real-time history provides no opportunity for a "tâtonnement" (of estimations) of commonly embraced and known-to-be embraced models—a process vastly beyond any Walrasian tâtonnement involving a sequence of (known and foreseen) prices.[17]

A "*tâtonnement* of expectations" concerns recontracting; the Frydman-Phelps argument amplifies established hostility to general equilibrium analysis, which obviously depends on the absurd stipulation that "false trading" can be neglected.

I propose a program more radical than that of Frydman and Phelps. They study a model in which there are "true," firmly planted parameters. They ask, "is there a learning process converging on an objective solution?" And they point the way to the hedged position of Marshall and Pigou. In particular, they say that Knight (1921) stresses the unique aspects of each economic situation: "but economics must also recognize the recurring elements . . . if it is to aspire to any explanatory power."[18] Of course, there are recurring elements, as indeed Knight also pointed out. But the commanding position cannot be outflanked: correct economics must be, *inter alia*, a study in history, duly identifying "recurrent elements." Joan Robinson would probably have rejected the consensus-building role I assign her, but she did build consensus across much of the economic spectrum.

Expanding and Deepening the Analysis: Kirman (1983) and Georgescu-Roegen (1971)

Kirman (1983) projects the radical idea that models learn from agents. Our perceptions of "reality" affect its properties—here, structural coefficients of macromodels. The upshot is observationally indistinguishable from one in which there is no true model—and so no equilibrium reference state.

Kirman may be too prudent about the implications of his model. He is hard put to describe resulting outcomes as *equilibria.* And he puts so much distance between Equilibrium and History that one suspects he is more estranged from the new classical macroeconomists than he owns.

My interpretation of Kirman's analysis hinges on what Georgescu-Roegen calls irreversible and irrevocable processes:

> The first category of "nonreversibility" consists of all processes which, though not reversible, can return to any previously attained phase. . . . We may refer to them as irreversible. . . . In saying "history repeats itself," history is conceived as an irreversible process in this narrow sense. . . . A process is said to be reversible if and only if it can follow the same course phase by phase in the reverse order. . . . The second category of "nonreversibility" consists of processes that cannot pass through a given state more than once. . . . Such a process is irrevocable. . . . The entropic degradation of the universe as conceived by classical thermodynamics is an irrevocable process: the free energy once transformed into latent energy cannot be recuperated.[19]

Strictly, history is irrevocable—although measurements of various aggregates may display repetitive properties. But the process of Walrasian theory is completely reversible; that is what recontracting is all about! Reversibility is obtained at high cost: the *tâtonnement* plays out in a fictional or notional time. In historical time, life generates irrevocable changes.

Georgescu-Roegen does not cite Joan Robinson, but she anticipated his explanation of why the equilibrium idea of Walrasian, or new classical, economics is preposterous:

> The very fact that an individual . . . may alter his preferences [means that an] equilibrium . . . is thus immediately defeated not by the intervention of exogenous factors but by endogenous causes. . . . Edgeworth (1932, p. 127n) once said that "to treat variables as constants is the characteristic vice of the unmathematical economist." But an economist [confined] to mathematical models is burdened with an even greater vice, that of ignoring the qualitative factors that make for endogenous variability.[20]

In effect, Georgescu-Roegen sums up one of Frank Knight's principal positions:

> It is their [wants'] essential nature to change and grow. . . . The chief thing which the . . . individual wants is not satisfaction for the wants he has, but more, and *better* wants.[21]

And Knight's evaluation of the equilibrium idea in economics is exemplary:

> [One interested in scientific economics] had better give up . . . such notions as force and tendency and equilibrium, and restrict the matter of his discourse to statistical trends, correlations, etc., in the field of physically measurable mag-

> nitudes. . . . If terms like equilibrium and tendency are used in such a system it must be in the sense of statistical modes and mathematical limits.[22]

Surely Keynes does not demolish these positions. Nor would he have wanted to. In the domain of "time in economic theory," the great neoclassical writers are friends, not enemies, of Joan Robinson.

Mrs. Robinson and the Classics: "Where We Agree and Where We Disagree"

Marshall's description of the stationary state, the culminating idea in classical economics, should have pleased Joan Robinson:

> [The stationary] state obtains its name from the fact that in it the general conditions of production and consumption, of distribution and exchange, remain motionless; but yet it is full of movement; for it is a mode of life. The average age may be stationary; though each individual is growing up towards his prime or downwards to old age.[23]

> [In the stationary state] it will suffice to suppose that firms rise and fall, but that the "representative" firm remains always of about the same size . . . and that the economies resulting from its own resources are constant; and since the aggregate volume of production is constant, so also are the economies resulting from subsidiary industries in the neighborhood.[24]

Robinson was ambivalent towards Marshall, and surely unfair to Pigou. She acknowledged that Marshall studied a "recognizable economy in a particular framework of law and accepted conventions,"[25] and she points up the "notorious dilemma" posed by the idea of the representative firm. Indeed, she sees Marshall's stationary-state problem from an "increasing-returns" angle rather than from that of the "macro-foundations of microeconomics," i.e., the necessarily statistical properties of any equilibrium concerning biological agents.[26]

So far so good. But she also writes:

> As soon as the uncertainty of expectations that guide economic behavior is admitted, equilibrium drops out of the argument and history takes its place. The post-Keynesian theory reaches back to clasp the hands of Ricardo and Marx skipping over the sixty years of dominance of neoclassical doctrines from 1870 to the great slump.[27]

Why skip the years 1870–1930 (or 1870–1936, Kalecki excepted)? Joan Robinson offers two reasons. One is quite intriguing: it hits the expectations nail on the head. The other reason seems to me improper. It is based on the claim that writers like Marshall, Pigou, Wicksell, Lavington, Hawtrey, Robertson, and Knight base their work on concepts of equilibrium we know they explicitly reject.

> When Keynes summed up what he felt to be the main difference between his theory and that from which he had had "a long struggle of escape," he pointed to the admission into his argument of the very obvious fact that expectations about the future are necessarily uncertain. . . . Keynes (1937) described equilibrium theory as "a pretty, polite technique" which tries to deal with the present by abstracting from the fact that we know very little about the future.[28]

The *General Theory* contains profound and original insights into expectations. But it is also strongly committed to Marshallian equilibrium constructions. Indeed the book is marred by Keynes's efforts to keep equilibrium at its center.[29] So the excerpt's final sentence—immediately following a virtual capsulization of Knight's (1921) risk/uncertainty dichotomy—must be decried.

The "equilibrium theory" which Robinson undermines is that projected by Walras, Hicks, the neoclassical synthesis based on IS/LM, and prospectively, the new classical macroeconomics. Tobin makes a related point: the stipulation of continuous market clearing comprises an intense commitment to Equilibrium against History.[30]

Defending the Non-Walrasian Neoclassical Macroeconomic Doctrine

Marshall and Pigou et al. were primarily concerned with characteristic secular features of economic history (e.g., manufacturing employment, savings rates, and rates of profit). I do not find any trace of general equilibrium modeling in their work. (This may explain Walras's loathing of English economics.[31]) And Marshall, Pigou, Robertson, Fisher, Hayek, et al. are surely in agreement with Friedman's (1946, 1949, 1955) trenchant criticism of Walrasian methodology, as is Harrod (1956). Their business (trade) cycle theory, flowing from the work of Henry Thornton and J. S. Mill, emphasizes uncertainty and expectations. "Expectational noise" reverberates in their monetary economics and in Robertson's theory of industrial fluctuations. Nor is the theory of economic fluctuations of the Austrians, Wicksell and Fisher, at all Walrasian.

The proper dichotomy between Keynesian and general equilibrium paradigms is displayed by Lange's *Price Flexibility and Employment* (1944)—although Lange extracts Keynes-like results from his elaborate, if mathematically unrigorous, model.[32] Lange's equation system crumbles into dust if exposed to History. And Keynes clouds up the picture: he approved Hick's (1937) "Mr. Keynes and the Classics."[33] It seems that the sharpest paradigmatic clash in the domain under study, until the advent of the new classical macroeconomics, is between the constructions of Oskar Lange and Joan Robinson.

Concluding Remarks

Joan Robinson's penetrating analysis of time in economics goes far to show that general equilibrium theory cannot validly interpret motions of observable quantities. But she improperly extended her stricture to include non-Walrasian neoclassicals: Wicksell, Marshall, Fisher, Hayek, et al. are indicted, along with Walras, Lange, IS/LM, and the new macroeconomists; the former must be exonerated, but the latter are convicted. Thus, the line of macroeconomic thought running from Adam Smith and Ricardo, through Mill, Marshall, and Irving Fisher, to Milton Friedman (for example), is oblivious to "logical" time; these economists sacrifice "rigor" in a way decried by the Walrasian school, who went on to "reform" theory by introducing concepts that make sense only in "logical" time.

Joan Robinson's analysis is monumentally important in its proper domain. Her analysis of time in economic theory nests in an extended theoretical setting, going back to Samuelson's *Foundations of Economic Analysis* and including studies by Frydman and Phelps (1983), Kirman (1983), et al., of the consequences of the dependence of agents' actions in their expectations of others expectations. Kirman's study of the ways in which "real time" events may impose parametric, or even structural, change on models leads naturally to reflection on thermodynamical concepts, studied by Georgescu-Roegen (1971), of (ir)reversible and irrevocable processes: economic actions lead to entropic transformation of the ambient environment, so that "realization of our purposes sets up a never-to-return journey."[34] This is just what Joan Robinson taught. Economics properly concerns processes unfolding in time that irreversibly, if not irrevocably, affect a cast of economic agents that birth and death are shuffling up in any case. Economists should resist the temptation to obtain specious precision by pretending that time can be made to stand still.

Remember Joan Robinson.

Notes

I am indebted to Avi Cohen and Ingrid Rima for valuable suggestions.

1. Robinson, 1962, pp. 23–24.
2. Ibid., pp. 24–25.
3. Ibid., pp. 2–3.
4. Ibid., pp. 28–29.
5. Ibid., p. 25.
6. Feynman, 1963, pp. 8–9.
7. Robinson, 1962, p. 29.
8. Robinson, 1969, chap. 6, p. 57ff.
9. Tobin, 1980, p. 44ff.
10. Robinson, 1956/1965/1969, p. 60.
11. Ibid.
12. Kirzner, 1979, 1984.
13. Thomsen, 1987, p. 16.
14. Robinson, 1979, p. 2.
15. Samuelson, 1947/1983, p. 315.
16. Ibid., p. 329.
17. Frydman and Phelps, 1983, p. 25.

18. Ibid.
19. Georgescu-Roegen, 1971, p. 197.
20. Ibid., pp. 334–36.
21. Knight, 1935, p. 22.
22. Ibid., pp. 162–63.
23. Marshall, 1920, p. 305.
24. Ibid.
25. Robinson, 1974, p. 6.
26. See Burstein, 1988.
27. Robinson, 1974, p. 1.
28. Ibid.
29. See Burstein, 1988, and Kohn, 1986.
30. Tobin, 1980, pp. 21–22.
31. Described by Blaug, 1985, chap. 13.
32. Friedman, 1946, 1953.
33. Burstein, 1988.
34. Georgescu-Roegen, 1971, p. 195.

References

Bergson, H. (1911/1944) *Creative Evolution.* Trans. by A. Mitchell, foreword by Irwin Edman. New York: Random House (Modern Library).

Blaug, M. (1985) *Economic Theory in Retrospect,* 4th ed. Cambridge: Cambridge University Press.

Burstein, M. (1968) *Economic Theory: Equilibrium and Change.* London: John Wiley & Sons.

———. (1986) *Modern Monetary Theory.* London and New York: MacMillan and St. Martin's Press.

———. (1988) *Studies in Banking Theory, Financial History and Vertical Control.* London and New York: Macmillan and St. Martin's Press.

Edgeworth, F. Y. (1953) *Mathematical Psychics: An Essay on the Application of Mathematics to the Moral Sciences.* New York: Augustus Kelley, first published in 1881.

Ekelund, R. B., Jr. and R. F. Hébert. (1983) *A History of Economic Theory and Method,* 2d ed. New York: McGraw-Hill.

Feynman, R. (1963) *Lectures on Psychics,* vol. 1. Reading, Mass.: Addison-Wesley.

Friedman, M. (1946/1953) "Lange on Price Flexibility and Employment: A Methodological Criticism," *American Economic Review,* 36:613–31. Reprinted in *Essays in Positive Economics.* Chicago: University of Chicago Press.

———. (1949/1953) "The Marshallian Demand Curve." *Journal of Political Economy,* 57:463–95. Reprinted in *Essays in Positive Economics.* Chicago: University of Chicago Press.

———. (1955) "Léon Walras and his Economic System." *American Economic Review,* 45:900–909.

Frydman, R. and E. Phelps, eds. (1983) *Individual Forecasting and Aggregate Outcomes.* New York: Cambridge University Press.

Georgescu-Roegen, N. (1971) *The Entropy Law and the Economic Process.* Cambridge, Mass.: Harvard University Press.

Gram, H. and V. Walsh. (1983) "Joan Robinson's Economics in Retrospect." *Journal of Economic Literature,* 21 (June): 518–50.

Harcourt, G. C. (1979) "Joan Robinson." In D. L. Sills, ed., *International Encyclopedia of the Social Sciences,* Biographical Supplement, vol. 18, pp. 663–67. New York: Free Press.

Harrod, R. (1956) "Walras: A Re-Appraisal." *Economic Journal*, 66:307–16.

Hayek, F. (1945) "The Use of Knowledge in Society." *American Economic Review*, 35:519–30.

———. (1948) *Individualism and Economic Order*. Chicago: University of Chicago Press.

———. (1960) *The Constitution of Liberty*. Chicago: University of Chicago Press.

Hicks, J. R. (1937) "Mr. Keynes and the Classics: A Suggested Interpretation." *Econometrica*, 5:147–59.

———. (1946) *Value and Capital*, 2d ed. Oxford: Clarendon Press.

Kaldor, N. (1960) *Essays on Economic Stability and Growth*. London: Duckworth.

Keynes, J. M. (1921) *A Treatise on Probability*. London: Macmillan.

———. (1930) *A Treatise on Money*, vol. 1. London: Macmillan.

———. (1936) *The General Theory of Employment, Interest and Money*. London: Macmillan.

———. (1937) "The General Theory of Employment." *Quarterly Journal of Economics*, 51:209–23. Reprinted in D. Moggridge, ed., *Collected Writings of John Maynard Keynes*, vol. 14. London: Macmillan for the Royal Economic Society.

Kirman, A. (1983) "On Mistaken Beliefs and Resultant Equilibria." In R. Frydman and E. Phelps, eds. *Individual Forecasting and Aggregate Outcomes*, p. 147. New York: Cambridge University Press.

Kirzner, I. M. (1979) "Knowing about Knowledge: A Subjectivist View of the Rôle of Information." In his *Perception, Opportunity and Profit*, pp. 137–53. Chicago: University of Chicago Press.

———. (1984) "Prices, the Communication of Knowledge and the Discovery Process." In K. R. Leube and A. H. Zlabinger, eds., *The Political Economy of Freedom: Essays in Honor of F. A. Hayek*, pp. 193–206.

Knight, F. H. (1921) *Risk, Uncertainty and Profit*. Boston: Houghton Mifflin.

———. (1922/1935) "Ethics and the Economic Interpretation." *Quarterly Journal of Economics*, 36:454–81. Reprinted in *The Ethics of Competition*, p. 19. New York: Harper, 1935.

———. (1923/1935) "The Ethics of Competition." *Quarterly Journal of Economics*, 37:579–624. Reprinted in *The Ethics of Competition*, p. 41. New York: Harper, 1935.

———. (1935) *The Ethics of Competition*. New York: Harper.

Kohn, M. (1986) "Monetary Analysis, the Equilibrium Method and Keynes's General Theory." *Journal of Political Economy*, 94:1191–1224.

Lange, O. (1944) *Price Flexibility and Employment*. Bloomington, Ind.: Principia Press.

Leijonhufvud, A. (1976) "Schools, 'Revolutions,' and Research Programmes in Economic Theory." In S. J. Latsis, ed., *Method and Appraisal in Economics*. Cambridge: Cambridge University Press.

Lerner, A. P. (1952/1953) "The Essential Properties of Interest and Money." *Quarterly Journal of Economics*, 66:172–93. Reprinted in *Essays in Economic Analysis*. London: Macmillan.

Lindsay, R. and H. Margenau. (1957) *Foundations of Physics*. New York: Dover.

Lotka, A. J. (1922) "Contributions to the Energetics of Evolution." Proceedings of the National Academy of Sciences, 8:147–50.

Marshall, A. (1920) *Principles of Economics*, 8th ed. London: Macmillan.

Patinkin, D. (1981) *Essays on and in the Chicago Tradition*. Durham, N.C.: Duke University Press.

Pigou, A. C. (1935) *The Economics of Stationary States*. London: Macmillan.

Robinson, Joan (1942/1966) *An Essay on Marxian Economics*, 1st and 2d eds. London: Macmillan.

———. (1956/1965/1969) *The Accumulation of Capital*, 1st, 2d, and 3d eds. (See esp. the 3d ed.) London: Macmillan.

———. (1962) *Essays on the Theory of Economic Growth.* London: Macmillan.

———. (1974) *History versus Equilibrium.* Thames Papers in Economics. London: Thames Polytechnic.

Samuelson, P. (1947/1983) *Foundations of Economic Analysis.* Cambridge, Mass.: Harvard University Press.

Smith, Adam. (1776/1910/1970) *The Wealth of Nations*, vol. 1. London: Dent (Everyman's Library), 1910, rpt. 1970.

Thomsen, E. F. (1987) "Knowledge, Discovery and Prices," *Humane Studies Review*, 5, 1 (Fall): 1–2, 17.

Tobin, J. (1980) *Asset Accumulation and Economic Activity.* Chicago and Oxford: University of Chicago Press and Basil Blackwell.

Veblen, Thorstein. (1899/1934) *The Theory of the Leisure Class.* New York: Random House (Modern Library), 1934.

JR

CHAPTER SIX

Mr. Harrod and the Classics

J. S. METCALFE AND IAN STEEDMAN

There have been many responses to the economic theory of Keynes's *General Theory* but two of the most influential have certainly been Hicks's IS/LM interpretation of that theory and Harrod's dynamic extension to take account of the capacity-creating effects of net investment.[1] We shall not be concerned here with whether the IS/LM analysis provided a faithful rendering of the *General Theory* or whether it represented Hicks's own view of macroeconomic theory. Rather, taking it as a fact that IS/LM analysis has been, and still is, widely used, we seek to show how one flaw may be removed from that analysis by recognition of Harrod's fundamental insight into the requirements of macroeconomic equilibrium.

Joan Robinson was not a great admirer, it will probably be agreed, of the IS/LM interpretation of Keynes.[2] But she did maintain a longstanding, if critical, interest in Harrod's attempts to interpret Keynes's insights in a growth framework—an interest lasting, at least, from her March 1949 *Economic Journal* article on Harrod's *Towards a Dynamic Economics* to her retrospective "Harrod after Twenty-One Years" in the *Economic Journal* of September 1970. In the former, she appeared to adopt a "steady-state" interpretation of Harrod's central point, writing that:

> [H]is world is dynamic in the sense that continuous change is going on through time, but it is a world without history. Every change that took place in the past was digested, so to speak, as it occurred. Time rolls on in a homogeneous stream, and it makes no difference at what point we dip into it.[3]

As will soon emerge below, we adopt a quite different interpretation of Harrod's economic dynamics. This difference may not suffice, however, to still all the reader's questions regarding Joan Robinson's concerns about history, time, and uncertainty—but the reader may wish to suspend judgment on this issue until after reading our closing remarks.

IS/LM Equilibrium

As is well known, an IS/LM equilibrium is a momentary one and there are two routes through which internally generated forces may disrupt such an equilibrium. One such route is that expectations may be falsified by experience and hence changed. Without in the least denying the importance of expectations and changes therein, we shall adopt one of Keynes's devices, considering equilibria premised upon given patterns of expectations and supposing that long-period expectations may or may not be satisfied.[4]

The other possible source of internally generated disruption is that the "equilibrium" flows determined by an IS/LM analysis are themselves changing the very stocks that are taken to be among the determinants of IS/LM "equilibrium." In this precise sense, then, an IS/LM equilibrium may be said to be an internally *incoherent* "equilibrium."

An internal incoherence of the type just defined is sometimes swept aside by reference to the fact that any stock discrepancies are likely to be small, relative to the total value of stocks, and can therefore be ignored. This response misses the point entirely, for it is not the relative magnitudes of stock disequilibria that are important but rather the *responsiveness* of flow decisions to *any* such stock disequilibria. Only if expenditure flows are completely independent of balance-sheet positions is the IS/LM framework free from internal inconsistency. Since an assumption of such complete independence would be quite unjustified, a reformulation of the concept of macroeconomic equilibrium is required, the obvious candidate being Harrod's conception of a dynamic equilibrium.

In recent writings it has been the widespread (and welcome) concern with the government budget constraint that has most clearly drawn attention to issues of stock/flow (in)consistency but, as Tobin has forcefully pointed out,[5] there is absolutely no good reason for worrying about one particular stock/flow (in)consistency while ignoring others. What is needed is a form of analysis to which complete stock/flow consistency is central, or, so to speak, "built in." *Ad hoc* adjustments to IS/LM analysis will not suffice to remove the internal incoherence to which that analysis is subject and it is for this reason that we propose a reformulation that starts from Harrod's work and generates an internally *coherent* concept of equilibrium.

Coherent Equilibrium versus Steady Growth

A concept of equilibrium that is to be coherent, in the sense of avoiding stock/flow inconsistencies, must necessarily be defined in terms not only of the levels of endogenous variables but also of their rates of change. It was, of course, precisely such considerations that led Harrod to his conception of dynamic equilibrium. It is essential at this point to recognize that an equilibrium defined in terms of both levels and rates of change can be defined perfectly well *for a given moment of time*. Such an equilibrium will be internally coherent, in the sense explained above, but *it may or may not* be a steady- (or semi-stationary) state equilibrium. Recall that in our treatment of expectations, while short-period expectations are satisfied, long-period expectations may or may not be fulfilled.

By contrast, any steady-state equilibrium necessarily involves that long-period expectations *are* fulfilled. The equilibrium concept that we shall suggest as an alternative to the IS/LM equilibrium *is* an internally coherent equilibrium; it *need not* be a steady-growth equilibrium in the usual meaning of this term.

Our purpose here is to propose a particular improvement to IS/LM analysis, and not to present an exegetically impeccable account of Harrod's equilibrium concept, but in view of the prevalence of steady-growth theorizing and the consequent danger that our proposed "coherent equilibrium" will be *mis*interpreted as "steady-growth equilibrium," it will be valuable to recall some of Harrod's own statements that bear upon the distinction. In his famous *Economic Journal* essay of 1939, Harrod wrote that "The analysis relates to *a single point of time*"; twenty years later he stressed that "My equation purported to specify what the steady rate of growth *at a given point of time* would be . . . I did not dare venture beyond that."[6] And, in *Economic Dynamics*, Harrod still insisted that "The most basic equations in dynamics relate to *a particular point of time*."[7] If further evidence is needed that Harrod was not referring here to steady-growth theory (as that term is now generally understood), we may note his statement that "the dynamic determinants themselves . . . are, of course, always changing."[8] For better or for worse, our "coherent equilibrium" is, like Harrod's equilibrium, defined for a given moment in time. We shall *not* be engaging, in this paper, in semi-stationary growth theory and the reader is asked to resist any temptation to suppose otherwise.

We have already explained why the "coherent" equilibrium concept is preferable to the IS/LM equilibrium, which involves *only* market clearing. It should now be clear that "coherent" equilibrium also differs significantly from the long-run steady-growth concept that underlies "monetary growth theory."[9] There is no reason to suppose that actual economies are either in, or undergoing a transition to, a steady-growth path and it is hardly self-evident that they are adjusting to an exogenously given labor-force growth rate. It is probably true that the fundamental determinants are always changing. There is, therefore, a case for seeking to avoid *both* the internal incoherence of IS/LM analysis *and* the strenuous artificiality of monetary growth theory; it is exactly this that the "coherent equilibrium" concept is designed to do.

"Intermediate" IS/LM Analysis

Monetary growth theory is not, of course, the only strand in the literature that seeks to add dynamic equations to IS/LM. It is a straightforward matter to add equations that trace out time paths for the components of effective demand and for stocks of financial assets, and thus create a sequence of moving IS/LM equilibria.[10] However, such effective demand dynamics miss the central point of Harrodian theory, i.e., that dynamic equilibrium entails a relationship between changes in effective demand and changes in productive capacity. Adding dynamic equations to treat components of effective demand alone is necessarily incomplete as a treatment of the dynamic inconsistencies of the IS/LM framework.

Our Procedure

It need hardly be said that the basic IS/LM framework has been embellished in many ways; for example, to allow for variable prices, wage dynamics, wealth effects, the government budget constraint, the openness of the economy, and so on. Yet the problem of internal incoherence both exists in the basic framework and remains after such elaborations. It is therefore appropriate, since our central concern is with that internal incoherence, that we first present our proposed reformulation in terms of the basic, simplest case. Indeed, it would hardly be sensible to set out our main points in anything other than the basic case! Consequently, just as *basic* IS/LM analysis takes the money stock and the price level as *given,* so we shall, at first, take both the ratio of the money stock to capacity output and the price level as *given.* As in *basic* IS/LM, we take expectations as given, ignore real balance effects, and suppose given consumption, investment, etc. functions. Of course, we *cannot* treat the capital stock as given, as is done in IS/LM analysis, but it will be required to meet the condition of Harrod (and Domar, 1947) that output and capacity expand at the same rate. In a later section of the paper the endogenous determination of the inflation rate will be considered. But the central point throughout will be the need for—and indeed the simplicity of—the concept of *coherent* equilibrium at a *given* moment of time.

Conventions and Definitions

In the interest of simplicity, time is treated as continuous and, in the spirit of Harrod's work, no attention is paid to time lags. We do not, of course, suggest that time lags are really unimportant; we simply wish to bring out that our central points do not depend on lag effects. The symbols, Y, Y_c, I, and S denote actual output, capacity output, investment, and savings flows, at time t. All questions of depreciation and obsolescence are ignored.

At the ruling structure of relative prices, taken to be independent of the degree of capacity utilization, entrepreneurs have a clear idea of a normal relation between the values of their capital stocks and the associated potential flows of capacity output. Taken in the aggregate, this leads to a normal ratio of capital to capacity output defined by:

$$v_n \equiv K / Y_c \tag{1}$$

where K is the capital stock at time t, and v_n summarizes the relationship between capital stock and productive capacity and thus represents "aggregate supply conditions.'' No doubt v_n will be influenced by many factors (the interest rate, the real wage, the composition of consumers' expenditure, technical possibilities, the rate of accumulation, entrepreneurs' psychology, etc.), but the net effect of these influences *at a given moment of time* will be complex. We shall therefore simplify by treating v_n as a constant. (Of course, it would be desirable to replace this simplification by an explicit theory of the determination of v_n; not forgetting that steady-state theories of v_n will not necessarily be appropriate.)

It is important to recognize that the concept of normal capacity does not depend on a technologically fixed relation between capital stock and actual output. There is a margin of capacity utilization either side of ''normal capacity working'' so that the actual capital:output ratio, $v \equiv K/Y$, can be above or below v_n. There must be a technically determinate lower limit to v but we shall only consider positions of equilibrium within this limit. If we define the degree of capacity utilization by $x \equiv Y/Y_c$ then $v_n \equiv vx$. When output is in excess of normal capacity, $x > 1$ and $v < v_n$; while when output is below normal capacity, $x < 1$ and $v > v_n$. The possibility of a macro dynamic equilibrium discrepancy between v and v_n is crucial to what follows and distinguishes our framework from the contributions of Harrod and of Domar. (Although we proceed entirely in terms of the determinants of x, the translation into the behavior of v relative to v_n can be readily made.)

Growth rates are defined as:

$$g_c \equiv \dot{Y}_c / Y_c;\ g_y \equiv \dot{Y} / Y;\ g_I \equiv \dot{I} / I;\ g_K \equiv \dot{K} / K \equiv I / K \tag{2}$$

Expansion and Capacity Utilization

Let s be the average savings ratio, so that the goods market flow equilibrium condition—with no government and no foreign sector—may be written as:

$$I = sY$$

or

$$\dot{K} = \left(\frac{sx}{v_n}\right) K$$

or

$$g_K = \left(\frac{sx}{v_n}\right) \tag{3}$$

Since $Y \equiv xY_c$, effective demand and capacity, at a given instant, will be growing at the same rate as one another if, and only if, $\dot{x} = 0$. And since we treat v_n as constant, we see from (1) that $g_c = g_K$. Hence, when $\dot{x} = 0$, $g_y = g_c = g_K$.

We suppose that $s = s(x,r)$, where r is a representative long-term interest rate. The dependence on x results from the probable facts that as x rises the share of profits in income rises, and that the savings ratio out of profits exceeds that out of wages and salaries. Now, since $I = sY$, $g_I = g_y$ if and only if $\dot{s} = 0$. If $\dot{x} = 0$, $\dot{s} = 0$ if and only if $\dot{r} = 0$. Thus:

$$\dot{x} = \dot{r} = 0 \tag{4}$$

if and only if

$$g_y = g_c = g_K = g_I \tag{5}$$

Relations (4) and (5) are *necessary* for coherent equilibrium—but they are *not* sufficient, for the *desired* growth rate of capital accumulation must also be equal to the common growth rate shown in (5).[11]

Desired Investment and Accumulation

We suppose that scientific discoveries, innovation possibilities, population growth, etc., are creating an *expanding* set of investment opportunities. Given the perceptions of these opportunities by entrepreneurs, together with their other expectations, we take desired investment and the growth rate of desired capital stock to depend on r and on x, the dependence on r being negative and that on x being positive.[12] Notice that there is no inconsistency in supposing that investment is positive when $x < 1$, even though capitalists currently plan that their new capacity will be fully utilized. Since we are concerned with coherent equilibrium, the marginal expected x may be unity even though the average actual x is less than unity and constant. Thus, it is quite consistent to suppose that at a given moment there is underutilization of existing capacity, and yet entrepreneurs perceive *new* investment opportunities, to benefit from which they must lay down qualitatively new plant and equipment. (By contrast, of course, we would impose $x = 1$ if we were engaged in steady-growth analysis.)

More formally, we follow Kaldor (1951), Robinson (1962), and Marglin (1984) in supposing that, for given long-term expectations, *desired* investment, I^D, and *desired* capital stock, K^D, are related by:

$$I^D = f(\rho, x, r)K^D \tag{6}$$

where ρ is the current average rate of return on capital assets, net of interest payments, and $f(\,)$ is increasing in ρ and x but decreasing in r.[13] There will be a positive value of ρ for which $f(\,)$ is zero. Now:

$$\rho \equiv (Y - W - rK)K^{-1} \equiv \left[\left(\frac{x}{v_n}\right)(1 - W/Y) - r\right]$$

where W represents aggregate wages and salaries, and (W/Y) will almost certainly not rise as x increases. Thus, ρ increases, at least linearly, with x but decreases with r. Eliminating ρ from (6) gives us:

$$(I^D/K^D) = h(x,r) \tag{7}$$

say, where $h(\ )$ increases with x but decreases with r, taking account of both the direct effects of x and r, as shown in (6), and their indirect effects via changes in ρ.

Coherent Schedules

Capacity Utilization and Growth

Whereas (3) shows the *actual* rate of capital accumulation (when $I = sY$) as a function of (x,r), (7) shows the *desired* rate of accumulation—call it g_K^D—as a function of (x,r). Figure 6.1 shows g_K and g_K^D as possible functions of x, for $r = r_1$ say. *Given* that r_1, x^*, and g^* are the coherent equilibrium values of the degree of capacity utilization and the growth rate; if $x = x^*$, $g = g^*$ and $\dot{x} = \dot{r} = 0$, then (r_1, x^*, g^*) will give a coherent equilibrium, with $g_Y = g_c = g_K = g_I = g^*$, at the instant in question. There is "real side" flow equilibrium *and* a desired accumulation rate equal to the actual rate. Note that the unique equilibrium shown in Figure 6.1 is stable; at $x < x^*$ $(x^* < x)$ the actual rate of accumulation would fall short of (would exceed) the desired rate, i.e., aggregate saving would fall short of (would exceed) desired investment, so that x would be tending to rise (fall).

Our two-sided relation bringing together desired and actual rates of accumulation, as in Figure 6.1, will no doubt remind many readers of Joan Robinson's closely related diagram employed in her "Model of Accumulation," in the second of her *Essays on the Theory of Economic Growth* (1962). It may also be useful to recall here that Joan Robinson introduced her diagram in the course of discussing "*Short-period Equilibrium*," just as our Figure 6.1 is concerned with coherent equilibrium, and *not* with long-period analysis.[14] But if our diagram is a close cousin of Joan Robinson's, as it is, it is not exactly equivalent to it. For we treat the degree of capacity utilization x as a variable, which she did not.[15] In her 1949 review of Harrod she had written, "However, if I have understood Mr. Harrod aright, the warranted rate of growth is that rate of growth of output $(\Delta Y/Y)$ which ensures the continuous full-capacity working of the stock of capital considered as a whole."[16] In contrast with both this interpretation of Harrod and Joan Robinson's own 1962 essay, we seek to treat the degree of capacity utilization as an important *variable* to be analyzed.

Now suppose that, in Figure 6.1, the given value of r is changed slightly. To see how g^* and x^* will change, we describe the equilibrium position (dropping

Figure 6.1

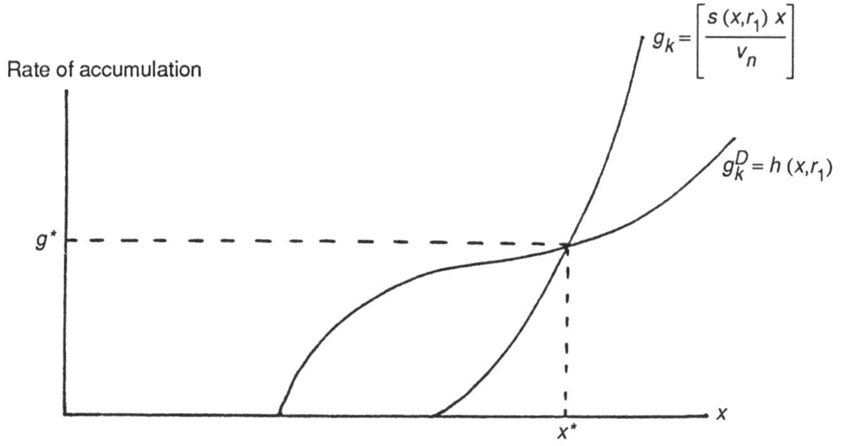

the asterisks from now on) by

$$g = h(x, r) = v_n^{-1}\, s(x, r)x$$

Stability in Figure 6.1 requires that g_K increases with x faster than does g_K^D, or:

$$(1 + Esx) > Ehx > 0$$

where Eij is the elasticity of i with respect to j. Now simple differentiation and manipulation shows that:

$$\left(\frac{dr}{dx}\,\frac{x}{r}\right) = \left(\frac{1 + Esx - Ehx}{Ehr - Esr}\right)$$

$$\left(\frac{dr}{dg}\,\frac{g}{r}\right) = \left[\frac{1 + Esx - Ehx}{(1 + Esx)\,Ehr - EhxEsr}\right]$$

The numerator is positive, in each case, from the stability condition. This same condition then ensures that if $Ehr \leq 0$, then $Esr > Ehr$ is necessary and sufficient to make both $(dr/dx)(x/r)$ and $(dr/dg)(g/r)$ negative. We shall assume $Esr > Ehr \leq 0$ from now on, so that both x and g are inversely related to r. It is, of course, another question whether such inverse relationships are defined for all non-negative values of r. It may (or may not) be the case, for example, that before r can fall to zero, x will reach some maximum possible value. At the other extreme, as r rises it may well reach a value at which the g_K and g_K^D curves in Figure 6.1 become tangential, implying that no higher value of r is compatible

Figure 6.2

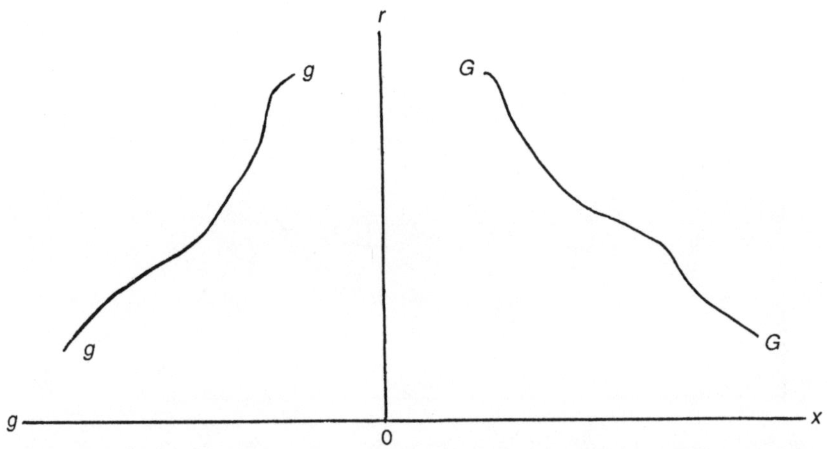

with coherent equilibrium, *given* the long-term expectations, animal spirits, attitudes to saving, etc.[17]

Figure 6.2 shows the relations between equilibrium g, r, and x, for the case in which there are both lower and upper limits to the relevant range of r. The GG schedule on the right of that figure is our coherent analog to the IS schedule; at every point on the GG schedule, investment = saving *and in addition, income, investment, actual capacity and desired capacity are all growing at the same rate*, shown as g on the left of Figure 6.2. Only combinations of (g, r, x) lying on gg—the "coherent growth schedule"—and GG are combinations implying *coherent* equilibrium on the "real side." (Note, more specifically, that GG is *not* merely an IS curve with Y replaced by $x \equiv (Y/Y_c)$ on the horizontal axis. The (r, x) lying on GG *both* ensure I = S *and* make the actual g_K = desired g_K. This is because account is taken of the normal supply conditions, represented by v_n, or, in other words, because Harrodian capacity expansion—as well as effective demand—aspects of investment are accounted for. Thus, it would not have been sufficient simply to take the IS curve and deflate it by capital stock, either actual or desired. By contrast, Turnovsky's presentation of intermediate IS/LM analysis does involve such a deflation; consequently his intermediate equilibrium does not involve $g_K = g_K^D = g_Y$.[18] Note that a higher v_n would imply a "northwest" shift in gg and a "northeast" shift in GG.)

With respect to gg, all (g, r) combinations lying on this schedule imply coherent growth, with income, capacity, and desired capital stock growing in step. Together with (7), they show why a given rate of growth could continue to be an equilibrium rate *if* underlying conditions were to be constant over time—thus avoiding Alexander's well-known objection to Harrod's formulation of the warranted rate.[19]

The interested reader will wish to consider now those cases in which the curves of Figure 6.1 have either no intersection or two intersections.[20] But we must move on to construct a coherent analog to the LM schedule—noting, however, that this second analog is independent of the *GG* schedule; one can accept either analog without necessarily accepting the other.

Money and Coherent Equilibrium

We now construct a schedule of those combinations of x and r for which the demand for money will both be equal to *and grow at the same rate as* the supply of money, when the latter is growing at the same rate as capacity output, Y_c, and the capital stock, K. We suppose, for simplicity, that when $\dot{x} = \dot{r} = 0$, marginal portfolio allocations will be the same as the prevailing average allocations (this is expressed in the homogeneity assumption made below). As in IS/LM analysis, the demand for money is assumed to reflect both transactions concerns and the desire to carry purchasing power through time. The absolute money price level is taken to be constant; a positive rate of inflation will be introduced in a later section.

We begin by writing a stock demand for money function in the form:

$$M^d = m(r, Y, \text{Wealth}) \tag{8}$$

where M^d is the demand for nominal money; $m(\,)$ is decreasing in r, increasing in Y and in Wealth, and linear homogeneous with respect to Y and Wealth. We assume that the aggregate value of the physical capital stock always equals the value of bonds held by households (this assumption will naturally have to be dropped in later work), but we do not wish to debate whether one should then define (Wealth $\equiv K$) or (Wealth $\equiv K + M^d$). In either case we divide through (8) by Y_c to obtain

$$(M^d/Y_c) = m(r, x, v_n)$$

or (9)

$$(M^d/Y_c) = m[r, x, v_n + (M^d/Y_c)]$$

where the presence of v_n as an argument of $m(\ )$ marks the influence of the "supply side."

Denote the exogenous nominal money *supply* by M. One condition of coherent equilibrium is, of course, that $M^d = M$. But this does not *suffice* for coherence, since stock-flow equilibrium requires in addition that M grow at the same rate as K, so that portfolio balance is maintained.

Replace M^d by M in (9), so that $M^d = M$ is built in from now on, and take (M/Y_c) as given. Then either form of (9) defines implicitly an upward sloping (x, r) schedule—to be called the *LL* schedule—showing those combinations of x and r

Figure 6.3

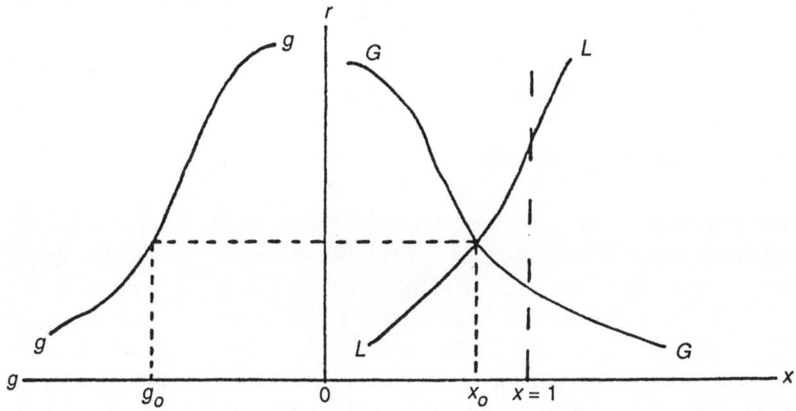

compatible with $M^d = M$ for the given ratio (M/Y_c). An increase in (M/Y_c) would displace this schedule "southeast"; a higher v_n would shift *LL* "northwest." Note that although (M/Y_c) is constant along *LL*—by definition—a move along *LL* in the direction of increasing x implies a fall in (M/Y) or, in other words, a rise in the income velocity of circulation.

It will not be forgotten that the *LL* schedule, like the *GG* schedule of Figure 6.2, is drawn for *given* expectations, attitudes, etc. It is *not* being suggested here that either schedule would remain unchanged in the face of shifts in confidence, unexpected inventions, or election results, and so on. We are concerned with coherent levels *and* rates of change *at a given moment*; we are not engaged in the analysis of persisting steady growth at an unchanging rate.

Coherent Equilibrium

Simply by adding the *LL* schedule of the previous section to Figure 6.2, we obtain Figure 6.3, which is our coherent analog to the IS/LM diagram. (We continue to focus on the case of a unique stable intersection in Figure 6.1.) Given the various determinants of the *gg*, *GG*, and *LL* schedules, the unique coherent equilibrium in Figure 6.3 is (x_o, r_o, g_o). This is the only position in which goods and money markets can clear *and* yield stock-flow equilibrium.

There is, of course, no reason why coherent equilibrium should involve full capacity utilization ($x = 1$) or, therefore, what Harrod defined as warranted growth (with $x = 1$). Indeed, the concept of a unique warranted growth rate is far too restrictive. In Figure 6.3, warranted growth *at full capacity* ($x = 1$) would require more active animal spirits, or a higher (M/Y_c), or in fact any combination of changes adequate to place the intersection of *GG* and *LL* above $x = 1$. The coherent counterpart to Keynes's underemployment theory is that there is no reason to expect full capacity utilization and growth at *Harrod's* particular warranted rate ($x = 1$).

A little more must now be said about the monetary side of coherent equilibrium. It was noted in the previous section that this requires both that $M^d = M$, which is implicit in the *LL* schedule, and that *M* grow at the same rate as *K* and *Y*. In Figure 6.3, then, coherent equilibrium requires that $g_M = g_o$, where g_M is the growth rate of the money stock. If (M/Y_c) had been higher, in Figure 6.3, *LL* would have been lower and thus g_o greater. Hence, holding the fundamental conditions constant, we may trace out those combinations of (M/Y_c) and g_M that are compatible with coherent equilibrium. Such combinations define a "coherent monetary policy schedule," along which (M/Y_c) and g_M are positively related. By construction, only those combinations of g_M and (M/Y_c) that lie on this schedule are consistent with coherent equilibrium. It would thus be quite futile to argue over whether the responsibility of the monetary authorities is to maintain an appropriate g_M *or* to maintain an appropriate (M/Y_c). Their task is, in fact, harder than either inappropriate characterization would suggest, for it is to maintain a suitable $(g_M, M/Y_c)$ combination.

Comparisons

It is naturally possible to use our (*gg*/*GG*/*LL*) diagram to compare the alternative coherent equilibria corresponding to different values of the fundamental data or different monetary policies. Perhaps two examples will suffice.

Monetary Policy

Starting from a given Figure 6.3, consider the effect of a notional increase in the exogenously given ratio (M/Y_c). The new *LL* schedule will lie to the "southeast" of the old one (if expectations, etc., are unchanged), so that the new coherent equilibrium will involve a *higher x*, a *lower r*, and a *higher g*. The "increase" in (M/Y_c) is "expansionary." Of course, the higher *ratio* (M/Y_c) would have to be accompanied by the appropriately higher *growth rate* of the money stock. The argument may be reversed, if the change in monetary policy is initially presented as a higher rate of growth of the money stock.

"Paradoxes" of Thrift and Accumulation

A *ceteris paribus* increase in the average savings ratio, at each pair (x, r), will imply that *GG* in Figure 6.3 shifts "southwest," while *gg* shifts "southeast." If nothing else changes, then, the new coherent equilibrium involves a lower *x*, a lower *r*, and a lower *g*. The *increased* desire to accumulate personal wealth results in a *lower* growth rate of that wealth. Conversely, an increase in "animal spirits" will shift *GG* "northeast" and *gg* "northwest," so that *x*, *r*, and *g* will increase. If an improvement in "animal spirits" is needed to eliminate *under*capacity working, it will do so by *increasing* the growth rate of capacity.[21] (In each case, the effects on x and on r will be clear diagrammatically but a more formal analysis is needed to show that the effect on g is indeed unambiguous.)

The reader may work through other comparative exercises but it will always remain central that *coherent* equilibrium ensures not only that goods and money markets clear but also that the actual and desired rates of accumulation are equal, with effective demand and capacity growing in step. Coherent equilibrium is superior to IS/LM equilibrium for the discussion of changes in policy, or in fundamental conditions, precisely because the former is free from the stock-flow contradictions inherent in the latter.

Inflation

In keeping with our aim of focusing attention upon the basic framework of coherent macroeconomic analysis, we could perhaps conclude our discussion at this point. However, the analysis of inflation is now so central to macroeconomic analysis that we shall extend our discussion to incorporate the determinants and effects of a positive rate of inflation. This extension is readily achieved, not least because our concern with coherent rates of growth of real output, etc., extends quite naturally to a concern with the rate of growth of the price level—and, by implication, the rate of growth of nominal income. Furthermore, the central role that the degree of capacity utilization plays in much analysis of inflation permits the latter to be incorporated, with minimum disturbance, into our relationships. In short, since growth is at the center of our discussion, it is easy to incorporate "growth" in the price level.

To be consistent with our prior treatment of expectations in the investment and money demand functions, we shall consider only coherent, inflationary equilibria for *given* inflation expectations. We recognize that the diversity of expectations should be an important component in inflationary analysis and that the determination and revision of inflation (and indeed other) expectations would be of prime concern in any extension of the analysis. However, given our Harrodian concern with events at a particular instant, we shall here treat the expected inflation rate as given. We simplify further by taking those expectations to be common to all decision makers in labor, money, and goods markets. Money illusion is also assumed absent from all economic decision processes. We may now recognize three consequences of a positive inflation rate for our coherent equilibria. First, the money rate of interest, i, will stand above the real rate of interest at the margin of investment, r in our previous discussion, by the uniformly expected rate of inflation, π. In the absence of taxes of any kind, we have the Fisher condition $i = r + \pi$. Second, to determine the actual rate of inflation we combine an expectations-augmented Phillips curve, Okun's law (relating x to the pressure of demand in the labor market), and a fixed markup pricing hypothesis (which converts the rate of growth of money wages into a corresponding actual

Figure 6.4

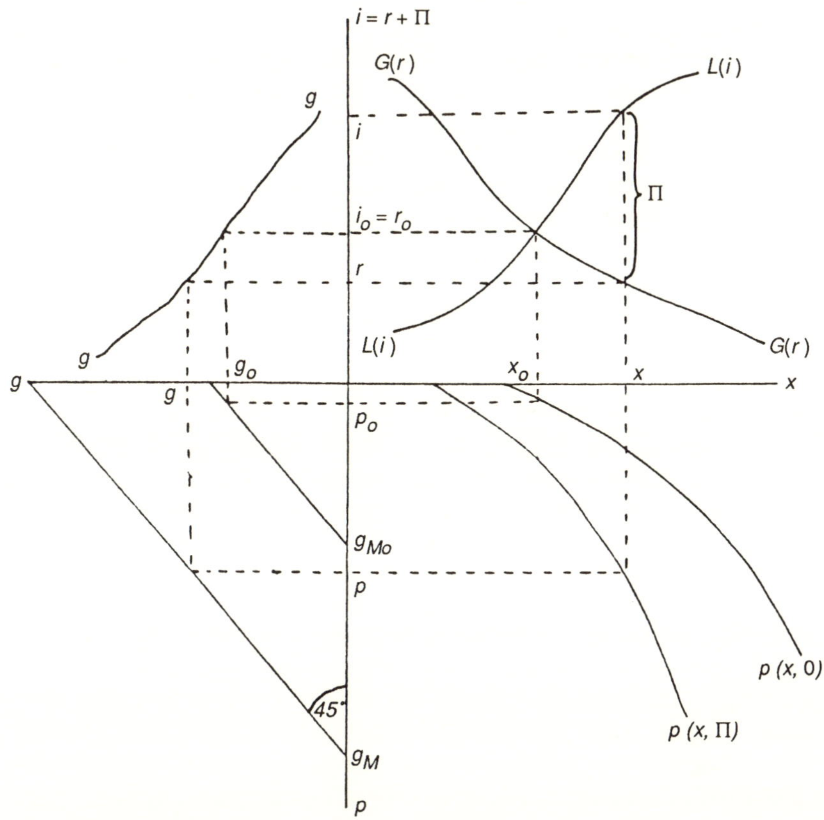

rate of price inflation, p). Thus $p = p(x, \pi)$, with $p(\,)$ increasing in both arguments and $(\delta^2 p/\delta x^2) \geq 0$. We could assume that there is a value of x that will equate actual and expected inflation rates but there would be no reason why this particular level should correspond to $x = 1$. Equilibrium inflation and full capacity utilization may simply be incompatible. Moreover, in the present framework, which is not that of steady-state analysis, no particular interest attaches to an equality between actual and expected inflation rates. Finally, a coherent equilibrium requires that the rate of growth of the money stock, g_M, exceed the growth rate of output by a margin equal to the actual rate of inflation ($p = g_M - g$). The various amendments to our framework are drawn together in Figure 6.4, in which the coherent equilibrium values for $\pi = 0$ are denoted by x_o, r_o, etc.

To the already familiar upper part of the diagram (Figure 6.3) we have added, in the lower right-hand quadrant, the expectations-augmented tradeoff $p(x, \pi)$. In the lower left-hand quadrant we have loci of constant rates of monetary growth marked by g_M, a higher rate of monetary expansion shifting the locus away from the origin in a parallel fashion. Along such a locus, the rate of growth of nominal income is constant, but at each point expansion is divided between inflation and real growth in a different way.

Consider now how the expectation of a positive inflation rate changes the coherent equilibrium (by comparison with that at $\pi = 0$). In equilibrium, $i = r + \pi$. Our money stock demand function, which previously had r as an argument, now has instead the *difference* between the real expected marginal returns to holding K or M, i.e., $[r - (-\pi)] = (r + \pi) = i$. In Figure 6.4, GG is a relation between (x, r) still but LL is now a relation between (x, i). As will be seen from that figure (with $\pi > 0$), x and g are higher than with zero expected inflation. With the expectations-augmented tradeoff also determined, for the given π, we see that p is the actual rate of inflation that corresponds to the coherent equilibrium value of x $(p > p_o)$. The rate of growth of nominal income is $(g + p)$ and this will be sustained by a rate of monetary expansion g_M $(= g + p > g_{Mo})$ that serves to maintain LL in its given position. Note that $i > i_o = r_o > r$.

It will be clear that these effects of a higher rate of expected inflation depend on our having held constant the ratio of nominal money stock to nominal capacity output, so that LL is unaffected. If, by contrast, we take g_M as given exogenously at the level $g_M = g_{Mo}$, then with the positive expectation of inflation π, both x and g will be lower than with zero expected inflation. The reduction in g will, of course, exactly offset an increase in p. Real and nominal rates of interest will *both* be higher than $i_o = r_o$ and the coherent equilibrium will be sustained by a reduced ratio of nominal money stock to nominal capacity, i.e., by an LL schedule that is appropriately displaced "northwest." It will be noted that while i is increasing in π, across coherent equilibria, in both cases, the value of r may increase or decrease with π, depending on the meaning attached to given monetary conditions.

From Figure 6.4 the reader will see immediately an opportunity to discuss the effects of other changes in data, now holding constant the positive, expected rate of inflation. We confine ourselves to one brief exercise, the comparison of coherent equilibria with alternative given rates of monetary expansion, the monetary growth rate and the money/capacity ratio being related by a "coherent monetary policy schedule," the slope and position of which also depends upon the expectations-augmented tradeoff between x and p. (The schedule is shifted "northwest" when π is raised.) It is readily established that a higher g_M corresponds to higher values of x, g, and p and to lower values of i and r. The precise split of the increased monetary expansion between inflation and real growth depends on the slopes of GG and gg, and upon $p(x, \pi)$. The higher is π, the higher is (p/g_M). It is easily shown that:

$$\left(\frac{dp}{dg_M}\,\frac{g_M}{p}\right) = \left(\frac{p+g}{p+gE}\right)$$

where

$$E = \left[\frac{(1 + Esx)\,|\,Ehr\,| + Ehx\,Esr}{Epx\,(\,|\,Ehr\,| + Esr)} \right]$$

so that, if $g > 0$, $(dp/dg_M)(g_M/p) \gtrless 1$ accordingly as $E \gtrless 1$. For example, if $Epx > (1 + Esx)$ then $E < 1$ and any given percentage increase in g_M provokes a larger percentage increase in p; more loosely, increased monetary growth spills more into increased inflation than into increased real growth. (It will be noted that $E \cdot Epx$ is simply the ratio of our earlier expressions for the elasticities of the gg and GG schedules. Hence these elasticities, together with that of the $p(x, \pi)$ tradeoff, determine the responsiveness of p (and g) to a change in g_M. These remarks may be compared with those of Keynes on the corresponding analysis of "levels," as opposed to our "rates of change.")[22] That our framework permits such clear-cut conclusions in this and other exercises is no accident. Coherent equilibria necessarily involve expansion—and how monetary expansion is divided between growth and inflation is naturally incorporated into our discussion, since both rates of expansion have the same dimension. By contrast, the dimensions and stock-flow inconsistencies of IS/LM analysis make it peculiarly difficult to incorporate inflation into that analysis.

Conclusion

Any IS/LM equilibrium is a momentary equilibrium that is liable to be disrupted both for reasons relating to the disappointment of expectations and for reasons stemming from stock-flow inconsistencies. Our coherent equilibrium, by contrast, is a momentary equilibrium that, while still vulnerable to unfulfilled expectations, is completely free from stock-flow inconsistency.

Just as with IS/LM equilibrium, any change in the data—not least in expectations or in government policy—will naturally imply a change in the position of coherent equilibrium. Some economists might argue that expectations are so volatile that none of our schedules will have a determinate position and that, as a consequence, coherent equilibrium is no more useful than is an IS/LM equilibrium. One might pause before accepting this view. While it may well be true that there are periods of historical time in which expectations are confused and rapidly changing—periods, that is, for which *any* formal method of analysis will have little power—it is hardly self-evident that the general state of expectations is always, or even usually, in such turmoil. The method of analyzing equilibrium positions for given expectations may therefore be a powerful way of understanding many actual economic situations.

However, the question does arise of whether actual output expansion will coincide with the long-term expectations of growth underpinning the investment function and, if so, through what process. When actual outcomes upset the expectations that gave rise to them, we may well entertain the presumption that expectations come to depend on history and that both expectations and actual outcomes come to be path-dependent. Of course, to say that an adjustment process is path-dependent is *not* to say that, *ipso facto*, the process will not converge to any equilibrium position; it may or may not do so. But one can certainly join Joan Robinson in suggesting that:

> the concept of "stability," based on a mechanical analogy, is inappropriate in economic analysis. For mechanical movements in space, there is no distinction between approaching equilibrium from an arbitrary initial position and a perturbation due to displacement from an equilibrium that has long been established. In economic life, in which decisions are guided by expectations about the future, these two types of movement are totally different.[23]

History and path-dependence may well matter and, as Joan Robinson put it, "To say how long it will take, or by what path, to find a new equilibrium (if there is one) we have to fill in a whole story about the behavior of the economy when it is out of equilibrium, including the effect of disappointed expectations on decisions being taken by its inhabitants."[24] We have not been able "to fill in a whole story" of the requisite kind; *has the reader*?

Notes

1. Hicks, 1937; Harrod, 1939.
2. See, for example, chapter 6 of *Economic Heresies* (1971), especially pp. 82–85.
3. Robinson, 1949, pp. 68–69.
4. Kregel, 1976.
5. Tobin, 1980, p. 163.
6. Harrod, 1939, p. 24; 1959, p. 454; both emphases added.
7. Harrod, 1973, p. 16; emphasis added.
8. Harrod, 1959, p. 459.
9. Tobin, 1955, and Johnson, 1967 are classic references; see also, among many others, Solow, 1970, chap. 4, the *Journal of Money, Credit and Banking*. "Symposium on Money and Economic Growth," 1969, and Possum, 1979.
10. Turnovsky, 1977, chap. 7; Backhouse, 1981.
11. A study of the case $\dot{x} \neq 0$ and g_c, etc., not all being equal to one another would lead us into cycle theory, which is left aside here.
12. Cf. Steindl, 1952, pp. 127–32; Domar, 1947.
13. Robinson, 1962, pp. 48–51; Marglin, 1984, pp. 121–22.
14. Robinson, 1962, pp. 46–47.
15. Ibid., p. 46.
16. Robinson, 1949, p. 80.
17. Cf. Robinson, 1962.
18. Turnovsky, 1977, chap. 7.
19. Alexander, 1950.
20. The second case formed the basis of Kaldor's (1940) trade cycle model; cf. Hudson, 1957.
21. Schelling, 1947.
22. Keynes, 1936, pp. 304–6.

23. Robinson, 1974, p. 2.
24. Ibid., p. 5.

References

Alexander, S. (1950) "Mr. Harrod's Dynamic Model." *Economic Journal*, 60:724–39.

Backhouse, R. (1981) "Keynesian Unemployment and the One-Sector Neoclassical Growth Model." *Economic Journal*, 91:174–87.

Domar, E. (1947) "Expansion and Employment." *American Economic Review*, 37:34–55.

Harrod, R. (1939) "An Essay in Dynamic Theory." *Economic Journal*, 49:14–32.

———. (1959) "Domar and Dynamic Economics." *Economic Journal*, 69:451–64.

———. (1973) *Economic Dynamics*. London: Macmillan.

Hicks, J. R. (1937) "Mr. Keynes and the Classics." *Econometrica*, 5:147–59.

Hudson, H. R. (1957) "A Model of the Trade Cycle." *Economic Record*, 32:378–89.

Johnson, H. G. (1967) "Money in a Neoclassical One-Sector Growth Model." In *Essays in Monetary Economics*. London: Allen and Unwin.

Kaldor, N. (1940) "A Model of the Trade Cycle." *Economic Journal*, 50:78–92.

———. (1951) "Mr. Hicks on the Trade Cycle." *Economic Journal*, 61:833–47.

Keynes, J. M. (1936) *The General Theory of Employment, Interest and Money*. London: Macmillan.

Kregel, J. (1976) "Economic Methodology in the Face of Uncertainty." *Economic Journal*, 86:209–25.

Marglin, S. (1984) "Growth, Distribution and Inflation: A Centennial Synthesis." *Cambridge Journal of Economics*, 8:115–44.

Possum, U. M. (1979) "The Long-Run Properties of an Income Expenditure Model." *Economica*, 46:159–73.

Robinson, J. V. (1949) "Mr. Harrod's Dynamics." *Economic Journal*, 59:68–85.

———. (1962) *Essays in the Theory of Economic Growth*. London: Macmillan.

———. (1970) "Harrod after Twenty-One Years." *Economic Journal*, 80:731–37.

———. (1971) *Economic Heresies. Some Old-Fashioned Questions in Economic Theory*. London: Macmillan.

———. (1974) *History versus Equilibrium*. Thames Papers in Political Economy (Autumn, 1974). London: Thames Polytechnic.

Schelling, T. C. (1947) "Capital, Growth and Equilibrium." *American Economic Review*, 37:864–76.

Solow, R. (1970) *Growth Theory: An Exposition*. Oxford: Oxford University Press.

Steindl, J. (1952) *Maturity and Stagnation in American Capitalism*. Oxford: Basil Blackwell.

"Symposium on Money and Economic Growth." (1969) *Journal of Money, Credit and Banking*, 1 (May):131–302.

Tobin, J. (1955) "A Dynamic Aggregative Model." *Journal of Political Economy*, 63:103–15.

———. (1980) *Asset Accumulation and Economic Activity*. Oxford: Basil Blackwell.

Turnovsky, S. J. (1977) *Macroeconomic Analysis and Stabilization Policies*. Cambridge: Cambridge University Press.

JR

CHAPTER SEVEN

History versus Equilibrium

KRISHNA BHARADWAJ

A theme that recurs prominently in the writings of Joan Robinson, involving a critical assessment of the significance and relevance of the neoclassical theory, is "the lack of a comprehensible treatment of historical time and failure to specify the rules of the game in the type of economy under discussion"; this lack "rendered the theoretical apparatus useless for the analysis of contemporary problems in the micro and macro spheres."[1] This criticism of theory with respect to its failure to deal adequately with historical time appears in Robinson's writings at various junctures and in various contexts of her analysis within the problems of value and distribution, accumulation, and technical change. As early as the early 1950s, Joan Robinson questioned the "meaning of capital";[2] the questions acquired a sharper focus on distribution theory in the capital controversy, following Piero Sraffa's *Production of Commodities* (1960) wherein the logical consistency of the explanation of the rate of profit in terms of the equilibrium between demand and supply of capital was challenged. In the 1980s, however, Robinson, a major participant in the debate, increasingly insisted that "the long wrangle about measuring capital" is a minor, secondary issue when compared with the methodological error of confusing comparisons of imagined equilibrium positions with a process of accumulation going through history.[3] It was in this context that she counterposed "history" against "equilibrium" and argued for abandoning the method of equilibrium. Her major argument rested on the role of uncertainty and expectations: "As soon as the uncertainty and expectations are admitted, equilibrium drops out of the argument and history takes its place."[4]

A number of issues are complexly intertwined in Joan Robinson's onslaught on theory and her passionate plea for a change of method—"getting economic theory out of the desert of equilibrium into fruitful fields."[5] Undeniably, Robinson is a pioneer of new critical thinking who persistently posed fundamental and significant questions for theory. Our attempt here is to argue that many of the inadequacies and the failure of the neoclassical theory to handle historical time, to which Joan Robinson justifiably points, arise from the logical structure of that theory, with its specific conceptualization of the mechanisms of change and choice that provide the basis for its explanation of prices and quantities. It would also seem that it is precisely the different structure of the classical theory of Smith, Ricardo, and Marx that enables these authors to deal with what Joan Robinson admiringly calls "a historical process of accumulation in a changing world while the Walrasians dwell in a timeless equilibrium."[6] In short, we suggest that it is the structural contrasts that distinguish the theories in terms of their openness to introducing historical changes and specificities in their analysis, i.e., in their ability fruitfully to combine historical elements abstracted from concrete observation and to bring them together in short chains of logical reasoning. The differences, we suggest, lie in the theory rather than the method *per se*. While Joan Robinson's contributions are in the realm of theory, her shift of emphasis onto the *method* in her critique seems to have helped her opponents divert attention away from the challenge thrown at the foundations of their theory, a challenge that Robinson herself, among others, initiated in her critical writings; her trenchant criticisms exposed the logical hurdles that the neoclassical theory faced in its notion of the aggregate production function, the marginal productivity explanations of distribution, the conceptualization of the choice of techniques, etc. It is when we examine closely the structure of the theory that we realize that the limitations and the difficulties are inherent in the basic structure of that theory.

How to tame the complexity and variety of historical observations so as to capture them within the logical framework of deductive reasoning has been a challenging problem for all system builders in economic theory, whether of the classical or the neoclassical school. The concrete events and experiences that constitute the empirical, observational base of theories are complex and manifold, varying not only from individual to individual, society to society, and time to time, but also reflecting ever-changing social and material interrelations. The application of logical reasoning however, requires that from this complex maze of interdependent activities that are changing over time, certain regularities and causal connections in the patterns of change be deciphered and hypothesized. These perceptions enter into the formulation of theoretical concepts and categories and into the structure of the theory. In particular, notions such as a state of equilibrium (as in the neoclassical theory) or of the natural position (as in classical theory) become necessary as organizing concepts: they indicate a position of the economy depicting the set of consistent outcomes of actions occurring under "normal" conditions of environment and under regular operation of behavioral rules as hypothesized by the theory. While such a notion of a "normal" position may be common to all theories, their explanations differ.

In the following discussion we first outline the structures of the neoclassical and the classical theory to illustrate the above point of view. In the third section we take up Robinson's critique of the neoclassical theory and its equilibrium methodology and conclude, in the last section, with a brief assessment of the strength of the critique, as well as some of its weaknesses.

The Structure of Neoclassical Theory (Demand- and Supply-based Equilibrium, or DSE Theory)

Neoclassical theory uses a specific theoretical framework and a methodological approach to the analysis of economic change and choice that has narrowly circumscribed the possibilities of incorporating into the analysis the complexity and variety of the historical processes. The theory visualizes the competitive capitalist economy as an aggregate of atomistic individuals (producers and consumers) who make their optimizing choices in pursuit of their respective returns, given the technological possibilities, the preference scales, and competitive prices. It is through the "fundamental and universal principle" of substitution that quantity choices are adjusted in response to variations in relative prices by individuals. (A pertinent question raised and not satisfactorily answered is who *is* the invisible auctioneer or helmsman who initiates these changes in relative prices?) Equilibrium is envisaged to be established when all markets clear, yielding *simultaneously* the equilibrium set of prices and of quantities. For such an equilibrium to exist, however, stringent conditions need to be established on the choice sets and on the price-quantity responses. Thus, the data for the demand- and supply-based equilibrium (DSE) theory are the initial endowment of primary resources and their distribution over individuals, the technological possibilities, and the system of preferences.

This explanation of prices and quantities has a number of analytical consequences. First, since the existence of equilibrium is explained in terms of balancing the opposite forces of demand and of supply, stringent conditions need to be imposed on the feasible sets of choices so that the "substitution" yields "well-behaved" demand and supply relations. The theory, thus, presupposes strict functional relations between, say, changes in outputs and per-unit costs (ruling out, for example, continuously decreasing per-unit costs) or between factor intensities and factor prices (e.g., a monotonic inverse relation, say, between capital intensity and the rate of profit). It is thus necessary to demonstrate that not only do markets clear (i.e., equilibrium occurs at the intersection of supply and demand) but that the price-quantity responses are of the appropriate signs in the neighborhood of the equilibrium (which are stipulated as first- and second-order conditions on the demand/supply relation). Should such conditions on the choice sets be violated—for example, as in the presence of increasing returns—the theory often has to rule out such possibilities by assumption. Similar difficulties on the demand side have to be tackled by relegating them to "paradoxes" or "anomalies." The logical difficulty surfaces dramatically in the capital theory debate where the presumed monotonic inverse relation between capital intensity and the rate of profit required to generate a well-behaved "demand function" for capital is challenged on the grounds of the theory's internal consistency (see Symposium on Paradoxes in Capital Theory in *Quarterly Journal of Economics*, 1966).

Further, the critique has deeper consequences: since the DSE theory determines all prices (commodity as well as factor) and all quantities (of commodities and also factor-utilization levels) *simultaneously* within the same framework of supply and demand, the capital-theoretic difficulty challenges the very *existence* of equilibrium and hence also the determination of all other prices and quantities in that theoretical framework. Thus, the reswitching controversy (characterized more generally as connoting the failure to establish the regular demand function for capital and covering the case of reverse capital deepening) remains a fundamental criticism of the neoclassical theory.

Further, the very notion of change is restrictively circumscribed in the neoclassical theory. First, all changes in quantities within the system are seen as outcomes of the ever-active principle of substitution. These changes are also primarily changes in relative quantities involving mainly allocational variations (e.g., given the budget constraint of the consumer, the changes in demand occur through substitution between different goods; given the primary resources, their use is discussed in terms of variations in factor proportions). These *allocational variations* emerge as an outcome of quantity decisions by *individuals* responding to changes in *relative prices*.

Critics of neoclassical theory often attack its methodological individualist perspective: that is, that the theory operates with the individual as the decision-making unit. However, it may be noted that it is not so much the fact *per se* that the concept of the individual as the decision-making unit creates the much-debated micro/macro cleavage; rather, the analytical divide originates in the manner in which individual choice is conceptualized in that theory. The individual is, as it were, cordoned off, through raising barriers of assumptions, from all influences emanating directly from other individuals or social relations by the assumption of no externalities. The individual operates atomistically from a black box, his feasible options (technology and preferences) already prespecified for him and given exogenously. The assumption of given technological possibilities and the conception of technical progress as a shift of this exogenously given set bypasses the entire issue of how these sets are themselves generated and the interaction between the availability of these options and the individual's access to the use of these options. Joan Robinson, as we shall see later, was quite justifiably critical of the neoclassical theory's conceptualization of "technology" and technical choice. Similarly, the given set of preferences evades the issues of the formation of demand as social consumption and the interrelation between "wants and activities," a theme that dominated the classical writers' discussion of demand. Through such conceptions of technology and demand, the neoclassical theory effectively rules out all feedback effects that impinge on the individual's mode and domain of decisions, emanating from the macro- or systemic-level social factors. At the same time, in the neoclassical theory, the influence of the individual's decisions on the macrosystem is also presumed to operate only through his quantity signals passed on to the market. These contribute to the collective demand and supply as aggregates that, in turn, form the basis for the relative price changes. The classical theory, even under the premise of competition, allows for a differential impact and influence of different decision makers belonging to different classes, as seen below.

The role of prices as predominantly one of resource allocating, emerges from such a structure determining variations in relative quantities and prices. *All changes are explained as induced by changes in relative prices and operate through individuals' quantity adjustments in response to these changes. In other words, in such a model of change, all influences affecting quantities are seen as being mediated through relative price variations on the market and are the outcomes of the atomistic responses of the individual.* In the real world, changes in activity levels, in social output and consumption, or in methods of production (what we may call "quantity" dynamics) can and do occur, as classical authors and also Keynes and Kalecki recognized, through causal processes that act directly through mechanisms other than relative prices. Keynes, for example, dealt with quantity changes in his multiplier analysis. In contrast, recent efforts at traversing from Keynes to Walras reflect precisely an attempt to transcribe the Keynesian results into the Walrasian price-quantity response mechanisms and thus call forward essentially the same criticisms that were directed at the DSE theory itself. I have elsewhere traced (Bharadwaj, 1985) the development of economic theory to argue how the supply and demand theory universalized its domain through extending the marginalist approach to all domains; consequently concepts like "competition," "supply and demand," and "equilibrium" acquired different content, scope, and analytical significance and roles.[7] Among these, changes in the notion of equilibrium are especially pertinent for understanding the exact content and meaning of Joan Robinson's critique of the equilibrium method.

Changes in the Notion of Equilibrium

With the universalization of the supply and demand approaches to the determination of all activities and the consequent restrictions that have to be imposed on the price-quantity responses, competition acquired a more restrictive content in the idea of "perfect competition." The assumptions of equal and uniform access to markets for all agents, perfect foresight, and complete information were adopted.[8]

The explanation of equilibrium in terms of the balancing of the opposed forces of supply and demand implied that the explanation of a position was now offered in terms of potential changes that are hypothesized to occur in the neighborhood of the position. Thus, in order to establish the existence of equilibrium, stringent conditions on the marginal changes had to be imposed. Equilibrium was also defined to signify the absence of incentive for change, given the data of the system. This further implied that if the system were not in equilibrium, there would be presupposed tendencies in the system to move towards the position. Although Marshall and the original neoclassicists appear not to have necessarily inferred from this that the system *actually reaches* or is required to *reach* equilibrium,[9] the increasing rigor and formalism, introduced in the theory in an attempt to give it cogency, led to stricter conditions on the equilibrium. The requirement that any deviation from equilibrium would set up forces for return to the position enjoined the question of the existence of the equilibrium with that concerning the stability. As we shall see, the arguments that Joan Robinson legitimately raised against the method of equilibrium arise, in fact, because of the specific way in which neoclassical theory explains equilibrium. We can appreciate the content of her critique better if we note also that the classicals fruitfully used the organizing concept of "natural position" without their theory requiring the imposition of restrictive conditions.

The Structure of the Classical Theory (Classical Political Economy, or CPE)

A methodological idea shared by the classical writers (the Physiocrats, Smith, Ricardo, and Marx) is that a particular social formation could be abstracted on the basis of observation, and viewed as a system governed by "discoverable" regularities or systemic tendencies.[10] The organizing concept is the "natural" (or "average") state of the economy, which is based on a methodological distinction between "stable" or "permanent" tendencies, and "temporary" or "accidental" forces. The role of the theory, in this context, is to analyze the conditions of reproduction of such a "natural position," which depicts representatively the production, exchange, and distributive relations within the economy as a basis for analyzing the forces of change operating on the system, their causes, and their consequences.

The central concept of the classical theory is that of "net product" or "surplus," defined as the difference between "gross product" and "productive consumption"; the latter constitutes material requisites of production that include the sustenance of labor embodied in production. An economic system is characterized in terms of the mode of generation and appropriation of surplus and the rules by which it is distributed among the revenue classes specific to that mode. For example, in the competitive capitalist mode—the mode most comprehensively analyzed in both theories—surplus is generated through wage labor, appropriated and realized through the market, and shared among the tripartite division of classes as wages, rents, and profits. Given the material structure of production, the rule of surplus distribution under the principle of uniform rates of wages and profits, and given also the form and condition of labor (i.e., waged labor), natural prices are defined as those that make the system and its relations reproducible.[11]

Certain consequences follow from this approach: the view of the economy as a circular, reproductive process gives rise to concepts and categories as well as a structure of the theory that is conducive to analyzing the generation, appropriation, distribution, and utilization of the surplus in the context of accumulation. The conceptualization of "change" and "choice" in classical theory is strikingly different from that of neoclassical theory, which, as noted earlier, explains changes in quantities primarily as the outcome of substitution behavior of optimizing individuals who respond to changes in relative prices. The data that determine the natural prices under competition in the classical theory are: effectual demand (or social demand), observed methods of production, and the socially determined wage. Given the uniformity postulate on the rates of profit and wages, prices of production (or "natural prices") are the exchange values consistent with these data. These quantity sets (outputs, input utilizations, and wages) are taken as given for price determination, *not, however, as invariable or static magnitudes*. In fact, it is precisely in the dynamics of these magnitudes that the classical theorists are interested. That is also the paramount task for economic theory in Joan Robinson's forceful perception.

There appears to be a separate determination of quantities and prices in the sense that the forces that explain social consumption, methods of production, and wages are considered as not entirely or exclusively subsumed within the price domain. Classical political economy (CPE) thus encompasses theories of the determination of wages, of methods of production, and of social demand, but these magnitudes are not simultaneously and co-terminously determined as a subproblem of relative price formation. The "changes" in these quantities are not explained as arising solely due to relative price fluctuations. Thus, CPE has a much more dynamic story to tell about the interrelationships between levels and changes in output *and* wages, or between the changes in output *and* techniques, and vice versa. These relations are analyzed as affected by the accumulation process as much as by the resource-allocative process.

One of the important consequences for the theory of distribution is that, in CPE, "factor prices" are not determined from within the same process and by the same mechanism as "commodity prices," as is the case in DSE. Thus, "full employment" is neither an assumption nor a conclusion of CPE: Marx considers the reserve army of the unemployed as more or less a permanent feature of the capitalist system. Second, the demand and supply, referring to labor or capital in CPE, are not schedules derived, as in DSE, on the basis of the changes in "relative proportions of factors" corresponding to "changes in relative prices" alone, but incorporate dynamic influences generated by the process of accumulation. To wit, in Marx, the "supply of labor" to industry is not only related to the growth of population and migration, but also to the generation of the "reserve army of the unemployed," linked with the process of "primitive accumulation." The "efficiency" and "optimality" of price-guided resource allocation which is at the center of DSE discussions, has thus no exact counterpart in CPE.

The formulation of choice and the position of the individual is also more complex and more interesting in CPE.[12] We may note that Smith's (or, in general, the classical/Marxian) conception of the "individual in the society" is far different from the atomistic individual of DSE, and needs to be understood within Smith's more complex "system of natural liberty."[13] Smith, for example, presented a much more complex conception of the motivation of the individual propelled by countervailing interests and passions. He insisted on the need to create appropriate institutions whereby the "self-interest" could be channeled into socially beneficial outlets. (He also had his Scottish optimistic Theism whence he derived his belief that commensurate moral systems develop that render a social system viable; i.e., a consistent morality develops that can sustain the reproduction of a system.)

What is remarkable, however, is that Smith's (or for that matter, the classical theorists') discussion of the behavior of the economic agents is not one of atomistic decision making; their activities are analyzed more as members belonging to "classes" or "ranks" and "orders." The constraints that operate on the individuals, as demanders and suppliers, are multiple: these include the physical and material resources at the individual's command as well as those systemic constraints that circumscribe his or her feasible options. There are thus constraints emanating from the macrosystem—the rate and pattern of accumulation influences the environment and the objective condition as well as the subjective perceptions of the decision makers. It provides their arena of action, as well as constraints on feasible choices. Thus, the process of accumulation has differential consequences on the various "orders." At the same time, not all individuals are equally or uniformly placed in terms of the power to make decisions or in terms of the influence their decisions can exert on the pace and path of accumulation, which they are seen so to exert, as members of a class. Moreover, the objectives pursued by different "orders" of decision makers can themselves be different. Smith, Ricardo, and Marx in particular, recognized explicitly the different roles played by different classes in the process of accumulation and the asymmetric power and influence of their decisions as, also, the divergent class interests promoted or obstructed by a particular process of accumulation. Thus, the "individual" in CPE is not an atomistic transactor nor is the domain of his choice autonomized to himself through an *ex-hypothesis* negation of "externalities."[14]

The separate determination of prices and quantities allows CPE to hypothesize different kinds of quantity and price interrelations between different economic activities and variables at the micro and macro levels, and to account for their changing historical causal interconnections. The different and varying patterns of causal relationships can be captured in terms of specific causal structures appropriate to the problem and to the "state of the economy." This contrasts with DSE's grand design to universalize a specific modeling of change and choice for all economic activities (as discussed above) and to impose symmetries in explanatory structures of all quantities (be they consumption, output, technology, investment, or factor utilization levels) and prices (be they of factors or of commodities).

An example, about which Joan Robinson had much to say, may be found in the manner in which technical change is treated in DSE and in CPE (Smith and Marx). For DSE, the primary force determining technical change is the producer's choice of technique, optimizing his return, given the factor prices, and operating mainly through the substitution of factors. In contrast, Smith's analysis of the interaction between "extent of the market" and the "division of labor" proposes a direct, dynamic "cumulative causation" between expanding effectual demand and productivity gains. Marx's analysis of the changes that transpired in the fast-advancing capitalist system of nineteenth-century Britain is a masterpiece combining historical observation with logical analysis. He analyses not only the microlevel strategies of exploitation of individual producers but also the macrolevel consequences in terms of output levels and composition, social demand, distribution, the rate and pattern of accumulation, etc. The dynamic interactions among the pace of accumulation, wage-profit distribution, the material advance of the form of production, as well as changing capital-labor relations are portrayed in a rich analytical account of history.[15]

Classical political economy also explains the different distributive revenues (rent, wages, and profits) on separate grounds, with wages conceived as determined by "historical and moral" elements.[16] Not only are wages thus determined by sociohistorical factors, but their explanations reflect the changing historical milieux of their own times. The explanation of rent and its relative significance as a part of distributive revenue (surplus) so changed historically, as did its treatment in their analysis of capitalist dynamics. Whereas landlords (and their rents) were a major concern for Ricardo in his *Essay on Profits* (1815), Marx proceeded directly to the crucial capital-labor relation and to profits as the central driving force of capitalist relations.

Classical political economy also considered a variety of influences operating on "effectual demand" or social demand, involving an interaction between "wants and activities." This dynamic, historical element in their analysis of wants was recognized explicitly by Marshall, but for the sake of "elementary but formal analysis," he himself moved on to the "theory of demand" of DSE wherein the demand schedules yielded hypothetical choices of consumers indicating their utility-maximizing levels of demand, at parametrically given prices.[17]

In the world of commodities, CPE also drew important analytical distinctions. The wage-good/luxury-good distinction was used to distinguish commodities (wage goods) whose methods of production and prices (and changes in them) affect the macro parameters of the economy, such as prices of all other goods, wages, and the rate of profit, from those commodities (luxuries) that, under similar circumstances of change in their prices or in their methods of production, have only limited and localized effects. Thus, CPE constructed short chains of logical reasoning that hypothesized causal connections to give a form to sharp analytical intuitions, themselves derived from observations on the ground level of reality. The object was to tame the complexity of reality, but not to superimpose on it *a priori* symmetries and uniformities, dictated by the logical requirements of a preconceived abstract theoretical model, as in DSE.

This is not to say that CPE did not analyze price-quantity relations. There was, however, no universal pattern attributed to these relations, uniformly conceived for all "markets." Nor was there a need to presume, as in DSE, specific properties of these price-quantity relations that were deemed uniformly applicable to all exchanges. Thus, no *a priori* relation between levels of output and per unit cost of production of a commodity needed to be universally presumed. (In the case of DSE, however, it was necessary to rule out the case of persistent declining unit costs.) In other words, the issue of returns to scale was not relevant to the determination of "natural prices." Similarly, CPE would have to face no "conundrums" in explaining the persistence of unemployment at a given wage level, or the fact that the wage level would not automatically adjust downwards to absorb more employment. In DSE, full employment is to be expected as a result of the theory when, given the normal functioning of the price-quantity responses, the labor market would be "cleared" at full employment in equilibrium. Even when allowing that the optimum techniques may change when wages/rate of profit changes, CPE theory did not have to presume that there need be a monotonic inverse relation between factor intensity and factor prices. Thus, while CPE did not deny that relative-price-induced substitution between commodities or factors could occur, this is neither generalized for all cases nor are any *a priori* assumptions made to explain their net outcome at the macro level.

Thus, we find that when discussing the effects of taxes on particular commodities, CPE discussed the possibility that consumers could substitute relatively cheaper commodities when such close substitutes indeed existed. However, whether the effects of the tax and the consequent plausible substitutions would have wider, macro-consequences on the economy depended upon the placement of the commodity in social consumption and in production. The tax on corn (a prime wage good) had "permanent" consequences on the methods of production in agriculture (e.g., moving on to inferior soils) and in turn on the (natural) rate of profits. Thus, Ricardo attributes tremendous significance to the duties on corn imports. The effects of a tax on a "luxury good," however, would be much more localized; such a tax may not disturb the "natural position" of the economy. (Such distinctions between wage goods and capitalist consumption were fruitfully employed by Kalecki and by Joan Robinson herself.)

Classical political economy makes an analytically significant and useful distinction between "permanent," or "stable," and "temporary," or "accidental," causes and effects. The "natural" position of the economy is defined in terms of the given effectual demand, the dominant methods of production, and the wage, all considered at their "natural level." The distinction between "permanent" and "temporary" causes is in terms of their qualitative intervention into the system: not all "changes," and in all economic variables, would induce a change in the natural position. Causes that necessitate a change in the natural position (i.e., in the "effectual demand" or "methods of production" or "wage") are studied for their effects on other interrelated variables and activities. Temporary causes may be "accidental," short-lived ones, e.g., an occasional disruption in supply or fluctuation in demand. These are too fitful, irregular, or short-lived to be analyzed. However, "short-period" analysis was carried out by Marx in the case of "disjunction" between purchases and sales due to hoarding, in turn due to the intervention of money. Similarly, Marx discussed periodic cyclical variations that arise because of disruptions in trade, credit, and commodity and capital circuits, i.e., the phenomenon of disproportionalities among sectors. These short-period phenomena could very well accumulate or accelerate into long-period crises. Although such macrodynamics were not worked out with sufficient rigor, the analysis can be made more rigorous to open up interesting dynamics. The methodological point at issue here is that the structure of CPE permits the possibility of dealing with historically specific relations and with the system's behavioral specificities. It was through such a device, capturing discriminating analytical insights into the mode of functioning of the material and social interrelations, that the classicists managed to keep their theory open to historical observations.

Marshall's Constructs

This distinctive advantage of CPE over DSE in allowing for analytical insights, with the possibility of discriminating between different causal structuring of economic changes, becomes evident when we look carefully at Marshall's attempt to adapt CPE's qualitative distinction of "natural" and "market" forces in a DSE framework. Marshall is pertinent here because, as we shall see, Joan Robinson's early critique focused on the Marshallian conundrums; on the other hand, Keynes, in his macroeconomics, made productive use of the Marshallian short- and long-period distinction.

Marshall, particularly in his early work, adopted the "natural" price and "market" price distinction from Adam Smith and Ricardo. In the *Principles* (1890, 8th edition, 1920), however, he introduced his well known periodization of markets—"market," "short-period normal," "long-period normal," and "secular." However, he maintained "a continuity not only through time" (in the sense that "there was no impassable gulf between these periods and that time was continuous") but also analytically, for he wished to demonstrate that the fundamental idea of Demand and Supply ran through all the analytical frames of production, distribution, and exchange; the same principle of price and quantity determination was active in all these "periods." The need for "periods" derived from the different "causes" operating on the demand and supply, and these causes took different time periods for their full effects to be worked out. Thus, on the question of price determination, the Marshallian periods identified the different time taken for the supplies to adjust to changes in demand. Marshall used the periodization scheme to argue that the Ricardian cost of production doctrine was a limited one, pertinent, if at all, to the long-period equilibrium, when the supply side dominated. Even in that case, Marshall argued, Ricardo unintentionally ignored the presence of the other blade of the scissors, the demand side.

Marshall also used another methodological tool—the short chain of reasoning—in the form of his partial equilibrium method. His reluctance to proceed directly to the full equilibrium of the system is well known. However, he believed in the analytical continuity; whether examining partial or general equilibrium, Marshall wished to use the same DSE theory. In fact, he argued explicitly that the determination of pricing of particular commodities under partial equilibrium was but the first step towards determining distribution or "prices of factors" by the same supply and demand mechanism. By gradually releasing conditions impounded in the *ceteris paribus* clause, Marshall sought to establish the fundamental and universal idea of Demand and Supply and the unity of all theory. That such an enterprise was riddled with difficulties was clear from Sraffa's (1925, 1926) demolition of Marshall's attempt to construct a supply schedule for a particular commodity, independent of the demand schedule in the partial equilibrium framework. More difficulties were perceived by Marshall himself in accommodating increasing returns into the competitive equilibrium framework.[18] Without entering into the logical dilemmas posed for DSE theory, we may nevertheless note that Marshall was well aware of the social and historical factors and the presence of "the element of time." His attempt to borrow certain methodological elements from CPE provided some "openness" but failed precisely because the basically mechanistic premises of the DSE theory that he steadfastly supported did not allow for such "openness."

The Element of Time

The DSE theorists have not been unaware of the shortcomings of their theory, particularly its tenuous link with the observational base and with the concrete experiences of economies.[19] However, the lacunae evident when the theory is confronted with internal logical difficulties have led to remedial attempts via the relaxation of certain restrictive assumptions (such as the introduction of increasing returns, of uncertainty, and of money) with only limited success.[20] A more powerful trend that is emerging with such efforts is toward diagnosing the theory's shortcomings as one of *method*. John Hicks is among the scholars who have put considerable emphasis on this way out, with his seminal discussions of methods of dynamic analysis.[21] How to introduce "the element of time" into theory, by distinguishing between statics (when time does not enter in an essential way) and dynamics is identified as the main problem.[22]

The attempt to introduce "the element of time," however, has been made while preserving the theoretical DSE framework and approach. Time has also been introduced into some econometric studies as an independent variable or in the form of dated variables with lagged interactions, as in the Cobweb models. Hicks viewed the deficiency of the earlier neoclassical theory in terms of its method, i.e., in its failure to have a general "dynamic" theory in which "all quantities are properly dated and time enters in an essential way."[23] In *Value and Capital*, he offered a model of intertemporal equilibrium wherein the analysis was in terms of plans and realizations during a single period within which prices were expected to be determined by the usual equilibrium analysis. The role of expectations was highlighted in this construction. John Hicks, himself not satisfied with this, later discussed alternative methods of dynamic analysis.[24] While we would not enter here into a detailed critique of these alternatives or provide a taxonomy of methods, it is relevant to note that the basic structure of DSE theory is present in all these constructions. Hicks himself observes that "these do not quite fit together into a single coherent whole."[25] What Hicks does is attempt to salvage the theory through introducing special assumptions regarding the period over which the supply and demand relations are considered effective in establishing equilibrium or through introducing lags in the price-quantity responses. The disintegration of DSE *theory* into separate *methods*, failing to add up to a coherent whole, is an indirect admission of the failure of the theory precisely because DSE theory, unlike CPE, is constructed on the premises of symmetries and of the universalizability of the supply and demand relations. The "failure" in any market has direct consequences for the rest of the system, and parts of the system cannot be treated separately piecemeal.

Joan Robinson's Critique of Equilibrium

A number of criticisms raised by Joan Robinson against the equilibrium method may in fact be seen as deriving from the neoclassical theory's mechanistic conceptualization of change and its specific mechanisms of change and choice. Her critique itself passed through various phases: In her early writings, she raised objections against the mechanistic notion of equilibrium in the context of price determination, with Marshallian concerns such as increasing returns, irreversibilities in time, and also the stability properties of equilibrium. In her later writings, when she took up the theme of accumulation in the generalization of the *General Theory*, the arguments reappeared in the context of accumulation, with greater stress on such Keynesian concerns as uncertainty of expectations, particularly the irreversible effects of investment decisions encountered in the form of the nonmalleability of capital. While still working in the equilibrium methodology, Robinson entered into debates with the neoclassicists on the issue of the meaning and the measurement of capital in the production function. She later retracted her own suggestion to use a "pseudo-production function" in its place, following the reswitching and the capital reversing controversies originating from Piero Sraffa's *Production of Commodities*. While initially appreciating the destructive critical power of this controversy, she was later inclined to consider the "wrangle about capital measurement" as only a minor part of the critique. In her last writings she maintained that the fundamental error of theory based on equilibrium was one of confusing comparison of equilibria with historical processes. By the time she had moved on to the production function controversy, three main arguments relating to "methodological error" were being stressed: movements in time versus movements in space, "stability" and "existence" of equilibrium, and uncertainty.

Mistaking a Metaphor in Space for a Process through Time

As early as 1953, Joan Robinson focused on the methodological error of confusing a metaphor based on space to explain a process through time: "In space bodies moving from A to B may pass bodies moving from B to A but in time the strictest possible rule of one way traffic is always in force."[26] The difference between movements across space and time refers to the phenomenon of "irreversibility" that was to trouble Marshall, particularly in connection with "increasing returns," when he realized that it was not possible to move forwards and backwards on the same supply curve: cost conditions would alter irreversibly when economies were established at higher scales of output so that when output levels declined, the supply curve needed to be redrawn.[27] Such a requirement implies that the curve so drawn is only a "historical" curve and could not be used to *determine* equilibrium. The notion of reversibility is implicit in the construction of the supply and demand relations, which are a set of hypothetical quantities (supplied or demanded) corresponding to a hypothetical set of prices. They are coincidental alternatives and have no sequential ordering.

The second point of Robinson's methodological critique is: "in space, the distance from A to B is of the same order of magnitudes (whatever allowance you like to make for the trade winds) as the distance from B to A; but in time the distance from today to yesterday is infinite as the poets have often remarked."[28] In this, Joan Robinson appears to suggest a lack of symmetry between movements to and away from equilibrium. In a later paper, *History versus Equilibrium,* she remarks that "the concept of 'stability' based on mechanical analogy is inappropriate in economic analysis. For mechanical movements in space, there is no distinction between approaching equilibrium from an arbitrary initial position and a perturbation due to displacement from an equilibrium that has long been established."[29] Here, Robinson appears to draw a distinction between the *existence* of equilibrium as a process of reaching equilibrium from an arbitrary position and the stability condition for equilibrium, a disturbance occurring from an equilibrium already attained, which sets up tendencies for the return to it. In the earlier Oxford Lecture she concentrated mainly on the first question and referred to the "cobweb" theorems, "shipbuilding" and "pig" cycles generated by the peculiar properties of the lagged supply and demand relations whereby equilibrium would not actually be attained.[30]

When Robinson turns her attention to the question of accumulation, she brings in the influence of time mainly through expectations and uncertainty: "In economic life, in which decisions are guided by expectations alone, the two types of movements (i.e., approaching equilibrium from an arbitrary initial position and a perturbation due to displacement from an equilibrium, long established) are totally different."[31] It is this position that develops into a "third ground" for opposing the extension of the metaphor of "space" and is considered "a profound methodological error which makes the major part of neoclassical doctrine spurious."[32] Her main argument could be put briefly as follows: In order to assert that there is a tendency towards (long period) equilibrium, the economy would have to be in equilibrium already:

> The neoclassical economist thinks of a position of equilibrium as a position towards which an economy is tending to move as time goes by. But it is impossible for a system to *get into* a position of equilibrium, for the very nature of equilibrium is that the system *is* already in it, and has been in it for a certain length of past time.[33]

A few general observations on Robinson's interpretation of the long-period equilibrium may be noted. First, it would seem that she presupposed that for a meaningful conceptualization, the equilibrium must be actually attained, or that the equilibrium prices and the (uniform) rate of profit actually rule at any particular moment of equilibrium.[34] However, as Robertson pointed out, "We must not think of the 'long-run-value' of a thing as something which will be attained after so many months or years and then stay put. It is more legitimate to think of it as a norm around which actual value oscillates."[35] Indeed, this was the Marshallian conception to which Robertson here refers. However, given the kind of theory wherein the long-period equilibrium is explained mechanistically in terms of balancing of supply and demand, and particularly in the case of long-lived capital, these forces had to be considered as operating over time. Conditions such as perfect foresight and complete knowledge were introduced to derive rigorous results.

Second, Joan Robinson denies the process of getting into equilibrium mainly on the grounds of uncertain expectations. "It is," she writes "characteristic of a position of equilibrium that it is fulfilling expectations which were held in the past and is therefore recreating expectations that will be fulfilled in future. In reality, this situation is never realized."[36] Such is the emphasis that she places on this factor that, "As soon as uncertainty of the expectations that guide economic behaviour is admitted, equilibrium drops out of the argument and history takes its place."[37] She argues that since no economic agent has any inducement to change his method of production, and no input is in excess demand whenever equilibrium prices rule, the condition for reaching equilibrium is perfect foresight.[38] The argument appears to be that, with uncertainty present, no system not already in equilibrium can achieve equilibrium; while a system already in equilibrium could not but have "perfect foresight" by virtue of its being in such a state. Thus, since uncertainty of expectations is ever present, a state of equilibrium cannot exist.

Uncertainty of Expectations

Thus, Joan Robinson attaches considerable significance to the element of uncertainty as a crucial ingredient in bringing historical time into analysis. For her, the mark of post-Keynesian analysis is the recognition that we live in a world where the past is irrevocable and the future unknown.

Two observations may be made briefly here: First, in the classical theory (of the "long-run position") uncertainty of expectations has a role to play. We recall John Stuart Mill's observation that it is the expectation of profits that governs production and that it is precisely through the falsification of expectations that the profits below or above the "natural rate" tend to be corrected and the tendency to the uniform natural rate of profits operates. "Market prices" deviate from the natural prices precisely because of "miscalculations." It was the belief, however, of the classical writers that the forces bringing about uniformity of profit rates were strong enough to guide the quantity movements toward such an outcome, although the uniformity may not actually be achieved.

The classical theory did not specifically analyze individuals' expectations and uncertainty but rather concentrated on their objective outcomes. Today we have reasons to believe that uncertainty of expectations plays a different role in advanced capitalist economies from that envisaged by the classical writers and with the expanse of financial capital and financial developments, the *objective* basis for the formation of expectations and the corresponding behavioral premises are now perhaps altered. We need to discover these objective bases of different states of expectations and we need to know what systematic objective outcomes arise from these different states of expectations.

As to the argument that the "future is unknown," we may recall Frank Knight's (1921) remarks:

> It is a world of change in which we live, and a world of uncertainty. We live only by knowing *some things* about the future; while the problems of life, or of conduct at least, arise from the fact that we know so little. The essence of this situation is action according to *opinion*, of greater or less foundation and value, neither entire ignorance nor complete and perfect information, but partial knowledge. . . . [Further] experience has taught us that certain time and space relations subsist among phenomena to be depended upon.[39]

It is this "experience" that becomes the basis of an individual's inferences about the future. Apart from past shared experiences, there appears to be another fact of life that helps transcend the apparently chaotic and "subjective" inferences by individuals regarding the future, and turns them into "macro" events—the role of imitation and mutuality of expectations. "Expectations" work in patterns and give rise to broadly "uniform" behavior.[40]

The perception of the classical writers probably is too simple for today's more complex world of finance and monopoly capital. But it should still be the aim of theory to grasp the influence of uncertainty and expectation through their objective outcomes. Indeed, Keynes appears to have adopted an interesting methodology to frame the complexity of the real world. He has been credited with working out the effects of different states of expectations on employment and income under the provisional assumption that differences between expectations and realizations would not affect general expectations. It was under these conditions that he established the role of the effective demand principle in determining employment, and achieved a clear demonstration that the system could produce an equilibrium at less than full employment.[41] In this methodology, a close resemblance may be seen between the use of "market" and "natural" distinction of CEP when the variations in market values were not considered as affecting "natural values" (although permitted and taken into account for certain analyses), barring exceptional cases where the "market values" persisted in deviating from the "natural," the latter itself varying.[42]

Kregel (1976) makes another significant point: that Keynes's method was distinctive; that he did not see uncertainty as linked purely and continuously with the passage of time. This is evident from his rejection of the Swedish approach of ex-ante–ex-post analysis. Keynes did recognize that uncertainty and expectations arise because time elapses between the taking of decisions and the emergence of their outcomes. But he rejected the Swedish approach because the passage of time between the decision and the outcome could not be made precise and no definite cause-effect relations could be specified. Keynes wrote:

> I used to speak of the period between expectations and result as "funnels of processes" but the fact that the funnels are all of different lengths and overlap one another meant that at any given time there was no aggregate realized result capable of being compared with some aggregate expectation at some earlier date.[43]

It was only by taming the expectations and uncertainty by the above methodological device that Keynes could arrive at the definite results of his quantity dynamics.

The Capital Theory Debate

While an enthusiastic participant in the capital theory debate in the early period, in her later writings Robinson came to believe that the main point of criticism lay elsewhere. Referring to the reswitching debate, she maintained:

> The major point is that what they pretend to offer as an alternative or rival to the post-Keynesian theory of accumulation is nothing but error of methodology—a confusion between comparisons and imagined equilibrium positions and a process of accumulation going through history.[44]

Robinson's attack is directed against the way the "pseudo-production function is used in the construction of a dynamic theory."[45] Taking Solow's (1963) definition that each point on the function represents an economy on an island that has no intercourse with any other, Robinson argues that "there could be no movement along the pseudo-production frontier." Substitution (of capital for labor) is an illusion in any case. Joan Robinson's contention is that there is no *moving* from one rate of profit to another as, in reality, two economies with different rates of profit "are separated either in time or space." Her complaint is that the process of change from one state into another is confused with comparisons of two equilibria.

Further, Robinson argues that such a comparison of equilibria itself is illegitimate because "a comparison of economies each with a different rate of profit, each with its own future and its own past and its own rate, but all facing the same spectrum of technological possibilities is an artificial construction." Or, "not only is every island at a different point but every point is on a different production function." In this criticism, however, Robinson appears to question the age-old treatment of the choice of technique, where techniques are postulated to be chosen from a set of feasible technologies. During the process of accumulation, it may not be denied that new techniques emerge and "no two economies separated in space have exactly the same technology for many accidents of geography and history enter into the choice of techniques as well as the design of machines."[46] However, this criticism too is much better directed to the particular conceptualization of technical choice in the DSE theory than the method of comparison. We have referred earlier to how attempts are made in CPE, to make "technology," viewed as "the labor process," endogenous within social and production relations and where the social factors as well as factors of "history and geography" count.

While Joan Robinson's opinion on the omnipresent uncertainty and the need to study the dynamics of the irreversible processes at work through time is acceptable, her solution is neither precise nor lucid:

> To make the argument applicable to actual situations we have to leave equilibrium analysis behind and approach the problem in terms of a historical process, the system continually lurching from one out-of-equilibrium position to another.[47]

This solution cannot circumvent the difficulty of conceptualizing a theoretical "position," even if it were considered as "out of equilibrium," and of analyzing the process that leads from one to the other. A theory would be required to define the position as well as the process, and such a theory would require specification of systematic and regular relations.

Joan Robinson's emphasis on uncertainty and expectations *per se* as the essence of historical reality, without adequate treatment of the theoretical framework within which these inescapable features of the real economies have to be rigorously incorporated, lessens the effectiveness of her own critique. The capital theoretic critique demonstrates the basic flaw in the neoclassical theory even in its simplest representation without the complications of uncertain expectations. The introduction of these complexities cannot ameliorate, and perhaps even exacerbates, these difficulties. Although we all should be grateful to her for raising fundamental questions that cannot—and must not—be bypassed by social scientists, Robinson's methodological critique could divert attention from the difficulties that are exclusive to neoclassical theory.[48] If Sraffa treats change as not appearing essential to his arguments, it is because in the theoretical propositions that he is involved in demonstrating, he does not require that change be postulated on an *a priori* basis. This is not tantamount to assuming that the system is stationary in the neoclassical sense so that no rationale for change remains.

We may here conclude that many of the shortcomings Joan Robinson records concerning the method of equilibrium relate to DSE theory "explaining" equilibrium. In fact, the classical authors Smith, Ricardo, and Marx, using the notion of the "natural position," derived considerably powerful results applying the method of comparisons. To answer similar questions, DSE theory found itself "in the rut of equilibrium" because of its mechanistic conceptualization of change and choice. Even when attempts are made to introduce "the element of time," the insistence on universalizing the supply and demand framework to all activities and to all domains of choice, and the imposition of symmetrical behavioral rules and of preconditions on price-quantity responses in an attempt to maintain consistency have prompted casting aside or ignoring historical variations in causes and effects. Attempts to dynamize through incorporation of the calendar time as a "third dimension," or to introduce discriminant lags and leads, have brought in "time" only in a sequential sense, i.e., as a sequential arrangement of variables.

The dynamics of history work through qualitative changes in social and in material-structural relations in the domains of production, exchange, or distribution, as much as through temporal (calendar time) sequences. The classical authors appear to have devised an analytical structure that was much less ambitious and universal in its scope but that kept open the possibility of bringing in the variety and complexity of forces that act upon and shape not only the material activities of production, exchange, and distribution, but also the social relations that bind the actors together in these activities. It is only through taming the complex uncertainty of expectations and of events, and constructing simple chains of logical reasoning, that the dynamics of the real economies can be captured, as illustrated by Smith, Ricardo, Marx, Keynes, and Kalecki. Dealing with complex historical processes, moving irreversibly through time, is a well-nigh impossible task, especially when multiple and diverse causes operate, with various speeds and having effects that traverse different domains in the economy and over different lengths of time. It is impossible, then, as Keynes and also Marshall realized, to associate rigorously a time period over which the cause-effect relation works, or to associate particular effects with particular causes, where effects are seen exclusively in terms of the temporal movements. By reducing all behavior to the atomistically defined individual, DSE theory excluded dynamics that arise from the changing structure of social relations. The attempt to introduce the element of time in DSE theory went along analogously with the extension of statics to dynamics, as in the mechanical sciences. History had to be reduced to some form of calendar time units and all changes in the social structural relations had to be "externalized."

It would seem that we are far from a full-bodied process analysis to capture historical dynamics with our present knowledge, techniques, and analytical skills. A more worthwhile approach is—as Ricardo, Marx, and Keynes have realized—the method of comparisons. However, while adopting the method, the user needs to be wary about the theory chosen for the task.

Notes

I have benefited greatly from Geoff Harcourt's comments on this paper. My thanks are also due to Arun Kumar and Ingrid Rima.

1. Robinson, 1979, p. 58.

2. I am grateful to Geoffrey Harcourt for drawing my attention to Joan Robinson's emphasis, from early on, on the question of "meaning" rather than "measure" of capital. In the supply and demand based explanations of profit, the two problems become almost identical: corresponding to every conception of profits as a "return" on capital is a "meaning" (homogeneous content) that is attributed to "capital," and its corresponding measure is constructed. For example, if profits were viewed as a return on foregone consumption, "capital" would be seen as "waiting" and measured as time intensity; if profits were seen as a productive contribution of "invested land and labor," capital would be seen as a subsistence fund and measured in terms of a consumption unit. In short, the "meaning" of capital is derived from the attribute associated with it that warrants it a "return," and the measure is the reckoning of this attribute.

3. Robinson, 1979, p. 57.

4. Ibid., p. 58.

5. Robinson, 1980, p. xiv.

6. Robinson, 1973, pp. 254–63 (originally published in 1953).

7. Bharadwaj, 1989b.

8. Robertson, 1957; Harrod, 1948.

9. Robertson, 1957, p. 94. In reacting to Joan Robinson's criticism that the tendency towards equilibrium makes no useful sense since equilibrium, in practice, would never be achieved, Robertson writes:

> Tends in long run to equal, not "equals." We must not think of the "long-run value" of a thing as something which will be attained after so many months or years and then stay put. It

> is more legitimate to think of it as a norm around which actual value oscillates. . . . Yet even that conception, though helpful, may be too clearcut for application to a changing world. It may be in such a world long-run equilibrium is never attained, if all the forces at work had time to work themselves out; but it may be that in any particular case they never will have time to work themselves out.

10. It is difficult to construct such theoretical average or normal positions not only because social interrelations change but also because the concepts and categories in economic theory themselves have a "penumbra" surrounding them so that no definite quantifiable or measurable characteristics can be accurately associated with them. Such is the penumbra surrounding such concepts as the rate of profit, competition, or wage. Also, even if these concepts and categories were viewed as "operational constructs" (see Bridgman, 1930; Nagel, 1961), these break down within stringently narrow ranges and the method of experimentation is not available to ascertain or verify their domain. This apart, the causal structures themselves vary over time—what Marx emphasized as the essentially dialectical character of change.

11. Although such a conceptualization was rigorously advanced in the classical theory for the capitalist mode it is generalizable to other modes as well. The classical theorists analyzed different stages and phases of capitalist development, adopting a different sectorization of the economy, different technical and institutional relations in production, and systems of surplus appropriation and distribution. They allowed for the different content and scope of concepts like "net product" and productive consumption, and specified different *forms* of wages and exchange value.

12. Adam Smith has been claimed by neoclassicals as the progenitor of the idea of the optimizing individual and the Smithian invisible hand has been equated with the Walrasian auctioneer. (For a detailed critique, see Bharadwaj, 1989b.)

13. The system of natural liberty advocated freedom of the individual to pursue self-interest and became the directing principle of laissez-faire propounded against the then prevalent system of interventions and restrictions imposed by the operation of monopoly privileges and mercantilist regulations. By competition, Smith meant mobility of labor, capital, and commodities on the market, not the perfect competition of the neoclassical theory. He also advocated that the initiative to decide should be left to the individual. It would be, however, too simplistic to assume that he arrived, syllogistically, at the conclusion that atomistic competition and mobility of resources would guarantee a harmony between social well-being and the unrestricted pursuit of self-interest (see Bharadwaj, 1989).

14. In the classical theory, therefore, there is no inherent contradiction between the possibility of "general progress" of the economy (in the sense that, in the man-nature relations, a general advance occurs in terms of what is attainable by human effort) and contradictory interests of classes. The former is reflected in terms of the forward thrust of the productive forces. It is quite conceivable in Smith (1776)—and inevitably so in Marx—that there are dialectical consequences of the development, differentially affecting the domain of choices and achieved goals of different classes and their members.

15. Marx, 1867, pp. 467–507.

16. Bharadwaj, 1985; Garegnani, 1984.

17. Bharadwaj, 1985.

18. Bharadwaj, 1972; Hahn, 1984.

19. Leontief, 1971; Phelps-Brown, 1972; Worswick, 1972; Hahn, 1984.

20. Hahn, 1984; Arrow and Hahn, 1971.

21. While the "market prices" reflected fixed supplies on the shelf, the "short period" allowed changing utilization levels of existing production capacities; the "long period" would take account of changing capacities themselves, while the "secular"

period could take account of technical progress, large changes in population, etc.

22. Pierangelo Garegnani (1976) has argued that the shift away from the long-period equilibrium to short-period equilibrium analysis has been prompted by the difficulty that the theory faced in its explanation of the rate of profit in terms of demand and supply of capital.

23. Hicks, 1968, p. 116a.

24. Hicks, 1982, pp. 217–35.

25. Ibid., p. 219.

26. Robinson, 1959, p. 120.

27. Marshall, 1920, appendix H, to which Robinson refers. See also Bharadwaj, 1972.

28. Robinson, 1959, p. 120.

29. Robinson, 1979, p. 48.

30. Robinson, 1973, pp. 256–57. It may be noted, however, that the cycles were depicted precisely with reference to the "equilibrium position" and that the early DSE theorists, including Marshall, did not need to maintain that equilibrium is actually attained; see Robertson, 1957.

31. Robinson, 1979, p. 49.

32. Robinson, 1959, p. 120.

33. Ibid., 130. This was further elaborated as follows:

> A state of equilibrium is one in which each individual is satisfied that he could not do better for himself by changing his behavior. Applied to long-lived capital equipment, this means that the stock in existence today is in all respects what it would have been if those concerned had known at relevant dates in the past, what expectations about the future they would be holding today. But periods affected by different decisions overlap, and the relevant past stretches back indefinitely. Thus, an economy can be following an equilibrium path today only if it has been following it for some time already.

34. "In space it is possible to go to and fro and correct misdirections, but time goes only one way. This is why equilibrium cannot be achieved by a process of trial and error" (Robinson, 1979, p. 8); or "We must therefore carry over from the last model the conclusion that equilibrium prices are never likely to be ruling at any particular moment" (Robinson, 1962, p. 17, n. 1); or, "It is absurd though unfortunately common to talk as though 'in the long run,' we shall reach a date at which equilibrium corresponding to today's conditions will have been realized" (Robinson, 1962, p. 17).

35. Robertson, 1957, pp. 92–93.

36. Robinson, 1979, p. 270.

37. Ibid., p. 80.

38. Ibid., p. 49.

39. Knight, 1957, pp. 199–204.

40. In a different context, Steindl (1982) observes: "The role of imitation and mutual dependence of expectations has not found enough attention in economics," and gives as an illustration: "A flock of crows feeding on a field after a time rises collectively to fly away. How is the uniform behaviour obtained? Some crows get impatient first, they flap their wings and rise tentatively in the air. In this way they stimulate others until the unrest spreads more and more until finally the whole flock departs." It is the "uniform collective behaviour" that would congeal into the "experience" that becomes the basis for the inferred, limited knowledge about future.

41. Kregel, 1976.

42. Ricardo, 1821.

43. Keynes, 1973, pp. 184–85.

44. Robinson, 1979, p. 58.

45. "The techniques are set out in a pseudo-production function in descending order of the net output per man. Each technique consists of the specifications of the input-output table for producing the machine that it requires. Running an eye down the pseudo-production function, we obtain the real wage rate falling and rate of profit rising" (Robinson, 1979, p. 78).

46. Ibid., p. 82.

47. Robinson, 1962, p. 6.

48. Joan Robinson's emphasis on method also appears to have misled her into drawing parallels between the neoclassical and the classical theory—the latter, particularly in the context of Sraffa's return to it. Her characterization of the Sraffa system as a "half-equilibrium" or as a stationary state suggests that such parallels were being drawn.

References

Arrow, K. and F. Hahn. (1971) *General Competitive Analysis*. Edinburgh: Oliver Boyd.

Bharadwaj, Krishna. (1972) "Marshall on Pigou's *Wealth and Welfare*." *Economica* (February):32–46.

———. (1978a) *Classical Political Economy and Rise to Dominance of Supply and Demand Theories*. Dutt Lectures, 1976. Calcutta: Orient Longmans.

———. (1978b) "The Subversion of Classical Analysis: Alfred Marshall's Early Writing on Value." *Cambridge Journal of Economics*, 2:253–71.

———. (1985) "Sraffa's Return to Classical Theory." *Political Economy, Studies in the Surplus Approach*, 2:3–31. Amended and republished in *Themes in Value and Distribution: Classical Theory Reappraised* (1989). London: Unwin and Hyman.

———. (1989a) "Adam Smith's Political Economy." In *Themes in Value and Distribution: Classical Theory Reappraised*. London: Unwin and Hyman.

———. (1989b) *Themes in Value and Distribution: Classical Theory Reappraised*. London: Unwin and Hyman.

Bridgman, P. W. (1930) *The Nature of Physical Theory*. Princeton, NJ: Princeton University.

Clower, R. (1965) "The Keynesian Counter-Revolution: A Theoretical Appraisal." In F. Brechling and F. Hahn, eds., *The Treaty of Interest Rates*. London: Macmillan.

Garegnani, P. (1960) "Il Capitale nelle teorie della distribuzione." Milan.

———. (1976) "On a Change in the Notion of Equilibrium in Recent Work on Value and Distribution." In M. Brown, K. Sato, and P. Zarembkha, eds., *Essays in Modern Capital Theory*. Amsterdam: North-Holland.

———. (1984) "Value and Distribution in the Classical Economists and Marx." *Oxford Economic Papers*, 26.

Hahn, F. (1984) "On the Notion of Equilibrium in Economics" and "General Equilibrium Theory." In *Equilibrium and Macroeconomics*. Oxford: Basil Blackwell.

Harrod, R. F. (1948) *Towards a Dynamic Economics*. London: Macmillan.

Hicks, J. R. (1968) *Value and Capital*. Oxford: Oxford University Press; 1st edition 1939.

———. (1982) "Methods of Dynamic Analysis." In *Money, Interest and Wages, Collected Essays in Economic Theory*, vol. 2. Oxford: Basil Blackwell.

———. (1985) *Methods of Dynamic Economics*. Oxford: Clarendon Press.

Keynes, J. M. (1973) *The Collected Writings of John Maynard Keynes*, vol. 14. London: Macmillan.

Knight, Frank H. (1957) *Risk, Uncertainty and Profit*. New York: Harper.

Kregel, J. (1976) "Economic Methodology in the face of Uncertainty: The Modelling Methods of Keynes and the Post-Keynesians." *Economic Journal* (June):209–25.

Leijonhufvud, A. (1960) *On Keynesian Economics and the Economics of Keynes*. New York: Oxford University Press.

Leontief, W. W. (1971) "Theoretical Assumptions and Non-observable Facts." *American Economic Review* 11 (March):1237–55.
Marshall, A. (1920) *Principles of Economics*, 8th ed. London: Macmillan.
Marx, K. (1867) *Capital*, vol. 1. London: Lawrence & Wishart.
Meek, R. L. (1977) *Smith, Marx and After*. London: Chapman and Mall.
Mill, J. S. (1909) *Principles of Political Economy* (1871), ed., Sir W. Ashley. New York: Longmans, Green. Republished Augustus Kelley (1973).
Nagel, Ernest. (1961) *The Structure of Science*. London: Routledge and Kegan Paul.
Phelps-Brown, E. (1972) "The Underdevelopment of Economics." *Economic Journal* 82, 325 (March):1–10.
Ricardo, D. (1821) *Principles of Political Economy. Works and Correspondence*, ed., P. Sraffa, vol 1. Cambridge: Cambridge University Press.
Robertson, D. (1957) *Lectures on Economic Principles*. London: Fontana.
Robinson, Joan. (1959) *Collected Economic Papers*, vol. 2. Oxford: Basil Blackwell.
———. (1962) *Essays in the Theory of Economic Growth*. London: Macmillan.
———. (1973) *Collected Economic Papers*, vol. 4. Oxford: Basil Blackwell.
———. (1974) "History versus Equilibrium." Thames Papers in Political Economy. In *Collected Economic Papers*, vol. 5. Oxford: Basil Blackwell, 1979.
———. (1979) *Collected Economic Papers*, vol. 5. Oxford: Basil Blackwell.
———. (1980) *Further Contributions to Modern Economics*. Oxford: Basil Blackwell.
Samuelson, P. (1941) "The Stability of Equilibrium: Comparative Statics and Dynamics." *Econometrica*, 9, 2.
———. (1975) "Steady State and Transient Relations: A Reply on Restructuring." *Quarterly Journal of Economics*, 89. Reprinted in *Collected Scientific Papers*, vol. 4, 1966.
Smith, Adam. (1776) *An Inquiry into the Nature and Causes of the Wealth of Nations*, ed. E. Cannan. London: Random House, Modern Library edition, 1937.
Solow, R. (1963) *Capital Theory and the Rate of Return*. Amsterdam: North-Holland.
Sraffa, P. (1925) "Sulle relazioni fra costa e quantita prodtta." *Annali di Economi*, 2:277–328.
———. (1926) "The Laws of Returns under Competitive Conditions." *Economic Journal* (December):535–55.
———. (1960) *Production of Commodities by Means of Commodities*. Cambridge: Cambridge University Press.
Steindl, J. (1982) "The Control of the Economy." Unpublished paper presented at the Conference on Theories of Accumulation and the Control of Economy, Udine, Italy.
Symposium on Paradoxes in Capital Theory. (1966) *Quarterly Journal of Economics*, 80: 503–83.
Worswick, C. D. N. (1972) "Is Progress in Economics Science Possible?" *Economic Journal* (March): 73–86.

JR

CHAPTER EIGHT

On the Generalization of the *General Theory*

J. A. KREGEL

Joan Robinson was among the first economists working around Keynes to recognize that the *General Theory* presented a new method of analysis as well as a new theoretical approach. She was thus already at work applying Keynes's new method of analysis to problems other than the determination of the level of output and employment on which Keynes had focused, even before his path-breaking book was published. For as a Marshallian taught by Pigou (but with serious doubts, as she tells us, raised by Piero Sraffa's arrival in Cambridge), it was natural to consider Keynes's theory as an application of the Marshallian short-period theory. From this perspective it appeared obvious that the way was open to use Keynes's method to produce an extension and generalization to the Marshallian long period. This Mrs. Robinson attempted in her 1935 essay on "The Long-Period Theory of Employment." As I have suggested elsewhere (Kregel, 1985), the remainder of her professional career may be viewed as the continuous perfection and refinement of the problems that were originally raised in that paper (or more precisely, in the revised version that was published in the 1937 book, *Essays in the Theory of Employment*, which applied the method to a number of additional areas).

In this first attempt at such a long-period theory, Joan Robinson employed a number of tools of traditional analysis that she subsequently criticized and replaced with new approaches. In this continuous process her work was stimulated by association with and criticism by the foremost economists of the generation, including Keynes. In addition to Piero Sraffa and Richard Kahn, Michal Kalecki and Roy Harrod played an important early role in provoking her to refine her approach to technical progress and growth, as did Nicholas Kaldor somewhat later. Joan Robinson thus had over twenty years of more or less constant work on these problems behind her when economists such as Meade, Swan, and Solow introduced their neoclassical versions of the Harrod-Domar growth model, which appeared to be starting off from more or less the same point where she had begun in the 1930s, but which Robinson had long since abandoned as unsatisfactory. It is indeed unfortunate that most interest in her work is associated with her criticisms of this neoclassical analysis which do not render full justice to her positive contributions to the problems of the relation of growth and technical progress. It is also unfortunate that her criticism of the neoclassical position has been linked so closely to the critique of the same theory by Piero Sraffa, when the two are best viewed as being independent of each other.

Joan Robinson's criticism of neoclassical growth theory does not come only from analysis of these models, but is in large part based on her own only earlier experience in applying the same neoclassical tools to these problems. She had first-hand experience of the defects and drawbacks of this approach because she had already experimented with it and found it incompatible with Keynes's theory.

There is one aspect of her early attempts at extending the method of the *General Theory* to the long period that bears closer scrutiny because of the way it conditioned the path she followed in her subsequent work. In Keynes's theory a fundamental proposition was the separation of the determinants of the rate of interest from those of the return to capital, or as we might put it in traditional terms, the separation of the rate of interest from the marginal productivity of capital. Keynes went to great lengths to insist that his theory was the direct opposite of Wicksell's theory in which the natural or real rate of interest, which would be established in the absence of money, determined the nominal or money rate of interest in equilibrium. Keynes not only reversed the causal link between the real and the money rate of interest, he rejected the idea of a real rate of interest or a marginal physical productivity of capital (as Myrdal had also done in criticism of Wicksell). It is money that is the "real" variable and the money rate of interest that determines the real rate or, as he called his version of the concept, the marginal efficiency of capital. This cut both the money rate of interest and the real rate of interest, or the marginal productivity, free from any "objective" or real physical factors associated with the technical aspects of the production process.

In chapter 14 of the *General Theory*, Keynes repeatedly insists that the marginal efficiency cannot determine the rate of interest because it is itself determined by the money rate of interest via the present value formula. A simpler way of stating this proposition is to say that the rate of interest and the rate of profit are determined by different factors.

Now Keynes had already noted in the *Treatise*, citing Schumpeter as authority, that investment is jointly determined by the expectation of future profits and the interest rate used to determine the present value of these profits relative to the present costs of the investment. This is virtually the same solution that Myrdal had applied in his *Monetary Equilibrium*. In almost all of the *General Theory* Keynes employed the simplifying assumption of a given state of general expectations. As I have suggested elsewhere (Kregel, 1976), this meant that the analysis was restricted to what might be called "static" and "stationary" analysis. On this assumption the marginal efficiency of capital as envisaged by entrepreneurs and the liquidity preference of the public have to be considered as being given or held constant in the *ceteris paribus* clause. Any discussion of an expansion in the level of investment, and thus any discussion of the accumulation of capital and the growth of output, is limited to an exogenous change in the rate of interest brought about by the Central Bank.

This is precisely the avenue that Joan Robinson pursued in her early work, analyzing the effect of a fall in the rate of interest on investment. But, in the pre-Keynesian tradition—whether Ricardian or neoclassical—a fall in the rate of interest should lead to a change in the remuneration of capital as a factor of production and thus to a substitution of capital for labor in the production process. This adjustment in inputs would lead to a change in the distribution of income from labor to capital that depends on the change in relative prices with respect to the changes in the relative quantities used in production.

If workers and capitalists have different propensities to consume, then any shift in distribution away from the former, who are assumed to have a higher propensity to consume, would reduce the multiplier and the expansion of output associated with any given change in the rate of interest. In this way, the theory of effective demand in the long period became intertwined with the problems of the distribution of income and the choice of technique. It was this interrelationship that Joan Robinson originally attempted to analyze by application of the concept of the elasticity of substitution. She eventually rejected its use and, on Harrod's suggestion, simplified the problem by adopting the concept of neutral technical progress, which assumed that the rate of interest was constant, and the idea of steady-state growth.

The first point to note about the way Joan Robinson approached the long-period problem, starting with an exogenous fall in the rate of interest, is that it produced a fusion of the problems of the determination of the level of output and the choice of technique, i.e., of relative prices. Sraffa, working on the problem from the other direction—i.e., not from the point of view of a long-period theory of output but from the point of view of a theory of prices of production—reached the conclusion that the problems could not be resolved simultaneously. Indeed, she was eventually led to adopt a very similar solution, carrying out her analysis in terms of steady-state models of growth with divergence of technical progress from neutral.

This was also a solution she was to reject vehemently in her later years as unsatisfactory when she reiterated: "there is no such thing as accumulation in a given state of technical knowledge."[1]

The second point that should be noted is that if Keynes's insistence on the independence of the rate of interest and the rate of profit is accepted, and the rate of profit is considered to be one of two distributive variables along with the wage, then it is inappropriate to consider the effect of a change in the rate of interest on the share of income going to capital. A change in the rate of interest in conditions of given expectations must imply that it leaves the marginal efficiency of capital and rate of profit unchanged. A fall in the rate of interest, if it increases the ratio of investment in national income, leads, following Keynes and Kalecki, to an increase in savings via an increase in aggregate profits in conditions of classical savings. If the wage is unchanged the problem of the substitution of capital for labor need not come into the question at all.

As Joan Robinson eventually recognized, in order to confront the problem of the choice of technique we need an explanation of changes in the rate of profit. It is the rate of profit, not the rate of interest, that will determine the choice of technique, or more simply of the relative employment of labor and capital in employment. This was a position taken by Kalecki: "The main stimulus to use more capital per worker is provided by new inventions. The advantage offered by them is usually so high that it will be taken whatever (within a wide range) the level of the rate of interest."[2] That is, if a new technique requiring an increase in capital expenditure per unit of labor offers a sharp increase in the expected rate of profit, it will be introduced irrespective of the rate of interest. On the other hand, a sharp rise in the wage, reducing the rate of profit, will bring about a reduction in the employment of labor, irrespective of any associated changes in the interest rate.

Kalecki summarized the general approach as follows:

> The idea that a reduction of the rate of interest stimulates the application of more capital per worker is based on the assumption that the planned *output* of the investing entrepreneur is given. On this condition a lower rate of interest makes it profitable to use more capital and less labor. If we assume, however, that the *capital* available to the firm for financing investment is given, the reduction of the rate of interest has no influence on the choice of the method of production when planning investment, because it affects the expected net profit equally, whatever the method of production adopted.[3]

It is interesting to note that the analysis of the choice of technique carried out in Joan Robinson's work in the 1950s proceeded on the assumption that the capital available to the firm to be invested in a new technique is given. By that time she had already started to analyze the choice of technique (what she called a change in technique within a given spectrum of techniques—the famous book of engineering blueprints) in terms of the impact of the rate of profits and the wage on firms' decisions. Indeed, the fundamental question posed by the *Accumulation of Capital* (Robinson, 1956) was the determination of the rate of profit.

This approach could have been introduced much more quickly had the early extensions of the *General Theory* started by discussing the effect on the rate of investment of a change in the marginal efficiency of capital, or more simply, a change in the rate of profit, rather than as the result of a change in the rate of interest. There are a number of reasons that might explain why this was not done. First of all there is the hold of "habitual modes of thought and expression" on the formulation of the problem. Second is the force of the assumption of a constant state of expectations. Keynes had already indicated where he thought the relaxation of this latter assumption would lead: to the model of "shifting equilibrium." This was far from the Marshallian definition of a long-period stationary state and it was not a path that Joan Robinson, or any other Cambridge economist (with the possible exception of Robertson who retained his interest in fluctuations), felt capable of pursuing.

Indeed, Joan Robinson was fond of repeating that it was first necessary to work out the simplified problems presented by the relation of accumulation and technical progress within the confines of the stationary state before moving on to the much more difficult terrain of change over historical time. But it was this latter problem that was to preoccupy her at the end of her professional career. Exhibiting a degree of impatience she would not accept of her students and colleagues, eager to pursue more interesting questions, she responded to her rhetorical question: History versus Equilibrium? by emphatically declaring in favor of the former.

This position was then echoed in her declaration in the *Quarterly Journal of Economics* in 1975 concerning the "Unimportance of Reswitching," and her exchanges with Piero Garegnani: "There is no such phenomenon in real life as accumulation taking place in a given state of technical knowledge"[4] because "the long-period aspect of investment is the change that it is bringing about in the stock of means of production often accommodating technical innovations."[5] The problem that had plagued analysis of the long period throughout her career was thus classified as a wild-goose chase that had only been introduced to make sense of traditional theory: Within Keynes's method the problem of the effect of the choice of technique on the rate of accumulation could be handled independently of the relation of the rate of interest to the choice of technique of production.

Notes

The author is Professor of Political Economy at the University of Bologna, Bologna, Italy.

1. Robinson, 1975, p. 39.
2. Kalecki, 1944, p. 61.
3. Ibid.
4. Robinson, 1975, p. 39.
5. Robinson, 1979, p. 179.

References

Kalecki, M. (1944) "Three Ways to Full Employment." In *The Economics of Full Employment*. Oxford: Basil Blackwell.

Kregel, J. A. (1976) "Economic Methodology in the Face of Uncertainty: The Modelling

Methods of Keynes and the Post-Keynesians." *Economic Journal*, 86:209–25.

———. (1985) "Post-Keynesian Distribution Theory in Relation to Growth and Technical Progress." *Economie Appliquée*, 37, 2:375–88.

Robinson, J. (1937) "The Long-Period Theory of Employment." In *Essays in the Theory of Employment*. London: Macmillan.

———. (1956) *The Accumulation of Capital*. London: Macmillan.

———. (1974) *History versus Equilibrium*. London: Thames Papers in Political Economy (Autumn).

———. (1975) "The Unimportance of Reswitching." *Quarterly Journal of Economics*, 89, 1 (February):32–39.

———. (1979) "Garegnani on Effective Demand." *Cambridge Journal of Economics*, 3, 2 (June):179–80.

JR

CHAPTER NINE

Joan Robinson

Journeys into Heterodoxy

LARRY LEVINE

Preliminaries

Even if much of the territory intrinsic to Joan Robinson's legacy has been dealt with in great breadth and depth elsewhere,[1] various links that connect her work both forward and backward in time, to a variety of destinations in the literature, remain for exploration.

If we are to single out some of the starting points in Mrs. Robinson's work for these journeys, perhaps first in order of importance would be her rejection of that "tight prior equilibrium" world view, to use Melvin Reder's felicitous phrase (1982), which is the stock in trade of present-day Walrasian general equilibrium theorists, in favor of a more Marshallian—and hence looser—approach to the analysis of economic process. (The intellectual kinship between Robinson and Marshall was clearly a love/hate relationship!) In that corner of the Marshallian edifice that she singled out for *favorable* comment, markets are inhabited by flesh-and-blood decision makers who do not possess perfect knowledge. Perhaps next in importance was her refusal to immerse herself in the lore of the neoclassical production function. (This was destined to be the source of much mischief, in the eyes of others.)

Where could paths from such positions lead? Rejection of Walras is a continuing theme; "replacement" of Walras by Marshall is an intermittent one. Her 1962 paper, "Normal Prices," is a *locus classicus* for points of departure *and* final destinations. It offers a *mise en scène* characterized, in its micro particulars, by Marshall's long-run normal supply prices, and connected with this, in her eyes, is the Sraffa (and Von Neumann) model of price determination in which relative commodity prices are determined solely by supply-side phenomena, by the technics of production, independently of demand phenomena.[2] A macro element in the same essay: the level of the independently coursing money wage drives the general level of prices. And the rate of profit? *It* is determined by the rate of investment. But the model is not closed with respect to the latter. In sum: her rejection of Walras here, guided in part by Marshall, leads to a Sraffian scenario into which a Keynesian additive has been introduced.

Although the model is not closed with respect to the determination of investment, and money wages can have an independent "history" of their own, we are not left with chaos. There is a set of mutual consistencies that includes the pattern of income distribution. Thus, the "level of normal prices has to be such that the rate of profit is such that the distribution of income is such that the ratio of saving to capital stock is equal to the rate of accumulation."[3] Notice, then, that the "main weight of the equalization of savings to investment (at normal prices) falls upon the distribution of income between classes."[4]

As intimated above, perhaps *the* starting point for paths to heterodoxy are Robinson's frequent reminders, often accompanied by an acknowledgment to Marshall, that markets are not lifeless structures, but are inhabited by fallible human beings who nevertheless harbor expectations, and who have to make decisions under uncertainty.

Not wholly unrelated to this is her abandonment of the neoclassical production function. Furthermore, it is possible to contend, without overburdening one's imagination, that her critique of the notion of a production function brings Mrs. Robinson into touch with that burgeoning current literature on team production and implicit contracting.

These are the principal issues, then—"equilibrium" placed in a parlous position with respect to "history" (the flow of events in historic time), decision making under uncertainty in a production-functionless world—on which much of the following examination of lines of communication from Robinsonian positions to sometimes startling destinations in the literature will center. Item: neo-"Austrian" airs (?) on a non-Walrasian theme—without, of course, "Austrian" policy implications! To Negishi, the diversity that can be subsumed under the head, "non-Walrasian" economics, includes the "Classical, Marxist, Austrian, Jevonian and Cambridge Schools."[5] What this ecumenical potpourri adds up to is concentration, not upon "state" or upon market as a "structure," as in the Walrasian system, but upon activity (behavior); that is, trading activity (Edgeworth, Menger, and Marshall, with some interfaces with Adam Smith), and production activity (Smith, Marshall, and Marx). In Negishi's hands, there is an important spin-off from reassembling these pieces, namely, the provision of microeconomic foundations for Keynesian macroeconomics—not wholly unlike Mrs. Robinson's micro-cum-Keynes "blending" endeavors in her theory of "normal prices."

We begin the section that follows with a conspectus of possible starting points—the potential—in Mrs. Robinson's work for advances into some decidedly non-Walrasian territory. In the third section a survey of some of this territory—the set of destinations—is undertaken.

The Starting Points

Mrs. Robinson's numerous dismissals of the neoclassical production function were invariably mordant. Here is a characteristic instance: "The dominance in neoclassical economic teaching of the concept of a production function . . . has had an enervating effect upon the development of the subject. . . . [T]he production function has been a powerful instrument of miseducation."[6]

Perhaps the most important point of departure for a heterodox destination is her treatment of the notion of long-run equilibrium. Here, too, the message was loud and clear:

> [W]e have to leave equilibrium analysis behind and approach the problem in terms of an historical process, the system continually lurching from one out-of-equilibrium position to another.[7]

This was a note that Mrs. Robinson struck repeatedly, but perhaps nowhere more forcefully than in her 1974 paper on "History versus Equilibrium." Like so much of her work, this, too, bears the marks of her prolonged encounter with Keynes—the Keynes who described himself as having "a long struggle to escape" into that universe of discourse in which "expectations about the future are necessarily uncertain."[8] A corollary, from the same source: "As soon as the uncertainty of the expectations that guide economic behavior is admitted, equilibrium drops out of the argument and history takes its place." Furthermore, equilibrium should never be taken to be the *terminal point of a process.* And, in the same vein: one of the great neoclassical errors is to build conceptual models of systems "getting into" equilibrium; for, *on the level of concept*, "the very nature of equilibrium is that the system is already in it."[9]

Appearances notwithstanding, there is nothing enigmatic about all this. If one pays heed to the problem of the formation of expectations in an uncertain world, one will get the "equilibrium" thing right and, at the same time, learn not to place too great a burden upon the notion of equilibrium. That is, if one *is* going to get it right, one must specify all of the system's pertinent physical data—technical conditions and the like—and, then, along with the "state of expectations" of the decision makers of the system, one simply "dumps [this model of a system] down," so to speak, at "a particular date in historic time and work[s] out what will happen next."[10] Of course, what actually "happens next" may not be what was *expected* to happen next.

And, one should never attempt to build a conceptual model of a system "getting into" long-run equilibrium not only because, to repeat, the system is, on the level of concept, "already in it," but more importantly, because "observed history cannot be interpreted as evidence to support any propositions" concerning "movement" along a fictitious "equilibrium path."[11] The "facts" of a real—and uncertain—world can never be crammed into anything purporting to be a *real-world* "equilibrium" path or equilibrium position. Reality is too full of incompatibilities for that. Nor can the properties of "stationary equilibrium" provide the context for modeling intertemporal change. "What has led us astray is the bad habit (which Marshall tried to resist, but Wicksell freely indulged) of conducting an analysis of movements through time as though they occurred in stationary equilibrium."[12]

But what about those sets of physical and expectational data, "dumped down" at particular points of historic time, as candidate equilibrium positions? Although not entirely chimerical, they can only be envisaged as *conceptual* (not actual) "equilibrium positions." And, if they are kept in their "logical place," there is "much to be learned" from *a priori* comparisons across these equilibrium positions.[13] "But they cannot be applied to actual situations; it is a mortal certainty that any particular actual situation which we want to discuss is not in equilibrium."[14] So, although equilibrium is not a chimera on the level of concept, still, when it comes to understanding problems of the real world, one is left yet again with Mrs. Robinson's aphorism that equilibrium must be permitted to drop out of the argument, its place to be taken by history—a history which is replete with those incompatibilities that can always be relied upon to knock an economy out of a "state" that, "from a short-period point of view,"[15] may have an equilibrium *appearance*.

The existence or nonexistence of equilibrium states (conceptual or actual) aside, people, not things, create "states"—and markets. Thus, given Mrs. Robinson's views on equilibrium, "history" (flow of events), and uncertainty, her rejection of that device that is a seemingly lifeless market—the Walrasian device—surely follows as an inevitable corollary. The Walrasian characterization "of the economy is not so much unreal as non-existent. Sometimes it means that there are no people in the market at all—only prices and quantities of commodities are mentioned."[16]

Destinations in Heterodoxy

Mrs. Robinson's positions on the production function, on equilibrium, on uncertainty and expectations, on models of markets for which flesh-and-blood non-omniscient decision makers must be postulated, have points of contact with a variety of stopping-off places in the literature. Some of the lines of communication from Robinsonian territory to other places are readily apparent. Others are far less so, and some connecting links may seem to be excessively tenuous, even if not wholly fanciful. Still, the enterprise—the search for links—is too full of promise not to be undertaken.

(1) Mrs. Robinson's aversion to the neoclassical production function brings her into close touch with Piero Sraffa's *Production of Commodities by Means of Commodities,* and of particular relevance here is Sraffa's rejection of the marginal productivity approach to the theory of factor pricing and income distribution.

(2) The Sraffa connection in the above is patently obvious. A less apparent "link" is the way in which Mrs. Robinson's disavowal of the production function interfaces with a body of literature that is not, at least in *all* its particulars, outside the mainstream (although some "mainstreamers" would no doubt enter a caveat here). We refer to latter-day extensions of the Coasian firm that feature property rights, transaction costs, principal/agency problems, and implicit contracts.[17] Mrs. Robinson would surely not be too upset by this "association." After all, in the eyes of some, this literature has had the consequence, for the theory of production and the theory of the firm, of shifting the focus of analysis from inputs in a physical sense, an assumed homogeneity on the input side, and what may generally be described as a (static) production-function world view, to that world view that brings within its ambit the services of human beings and the contractual arrangements—typically implicit—under which these services are engaged. In a word, this literature views the firm as a "nexus of contracts" or as a team or set of teams, and production as team production.[18]

The consequence of this for the conventional notion of a production function could be profound. After all, where there is, literally, team production (and this is surely the norm), there cannot exist a production function in the sense of assuming one factor or factors conceptually "fixed" and another factor variable in order to "compute" the marginal product attributable to the "variable" factor. In other words,

$$\frac{\partial^2 x}{\partial y_1 \partial y_2} \neq 0,$$

where x is product and y_1 and y_2 are factors of production.[19]

(3) What we have just described may be thought of as a "people-oriented" approach to the theory of production and the theory of the firm. Furthermore, this approach to the theory of production and the firm should be twinned with what we might refer to as Mrs. Robinson's people-oriented view of equilibrium; that is, if we are in fact entitled to introduce anything smacking of "equilibrium" into an overview of her legacy. We have suggested that we are so entitled: "logical places," *a priori* comparisons across positions—and all that. However, we have also mentioned Mrs. Robinson's insistence that "equilibrium" must be allowed to drop out of the analysis when the uncertainty of expectations that "guide economic behavior is admitted," its place to be taken by "history." And we have suggested that to "history" should be added "real people." If this is done, Mrs. Robinson will be brought into touch with Marshall, and with Marshall's not always abundantly clear lucubrations on equilibrium. Indeed, at this juncture, that is, when Mrs. Robinson beholds the Alfred Marshall who "retained something of the classical tradition," and more pertinently, when she reflects upon the fact that Marshall's analytical "world" is "inhabited by busi-

nessmen, trade union leaders, bankers and traders,''[20] ''love'' replaces ''hate'' in the love/hate relationship that Mrs. Robinson had with the man whom she once (mildly) pejoratively referred to as the ''old fox.'' With this Robinson-Marshall mutual concern for ''life as it is lived'' in mind, we might consider that sense of ''real people'' that animates Marshall's treatment of trading in the market period (in a country-town corn market) in chapter 2 of Book 5 of the *Principles.*

What one discovers there is a scenario that can accommodate both an ''anchor'' notion of *market* equilibrium—i.e., a ''fixed point,'' or market-clearing price, to which individual planning and decision-making behavior may be said to be ''anchored''—and a reality of agents who endlessly adjust their (quantity) offers in real time. Price bargaining is not explicitly mentioned, but it is surely not precluded: after all, Marshall does speak of (market) price moving about ''like a shuttlecock,'' presumably as a result of divergences of realizations from plans. Whether one regards these agents as being in or out of ''equilibrium'' is quite beside the point. Real behavior, and uncertainty, there is in plenty. And one can envisage activity that is not *necessarily* equilibrating; that is, one can conceive here of trading that is not genuinely non-*tâtonnement* (if it were, there would be convergence to equilibrium). True, Marshall writes that the market will close at the end of the interval of *real* time in question (a market day) at a price that will ''probably'' be at the equilibrium level.[21] However, the very ''model'' that Marshall presents here perhaps may be more aptly described as one of *quasi*-non-*tâtonnement*, rather than non-*tâtonnement*, since the trading activity will not necessarily be equilibrating.

The point is worth pursuing. What has happened to the ''anchor'' in this scenario? There *seems* to be a ''market-equilibrium'' price in the conventional market-clearing sense, but will all agents perceive it to be such? There is scope for a negative reply. At any rate, Marshall literally opens the floodgates to a host of problems having to do with decision making under uncertainty.[22] So where are we? The demand/supply schedule Marshall introduces here shows 36s a quarter as the apparent equilibrium price in the market-clearing sense. But Marshall, ever with his eye on reality, offers the following account: many traders who could have been counted on to sell their corn for 36s were in fact only willing to sell at that price because they were ''in urgent need of a certain amount of ready money.''[23] If they had been able to surmount this ''need'' and had actually succeeded in selling at a somewhat higher price, there might have been a diminution in the marginal utility of money to them, and if *that* had happened, they might have refused to sell at 36s ''all the corn they could have sold if the price had been at 36s throughout''; thus, such sellers, as a consequence of ''getting an advantage at the beginning of the market,'' might hold to the end to a price higher than the ''equilibrium'' price. In this situation, one should envisage the market closing at ''*an*'' equilibrium price rather than ''*the*'' equilibrium price—although, in a somewhat hesitant afterthought, Marshall wrings from himself the concession that the price, ''*an*'' equilibrium price, as we have already noted, would be very unlikely to diverge widely from "*the*" equilibrium price.[24]

Again, where are we? The notion of *the* equilibrium that is determinate, in the Kaldor-Negishi sense, and unique has taken a buffeting in the face of problems of decision making under uncertainty.[25] Succumbing to, or resisting, the urge for cash flow in the here and now might well be associated with little market-testing or information-enhancing experiments on the part of agents, the result of these experiments being different perceptions across agents of the market-clearing price, which will have changed one of the "conditions" (in Kaldor's sense[26]) of market equilibrium: namely, the set of prices that *could* result in an equilibrium "position" (price/quantity set). In sum, there would appear to be the possibility of equilibria that may not be invariant to modes of information gathering (perception formation).

What we have described as quasi-non-*tâtonnement*, in Marshall, was indeed worth examining in some detail. After all, it was *this* Marshall who was separated from the Walrasian tradition by a yawning chasm, and it was *this* Marshall (he who was "studying a recognizable economy," as Mrs. Robinson put it) who had caught Mrs. Robinson's fancy. And it is this Marshall whom one can discern in the opening pages of Mrs. Robinson's 1962 "Model of Accumulation," where she deals with the alleged "tendency" for market price to move to the "equilibrium" (market-clearing) level. More specifically, she identifies what is really *the* problem here: in order to be able to speak of a "tendency" to equilibrium, it is necessary to assume that "there is a clear concept in the mind of the dealers as to what the equilibrium position is."[27] Finally, the intimation here that there is no guarantee that there will in fact be such a "clear concept" in the minds of all dealers puts Mrs. Robinson into touch with Arrow's (1959) problem of the possibility of price dispersion in a "competitive" market.

(4) Before we put "paid" to the notion that the world is inhabited by real people—a notion shared by both Mrs. Robinson and her not-always-discredited (in her eyes) "mentor"—we might advance the (strange?) notion—with, of course, appropriate misgivings—that it is possible to perceive an "Austrian" element here as well; specifically, Menger's *Absatzfahigkeit* ("marketability") as another candidate "destination" that can be reached from Mrs. Robinson's *Weltanschauung*. If we could put words into her mouth, might we almost hear her saying, "*anything* to distance one's self from Walras's frictionless void"? At any rate, as Negishi has recently reminded us in his *Economic Theories in a Non-Walrasian Tradition*, the markets of the Walrasian system are well organized; those in Menger are, typically, poorly organized (" 'marketability' is not high").[28]

From treatment of economic activity and human foibles in the Austrian manner, we might move on to another non-Walrasian variant of general equilibrium theory, with, of course, "general equilibrium" *per se* suppressed if we are to maintain contact with Mrs. Robinson. A central feature of this reformulation is the relative subordination of the "market" to the "individual," in so far as the focal point of analysis is concerned.[29] It is a reformulation that builds to some considerable extent upon foundations laid by F. Y. Edgeworth: he of the "Art of Bargaining," which consists in "higgling dodges and designing obstinacy and other incalculable and often disreputable accidents."[30] We dealt above with a "humanized" version of "equilibrium" in Marshall's *market period.* Let us return, now, to the notion of *long-run* equilibrium, and to Mrs. Robinson's theory of "Normal Prices." Let us remind ourselves once again that there is, on the level of concept, a notion of equilibrium there (and elsewhere). It emerges from those "*a priori* comparisons of equilibrium positions," which, to Mrs. Robinson, are legitimate, provided they are "kept in their logical place and not applied to *actual* situations."[31] To Mrs. Robinson, one such "logical place" is the set of relative commodity prices which can become Marshall's normal long-run supply prices "when expectations are realized."[32] And it is this that brings Mrs. Robinson, both directly and through Marshall, into another interface with Sraffa (and with the von Neumann model of price determination, too); that is, with a model of an economy in which relative commodity prices are determined entirely by supply-side phenomena (technics of production).

Continuing with long-run equilibrium: having brought Mrs. Robinson into touch with Sraffa yet again, a further leap in a Sraffian direction might be taken. The conceptual equilibrium that is to be kept in its "logical place" in Mrs. Robinson's "Normal Prices" is surely at one with the open, bounded set of mutual-consistencies view of equilibrium that is appropriate to the Sraffa system. Consider Sraffa's equations of production that could generate an "equilibrium" relative commodity price set, with a given wage *or* rate of profit (Sraffa eventually opted for the latter), and a given input-output structure. There is indeed an equilibrium set-up here. Relative commodity prices, distributive shares, and the input-output structure must all be consistent with one another, although the Sraffa system is "open" with respect to *absolute* levels of activity—i.e., the equations of production can take on any set of scalar multiples without disturbing the (relative) commodity-price solution (it is open, too, with respect to the absolute price level). Furthermore, this "mutual-consistencies" view of equilibrium accords with Frank Hahn's characterization of the "traditional" notion of equilibrium as a state of the economy "in which the intended actions of rational . . . agents are mutually consistent and can therefore be implemented."[33]

What is important in Hahn's treatment of equilibrium, though, is that he concedes that the activities of entrepreneurial decision makers are not necessarily "equilibrating"; that is, when he envisages decision makers in capitalist economies attempting to adapt to fluctuating prices and "noise"—a vision that leads Hahn to reject any "global stability" claims in so far as his concept of equilibrium is concerned.[34] Hahn appears, then, to be rejecting the *gridlock* of tight prior general equilibrium. With his "mutual-consistencies" view of equilibrium, he is surely on the right track—the Robinsonian track—and even more so when he insists that a truly serviceable notion of equilibrium must be able to do what Arrow-Debreu does not do: namely, bring within its compass (and this explicitly) uncertainty, expectations, modes of acquiring information, etc.

Yet another inferface with Robinson: to Hahn, equilibrium should not be looked upon as the termination of a process (so much for questions of convergence!). Good Robinson stuff this, in spite of the (seemingly anomalous) lesson that Hahn extracts from his line of reasoning: since equilibrium is not necessarily the terminal point of a *process*, the behavior of individuals is not relevant to the notion of equilibrium. In this context, "the individual is of no importance—he is of measure zero. . . ."[35] But why the *need* for an equilibrium notion at all? The need is there, he argues, because we have to make precise the *limits* of the kind of economic analysis that might be deployed, if we do insist upon bothering at all about "equilibrating" behavior.[36] Well, knowledge about limits is still knowledge, and it does accord with Joan Robinson's assignment of a "logical place" to a suitably circumscribed notion of equilibrium that should never be permitted to carry too much weight.

Epilog

We have, in this retrospective, paid scant heed to the Joan Robinson of the Cambridge Circus, to the young woman, that is, who read and discussed with the master himself the *General Theory* as it circulated in manuscript form among members of the Circus. Unlike that same young woman's *Economics of Imperfect Competition*—eventually to be abjured by its author in a prefatory declaration in a reprint—she carried Keynes's message with her to the end. And those Robinsonian "positions" with which we have dealt are, none of them, out of touch with her Keynesian inheritance—and *vice versa.* As if to firm up the *vice versa*, she wrote that although the "most obvious application of post-Keynesian analysis (the behaviour of an economy in conditions of uncertainty) is to Keynes's own problems—investment decisions, the determination of the pattern and level of interest rates, and the evolution of the general price level . . . *it is equally necessary to apply it to so-called micro-economics, and the behaviour of markets.*"[37]

Notes

1. E.g., Gram and Walsh, 1983.
2. Robinson, 1962a, p. 8.
3. Ibid., p. 12.
4. Ibid.
5. Negishi, 1985, p. xi.
6. Robinson, 1960a, p. 114.
7. Robinson, 1962a, pp. 6–7.
8. From Keynes's 1937 article in the *Quarterly Journal of Economics,* "The Theory of Employment," cited in Robinson, 1980, p. 48.
9. Robinson, 1960a, p. 120.

10. Robinson, 1962b, p. 25; 1960a, pp. 141–42.
11. Robinson, 1962b, p. 25.
12. Robinson, 1960b, p. 142.
13. Robinson, 1962b, p. 25.
14. Ibid.
15. Ibid., p. 26.
16. Robinson, 1980, p. 54.
17. E.g., Alchian and Demsetz, 1972; Jensen and Meckling, 1976; Fama, 1980; Faith, Higgins, and Tollison, 1984; and Williamson, 1986.
18. Fama, 1980, p. 294.
19. Alchian and Demsetz, 1972, p. 779.
20. Robinson, 1980, p. 53.
21. Marshall, 1920, p. 333.
22. Ibid., p. 325, n. 1.
23. Ibid.
24. Ibid., emphasis in original.
25. Kaldor, 1933–34; Negishi, 1961.
26. Kaldor, 1933–34.
27. Robinson, 1962b, p. 23. Compare with Gram and Walsh, 1983, p. 531.
28. Negishi, 1985, p. 165.
29. Compare with Weintraub, 1977, p. 14.
30. Edgeworth, 1881, p. 46.
31. Robinson, 1962b, p. 25, emphasis added.
32. Robinson, 1962a, p. 8.
33. Hahn, 1973, p. 2.
34. Ibid., p. 28.
35. Ibid., p. 33.
36. Ibid., pp. 21 and 38, emphasis added.
37. Robinson, 1980, p. 50, emphasis added.

References

Alchian, A. A. and H. Demsetz. (1972) "Production, Information Costs, and Economic Organization." *American Economic Review*, 62 (December):777–95.

Arrow, K. J. (1959) "Toward a Theory of Price Adjustment." In M. Abramovitz et al., *The Allocation of Economic Resources. Essays in Honor of B.F. Haley*. Stanford: Stanford University Press, pp. 41–51.

Edgeworth, F. Y. (1881) *Mathematical Psychics*. London: Kegan Paul.

Faith, R. L., R. S. Higgins, and R. D. Tollison. (1984) "Managerial Rents and Outside Recruitment in the Coasian Firm." *American Economic Review*, 74 (September):660–72.

Fama, E. F. (1980) "Agency Problems and the Theory of the Firm." *Journal of Political Economy*, 88 (April):288–307.

Gram, H. and V. Walsh. (1983) "Joan Robinson's Economics in Retrospect." *Journal of Economic Literature*, 21 (June):518–50.

Hahn, F. H. (1973) *On the Notion of Equilibrium in Economics*. Cambridge: Cambridge University Press.

Jensen, M. C. and W. H. Meckling. (1976) "Theory of the Firm: Managerial Behavior, Agency Costs and Ownership Structure." *Journal of Financial Economics*, 3 (October):305–60.

Kaldor, N. (1933–34) "A Classificatory Note on the Determinateness of Equilibrium." *Review of Economic Studies*, 1:122–36.

Keynes, J. M. (1937) "The General Theory of Employment." *Quarterly Journal of Economics*, 51:209–23.

Marshall, A. (1920) *Principles of Economics*, 8th ed. London: Macmillan.

Negishi, T. (1961) "On the Formation of Prices." *International Economic Review*, 2 (January):122–26.

———. (1985) *Economic Theories in a Non-Walrasian Tradition*. Cambridge: Cambridge University Press.

Reder, M. (1982) "Chicago Economics: Permanence and Change." *Journal of Economic Literature*, 21:1–38.

Robinson, J. (1960a) "The Production Function and the Theory of Capital." Originally published in *Review of Economic Studies*, 21 (1953–54). Reprinted in Joan Robinson, *Collected Economic Papers*, vol. 2. Oxford: Basil Blackwell.

———. (1960b) "Accumulation and the Production Function." *Economic Journal* (September 1959). Reprinted in *Collected Economic Papers*. vol. 2. Oxford: Basil Blackwell.

———. (1962a) "Normal Prices." In *Essays in the Theory of Economic Growth*. New York: St. Martin's Press.

———. (1962b) "A Model of Accumulation." In *Essays in the Theory of Economic Growth*. New York: St. Martin's Press.

———. (1980) "History versus Equilibrium." *Thames Papers in Political Economy* (1974). Reprinted in *Collected Economic Papers*, vol. 5. Cambridge, Mass.: MIT Press.

Sraffa, P. (1960) *Production of Commodities by Means of Commodities. Prelude to a Critique of Economic Theory*. Cambridge: Cambridge University Press.

Weintraub, E. R. (1977) "The Microfoundations of Macroeconomics: A Critical Survey." *Journal of Economic Literature*, 15 (March):1–23.

Williamson, O. (1986) "Transaction Cost Economics." *Law and Economics Workshop Series*, Law and Economics Programme, Faculty of Law, University of Toronto, Working Paper 7 (January).

JR

CHAPTER TEN

Value and Capital, Robinson Style

HARVEY GRAM

Introduction

Capital *theory* is arcane. Students of *capitalism* are instructed in basic arguments first, beginning with the pure theory of exchange, purified of production and of process—and thus of time, error, and experience. This is sound pedagogy, for when production is added on, it takes the form of an indirect exchange of factors for commodities, among households, via the intermediation of producing agents—bloodless actors who, without experience, never err in moving the props about the stage as efficiently as possible.

Of course, the word "capital" keeps turning up. The student is told to treat it in the same way as land: to allocate it efficiently so as to equalize the value of its marginal product in different uses and to interpret this value as a rental for its services. This, too, is sound practice, for what is being learned is not the real theory—it is only a parable. The real theory of capital concerns allocation over time; it cannot be presented in static terms and, while one is learning principles, complexity is properly avoided. Curiously, when the time comes for induction into the mysteries of the subject, the variables and parameters of the static resource-allocation model are simply relabeled, giving physical inputs and outputs an added time dimension. On the demand side, pure time preference is added to the interpretation of income and substitution effects. On the supply side, investment is assumed to be productive: an increase in future output per unit sacrifice of current output exceeds one in absolute value over some range of feasible allocations.[1]

On the one hand, the student finds that capital theory, despite its complexity, involves no new concepts. It is essentially a generalization of the pure theory of exchange for which appropriate mathematical tools (such as optimal control theory and dynamic programming) exist to solve what amounts to a multiperiod allocation problem. On the other hand, even a cursory reading of the major works of the classical economists, from Petty to Marx, or of the *original* neoclassics, may give pause.[2]

Capital theory has long been a battleground. The most recent controversy began with Robinson's attack on the concept of aggregate capital in "The Production Function and the Theory of Capital."[3] It is unnerving for the unsuspecting student, brought up on her well-known early work,[4] to read that " 'Capital' is not what capital is called, it is what its name is called."[5] Only the initiated are inoculated against doubt about the meaning of capital by a clear understanding of the logical requirements of the neoclassical theory of the allocation of scarce means among alternative uses. They are not bothered by Robinson's early warning: " 'The formulae are wiser than the men who thought of them,' and the technique knows a great deal more about the assumptions that it requires than the economist who is expounding it."[6]

Normal Prices

In order to understand Robinson's contributions to the theory of value and capital, it is necessary to recognize a distinction between two theories of relative price, a distinction that finds no place in neoclassical orthodoxy. It is also necessary to appreciate the importance of time in Robinson's analysis since it marks her off from everyone else, friend and foe alike. Her clearest statement on these issues is contained in "Normal Prices," the first chapter in her *Essays in the Theory of Economic Growth.*[7] She begins by remarking, "The traditional teaching that goes under the title of the theory of Value and Distribution does not depict a single system of prices. . . . The models can be divided into two broad classes, with a variety of intermediate types combining elements of each."[8] Their general properties are summarized under two headings: Supply and Demand, and Wages and Profits. Robinson's purpose is to argue that the theory of market equilibrium has nothing to say about the division of income between work and property.

In the Walrasian theory of general equilibrium, the "conditions of supply and demand . . . depend on the tastes and habits of the individuals concerned and the distribution of purchasing power between them; and on the prevailing techniques of production, the number of producers with different aptitudes, the natural resources available to them and the stock of produced means of production in existence."[9] A feature of the model's solution, not always pointed out, comes in for special emphasis: "The prices that rule in equilibrium, at a particular moment, may very well be such that some of the individuals in question are in the process of being starved out of existence."[10] No serious attempt has been made to deal with this aspect of neoclassical theory in so far as it raises an economic problem as opposed to a purely formal one.[11]

Robinson also emphasized the possibility of sharp differences in supply and demand prices associated with small differences in the underlying parameters of the model. For her, this was the most enlightening feature of the Walrasian scheme, revealing an unavoidable political element in the operation of free markets. The devastating effects of *unforeseen* changes in the conditions affecting supply and demand suggest the need for policy intervention to stabilize commodity prices at a level appropriate to maintaining a flow of production consistent with a normal long-run flow of consumption. The lessons usually drawn from the Walrasian model, however, run entirely in terms of the efficiency properties of a system of market-clearing prices.

It was typical of Robinson to use economic theory, not for the purpose of finding sets of assumptions sufficient to establish equilibrium solutions for particular models, but rather to sharpen her understanding of the political aspects of economic problems. She did not consider the central structure of neoclassical economics—the theory of the allocation of scarce means among alternative uses—as totally without application.[12] She simply regarded it as a very thin base on which to build. It says nothing about the determinants of the pattern of ownership of an economy's "given resources" and so precludes discussion of one of the most important determinants of the pattern of consumption. It allows, only as an exception to be accommodated by the creation of further markets, the many kinds of consumption that create disutility for others. It is silent on the question of how the circular flow of production and consumption is continually stimulated by the introduction of new commodities and newly perceived needs.[13] Robinson applauded what she saw as Arrow's rejection of the principle of individualism upon which neoclassical theory is built.[14] It is this principle that precludes consideration of the constraints imposed on individual behavior by the authority of institutions, ethics, and morality. Finally, she regarded the concept of scarce means with alternative uses not only as an exaggeration, for "at any moment, . . . [scarce] resources . . . have hardly any range of alternative uses . . . , [but also as] self-contradictory when it is set in historical time, where today is an evermoving break between the irrevocable past and the unknown future."[15] The "full information required to make a correct choice can never be available because of the inescapable fact that: 'the basic data simply do not exist, and cannot exist, no matter what information is devised. There is no certain knowledge about the future, not even certain knowledge of probability distributions.' "[16] And, with this remark, she would, no doubt, have dismissed the recent fashion for models incorporating "consistent expectations."[17]

In "Normal Prices," Robinson set aside these objections in order to construct a Walrasian model in which capital accumulation is taking place. She wanted to find out what the theory has to say about the distribution of income between work and property, i.e., between wages and profits.

Orthodox treatments of capital accumulation in an intertemporal Walrasian framework are elsewhere dismissed: "For my part, I have never been able to make that theory stand up long enough to knock it down."[18] It is easy to see why. One version assumes that all transactions in time-dated goods and services of all kinds are agreed to in the present for all possible future states of the world. Suspending disbelief as to how everyone is to be informed about such future states, to comprehend fully their implications, and to guarantee the enforcement of all contingent contracts, one might wonder, as Robinson did, why all such contracts were not completed, as it were, yesterday, in which case we would now be living out our predestined roles. It must be because an unforeseen change has taken place, today, but if this normally happens we will normally be out of equilibrium and so the theory will normally be without application.[19] Another version of the Walrasian model treats the future as if it were the moon. The moon moves, but because its position is predictable, astronauts can be fired off at an angle calculated in such a way that they and the moon converge. In the economics of intertemporal equilibrium, initial stocks of resources, including heterogeneous capital goods, take the place of the astronauts' initial, earth-bound position; final stocks correspond to the astronauts' final position (and that of the moon); and an initial calculated set of relative prices replaces the calculated angle of take-off. Prices start to change in response to the production and consumption decisions of optimizing, atomistic decision makers taken in light of the initial price vector, just as the path of the space ship begins to adjust itself in such a way as to hit the moon in due course. Indeed, the theory of optimal control is used to solve both problems.[20] But, as is well known, the efficiency properties of this model, reflecting the "very important 'invisible-hand' principle [characterizing a competitive price system, presume] no uncertainty so that *ex ante* expected prices or rates of change of prices—which each competitor knows but cannot himself affect—will correspond exactly to *ex post* observed prices. Under these strong assumptions of perfect certainty, where the *ex ante* future must agree with the *ex post* past, the whole future pattern of prices is knowable."[21]

Robinson had little patience with such arguments. Her own version of the Walrasian theory was quite different—she called it a model of the artisan economy. In this story, there are capital goods which are, of course, produced commodities. Investment has occurred in the past and may be continuing in the present as individual artisans make further additions to their individual stocks. But, for each artisan, the rate of return on investment has a different significance depending on the expected future expenditures of his family. Robinson concludes that, even in a stationary state:

> There is nothing in [this] picture that corresponds to a *rate of profit on capital.* We can, if we like, value all the goods in existence at their equilibrium prices in terms of some *numeraire*, and call the resulting sum "capital"; and we can value the total flow of production in the same terms, but there is no way of telling what part of that flow belongs to the "capital" [so measured] and what part to the work being done with the aid of the means of production which it comprises.[22]

In short, Robinson's criticism of the Walrasian model of supply and demand with a given number of producers in each line of activity is that it does not admit a concept of capital that would allow us to ask the question: What determines the distribution of income between work and property? There is the property of each family in its own means of production, just as an individual worker has property in his own human capital, but there is no generalized notion of capital associated with the free movement of profit-seeking employers from one line of production to another. Were such mobility allowed, Robinson concludes, "the model dissolves, for there are then no given supplies of specific factors."[23] What she saw as essential to the logical coherence of the Walrasian theory is the assumption that investors stick to their own lines of activity. In effect, she has specified investment functions.[24]

Perhaps no one has ever claimed that the purpose of Walrasian models of intertemporal equilibrium is to elucidate the determinants of the division of income between work and property. Their main use lies in analyzing the properties of intertemporally efficient consumption paths. In such models, it is the presence of transformations of resources, not into present consumption goods, but into new resources to be used to produce future consumption goods that complicates the analysis. The virtue claimed for the theory is that it shows that there are many efficient paths (just as there are many efficient static allocations) and that for each such path there is a sequence of prices that supports it, assuming all agents to be engaged in price-taking, optimizing behavior. To claim that there is no uniform rate of return on the value of stocks of produced inputs is incorrect.[25] A competitive price system has the property that *correctly anticipated* capital gains and losses serve to equalize rates of return even though current rental rates for the services of capital goods, *exclusive* of such gains and losses, do not all bear the same proportion to current prices of those same reproducible inputs.[26] To point out that the theory fails to show how prices are established in such a way as to generate mutually consistent and correct expectations is simply to state a fact well known to those engaged in current research on general equilibrium theory.[27]

So why not let the priests of high theory work in peace? Robinson wanted their project called off because she regarded the notion of equilibrium over time as internally contradictory, based as it is on the implicit requirement of perfect foresight or its stochastic counterpart, the hypothesis of rational expectations. Why waste the immense amount of intellectual effort needed to master the intricacies of a theory that can have no point of contact with the world in which we live (while running the unnecessary and serious risk of forgetting how to think in any other way)?

As a basis for analyzing accumulation and distribution under capitalism, a model of an artisan economy is clearly inappropriate, and yet, for Robinson, it and certain planning models were the only sensible interpretations of the Walrasian scheme. For this reason, she directed attention in "Normal Prices" to an alternative theory associated with Marx and Marshall, and more particularly, Sraffa and von Neumann. She regarded this theory as relevant to certain questions about the long run that arise whenever an attempt is made to extend

Keynesian short period analysis to encompass the process of accumulation. It was in this context of generalizing Keynes's *General Theory* that Robinson took up the question of the meaning of capital. Her point was this: In the short run, we do not have to ask what capital means, "since the organization of industry, stocks of equipment, the training of the labour force and the habits of consumers are already settled . . . and for practical purposes may be taken as constant."[28] All that mattered for Keynes's theory was "the flow of actual gross profits today and the expected return in the future on finance invested today."[29] The present was not correctly anticipated when finance was committed in the past and the future is not known today so that the value of capital is vague and imprecise just as the profit rate is vague and imprecise. But for a theory of the accumulation of capital and the distribution of the net product between wages and profits, these concepts must somehow be *made* precise.

For Robinson, the neoclassical argument turned on a pun: "putty" capital is simply a clever device for ignoring the fact that at one moment capital is a sum of finance, and at another moment it is a stock of capital goods.[30] In 1974, she recalled her experience of twenty years earlier:

> In 1953 I tried to find out what [capital] meant. . . . Does a quantity of capital mean a number of dollars or a list of machine tools, railway lines and other hard objects? And which is it that has a "marginal product"? The only answer we got was: Let us pretend that it doesn't make any difference.[31]

Robinson's version of Sraffa's argument and her criticisms of his followers are instructive. In this type of model, "there are no persistent differences between factors of production. Labour can be trained and equipment designed for any use."[32] There are no fixed supplies of nonproduced inputs such as land and neither the stock of capital goods nor the skills of the labor force are arbitrarily specified in advance. The theory of supply and demand has nothing to bite on. That is the point of the assumptions and, of course, those who reject Robinson's distinction between two theories of price regard the assumptions as absurd. But Robinson is not describing an existing state of the world. She is defining a concept, that of long-period equilibrium corresponding to a hypothetical state of affairs. She never intended this concept to be interpreted as the end point of a process of accumulation to which an economy might converge. Its purpose was to provide a starting point for the discussion of various types of disequilibrium.

Robinson's description of long-period equilibrium takes, as given, the technique of production, the composition of output, and the class structure: "Workers own no property and must take service with those who can provide means of production for them to operate."[33] The neoclassical theory of supply and demand has no particular class structure; the distribution of ownership of the arbitrarily given factors of production is itself arbitrarily given and, in any case, affects only demand. The organization of production is, in neoclassical theory, unrelated to the distribution of ownership of the factors; this is presumably intended to make the theory universally applicable. Robinson is interested in a theory that is specifically concerned with capitalist institutions. Workers are paid in money and values are calculated relative to the level of money wages. Capitalist firms are free to

> set labour to work upon whatever promises the best return. . . . [It] is necessary that there should be no limitation on access, given time, to any market, so that an equal rate of expected profit on investment tends to be established throughout the system. In a state of tranquillity, when expectations are realized, the criterion that competitive conditions prevail, in this sense, is that there is a uniform rate of net profit on the value of capital in all lines of production.[34]

Summing up, Robinson remarks:

> The difference between this system of prices and the Walrasian system is that here the equilibrium stock of means of production is determined by the flow of ouput, given the technical conditions and the rate of profit, whereas in the Walrasian system there is an arbitrarily given stock of means of production and outputs are determined by the technical and psychological conditions which govern the pattern of supply and demand.[35]

In Robinson's Sraffa-type model, the distribution of income between wages and profits is first and foremost a function of the rate of investment:

> Whatever the ratio of net investment to the value of the stock of capital may be, the level of prices [relative money wage rates] must be such as to make the distribution of income such that net saving per unit of value of capital is equal to it. Thus, given the propensity to save from each type of income (the thriftiness conditions) the rate of profit is determined by the rate of accumulation of capital.[36]

This throws the question forward to what determines the rate of accumulation. Robinson regarded the acceleration principle as a useful idea: "Carrying itself by its own bootstraps is just what a capitalist economy *can* do."[37] And the inflation barrier is also important: "The limit to [the process by which accumulation generates the savings it requires] is set by the level to which it is possible to force down real wages."[38]

The common practice of setting the rate of accumulation equal to the rate of growth of the (effective) labor force, however, is indefensible since the latter sets neither a maximum nor a minimum value to the rate of growth of capital. To claim that it sets a maximum value is to ignore technical progress, which is the very essence of the process of accumulation. To claim that it sets a minimum is to ignore all the various ways in which the nonindustrialized sectors absorb labor when accumulation lags behind the rate of growth of the industrial labor force. Robinson concluded that:

> there is no way to close the model which is both neat and plausible. We must be content to leave it open. To account for accumulation, we have to fall back upon human nature and the structure of society. Firms once established have an urge to grow, or, at least, an urge to resist the encroachment on their markets of others who are striving to grow, and in each generation new men who own wealth or command credit have an urge to try their fortune. Amongst them, the overall rate of accumulation somehow emerges.[39]

Those theorists who embrace the mechanical idea that whatever exists is either *in* a state of equilibrium or rapidly approaching one will find Robinson's argument unscientific. But it was just such a mechanical metaphor, appropriate at best to a spatial model, that Robinson rejected in her use of golden (and other metallic) age models. Her models were meant to raise questions.

Is a particular rate of accumulation maintainable? Latent imbalances in the structure of the capital stock may create bottlenecks that preclude any sustained period of economic growth. It is only in equilibrium that the composition and age structure of the stock of capital goods embodies correct anticipations concerning the flow of output that can be sold at prices corresponding to a uniform rate of return on past investment.

Will the ratio of unemployed workers to the population be increasing or decreasing as capital accumulation takes place? Capital goods embody a particular technique of production, and, as the capital theory controversy made clear, there is no systematic relationship between the wage rate (or profit rate) and the relative capital intensity of production. A lower real wage may not be associated with a more labor-intensive technique.

If unemployment increases, will it result in misery and social tension or will it be accommodated by a shortening of the work week? If unemployment falls, will this ignite an inflationary spiral of wages and prices followed by restrictive policies designed to protect the purchasing power of the currency? Or will it be accompanied by a rationing of the labor force, technical progress, and all the imbalances that follow in the wake of uneven growth of firms, industries, and nations?

Finally, should sustained growth be possible, what is it for? By recognizing that decisions to invest are undertaken by profit-seeking firms, the obvious question comes up as to whether or not the corporate view of what can be sold in the way of new commodities corresponds to a rational long-term view of what is in the best interests of consumers as a whole. It is the allocation of *investible resources* in the light of expected profits and according to the most recently invented production processes that is at issue—not the allocation of existing physical inputs already committed to particular uses. As for the resulting output:

> There is a . . . fundamental bias in our economy in favour of products and services for which it is easy to collect payment. Goods that can be sold in packets to individual customers, or services that can be charged for at so much

per head, provide a field for profitable enterprise. Investments in, say, the layout of cities, cannot be enjoyed except collectively and are not easy to make any money out of; while negative goods, such as dirt and noise, can be dispensed without any compensation being required. When you come to think of it, what can easily be charged for and what cannot, is just a technical accident.[40]

Conclusion

The methodological position that Robinson defended, and around which swirled a flood of criticism of orthodox theory, often seemed to her in danger of being abandoned. In her final years, she felt disillusioned by the direction in which her allies had taken some of the theoretical arguments that she had been so instrumental in establishing. Her impatience with the protracted attention given to the phenomenon of reswitching is well known. The "construction of a spate of pseudo-production functions [Robinson's version of the wage-profit frontier] exhibiting switches of all kinds . . . are now so elaborate, elegant and beautiful and their designers have become so fond of them that it seems cruel to point out that they are unable to say anything without falling into Samuelson's fallacy."[41] This was the fallacy of equilibrium, namely, the false notion that it is possible to discuss the effects of unanticipated changes using a framework of analysis in which all actions are the result of optimizing behavior and therefore require (at least probabilistic) knowledge of the future.[42]

Robinson chose to focus her criticism of neoclassical economic theory on what she regarded as its Achilles' heel: the problem of getting into equilibrium, or what neoclassical theorists call the stability problem. The difficulty with this strategy is that it appears to leave unchallenged the theory whose stability is being questioned. And, since the general equilibrium theorists have, for some time, been engaged in precisely the task of developing a proof of stability (based on a theory of how expectations are formed), defenders of Robinson's point of view run the risk of being regarded simply as good neoclassical economists.[43]

A Robinsonian is not, however, in quite such an exposed position. First, there is a great deal more to Robinson's economics than her penchant for criticizing equilibrium as a logically incoherent idea. She insisted that good theory cannot be formulated independently of ideology. Conflicts of interest must be recognized whether or not particular models contain mechanisms to resolve them. Robinson's concern for these explicit or implicit rules of the game raises questions that neoclassical theory also considers, but usually in formalistic ways.[44] Second, the recent work of general equilibrium theorists[45] does not encourage one to think that the problem of getting into equilibrium is about to be solved. Indeed, the claim that the capital theory controversy was nothing more than a "barrage of soap bubbles"[46] may finally come home to roost.

At the same time, there is something to be said for caution in adopting

Robinson's position *vis-à-vis* neoclassical theory. To attack that theory mainly on the grounds that it lacks a satisfactory explanation of how a general equilibrium comes into being is to grant a certain legitimacy to the underlying theoretical structure that is nowadays identified with neoclassical economics as a whole. And yet, it strains credulity to think that a great intellectual following could have been founded on the nihilism implicit in the recognition that what is now claimed to be neoclassical theory "can make no causal claims at all."[47] On this view, baroque variations on the stability theme are simply irrelevant and need not take up the valuable time of theorists attempting to understand the dynamics of a capitalist society. This was Robinson's main interest and it goes without saying that stability was, for her, a broadly defined notion eclipsing the narrow concerns of the general equilibrium theorists.[48] It is that much broader conception of the laws of motion of the capitalist system that deserves the attention of those engaged in the development of modern classical theory.[49] To become entrapped within the narrow confines of a debate concerning the stability analysis appropriate to a theory that has cut itself off from its original heritage is to blind oneself to more exciting vistas. It is only by abandoning this neo-neoclassical theory, a term Robinson used frequently in her later writings, and replacing it with an alternative conceptual framework, that those vistas will finally be opened up.

Notes

1. See, for example, Hirshleifer, 1970, chaps. 2–4.

2. Garegnani (1976) and Bharadwaj (1985) argue that the methods of analysis of the classical economists and of the original neoclassics were essentially the same. However, in their view, the attempt to find an explanation for the distribution of income between wages and profits within the theory of supply and demand equilibrium resulted in the eventual abandonment of that common method of analysis by the later neoclassics. The reason for this abandonment of the classical method was rooted in the logical requirements of a supply and demand theory of simultaneous price and quantity determination in which substitution in response to price changes is a central feature of the analysis. The work of Sraffa (1960) and, more particularly, the results of the capital theory controversy, undermined this notion of substitution of capital for labor in response to factor price changes and, partly for this reason, inspired a revival of interest in the classical method.

3. Robinson, 1953; *CEP*, vol. 2. References to Robinson's works will be given by original year of publication followed, where appropriate, by a reference to the relevant volume of her *Collected Economic Papers* (1951, 1960a, 1965a, 1973, 1979, abbreviated *CEP*) with page numbers where needed. Although in certain cases, such as the present one, papers reprinted in *CEP* are abbreviated versions of the original journal articles, *CEP* also includes postscripts to many of Robinson's more controversial arguments, original papers, and translations of foreign language articles, and, in the case of volumes 2 and 3, lengthy introductions to second editions published in 1975.

4. Besides *The Economics of Imperfect Competition* (1933), three of Robinson's best known early contributions are "The Foreign Exchanges" (1937a; *CEP*, vol. 4); "Beggar-My-Neighbour Remedies for Unemployment" (1937b; *CEP*, vol. 4); and "Rising Supply Price" (1941; *CEP*, vol. 1).

5. Robinson, 1953, p. 83; *CEP*, vol. 2, p. 117.

6. Robinson, 1932, p. 8.

7. Robinson, 1962b. In the preface, Robinson writes: "The essays in this volume might be regarded as an introduction rather than as a supplement to my *Accumulation of Capital*. That book was found excessively difficult" (p. v).

8. Ibid., p. 1.

9. Ibid., p. 2. In Walrasian theory, the distribution of purchasing power depends on (parametric) ownership of factors and (variable) factor prices, where the latter are imputed values. In equilibrium, all prices (and therefore purchasing power) are determined *simultaneously* with factor and commodity allocations. Robinson appears to regard the distribution of purchasing power as a *given* in a Walrasian model, even though it is part of the solution to the allocation problem once ownership of factor supplies is specified. In this connection, Maurice Dobb argued that the "inclusion of a theory of distribution *within* the theory of the pricing-process, as a constituent set of the larger set of market processes viewed as an interrelated whole, is question-begging in an important respect" (Dobb, 1973, p. 34).

10. Robinson, 1962b, p. 3.

11. It is true that in rigorous treatments of the subject, individual factor endowments with a zero equilibrium value are ruled out by an appropriate assumption concerning the distribution of factor endowments. This is done to ensure the upper semi-continuity of demand correspondences rather than to address the problem of subsistence or survival of the model's consuming agents. See the discussion of "resource relatedness" in Arrow and Hahn (1971, pp. 116–19).

12. Robinson, 1977b, pp. 1320–23; *CEP*, vol. 5, pp. 4–9.

13. Ibid., p. 1337; p. 30.

14. Ibid., p. 1323; p. 9. The reference is to Arrow (1974).

15. Ibid., p. 1322; p. 8.

16. Ibid., p. 1322; p. 7. The passage cited is from Loasby (1977).

17. Simon, 1978, p. 2, n. 1. Simon writes: "Perhaps we would mislead ourselves and others less if we called [rational expectations] by the less alluring phrase, 'consistent expectations.' " The only explicit reference in Robinson's work to the modern concept of rational expectations occurs in a posthumously published paper, originally entitled "Spring Cleaning," where Robinson remarks: "It is strange that the concept of 'rational expectations' over the long run has come into fashion among economists just at a moment (1980) when prospects for the capitalist world are more uncertain and more threatening than they have been ever since capitalism came into existence" (Robinson, 1985, p. 160). It may be noted that the argument of the rational expectations theorists that monetary policy can lose its effectiveness when it is is predictable was also pointed out by Robinson (1960b, p. 794; *CEP*, vol. 3, p. 129).

18. Robinson, 1980, p. 128.

19. Franklin Fisher (1983, pp. 2, 90) argues that one should not even try to obtain a proof of stability of equilibrium in a world in which *favorable* surprises are taking place, including Schumpeterian innovations of all kinds, windfall gains, and sudden bursts of optimism.

20. See the reference by Bruno (1967, p. 184, n. 6) to Pontryagin et al. (1962, chap. 6). Note also the similar assumptions concerning the heterogeneity of capital goods in Bruno (1967, section 4) and Garegnani (1970). Together, the two articles are a study in how different schools of thought have interpreted the significance of this heterogeneity.

21. Dorfman, Samuelson, and Solow, 1958, p. 319.

22. Robinson, 1962b, p. 5.

23. Ibid., p. 6, n. 1 continued from p. 5.

24. It is the *lack* of such functions that leads to the indeterminacies known as the "Hahn problem" in neoclassical models of capital accumulation with heterogeneous capital goods. Hahn (1966) and Samuelson (1967).

25. It is misleading to suggest, as in Walsh and Gram (1980, pp. 304–7), that the presence or absence of a uniform rate of profit identifies a model as either classical or neoclassical. All economists, at least since the time of Adam Smith, have recognized that competition, in the sense of free entry, implies a tendency towards equalization of rates of return on the value of reproducible assets. The point made in the text is that modern intertemporal general equilibrium theory has achieved this by collapsing the future into the present so that there is no longer any *tendency* or disequilibrium dynamics to consider. This change in the method of analysis of the neo-neoclassics, to use Robinson's useful label, marks them off from both the classics and the original neoclassics. It is a change that, in the views of Garegnani (1976) and Bharadwaj (1985), has been forced on modern orthodoxy by the logical requirements of a supply and demand based theory of the rate of profit. See n. 2 above.

26. It is interesting to note that in models employing the theory of optimal control, relative prices and their rates of change serve to maintain at a constant level the *present value* of the stock of capital. See Dorfman, Samuelson, and Solow (1958, p. 322). In a well-known price theory textbook, the assumption is also made that the *value* of capital is constant even though its *form* is variable. See Stigler (1987, p. 136).

27. Some of the most prescient criticisms of the theory are expounded by its defenders. See, for example, Fisher (1983) and, especially, Hahn (1984).

28. Robinson, 1977a; *CEP*, vol. 5, p. 59.

29. Ibid., p. 60.

30. Robinson, 1974a, p. 7; *CEP*, vol. 5, p. 55.

31. Robinson, 1974b, p. 60; *CEP*, vol. 5, p. 38.

32. Robinson, 1962b, p. 7.

33. Ibid.

34. Ibid., p. 8.

35. Ibid., p. 10.

36. Ibid., pp. 11–12.

37. Ibid., p. 13.

38. Ibid.

39. Ibid., pp. 15–16.

40. Robinson, 1962a, p. 132.

41. Robinson, 1980, p. 139. Her own examples are presented in a paper written with K. A. Naqvi (1967). Of course, Robinson agreed that what the designers of these technologies *can* say is, in a negative sense, very important: there is no one-to-one relationship between the real wage rate and *any* property of the technology matrix one might care to consider. Thus, the notion, fundamental to neoclassical theory in all its forms, that substitution of one input for another, in response to relative price changes, is systematic and predictable, has no firm analytical foundation. This startling conclusion gets shunted aside when neoclassical theorists make new assumptions, such as that of a "regular economy" (Burmeister, 1980, pp. 206–7), in order to rule out awkward transition paths for, say, per capita consumption, which characterize intertemporal equilibrium models that *do* allow for reswitching.

42. That the argument between Samuelson and Robinson turns on the issue of perfect foresight, and could be conducted by her in terms of the most well-behaved pseudo-production function, is made clear in their discussion of the unimportance of reswitching. See Robinson (1975a) and Samuelson (1975). One cannot entirely agree with Robinson that she and Samuelson simply had a difference of opinion about a purely logical point.

See the final section of Samuelson (1967, pp. 228–30), in which the perfect foresight assumption is attacked in a way that Robinson could only have applauded.

43. Robinson claimed that she did better neoclassical economics than her neoclassical colleagues because she understood it better, having been brought up in the Marshallian tradition which permeated the Cambridge of her undergraduate days. The Walrasian tradition, however, was not part of her intellectual background. See Robinson, 1951, p. vii.

44. As already pointed out (in n. 11 above), equilibrium prices for certain commodities can be zero in a model of pure exchange, in which case, zero purchasing power is not ruled out for certain consumers. The analysis thus points to the problem of survival in a free market economy, but, if the theorist only sees the problem as one of guaranteeing the upper semi-continuity of demand correspondences, it will be this difficulty rather than the economic one that receives attention. See Gram (1989, pp. 287–89) for further discussion and references.

45. See, for example, Fisher, 1983; Grandmont, 1982; and Hahn, 1984.

46. Hahn, 1984, p. 78.

47. Ibid., p. 47.

48. "The New Mercantilism" (Robinson, 1966) can be seen in this light as a general discussion of the stability problem facing the modern international system of world trade and payments.

49. A full-blown neoclassical theory is incapable of dealing with any situation that is *not* an equilibrium, however complicated the equilibrium path of prices and quantities may be. It has no center of gravitation *around which fluctuations take place*. In this sense, there is nothing for the laws of motion to describe even though there may be a formal dynamic analysis that generates the equilibrium path.

References

Arrow, K. J. (1974) *The Limits of Organization*. New York: Norton.

Arrow, K. J., and F. H. Hahn. (1971) *General Competitive Analysis*. San Francisco: Holden-Day.

Bharadwaj, K. (1985) "Sraffa's Return to Classical Theory: Change and Equilibrium." *Political Economy, Studies in the Surplus Approach*, 1, 2:3–31.

Bruno, M. (1967) "Optimal Accumulation in Discrete Capital Models." In K. Shell, ed., *Essays on the Theory of Optimal Economic Growth*. Cambridge, Mass.: MIT Press.

Burmeister, E. (1980) *Capital Theory and Dynamics*. Cambridge: Cambridge University Press.

Dobb, M. (1973) *Theories of Value and Distribution since Adam Smith*. Cambridge: Cambridge University Press.

Dorfman, R., P. A. Samuelson, and R. M. Solow. (1958) *Linear Programming and Economic Analysis*. New York: McGraw-Hill.

Fisher, F. M. (1983) *Disequilibrium Foundations of Equilibrium Economics*. Cambridge: Cambridge University Press.

Garegnani, P. (1970) "Heterogeneous Capital, the Production Function and the Theory of Distribution." *Review of Economic Studies*, 37(3), 111:407–36.

———. (1976) "On a Change in the Notion of Equilibrium in Recent Work on Value and Distribution." In M. Brown, K. Sato, and P. Zarembka, eds., *Essays in Modern Capital Theory*. Amsterdam: North-Holland.

Gram, H. N. (1989) "Ideology and Time: Criticisms of General Equilibrium." In G. R. Feiwel, ed., *Joan Robinson and Modern Economic Theory*. London: Macmillan.

Grandmont, J. M. (1982) "Temporary General Equilibrium Theory." In K. J. Arrow and M. D. Intriligator, eds., *Handbook of Mathematical Economics*, vol. 2. Amsterdam: North-Holland.

Hahn, F. H. (1966) "Equilibrium Dynamics with Heterogeneous Capital Goods." *Quarterly Journal of Economics*, 80:633–46.

———. (1984) *Equilibrium and Macroeconomics*. Cambridge, Mass.: MIT Press.

Hirshleifer, J. (1970) *Investment, Interest, and Capital*. Englewood Cliffs, N.J.: Prentice-Hall.

Loasby, B. J. (1977) "Imperfections and Adjustment." University of Stirling Discussion Papers, No. 50.

Pontryagin, L. S., V. G. Boltyanski, R. V. Gamkrelidze, and E. F. Mishchenko. (1962) *The Mathematical Theory of Optimal Processes*. New York: Interscience (John Wiley).

Robinson, J. (1932) *Economics Is a Serious Subject, The Apologia of an Economist to the Mathematician, the Scientist and the Plain Man*. Cambridge: W. Heffer and Sons.

———. (1933) *The Economics of Imperfect Competition*. (2d ed., 1969a.) London: Macmillan.

———. (1937a) "The Foreign Exchanges." In *Essays in the Theory of Employment*. London: Macmillan. Reissued in 1947, Oxford: Basil Blackwell. Reprinted in *Collected Economic Papers*, vol. 4.

———. (1937b) "Beggar-My-Neighbour Remedies for Unemployment." In *Essays in the Theory of Employment*. London: Macmillan. Reissued in 1947, Oxford: Basil Blackwell. Reprinted in *Collected Economic Papers*, vol. 4.

———. (1941) "Rising Supply Price." *Economica* (New Series), 8:1–8. Reprinted with a postscript in *Collected Economic Papers*, vol. 1.

———. (1951, 1960a, 1965a, 1973, 1979) *Collected Economic Papers*, vols. 1–5. Oxford: Basil Blackwell.

———. (1953) "The Production Function and the Theory of Capital." *Review of Economic Studies*, 21(2), 55:81–106. Partially reprinted with a postscript in *Collected Economic Papers*, vol. 2.

———. (1956) *The Accumulation of Capital*. (Rev. ed. 1965b; 3d ed., 1969.) London: Macmillan.

———. (1960b) "General Liquidity." *The Banker*, 110, 418:790–95. Reprinted in *Collected Economic Papers*, vol. 3.

———. (1962a) *Economic Philosophy*. Based on the Josiah Mason Lectures, 1959. Chicago: Aldine.

———. (1962b) *Essays in the Theory of Economic Growth*. London: Macmillan.

———. (1966) *The New Mercantilism*. Cambridge: Cambridge University Press. Reprinted in *Collected Economic Papers*, vol. 4.

———. (1974a) *History versus Equilibrium*. Thames Papers in Political Economy. London: Thames Polytechnic. Reprinted in *Collected Economic Papers*, vol. 5.

———. (1974b) "The Abdication of Neo-Classical Economics." In Ashok Mitra, ed., *Economic Theory and Planning: Essays in Honour of A. K. Das Gupta*. Calcutta: Oxford University Press. Reprinted in *Collected Economic Papers*, vol. 5.

———. (1975a) "The Unimportance of Reswitching," and "Reply." *Quarterly Journal of Economics*, 89:32–39, 53–55. Reprinted with a postscript in *Collected Economic Papers*, vol. 5.

———. (1975b) "Introduction 1974" to *Collected Economic Papers*, vols. 2 and 3. Oxford: Basil Blackwell.

———. (1977a) "Qu'est ce que le capital?" *Revue d'Economie Politique*, 87:165–79. Original English draft, "The Meaning of Capital," printed in *Collected Economic Papers*, vol. 5.

———. (1977b) "What Are the Questions?" *Journal of Economic Literature*, 15:1318–39. Reprinted in *Collected Economic Papers*, vol. 5, and in Robinson (1980).

———. (1980) *What Are the Questions? and Other Essays, Further Contributions to Modern Economics*. Armonk, N.Y.: M. E. Sharpe.

———. (1985) "The Theory of Normal Prices, A Reconstruction of Economic Theory." In G. R. Feiwel, ed., *Issues in Contemporary Macroeconomics and Distribution*. London: Macmillan.

Robinson, J., and K. A. Naqvi. (1967) "The Badly Behaved Production Function." *Quarterly Journal of Economics*, 81:579–91. Reprinted in *Collected Economic Papers*, vol. 4.

Samuelson, P. A. (1967) "Indeterminacy of Development in a Heterogeneous-Capital Model with Constant Saving Propensity." In K. Shell, ed., *Essays on the Theory of Optimal Economic Growth*. Cambridge, Mass.: MIT Press. Reprinted in R. C. Merton, ed., *The Collected Scientific Papers of Paul A. Samuelson*, vol. 3. Cambridge, Mass.: MIT Press.

———. (1975) "Steady-State and Transient Relations: A Reply on Reswitching." *Quarterly Journal of Economics*, 89:40–47. Reprinted in H. Nagatani and K. Crowley, eds., *The Collected Scientific Papers of Paul A. Samuelson*, vol. 4. Cambridge, Mass.: MIT Press.

Simon, H. A. (1978) "Rationality as Process and as Product of Thought." *American Economic Review*, 68, 2:1–16.

Sraffa, P. (1960) *Production of Commodities by Means of Commodities, Prelude to a Critique of Economic Theory*. Cambridge: Cambridge University Press.

Stigler, G. J. (1987) *The Theory of Price*, 4th ed. New York: Macmillan.

Walsh, V. C. and H. N. Gram. (1980) *Classical and Neoclassical Theories of General Equilibrium, Historical Origins and Mathematical Structure*. New York: Oxford University Press.

JR

CHAPTER ELEVEN

Robinson's Classic Question Revisited

How to Measure Capital?

EDWARD M. MILLER

Probably the best known of Joan Robinson's passages is her complaint that neoclassical economists did not state the units in which capital is measured:

> The student of economic theory is taught to write O = f(L,C) where L is a quantity of labor, C a quantity of capital and O a rate of output of commodities. He is instructed to assume all workers alike, and to measure L in man-hours of labor; he is told something about the index-number problem involved in choosing a unit of output; and then he is hurried on to the next question, in the hope that he will forget to ask in what units C is measured. Before ever he does ask, he has become a professor, and so sloppy habits of thought are handed on from one generation to the next.[1]

The question "In what units is 'capital' to be measured?" (Robinson, 1971) was repeatedly asked in her writings. Although her complaints help lead to the Cambridge Capital Controversy[2] (which this paper is *not* about) neoclassical writers continued to refer to capital and wrote equations containing K without even stating the units in which they were working. It will be argued here that by obfuscating the use of inconsistent definitions, Robinson's omission of an explicit definition, made the neoclassical methodology with its apparent rigor of mathematical method appear more rigorous than it really was.

Joan Robinson's question was a key one. This paper will not restate her answers to the question,[3] but will try to point out which issues must be dealt with in answering her question. As far as practical, the neoclassical questions are presumed to be meaningful, and efforts are made to find capital concepts that answer them. Robinson herself probably would not concede that the questions were meaningful.

It will be argued here that there is no definition of the quantity of capital services for which all of the implications of neoclassical theory hold. One must either abandon the idea that the "law of one price" holds for factor services, or one must abandon the idea that there are unique factor inputs determined by technology, factor prices, and the desired level of output. If quantities of capital services are defined so that the services of all items are proportional to the prices of their services, it follows that the production function cannot be strictly quasi-concave and that factor inputs are not unique. These logical difficulties would have been noticed long ago if Joan Robinson had been listened to and if the units in which capital or its services[4] were measured had been stated.

Capital in Growth Accounting

Since much of Joan Robinson's work on capital grew out of an exchange with Professor Solow, let us start by considering the units in which capital services must be measured in order for Solow's growth accounting method to work.[5] Surprisingly, Solow's response to Robinson's critique did not include a clear definition of the symbols in his equations, although he did state why he disagreed with what he understood to be her proposed definition.

In "Technical Progress and the Aggregate Production Function" (1957), Solow proposed a simple formula for calculating the output growth that could be attributed to growth in per capita capital input. His formula states that the contribution of capital growth to output growth is the product of the growth rate of capital input and capital's share of total factor input. He did not give the units in which capital was to be measured, stating only that they were physical units. In a footnote he stated that he did not wish to be involved in complicated disputes about the definition of capital. Although one can understand a desire to stay away from the capital controversy, the merits of a proposed quantitative formula cannot be evaluated without a clear definition of the units.

Because the Solow derivation was a mathematical proof, it is easy to imagine that it holds for all definitions of capital quantity, or at least for all plausible ones. However, this is not so (Miller, 1989b). A necessary assumption for Solow's method is that the units of capital be defined in such a way that the services of old and new capital goods sell for the same price. This assumption is not satisfied by all possible definitions for the quantity of capital services. For instance, if the quantity of services provided by an obsolete good is considered equivalent to that provided by a new good, this condition is not met.

To see this, it is useful to derive the Solow equation in an alternative way that makes clear all of the assumptions behind it. The problem in capital service growth is in knowing the marginal product of the new items of capital added to the stock or removed from it. Solow's basic insight was that in equilibrium the value of capital's marginal product equaled the price of capital services. If the price for the services of new capital were known, its contribution to output growth could be estimated.

The average price of capital services is easily determined. This is the ratio of income from capital to the number of units of capital services consumed. If there is only one price for capital services, the price of the services of the newly added capital goods must equal the price of the services of the older goods. Once this is accepted, Solow's formula follows.

The argument can be simply set out in symbols. Let Y be total income and a specific factor's share of national income a, making total earnings of the factor aY. With F the total input of the factor, the per unit earnings are aY/F. If the increment in factor input is DF, and the factor's marginal product equals the average per unit earnings of the factor's service, the income increment due to the growth in the factor's input is $DFaY/F$. As a fraction of income, it is $DFaY/FY$, or DFa/F after canceling. After rearranging terms, this is $(DF/F)a$ which, in words, is the factor's growth multiplied by its income share. This is Solow's growth accounting formula.

The above argument has the virtue of not requiring the existence of an aggregate production function. For the derivation of the growth accounting formula via a production function to be logically rigorous, the necessary conditions for a perfect capital aggregate must be met (Fisher, 1965). It is agreed that these are generally not met. Even Solow (1956) views them as unmet, an admission that leaves his later derivations using aggregate production functions on shaky ground.

The above derivation makes very explicit the key assumption, which is that the marginal product of an increment to capital can be estimated from the average earnings of all capital. It might be thought that if the services of all items of capital sell for the same price, which would follow from the law of one price, their marginal products are equal. However, the law of one price is a theoretical argument that identical items and services should sell for the same price in a single market. There is no economic reason why the services of items differing in economically relevant ways should sell for the same price. It is easy to think of aggregation systems or definitions of capital quantity where the prices per unit differ. For instance, if quantity is measured by tons or cubic feet of machinery (or tons or cubic feet per hour), there is no reason to believe all prices will be identical.

A key part of the logic of Solow's method is to estimate the price of the services (and hence their marginal products) for the added capital items from the average price of the services of all capital in the economy. Thus, correctly measuring the ratio of the price of the services of the newer capital goods (being added by investment) to that of the older capital goods is critical. The prices of the services of the older goods fall below the service prices for new goods because of obsolescence and deterioration.

If the services of the old and the new goods of a certain type are to be regarded as selling for the same price per unit of capital (necessary for growth accounting), the total number of units of services the old good provides must be proportional to the total price of the services of the good. If a steam locomotive rents for one-fifth of the amount per year of a diesel locomotive, the steam locomotive must be regarded as providing only one-fifth of the units of capital services of the diesel locomotive. Then the price of the services of the two locomotives per unit of physical service provided will be the same, permitting the marginal product of new capital to be estimated from the average prices of the services of the old capital.

It is not clear that Solow's "physical" concept of capital is the correct one for his formula. The term "physical" implies that an unchanged capital good will always represent the same number of units of capital as it ages, even if it becomes obsolete. Solow appears to be supporting the model (traceable back to J. B. Clark) of capital as a physical something that changes shape as circumstances change, but always represents the same number of units of capital. Joan Robinson disagreed strongly with this view, with reason.

Having the quantity of capital represented by a good remain unchanged over time is inconsistent with the number of units of capital that goods of different ages represent remaining proportional to the prices for the good's services. Thus, if "physical" had the above meaning Solow's theory would appear inconsistent with his capital concept. However, the actual data Solow chose (Goldsmith's) can be argued to fit the equal priced condition since it reduced the quantity of capital for accumulated depreciation on a straight-line basis, thus allowing for the effects of deterioration and depreciation.

Other authors also appear to have erred in their choice of capital concept. With the growth accounting equation derived without the units ever being specified, authors chose the capital concepts they thought the most useful in general, rather than those that met the necessary conditions for the growth accounting exercise being conducted. Denison (probably the best-known practitioner of growth accounting) had argued in 1957, using quite good reasoning, for a cost-based concept of capital quantity. Naturally, when he turned to growth accounting he retained this concept of capital.

In particular, Denison argued that the quantity of capital a good represents should not be adjusted for the obsolescence of that good prior to the good's retirement. He even went so far as to state that an obsolete steam locomotive that was still as good as new should be regarded as representing the same quantity of capital as it represented when new, or a quantity based on its reproduction cost.[6] This violates the condition pointed out above that the quantity of capital must be measured so that the quantity of services provided by an old good is proportional to the price of that good's services, thus making it possible to deduce the marginal product of new capital from the average price of the services of old capital goods. If the quantity of capital services provided by a good is not adjusted for its obsolescence, the price of the services of the existing capital stock (much of which is obsolete and deteriorated) will not be a good approximation to prices for new goods' services.

To use the locomotive example, the rent of steam locomotives should not be expected to reveal the marginal product of new diesel locomotives unless the quantity of capital services provided by the different types is considered to be equal, which requires that the quantity of capital services has been defined as proportional to the rents of the different items being aggregated. If the rate of return is estimated as equaling the ratio of all income from capital to a capital stock that values obsolete goods at their reproduction cost, the rate of return will be underestimated. When this rate of return is then applied to the recently added goods, which can be presumed to contain few obsolete goods, the contribution of capital growth to output growth will be underestimated.

Similar errors have been made elsewhere. This problem appears in the description of the official U.S. productivity estimates, which at one point states: "The pattern of services is proportional to the rental income, in constant prices, which the good is capable of generating."[7] It is not clear whether this is meant to describe how the data were constructed, or whether it is merely a belief. It appears to be the latter since the paper then goes on: "The assumption of a concave form was settled on because of the *cursory observation* that many capital assets do not tend to decay rapidly during their initial years."[8] It is discouraging to discover that calculations that appear so very precise depend on "cursory observation."

Even worse, the Bureau of Labor Statistics report does not explain on what basis it is reported that assets "do not tend to decay rapidly during their initial years." Most likely the observer (not identified) was looking at the services in "physical" terms and noting correctly that they decrease slowly. He probably was not observing obsolescence, since that cannot be directly observed but must be deduced by comparing the services of the older good with that of newer goods. The absence of reference to such comparative observations suggests that obsolescence was excluded.

Elsewhere there are references to an "efficiency" function relating capital services to age, but "efficiency" is never defined. It is the rate of decline in the quantity of capital services, but "capital services" are not defined in a quantitative manner. Here again we see that the lesson of Joan Robinson has not been absorbed. Economists still talk about the quantity of capital without being clear in what units their quantity is expressed.

A reference to efficiency decline being a function of age[9] only suggests that the concept is meant to measure deterioration alone without reflecting obsolescence, since the obsolescence depends on the embodied technical progress, which depends on more than age. If obsolescence is not adjusted for, the service decline cannot be proportional to the rent decline. The actual shape of the "efficiency decline" curve used resembles that used by Denison, who, as noted above, is explicit about not having adjusted for obsolescence or capital embodied progress in the newer goods.

Although the Bureau of Labor Statistics never states which aspect of capital services is observed to discover the capital service decline rate, it apparently is not rent. Unfortunately, the concept of capital being used appears inconsistent with the requirement that the rents per unit of capital must be the same at all ages.

Is the Neoclassical Capital Concept Consistent?

So far it has been argued that a necessary condition for neoclassical-based growth accounting is that the capital service units provided by a good be proportional to the good's rent, giving all goods the same rent per unit of capital services. Note that this condition is necessary for capital services to have a single price, and that neoclassical theory routinely talks about the price of capital, or differentiates a cost function with respect to the price of capital.

It might be hoped that the above discussion had resolved the problem raised by Joan Robinson concerning the units in which capital is to be measured. Although Denison and the U.S. Bureau of Labor Statistics got the units wrong, most neoclassical economists appear to be measuring capital in a way that permits one to argue that the quantity of capital services provided by a good declines with age in proportion to its rent decline, and that different items have rents proportional to the services they provide. For instance, although Jorgenson never defines his capital concept, it could be argued that the numbers he uses have the above properties. He appears to choose his rates of decline in capital quantity with age to equal empirically determined rent decline rates.[10]

Are we then to conclude that Joan Robinson's measurement problem can be answered merely by explicitly adopting the above definition? Is it enough to state that new capital goods of different types have been given weights proportional to their rents when new, and the weights of older goods have been reduced in recognition of deterioration and obsolescence by the percentage by which the rents are estimated to have declined? The answer is an emphatic no!

The problem in the neoclassical literature is deeper than a mere failure to state the units being used, or even to realize what units must be used. If the above system of units is adopted, it follows that production functions do not have the usual strictly quasi-concave shape. This implies that the standard neoclassical theory of factor inputs (that profit-maximizing firms choose the factor inputs that minimize their cost of production given the factor prices, technology used, and output mix) does not give unique factor inputs.

Since the argument regarding the quasi-concavity of production functions with the usual definition has been presented elsewhere (Miller, 1988), it is only summarized here. Let us consider the simplest possible production system, one where labor and capital are used to produce a single output. If the reader prefers, labor can be thought of as a composite factor including all of the non-capital inputs. Capital can be presumed to take the form of a single machine that can vary in age. This does not alter the argument.

To provide a notational system suppose:

R = the rent of the machine

w = the wage rate

L = the labor input

Q = value of the output of the machine.

From the basic theory of rent we know that $R = Q - wL$. Rent is the part of the product that is not paid out as payments to other factors. If the owner of the capital good were to set the rent any higher, production using the good would be unprofitable, and hence the good would not be rented. If the rent were set any lower, there would be many applicants to rent the good and the owner would be leaving money on the table. Thus, the rent will be exactly the amount that is not paid out to other factors. Let the number of units of capital services provided by an item be K, and r the rent of one unit of capital services, so that $R = rK = Q - wL$. With r, w, and Q constants, if L varies, K will vary in an offsetting way, and the amounts of L and K capable of producing the output Q will fall on a straight line. It now remains to consider whether the L used to produce a specified output at minimum cost can vary.

The world is such that a firm typically can achieve the minimum possible cost of production by using either new or old goods. Old goods typically require more of other factors. This is because old goods are either deteriorated and need more maintenance, or are of an older design not incorporating certain labor- or fuel-saving features.

Conceivably, as a machine aged, its output and inputs of all variable factors could decline in proportion. In this case rent could decline without changing the rent expended for a given output. Observation of the world shows that this seldom, if ever, happens. Typically, inputs change while output remains unchanged, or changes at a different rate from inputs.

Where older capital goods require more labor, the point representing the combination of labor and capital used to produce a specified quantity of the final consumption good lies on the straight line, $rK = Q - wL$. Since the different points on this line can produce the specified output and there is no other factor combination that can produce it at lower cost, the points lie on the isoquant. If all factor inputs between those used by new goods and those used by goods on the margin of retirement (zero rent) are available to the firm (and these two points differ in labor inputs), it follows that the isoquant has a linear segment coinciding with the isocost line. This is quite a contrast with the textbook vision of a curved isoquant that touches an isocost line at only one point.

This surprising conclusion results because of the nature of the physical world. It is such that as goods age, their quality changes in such a way that their use of factors per unit of output changes, while the prices charged for the services of capital goods of different ages adjusts so that minimum cost production is possible with each. If the quantity of capital services a good provides is then defined to make it meaningful to talk about a single price for capital services, the isoquant must have a linear segment.

As Joan Robinson has emphasized, capital is not a perfectly flexible ectoplasm or "leets" (Robinson, 1970) that can be effortlessly reshaped into any desired form. If capital were perfectly flexible, old machines in a meaningful sense would not exist because they would be reshaped into new ones. Likewise, obsolescence would not occur because the capital could be reshaped as necessary. In the absence of obsolete or deteriorated capital, the case of capital goods differing in quality in such a way as to differ in variable inputs per unit of output would not arise. Observation shows that leets do not exist and that obsolescence and deterioration do, causing the effect discussed above to occur.

With capital quality varying and this quality variation affecting the variable inputs, the prices for renting the goods (and the prices for buying the goods outright) adjust so that the typical firm is indifferent between using the capital goods of different ages. When this happens, there is no unique input of the non-capital factors as predicted in the neoclassical theories. If the quantity of capital services provided by an older good is defined to be proportional to the rent, there is also not a unique input of capital services.

The neoclassical theory attempts to explain factor inputs as determined by firms' efforts to maximize profits subject to the prevailing factor prices, the desired output, and technological constraints. If one adopts the commonly used definition of the quantity of capital services as proportional to the rent, the quantity of capital input is not determined by the neoclassical elements of relative factor prices, technology, and output. Should neoclassical theory be regarded as having a theory of factor inputs when the variables in this theory are incapable of providing a prediction of the inputs chosen by a firm? To answer the question of how much capital will be employed, additional information is required. Joan Robinson has emphasized one of the missing variables, history, which determines whether the capital will be relatively new (and hence represent a large input of rent-defined capital) or relatively old (representing a smaller input).

An Original Cost Definition

Our intuition is that the concept of quantity of capital does have some meaning, and that an optimum capital input depending on (among others things) the price of capital services can be a useful concept. While with the standard neoclassical concept of capital services (in which the quantity of services is proportional to the rent) there is not a unique capital input, with other capital input definitions, the desired unique capital input may exist. As Robinson points out, in one country, "a length of roadway is being cleared by a few men with bulldozers, in Beta a road (of near enough the same quality) is being made by some hundreds of men with picks and ox-carts. In Gamma thousands of men are working with wooden shovels and little baskets to remove the soil," and the reason for this is "that capital in some sense is more plentiful in Alpha than in Gamma."[11]

Joan Robinson has proposed thinking of the firm as having a book of blueprints and picking the production process from this, along with the machine designs used, etc. In the Robinson concept, the quantity of capital services may vary greatly with the passage of time as it relates to the firm's production process. If the firm has just begun production, one might expect it to have more capital committed than if the production plan had been in use for a number of years and the machines were virtually worn out. Notice how subtly this concept differs from the neoclassical production function based concept with its unique capital input.

The neoclassical assertion is that there is a unique capital input for the typical profit maximizing firm, although observation shows less rent measured capital is required when older goods are used. One way to avoid the complications of older capital goods is explicitly to limit the concept of optimal factor inputs to a firm that is just choosing its production technique, leaving the question of how to measure the capital input of firms with older machines, obsolete machines, or work in progress to be handled separately. If this is done, the production function becomes an *ex ante* one, restricted to the firm using new capital goods. In this case, there is less conflict with reality in the idea of a production function having the mathematical properties needed for capital to be unique.

If the quantity of capital input is defined to be proportional to the cost of producing the capital goods, it is plausible (but certainly not necessary) that at a particular set of factor prices and technology there will be a single profit maximizing design for the machines and building being used (selected from Joan Robinson's book of blueprints), and hence a unique optimum capital input. While a single input is likely, there can, of course, be switch points where two different techniques have the same production costs and the firm is indifferent between them. Unfortunately, an *ex-ante* production function is not easily estimated from aggregate data, since the available data are seldom restricted to firms using only new capital goods.

Joan Robinson's preferred concept of capital was not a monetary production cost, but the quantity of labor embodied in the good discounted at the prevailing rate of profit. For a new good, this would be equal to the cost of the good. She doesn't discuss in detail how much capital an obsolete good might be considered to represent. Solow raises the objection that if the amount of labor required to produce the good had changed (perhaps because of technical progress), one could have two identical goods that represented different quantities of capital.

While one can only speculate[12] about Joan Robinson's answer to this objection (since there was no further exchange), most likely, it would have been that the quantity of capital represented by a good should be based on the embodied labor when produced in the most efficient manner, and that if the most efficient manner changes, the older goods have to be considered as representing less capital than they represented when built. Robinson appeared to have no commitment to the idea that a particular item of capital had to represent the same quantity of capital, or be considered as providing the same quantity of services over time, even while circumstances and the quantities of other factors were changing.

Cost Function Differentiability

One of the prouder moments for a teacher of microeconomics comes when he shows that if a cost function is differentiated with respect to the price of a factor, the result is the optimum input of that factor. Unfortunately, in all of the pages leading up to this idea, the typical textbook never defines the units being used. This is a necessary omission because there is no set of units that can be used without making it painfully obvious that the theory does not correctly describe the world.

The problem is that for a cost function to be differentiated with respect to a factor price, it is necessary both that the function actually be differentiable and that the price with respect to which differentiation is done be well defined. Unfortunately, the world is such that definitions of quantities that satisfy both of these conditions cannot be found.

It was shown above that for growth accounting the quantity of capital must be defined so that the quantity of capital services provided by any item is proportional to the item's total rent. This then makes it possible to talk about *the* price of capital services. Given a single price for capital services, it is then logically possible to talk about differentiating a cost function with respect to the price of capital services. If any other definition of capital quantity is used, even with the perfect competition assumption, there will be multiple prices for capital services and it will not be meaningful to talk about differentiating any function with respect to the cost of capital services.

If the quantity of capital services is defined to be proportional to the rents of different items, there will be a well-defined price for capital services, but as pointed out above, the production function will not be strictly quasi-concave. This implies that the cost function will not be differentiable.

Perhaps the most direct way to see that differentiation of the cost function with respect to the prices of factor services cannot give the optimum factor input is to note that the firm simply has no cost-minimizing capital input. The firm can achieve minimum cost of production by using either new capital goods or by using older capital goods whose deterioration or obsolescence causes them to rent for less, but that require greater use of other factors. Naturally, with no unique cost-minimizing factor input to be found, differentiating the cost function cannot reveal a unique cost-minimizing factor input.

There are other reasons why the absence of a unique capital input is important. There has been much discussion of the neoclassical model of investment in which the firm is presumed to have a desired capital stock and adjusts its investment to achieve this.[13] If there is no unique desired capital stock, it would be irrational for firms to act as predicted.[14]

Thus, close consideration of Joan Robinson's question concerning the units in which capital is measured reveals a serious flaw in the neoclassical system. There appears to be no way to measure capital so that all of the theory's predictions hold. It is not that one could not imagine a world in which the theory would hold if factors of production were homogeneous. If the conditions for perfect aggregation were met (Fisher, 1965), there could be both a well-defined price for capital services and strictly quasi-concave production functions. The real world, however, does not meet the necessary conditions.

Why These Problems Were Not Recognized Earlier

It may be asked why these problems were not recognized earlier. The answer lies in a failure to define terms so that they had only one meaning, and in the way the brain interprets sentences with ambiguous words in them. If a word has several possible meanings, when we hear a sentence containing that word we automatically insert a meaning in which the sentence makes sense and is correct. If later the same word is used in another sentence and makes sense with a slightly different meaning, that meaning is automatically inserted as well. We are usually not even conscious of this process. For instance, when reference is made to the cost of capital services, we imagine that the quantity of capital services has been defined so that it is meaningful to talk about a single price for capital services (perhaps with some adjustment for risk, liquidity, etc., as applied to particular items).

If later, it is announced that a cost minimizing firm with access to particular technologies and faced with certain factor prices has a unique input of capital or capital services, we do not find this bothersome. Like Joan Robinson, we can imagine a book of blueprints for production of a particular good, and we find it easy to imagine that with particular factor prices there is only one production plan that permits minimum cost. The quantity of capital required is the quantity required to implement this plan. Thus, the neoclassical theory's prediction of unique factor inputs does not strike us as contrary to observation.

The question of how to define the capital quantity represented by deteriorated or obsolete goods does not immediately occur to us. Instead, we identify the capital quantity with the quantity required at the start of production (when new machines are bought). Thus, no red flags are raised when neoclassical economists, after solving a constrained optimization problem with a production function having certain properties, announce that there are unique factor inputs. Nor are flags raised when they claim to have a theory of factor inputs. Unless the reader has given the issue much thought, he is unlikely to notice that unique capital inputs are likely only with certain definitions of the quantity of capital services and that these definitions are not the same ones that lead to a single price for capital services.

However, if neoclassical writers followed the physical science tradition of stating the units for all of their equations, whenever an implication of the theory was stated the reader would ask if that result was really to be expected, given the definition used. If the author tried casually to assume that the production function was strictly quasi-concave after having defined the quantity to be proportional to rent under normal conditions for capital of widely varying ages, the alert reader (or the referee for a submitted manuscript) would realize that a typical firm had the option of substituting old capital goods for new capital goods. When this was done, the quantity of capital a cost-minimizing firm used varied (as did the quantity of other factors). He would realize that the theory of a strictly quasi-concave production function was falsified by observation.

If at the start of the argument the units in which capital is measured were stated to be proportional to the cost of production of a good, the reader might agree that there was a unique input of capital services. Similarly, he would probably realize that because not all capital services sell for the same price in equilibrium, that part of the textbook theory is vitiated. But unfortunately, not all readers will notice this critical point.

Other Factors of Production

The above argument was presented for capital. It is for capital that the definitional question is most important, and it is capital for which Joan Robinson first raised the question of the units being used. However, very similar problems arise for other factors. There is a simple argument to show that production functions in the real world are seldom strictly quasi-concave.

An isocost line is defined as the line showing the alternative combinations of different items whose costs add up to a specified amount. At any given set of factor input prices there will be a minimum possible cost for producing a specified output, *Q*. If the quantities of factors have been defined to make it meaningful to refer to an isocost line, the line represents the minimum production cost. All points on the minimum cost isocost line must be on the isoquant since they represent factor input combinations capable of producing the specified output. If two different input combinations can produce the same output at minimum cost, there must be at least two different points on *both* the minimum cost line and the isoquant.[15]

Having two different points on the isocost line that are also on the minimum cost isocost line is, of course, inconsistent with the neoclassical idea that isoquants have the conventional, smooth, strictly convex shape at all points, and is inconsistent with the idea that production functions are strictly quasi-concave. Thus, a simple way to look for violations of the neoclassical, strict, quasi-concavity assumption is to ask whether there are two or more factor combinations that permit minimum cost production. While in a few cases production using radically different methods will be found to have the same cost, most of the cases where the same product can be produced with differing factor proportions will be found to be cases where, when the *quality* of one factor is varied, the *quantity* of other factors employed varies. Cases of this type are easily found.

When land quality varies, the quantity of fertilizer, labor, and other factors varies. As Ricardo and others have recognized, the rent of the land adjusts so that farmers are indifferent between high or low rent land. The farmer achieves the same cost by employing a few acres of good land and little of other inputs, or by employing more acres of poor land and more of other inputs.

When the quality of workers varies in such a way that the percentage of the raw materials spoiled varies, the wages of the workers are expected to vary to make the costs of production the same. Once this has happened, firms have a choice between using a few high-quality workers and less raw materials, or using more, but lower-quality, workers and more raw materials.

Production is often by a unit that can be thought of as certain workers and the equipment they use (a tractor and driver, mill and associated workers, etc.). However, the output of each production unit varies with the quality of one or more of the inputs.

Likewise, workers frequently differ in skill, such that more skilled workers work faster. Wages adjust so that workers of different skills are equally profitable to employ. Firms then have a choice between employing a few skilled but highly expensive workers and fewer machines, or employing more machines and more workers, but paying the workers less. Both strategies produce at minimum cost.

In all of these cases there are multiple factor input combinations that permit minimum cost production. The production functions cannot be described as strictly quasi-concave, and standard production function based neoclassical theory cannot discover a particular firm's factor inputs. In most cases it cannot predict an industry's factor inputs because that requires knowing the factor quality distribution, and this is not a variable in the standard theory.

Note that the above result is not merely a failure of aggregation. Even when there is no aggregation between factors of different qualities with each quality being considered a separate factor, it still follows that the production function is not strictly quasi-concave. If high- and low-quality workers are considered different factors, and a firm can produce at the same cost using either high- or low-quality workers (which normally implies differences in the inputs of any homogeneous factors), the production function will not be strictly quasi-concave.

Leaving aside any effects that result from any disadvantages of mixing workers of different qualities and any economies of scale, the output of a firm that employs low-quality workers and high-quality workers, each with the associated machines, will simply be the sum of the output of a firm that employed the same number of low-quality workers with the machines they work on (and no high-quality workers) and the output of a firm that employed the same number of high-quality workers and their machines (and no low-quality workers). This observation is inconsistent with strict quasi-concavity. One will not be able to predict a firm's factor inputs, even knowing the production function (i.e., the technology), the factor prices, and the desired output.

For years the neoclassical textbooks at the basic level have been expounding at the two factor level a theory in which factor inputs are determined by finding the point of tangency of a curved isoquant with an isocost line. More advanced textbooks use the same logic expressed in a mathematical form, casually assuming that production functions are strictly quasi-concave. The above discussion shows that a major implication of the theory that production functions are strictly quasi-concave is that no quality differences will be observed that affect the use of other factors. This is a testable implication. It is falsified by observations of fertility and climate variations among land parcels, differences in speed and accuracy among workers, and the requirement for more maintenance for aging machines.

Conclusions

The attempt to answer Joan Robinson's question, "In what units is capital measured?" exposes some very weak points in neoclassical production function based theory. No matter how the theory is expressed, one comes up against the problem that the quantity of capital (and other factors also) cannot be defined to produce both a single well-defined price for a factor and a unique input of that factor for the cost-minimizing firm.

Notes

1. Robinson, 1953–54, p. 81.
2. See Harcourt, 1972.
3. She summarizes four different definitions in Robinson, 1965, chap. 11.
4. Joan Robinson and other writers of her time talked simply of the capital input. Dale Jorgenson and others have pointed out that if labor is to be measured in man-hours, capital should be measured in units of its services for compatibility, with the correct measure being a weighted average of machine hours. Thus, one should think of references to capital input as just shorthand for references to capital services input. The writings of Joan Robinson are not altered in any essential way if her references to capital are replaced with capital services.
5. Joan Robinson doubted whether the questions Solow asked were meaningful. The goal here is to meet the neoclassical analysis (or at least, the versions of it found in textbooks) on its own grounds, and to ask whether there is a set of units for which its predictions would hold.
6. Denison, 1962, pp. 95–96; 1967, p. 135.
7. U.S. Department of Labor, 1983, p. 41.
8. Ibid., p. 43, emphasis added.
9. Ibid., p. 41.
10. Jorgenson, 1980; Jorgenson, Gollop, and Fraumeni, 1987. However, in Jorgenson, 1989, he introduces the concept of efficiency decline without defining it, discusses how it might be measured using rates of decline in asset prices and rates of decline in rents and then later (p. 20) states that "A second alternative to the vintage price approach is to analyze investment for replacement purposes." Unfortunately, as is made clear in this essay, these are two different concepts. Coen (1975) has made the same mistake where he introduces efficiency decline as the rate of decline in rent, assigns it a symbol,

and then without changing symbols proceeds to estimate the rate of decline in capacity, a conceptually different concept.

11. Robinson, 1953–54, p. 78.

12. This speculation is based on Robinson's (1962, p. 43) comments about combining labor into an aggregate labor input measure and apparent approval of using socially necessary time to produce something.

13. Jorgenson, 1963; Jorgenson and Siebert, 1968.

14. Miller, 1989a.

15. Textbooks, starting with the idea that isoquants are curved at all points, suggest that if there are two points on both an isoquant and an isocost line, these are points where the isoquant is cut by the isocost line. In the above argument, the possibility that the two points are where the isocost line cuts the isoquant is excluded because the isocost line is the minimum cost isocost line. If the specified output could be produced by any combination of inputs purchasable at the cost represented by a lower isocost line, the original isocost line could not be the minimum cost isocost line.

References

Clark, John Bates (1914) *The Distribution of Wealth.* New York: Macmillan.

Coen, Robert M. (1975) "Investment Behavior: The Measurement of Depreciation and Tax Policy." *American Economic Review*, 65, 1 (March):59–74.

Denison, Edward F. (1957) "Theoretical Aspects of Quality Change, Capital Consumption, and Net Capital Formation." In Conference on Research in Income and Wealth, A Report of the National Bureau of Economic Research, *Problems in Capital Formation, Studies in Income and Wealth.* Princeton: Princeton University Press.

———. (1962) *The Sources of Economic Growth in the United States and the Alternatives before Us*. New York: Committee for Economic Development.

———. (1967) *Why Growth Rates Differ: Postwar Experiences in Nine Western Countries.* Washington, D.C.: Brookings Institution.

———. (1988)"The Unimportance of the Embodiment Question: Reply." *Journal of Macroeconomics*, 10, 1 (Winter):139–42.

Fisher, Franklin M. (1965) "Embodied Technical Change and the Existence of an Aggregate Capital Stock." *Review of Economic Studies*, 32, 4:263–88.

Goldsmith, Raymond, W. (1956) *A Study of Savings in the United States*, vol. 3. Princeton: Princeton University Press.

Harcourt, G. C. (1972) *Some Cambridge Controversies in the Theory of Capital.* Cambridge: Cambridge University Press.

Jorgenson, Dale W. (1963) "Capital Theory and Investment Behavior." *American Economic Review*, 53, 2 (May):247–59.

———. (1967) "The Theory of Investment Behavior." In R. Ferber, ed., *The Determinants of Investment Behavior*. Conference of the Universities—National Bureau Committee for Economic Research. New York: Columbia University Press.

———. (1980) "Accounting for Capital." In George M. von Furstenberg, ed., *Capital, Efficiency and Growth.* Cambridge, Mass.: Ballinger.

———. (1989) "Capital as a Factor of Production." In Dale W. Jorgenson and Ralph Landau, eds., *Technology and Capital Formation.* Cambridge, Mass.: MIT Press.

Jorgenson, Dale W., Frank M. Gollop, and Barbara M. Fraumeni. (1987) *Productivity and U.S. Economic Growth.* Cambridge, Mass.: Harvard University Press.

Jorgenson, Dale W. and Calvin D. Siebert. (1968) "Optimal Capital Accumulation and Corporate Investment Behavior." *Journal of Political Economy*, 76, 6 (November/December):1123–51.

Miller, Edward. (1985) "On the Importance of the Embodiment of Technology Effect: A Comment on Denison's Growth Accounting Methodology." *Journal of Macroeconomics* (Winter):85–99.

———. (1988a) "Used Capital: Implications for Isoquants, Production Functions, and Shephard's Lemma." *Eastern Economic Journal*, 14, 2 (April–June):141–52.

———. (1988b) "A Capital Paradox: An Upward Sloping Demand Curve." *Review of Business and Economic Research*, 24, 1 (Fall):68–76.

———. (1989a) "The Unique 'Rent Defined' Capital Input Assumption in Investment Theory." *Southern Economic Journal*, 55, 4 (April):987–93.

———. (1989b) "The Definition of Capital for Solow's Growth Accounting Formula." *Southern Economic Journal*, 56, 1 (July):157–65.

Robinson, Joan. (1953–54) "The Production Function and the Theory of Capital." *Review of Economic Studies*, 21(2), 55:81–106.

———. (1962) *Economic Philosophy*. Chicago: Aldine.

———. (1965) *The Accumulation of Capital*. New York: St. Martin's Press.

———. (1970) "Capital Theory Up-to-date." *Canadian Journal of Economics*, 3:309–17. Reprinted in Robinson, 1980.

———. (1971) "The Measure of Capital: The End of the Controversy." *Economic Journal*, 81 (September):597–602. Reprinted in Robinson, 1980.

———. (1980) *Collected Economic Papers*, vol. 4. Cambridge, Mass.: MIT Press.

Solow, Robert M. (1955–56) "The Production Function and the Theory of Capital." *Review of Economic Studies*, 23:100–108.

———. (1957) "Technical Progress and the Aggregate Production Function." *Review of Economics and Statistics*, 39 (August):312–20.

U.S. Department of Labor, Bureau of Labor Statistics. (1983) *Trends in Multifactor Productivity, 1948–81*. Washington, D.C.: U.S. Government Printing Office.

JR

CHAPTER TWELVE

Marx after Robinson

Production, Exchange, and Related Matters

GEOFFREY M. HODGSON

Although Joan Robinson's economic thought covers a great number of diverse topics it contains some unifying and persistent themes. Two in particular are considered here. The first is that orthodox analysis applies in the main to problems of the allocation given resources, and not to the creation or accumulation of goods or services through time. The second, an alleged limitation of orthodox theory and its link with pro-capitalist ideology, is that conceptual and normative distinctions must be made between incomes from work and incomes from property.

It is somewhat surprising, given the persistence of these themes, that they have not received more evaluation and attention, by either supporters or opponents of the arguments. This paper begins to rectify the deficiency. It proceeds by arguing, first, that these two linked Robinsonian themes are more problematic than may appear at first sight. Second, there is a connection with the radical literature on the labor process and, third, with modern developments in the theory of the firm. It will be argued that the Robinsonian themes can only be sustained by introducing a Knightian or Keynesian concept of uncertainty.

The Economics of a Prisoner-of-War Camp

"There is one very special case to which the Walrasian analysis applies pretty well," writes Joan Robinson, "that is the market in a prisoner-of-war camp."[1] In this system, nothing is produced and prisoners swap the contents of their Red Cross parcels using cigarettes as money. "It makes sense also, with some modifications," she writes elsewhere, "in an economy of artisans and small traders. . . . Two essential characteristics of industrial capitalism are absent in these economic systems—the distinction between income from work and income from property and the nature of investments made in the light of uncertain expectations about a long future."[2]

These ideas are recurrent.[3] They are not raised once or twice and then dropped, through doubt or frustration, but are repeated with increasing persistence, clarity, and confidence. Harvey Gram and Vivian Walsh, in a timely evaluation of Joan Robinson's work published the year of her death, saw the "distinction between income from work and income from property" as fundamental to her thought and to the questions she raised concerning distribution and accumulation.[4]

However, a number of outstanding conceptual issues still remain. Despite repetition of these distinctions—between incomes from work and from property, and between allocation and production—the reasons why orthodox theory has not embraced them still deserve further examination. A clue is provided by Joan Robinson herself in one of her later essays, where she provides an instructive quotation from Robert Clower:

> An ongoing exchange economy with specialist traders *is* a production economy since there is no bar to any merchant capitalist acquiring labour services and other resources as a "buyer" and transforming them (repackaging, processing into new forms, etc.) into outputs that are unlike the original inputs and are "sold" accordingly as are commodities that undergo no such transformation. In short, a production unit *is* a particular type of middleman or trading specialist.[5]

Typically, neoclassical economists refer to production as an "exchange with nature," and for at least some members of the Austrian School, all purposeful human action, including production, is exchange.[6] These approaches have common roots and some of the key ideological presumptions of classic liberalism. The choosing, propertied individual is regarded as the primary and animating force in the social system. Decisions to buy and sell impel and determine production, as expressed in the idea of "consumer sovereignty." Decisions in the marketplace are primary and active, production is merely consequent and passive.

The implications of this orthodox view are clear. First, there is no substantial distinction between production and exchange, as the former is seen as being animated by (and even taking the form of) the latter.[7] Once the deal is struck, the wheels of production are essentially predetermined. The law of contract, through appropriate penalties, ensures that the goods will appear at the appointed time and in good order. In this case all the key choices and actions take place in the determination of the contract itself. Production is merely an annex of the market: a place where agents act in accordance with the relevant clauses of the deal.

There is another consequence of this point of view. If all action is animated by exchange, and exchange involves property, then work itself is part of an exchange. After all, in the labor market the worker agrees to an employment contract that is supposed to specify the kind of work to be carried out. Labor time is bought (or "hired"), perhaps by the hour, in return for an agreed wage.

In this case the employee is exchanging his or her property, i.e., labor time, for an income, i.e., wages. Thus, Joan Robinson's distinction between income from work and income from property dissolves. Work itself, according to this view, is simply the hourly consumption of the property that has been bought by the employer. The wage thus appears as an income from the sale or rent of this particular property, just like any other.

Consequently, in the classic liberal view of the world—the view that is still taken by most economists—Joan Robinson's two distinctions are not meaningful or substantial. Production is animated by exchange, and wages too are an income from property, albeit in a special sense. Thus, without further theoretical support, the Robinsonian distinctions are condemned to future obscurity. The economics of the prisoner-of-war camp will continue to be applied, with amendments and additions, to the modern dynamic and corporate world. The question remains: Are the distinctions substantial, and if so why?

The escape route proposed here from this theoretical incarceration is as follows: Clearly, the issues involved relate directly to the nature of the employment contract and of productive institutions such as the firm. First, a Marxian view that the Robinsonian distinctions can be sustained mainly by distinguishing between labor and labor power will be examined and found wanting. Next, some related work on the employment contract by Herbert Simon will be shown to have taken a further but insufficient step in the right direction by introducing an element of indeterminacy. This leads on to the Coase-Williamson argument that the existence of the firm, and the peculiarities of the employment contract, are explicable in terms of transaction costs. On the basis of recent discussions of the nature of transaction costs, it is argued that the information problems associated with the firm and employment contracts cannot be properly understood without the recognition of true uncertainty. This leads directly to the rehabilitation of the Robinsonian distinctions.

Labor, Labor Power, and Indeterminacy

The distinction Marx made between labor and labor power is a useful entry for examining the distinctions between production and exchange, and between work and property incomes. Harry Braverman (1974) is largely responsible for the current renewed emphasis on the distinction between labor and labor power in Marxian theory.[8] As in Marx's writings, labor, the activity of work, is distinguished from labor power, the potential for work. It is the latter that is bought and sold on the marketplace by the hour. Marxian labor process theorists have thus concerned themselves with the specific social arrangements and practices concerned with the extraction of the maximum possible amount of labor out of a given quantity of labor power.[9] They are able to do this by asserting that no predetermined quantity or quality of labor flows automatically from the sale of the labor power that is specified in the contract of employment. Instead, the outcome depends on a struggle and trial of strength between management and employees.

While labor does not flow automatically from labor power, does this also mean that there is virtually no connection between them? Is it possible, for instance, to go so far as Richard Edwards in the following statement?: "Workers must provide labor power in order to receive their wages, that is, they must show up for work; but they need not necessarily provide *labor.*"[10] Perhaps in response to such overstretched arguments, Ian Steedman writes:

> In normal circumstances, to have disposal over workers' ability to work means precisely to get them to perform a certain number of hours of a certain kind of work: if they remain idle, or even work less hard than was anticipated by the capitalist, then the latter *does not have* full disposal over the workers' capacity for labour.[11]

Steedman's conclusion is not simply to reestablish a linkage between labor and labor power but to assert that the concept of labor power is itself "redundant."[12] While this conclusion is not endorsed here, it is notable that Marxian labor process theorists have failed to give an adequate response to such arguments.

Furthermore, and strikingly, much of Braverman's analysis can be turned against his own assertion of the distinction between labor power and labor. In giving great emphasis to the methods through which it is ensured that the maximum labor is extracted from labor power, such as hierarchical organization, incentives, discipline, and managerial supervision, Braverman is implying that the amount of labor performed is essentially under capitalist control. As Craig Littler and Graeme Salaman put it: "the overall theoretical thrust of *Labor and Monopoly Capital* is to suggest that capitalists no longer face the problem of labour power as a variable and indeterminate component of the production process."[13]

It is questionable that recent work by Marxists is more successful in overcoming this problem. In a major study of the growth slowdown of the U.S. economy, Samuel Bowles, David Gordon, and Thomas Weisskopf (1984) also draw on the distinction between labor and labor power. In their analyses they stress the possibility of a "free lunch": i.e., due to waste and slack in the economy, the possibility of extra output being obtained without an increase in inputs.[14] Going further than Harvey Leibenstein's (1976) identification of "X-efficiency," they claim to explain variable productivity through reference to the balance of class forces within the firm.

Similarly, Samuel Bowles's (1985) analysis focuses on the (costly) processes through which employers exercise power over labor, and the ability of workers to resist. Likewise, the amount of labor performed, and consequently the output, depends on factors such as the level of unemployment and the degree of unionization, both of which help to determine (positively or negatively) "employer leverage" over workers.

The relevance of the difference between labor and labor power for the Robinsonian distinctions is obvious. Yet, given the parameters that determine "employer leverage," a fixed amount of labor will exude from a given amount of labor power. Output is not simply a function of capital and labor, but a determinate (more complex) "production function" exists nevertheless. One is left asking what is the purpose of the distinction between labor and labor power in this analysis, especially given such orthodox features as the assumption of maximizing behavior by both employers and employees, which results in a predetermined equilibrium solution?[15] There is, in fact, despite claims to the contrary, no "free lunch" in this model. Anything "extra" must flow from a change in the parameters governing output.

Formally, Bowles's (1985) theoretical model is virtually identical to that of Carl Shapiro and Joseph Stiglitz (1984). Their important shared feature is an equilibrium solution in which profits are maximized, with a level of employment that is at an equilibrium in the sense of ensuring a degree of discipline over the workforce that is consistent with an optimal level of output:

> If there were no unemployment and if all firms paid the market-clearing wage, then the threat of being fired would not lead individuals to reduce their shirking: they would know that they could costlessly obtain another job. But if . . . there is unemployment . . . then workers have an incentive not to shirk: there is a real cost to being fired.[16]

What is not essential to a model of this type is the phraseology of class struggle; indeed, real struggle is actually excluded. While in some sense there is a distinction between labor and labor power—in that performed labor will depend upon factors that are additional to the employment contract—given those factors the amount of labor is predetermined once the contract is agreed. Once again, the Robinsonian distinctions disappear.

Braverman, Bowles, and others, like Marx before them, all fail to emphasize an essential element in the argument, without which the distinction between labor and labor power collapses into verbiage and irrelevance. To sustain the distinction, and the very autonomy of production from exchange, it is necessary to show that (within limits) the amount of labor-extracted labor power is in some sense *indeterminate.*

As far as this author is aware, the first theorist to give a substantial treatment of indeterminacy in the employment contract is Simon (1951).[17] Simon attacks the traditional view in economic theory that labor is a "passive factor of production," and asserts that the orthodox view "abstracts away from the most obvious peculiarities of the employment contract."[18] This is seen to differ "fundamentally from a sales contract—the kind of contract that is assumed in ordinary formulations of price theory.'' In a sales contract a ''completely specified commodity'' is exchanged for an agreed sum of money.[19] Even in cases where complete specification is absent, the details of the agreement are often regarded by law as implicit or ''understood.'' In contrast, in the employment contract the worker agrees to perform one from a mutually agreed and limited range of patterns of work, and allows the employer to select and allocate the tasks. In effect, the worker agrees to accept the authority of the employer, notably concerning the specification of the particular work to be performed.[20]

While noting the frequency of contracts of this type in the real world, Simon does not examine the reasons why employers do not or cannot fully specify the work in advance. Fortunately, however, these reasons are fairly well understood today. Imperfectly specified employment contracts are widely attributed to the possibility of unforeseen changes in product demand or in the supply of materials or components, or of interruptions in production as a result of mechanical malfunctions or industrial disputes. Herein is a source of the indeterminacy in production. We shall suggest below that this indeterminacy is of a type for which probabilities cannot be known.[21]

The nature of ''imperfect specification'' in a labor contract must be further clarified. It does not simply mean that the terms of the contract are not spelt out in detail: in this case they may still be ''understood'' by the parties. The imperfection of the labor contract goes further in that it covers a range of possible outcomes. Thus, ''imperfect specification'' here connotes also a degree of indeterminacy of outcome, whereby the contract cannot be generally ''understood'' to refer to something that is well defined and specific.

The pecuniary consequence of this indeterminacy, Simon argues, is that the capitalist will pay a higher wage—compared to a sales contract where the worker is contracted to supply a well-specified commodity or service—for the privilege of asserting authority over the worker and of postponing the precise specification of the work to be performed.

The key indeterminacy in Simon's model is the fact that the outcomes (i.e., profits, work satisfaction, etc.) for each pattern of work are not known precisely at the time of contracting. Simon formalizes this by considering the probability density function of outcomes for each feasible pattern of work. At the time of contracting, both employer and employee are assumed to know the relevant probabilities but not the precise outcomes.

While Simon advances our understanding of the employment contract by recognizing its essential indeterminacy, it is notable that he treats this as a matter of calculable probability. Herein lie some problems. For if the probabilities are known, then it not only makes possible a complete specification of the contract at the start,[22] but it also undermines the concept of authority that is central to Simon's argument. Given the probability distributions, the worker can compute the likelihood that each pattern of work will be selected by the employer. Thus, the acceptance of authority is not simply within limits but also with known probabilities of employer behavior. The ruling authority is not the employer, but, as it were, the random throw of the dice. Given maximizing behavior, the employer has no more power over the choice of outcome than the employee. The only significant difference is that the choice of pattern of work has the employer's utility as the maximand, given that the worker has maximized first.

While Simon's attempt to differentiate between employment contracts and sales contracts is a forward step, serious internal problems remain. These are not simply problems of "lack of realism" to which Simon himself openly draws our attention; they are problems regarding the internal coherence of the analysis itself.

Coase, Williamson, and Transaction Costs

A more recent and better-known approach to the peculiarities of the employment contract, which also relates to the issues at hand but is also inadequate in that context, has been developed primarily by Oliver Williamson (1975, 1985) on the basis of the classic article by Ronald Coase (1937). Coase's principal concern was with the capacity of the firm to supersede the price mechanism and allocate resources by command rather than through price. As Coase puts it:

> Outside the firm, price movements direct production, which is co-ordinated through a series of exchange transactions on the market.
>
> Within a firm, these market transactions are eliminated and in place of the complicated market structure with exchange transactions is substituted the entrepreneur-co-ordinator, who directs production.[23]

Coase's well-known explanation of why this occurs is in terms of the "cost of using the price mechanism."[24]

Following on from this approach, Williamson developed his central thesis that economic institutions such as the firm "have the main purpose and effect of economizing on transaction costs."[25] However, the idea of transaction costs "has become a catch-all phrase for unspecified interferences with the price mechanism."[26] Furthermore, the typical formal representation of transaction costs among mathematical economists, as a fixed proportion of the value of the goods that are exchanged, differs "in no significant way" from a regular transportation cost.

Dahlman suggests that all types of transaction cost "reduce to . . . resource losses due to lack of information."[27] It can be accepted that for purposes of theoretical clarification, Dahlman's argument is an important step forward; but it is not clear what a reduction of costs to matters of information could mean. Indeed, it could be fitted neatly into a neoclassical paradigm. One possibility, following the lead of George Stigler's classic (1961) article, is to accommodate search and information costs in a probabilistic framework. Information is then being treated just like any other commodity, and is subject to the marginalist rule that its consumption is optimal when the marginal cost of information search and acquisition is equal to its expected marginal return.

However, Keynes's insights have rendered the very idea of a rational calculus of information costs objectionable; in the normal circumstances of uncertainty we are forced to abandon full, rational calculation and are obliged to fall back on "the convention," or "average opinion."[28] Further, if such a rational calculus were possible, it is not clear why market contracting is superseded by the organization of the firm. After all, if information is simply a commodity like any other, there is no apparent special rationale for the firm to act as the minimizer of these information-related, transaction costs. The "information costs" version of the transaction costs argument does not appear to supply a convincing reason for the existence of the capitalist firm and for the relative rarity of alternative arrangements, in real life. As Brian Loasby (1976) has argued, there is no need in theory for non-market forms of organization in the general equilibrium model. Even the probabilistic version of general equilibrium theory, which implies information problems of a stylized and limited kind, provides no reason why firms, as such, should exist.

Richard Langlois's (1984) solution to this problem is to make a distinction between different kinds of information problem, which parallels Frank Knight's (1921) famous distinction between risk and uncertainty. The essence of the argument is that "parametric uncertainty" (akin to Knight's "risk") cannot be used to find the source of transaction costs that are relevant to the explanation of the relative efficiency of organizations such as a firm. A similar argument has been offered by Neil Kay (1984) who has shown that, in a neoclassical world of perfect knowledge, the firm is stripped of most, if not all, of its familiar structures and functions. Furthermore, there is no decisive difference if problems of probabilistic risk (or "parametric uncertainty") are introduced, because there "is a close affinity between perfect knowledge and risk in terms of homogeneity and replicability of associated events." He concludes: "True uncertainty and information costs represent the dominant consideration in areas of firm, market and state organization."[29]

By emphasizing true uncertainty (as opposed to risk), but with different features and qualifications, Loasby, Kay, and Langlois are all returning to Knight's *Risk, Uncertainty and Profit* and a core idea in its discussion of the firm that its "existence in the world is the direct result of the fact of uncertainty."[30] In the light of these theoretical developments it seems that an answer to Coase's question as to why firms exist is reemerging in terms of a nonprobabilistic concept of uncertainty. Transaction costs may or may not remain an intermediate category in the argument. But it is clear that transaction costs as a category are not meaningful without some concept of true or radical uncertainty, and this, either directly or indirectly, seems to be a necessary concept to explain the existence of the firm.[31]

A Rehabilitation of the Robinsonian Distinctions

While we are concerned with production *per se* and not simply with the specific institution of the capitalist firm, it is arguable that some of the uncertainty pertaining to the latter relates to the suggested indeterminacy of the production process itself, as suggested above, i.e., in terms of its inherent and unavoidable vagaries and variations. Thus, it is proposed here that there is some degree of objective indeterminacy in the production process: partly as a result of which agents are uncertain, in the sense of Knight or Keynes, as to the outcomes.[32]

In general, we can never demonstrate the existence of indeterminacy because there is always the possibility of a hidden and unknown causal mechanism at work. However, what we do know from the mathematical theory of chaos (Gleick, 1988; Stewart, 1989) is that even if the world is deterministic, it would almost certainly behave in a nonprobabilistic and unpredictable way. The possibility of "deterministic chaos" is thus established. Consequently, even if the world is deterministic, we should have to treat it as if it were indeterministic and unpredictable. Even if all our choices are caused, many of them will appear spontaneous and free. There is thus established a strange ground upon which determinists and indeterminists can meet.

On such a basis the Robinsonian distinctions between production and exchange can be rehabilitated, by the inclusion of an element of indeterminacy in production. Because the consequences of contracts pertaining to employment and production are not known precisely, even in terms of calculable probabilities, even when all contracts are concluded, real uncertainty is unavoidable and there is a functional distinction between production and exchange; a distinction that has eluded many orthodox theorists. Production is no longer an annex of the market because of the indeterminate outcome of production itself. All agents in the productive process confront the unforeseen and have to react to the unexpected. The forthright will engage with others to create stratagems and institutions to deal with the problems that are foreseen. But, essentially, the notion of an "optimum" or "equilibrium" is without much meaning, for eventualities depend on imagination and expectation concerning an unfolding but uncertain future.

Of course, for Keynes (1936, 1937) the existence of uncertainty was crucial in his theory of macroeconomic behavior. But, with a few exceptions, the importance of radical uncertainty to the analysis of microeconomic institutions, such as the firm, is not widely appreciated. An important exception is George Shackle, who asserts that "business is contest rather than co-ordination, that its appropriate theory is the theory of battle rather than that of pre-reconciliation."[33] Such real struggle and conflict depends, as Shackle shows with his customary brilliance, on such elements as incomplete specification of the "rules" and the exploitation of ignorance or surprise.

We now turn to the second Robinsonian distinction: between incomes from property and incomes from work. Given that production has an indeterminate outcome, it could be argued that a trader who hires a machine or other productive facilities to a capitalist is subject to a similar degree of uncertainty as the worker who hires his labor power. In both cases remuneration is fixed, once certain conditions are met.

What is different, however, is that while the worker is actively engaged in production, the owner of capital goods is not actively involved in the process, unless he or she takes managerial responsibilities and works as well. (In this case the individual combines roles as both owner and managerial worker.) To receive an income from work, the provision of an object of property, i.e., labor power, is not sufficient. The worker must submit to the authority of the employer but also continue as a purposeful agent, i.e., provide deliberate and purposeful work.

The elaboration of this distinction between two different sources and types of income cannot be carried out in full here,[34] but the argument is partly based on the view that human agents are capable of purposeful behavior but capital goods are not. Essentially, one is active and the other is passive. The owners of labor power and the owners of capital goods are both active and purposeful decision-making agents in the sphere of exchange. But during the process of production, capital goods themselves are passive instruments, subject to the purposeful activity of the workers (and managers). Owners, as such, here play no direct role.

Thus there is an essential distinction between income from property and income from work. The owner of property may obtain an income from hiring the goods, simply as a consequence of concluding a contract on the market. The goods themselves are not active agents, so they play no part in varying potential output. In contrast, the worker agrees to provide labor but to an imperfectly specified pattern, subject to some indeterminacy as elaborated above.[35]

Given the indeterminacy inherent in production, there must be choices and clashes of will: matters are not resolved *ex ante* by contractual or marketplace decisions, despite the orthodox assertion that the employment contract is subject to "continuous renegotiation" during production, so that payments actually reflect productive contributions *ex post*.[36] But this ignores the arguments of Coase, Simon, Williamson, and others to the contrary. What has been established here is that the distinctions they make between employment and other contracts, and between firms and markets, can be sustained only on the basis of the concept of true uncertainty.

Strikingly, just as these distinctions depend upon the concept of uncertainty, an element of indeterminacy is also required to define the concept of purposeful behavior. As Russell Ackoff and Fred Emery (1972) have argued, a key feature of purposeful behavior is that its goals are not predetermined. Unlike a programmed, goal-seeking device, such as a thermostat, the human agent can potentially change his or her goals *without any external stimulus*. Even with a sophisticated computer program that enables a kind of "learning," where past experience leads to a different response to a repeated problem, the outcome is not truly purposeful behavior because the output is still predetermined and the goals themselves are fixed. The capacity to change both behavior and goals without external stimulus is an essential component of *will* and real *choice*. Yet this is essentially to include an element of indeterminacy: a feature that is not only absent from orthodox economic theory,[37] but is also essential if Joan Robinson's distinctions, between production and exchange, and between incomes from work and property, are to be sustained.

In a very real sense, we have arrived at a modernization of some of the key themes of the economics of Marx, with the introduction of uncertainty in the sense of Knight or Keynes.[38] This is also an essential thrust of Joan Robinson's work, and sustains her constant reminders of the stature and complementarity of Keynes and Marx as economists.

Notes

The author is grateful to Ingrid Rima, Ian Steedman, and the participants of a joint Keele University–Staffordshire Polytechnic economics seminar for critical comments on earlier versions of this work.

1. Robinson, 1979, p. 153.

2. Ibid., p. 34.

3. See, for instance, Robinson (1942, pp. 18, 92; 1960, pp. 92–93; 1965, pp. 75, 141; 1969, pp. 3–4; 1973, p. 115; 1979, pp. 5, 29–30, 34, 68, 153, 157). These ideas almost certainly owe their origin to the influence of Marx on Robinson's economic theory; see, for example, Marx (1972, pp. 480, 499; 1973, pp. 274–75; 1976, pp. 675–84; 1981, p. 501). In one passage Robinson (1979, p. 5) makes explicit reference to Bukharin's (1972, pp. 54–56) discussion of the importance of production and accumulation as opposed to the "point of view of consumption," as allegedly typified in the economic theory of Böhm-Bawerk and the Austrian School.

4. Gram and Walsh, 1983, pp. 519, 547.

5. Clower, 1976.

6. For example, Jack Hirshleifer (1970, p. 12) and Ludwig von Mises (1949, p. 97). Notably, recent exponents of the "Property Rights School" (e.g., Furubotn and Pejovich, 1974) have failed to criticize, with or without their customary vigor, their neoclassical and Austrian colleagues for assuming that "nature" has property rights to exchange.

7. While orthodox economists have traditionally ignored the "black box" of production, some recent orthodox attempts to look inside it have typically reduced production and the employment contract to a more-or-less straightforward exchange. For a classic statement in this regard see Alchian and Demsetz (1972), and for critiques, see Hodgson (1988, chap. 9), Nutzinger (1976), and Tomlinson (1986).

8. After a century of neglect, by the late 1970s much Marxist scholarship was focused on the chapters in *Capital* that are devoted to the processes of production (Marx, 1976, chaps. 7–18). In addition to the inspiration of Braverman (1974) note the remarks in Rowthorn (1973) on the significance of the distinction between labor and labor power and on "despotism in the labour process" (p. 10).

9. For reviews of the literature on the labor process, see Littler and Salaman (1982); Nichols (1980); Thompson (1983); Zimbalist (1979).

10. Edwards, 1979, p. 12.

11. Steedman, 1982, p. 151.
12. Ibid., p. 153.
13. Littler and Salaman, 1982, p. 252.
14. Lest we ridicule such a suggestion, note that a recent theory of the origin of the universe considers that matter itself can be created, as it were, from nothing: "I have heard it said that there is no such thing as a free lunch. It now appears possible that the universe is a free lunch" (Guth, 1983, p. 215).
15. Indeed, Bowles (1985, p. 20) explicitly assumes that "workers have complete information about job and wage conditions throughout the economy, that employees know all (actual and potential) employee characteristics" and assumes away "problems of risk aversion and issues of reputation (workers and capitalists alike have no memories)." It is a defect of the classical, Marxian, and neoclassical traditions in economics that insufficient attention is paid to problems of information, uncertainty, cognition, and knowledge. It is mainly due to their attempts to deal with these issues that Knight and Keynes offer signposts into the twentieth century. Note, however, that in some passages of Marx's work, and unlike the Bowles (1985) model, there is a sense of an ongoing and nonequilibriating, historical process (e.g., Marx, 1976, chaps. 7–17) and more than a hint of post-Keynesian indeterminacy (e.g., Marx, 1969, pp. 504–9). On the latter, see Kenway (1980) and Hodgson (1982, chap. 13).
16. Stiglitz, 1987, p. 20.
17. Gintis (1976) is one of the few theorists to offer a sizeable discussion of Simon's article, but, despite making some valid criticisms, he does not give sufficient credit to the innovative character of Simon's theory. Notably, Simon's article is included in Putterman's (1986) excellent collection.
18. Simon, 1951, p. 293.
19. Ibid., p. 294.
20. Many years ago Knight (1921, p. 270) argued that "with human nature as we know it it would be impracticable or very unusual for one man to guarantee to another a definite result of the latter's actions without being given power to direct his work." As Coase (1937, p. 401) rightly points out, this statement is not universally true; consider the counter-example of a contractor who "is guaranteed a certain sum providing he performs certain acts." Nevertheless, while the indefinite character of labor is not a universal condition of human existence, it is a feature of typical employment contracts in a capitalist firm, and is thus associated with the existence of employer authority. Also, notably, Coase foreshadows Simon's emphasis on the authority relation as a key characteristic of the employment contract when he quotes Batt (1929, p. 6) to the effect that the "right of control or interference . . . marks the servant [i.e., employee—G.M.H.] from an independent contractor" (Coase, 1937, p. 404). Strangely, Simon (1951) does not refer to Knight or even to Coase's seminal paper on the firm.
21. Note that uncertainty could result from either the fact that there are no objective probabilities to be ascertained, i.e., there is indeterminacy in a full and radical sense, or that they exist but they cannot be known. On this distinction, see Elster (1983, pp. 27–28) and Lawson (1988).
22. Clearly, Simon (1957) has an answer to this question in terms of bounded rationality, i.e., the difficulty in making all the computations and assessments that are involved in such a fully specified, contingent-claims contract. This does not appear, however, in his 1951 article. Furthermore, bounded rationality, as Simon later made clear, relates to uncertainty in the true sense, as used by Keynes and Knight. A further response to the question could be made in terms of transaction costs in the manner of Coase (1937) or Williamson (1975), as discussed below.
23. Coase, 1937, p. 388.

24. Ibid., p. 390.

25. Williamson, 1985, p. 1.

26. Dahlman, 1979, p. 144.

27. Ibid., p. 148. As noted elsewhere (Hodgson, 1988), this is an example of the mistake of "informational reductionism."

28. Keynes, 1936, chap. 12; 1937.

29. Kay, 1984, p. 83. An important feature of this line of argument is that it does not rely on the conception of the human agent as opportunistic. Consider, as an example, the possibility of a person reneging on a half-completed contract. The problem here is not fundamentally one of opportunism *per se*: it is because one party to the contract is uncertain if the other will renege or not. The other person may, or may not, be opportunistic and self-seeking; that is a secondary question. Indeed, it might even be possible that he or she might break the contract for altruistic rather than selfish reasons. Strictly, the question of opportunism is not the basic issue and Williamson's emphasis on opportunism as the central element of transaction costs is quite inappropriate. The key point is the existence of the uncertainty as to whether or not the contract will be completed.

30. Knight, 1921, p. 271. Coase (1937, p. 401) points out that "nowhere does Professor Knight give a reason why the price mechanism should be superseded" in the firm. If the reason for the existence of the firm is due to relatively high transaction costs, then, as argued above, these costs are largely informational in character and nevertheless depend upon the existence of (Knightian) radical uncertainty. Thus, in attacking some of Knight's genuine limitations, Coase almost throws out the baby with the bathwater.

31. Note also the parallel with the well-established Keynesian argument that money exists largely to deal with an uncertain future, and the role of money is very much to do with this uncertainty. Consequently, types of analysis that rule out true uncertainty, such as neoclassical general equilibrium theory, cannot cope with relevant modern phenomena such as money and the firm.

32. Of course, it is not being argued that uncertainty is the *only* important feature here. See Hodgson (1988, chap. 9) for a further discussion of the essential characteristics of the firm.

33. Shackle, 1972, p. 423.

34. For a further discussion, see Hodgson (1982, chaps. 16–18).

35. Note, however, that the variable and indeterminate character of output renders a variable and indeterminate quality not to wages, which are normally fixed by the employment contract (albeit sometimes with the addition of output or profit related bonuses), but to profits. Thus, there is a further parallel with Knight's (1921) explanation of the origin of profit in terms of uncertainty.

36. Alchian and Demsetz, 1972, p. 794.

37. Loasby, 1976, p. 5; Hodgson, 1988, pp. 10–12.

38. It should be stressed that, contrary to the more common interpretation, emphasis on the concept of uncertainty does not necessarily lead to a subjectivist outlook regarding individual knowledge and the springs of action. In contrast, as Tony Lawson (1985) has argued, there is a view in Keynes's own writings that stresses the function of social conventions in providing a basis upon which to form expectations of the future and to act accordingly. We cope with uncertainty not simply on the basis of our own subjective resources, but with conscious or habitual recourse to the rules and conventions with which we interact. Thus, as suggested elsewhere (Hodgson, 1988), the introduction of the concept of true uncertainty makes possible an alternative line of theoretical development along institutionalist lines. The argument, in short, is that in a world of uncertainty, where the probabilistic calculus is ruled out, rules, norms, and institutions play a functional role in providing a basis for decision making, expectation, and belief. Without these "rigidi-

ties,'' without social routine and habit to reproduce them, and without institutionally conditioned conceptual frameworks, an uncertain world would present a chaos of sense-data in which it would be impossible for the agent to make sensible decisions and to act. See also Heiner (1983).

References

Ackoff, R. L. and F. E. Emery. (1972) *On Purposeful Systems*. London: Tavistock.

Alchian, A. A. and H. Demsetz. (1972) ''Production, Information Costs, and Economic Organization.'' *American Economic Review*, 62, 4:777–95. Reprinted in Putterman (1986).

Batt, F. R. (1929) *The Law of Master and Servant*. New York: Pitman Publishing.

Bowles, S. (1985) ''The Production Process in a Competitive Economy: Walrasian, Neo-Hobbesian, and Marxian Models.'' *American Economic Review*, 75, 1 (March):16–36. Reprinted in Putterman (1986).

Bowles, S., D. M. Gordon, and T. E. Weisskopf. (1984) *Beyond the Waste Land: A Democratic Alternative to Economic Decline*. New York: Anchor.

Braverman, H. (1974) *Labor and Monopoly Capital: The Degradation of Work in the Twentieth Century*. New York: Monthly Review Press.

Bukharin, N. (1972) *The Economic Theory of the Leisure Class*. New York: Monthly Review Press.

Clower, R. W. (1976) Letter to Joan Robinson. Quoted in Robinson (1979, p. 6).

Coase, R. H. (1937) ''The Nature of the Firm.'' *Economica*, 4 (November):386–405. Reprinted in Putterman (1986).

Dahlman, C. J. (1979) ''The Problem of Externality.'' *Journal of Law and Economics*, 22, 1 (April):141–62.

Edwards, R. (1979) *Contested Terrain: The Transformation of the Workplace in the Twentieth Century*. New York: Basic Books.

Elster, J. (1983) *Explaining Technical Change*. Cambridge: Cambridge University Press.

Furubotn, E. G. and S. Pejovich, eds. (1974) *The Economics of Property Rights*. Cambridge, Mass.: Ballinger.

Gintis, H. (1976) ''The Nature of Labor Exchange and the Theory of Capitalist Production.'' *Review of Radical Political Economics*, 8 (Summer):36–54.

Gleick, J. (1988) *Chaos: Making a New Science*. London: Heinemann.

Gram, H. and V. Walsh. (1983) ''Joan Robinson's Economics in Retrospect.'' *Journal of Economic Literature*, 21, 2 (June):518–50.

Guth, A., ed. (1983) *Asymptotic Realms of Physics*. Cambridge, Mass.: MIT Press.

Heiner, R. A. (1983) ''The Origin of Predictable Behavior.'' *American Economic Review*, 73, 4:560–95.

Hirshleifer, J. (1970) *Investment, Interest and Capital*. Englewood Cliffs, N.J.: Prentice-Hall.

Hodgson, G. M. (1982) *Capitalism, Value and Exploitation: A Radical Theory*. Oxford: Martin Robertson.

———. (1988) *Economics and Institutions: A Manifesto for a Modern Institutional Economics*. Philadelphia: University of Pennsylvania Press.

Kay, N. M. (1984) *The Emergent Firm: Knowledge, Ignorance and Surprise in Economic Organization*. London: Macmillan.

Kenway, P. (1980) ''Marx, Keynes and the Possibility of Crisis.'' *Cambridge Journal of Economics*, 4, 1 (March):23–36.

Keynes, J. M. (1936) *The General Theory of Employment, Interest and Money*. London: Macmillan.

———. (1937) "The General Theory of Employment." *Quarterly Journal of Economics*, 51:209–23
Knight, F. (1921) *Risk, Uncertainty and Profit*. New York: Houghton Mifflin.
Langlois, R. N. (1984) "Internal Organization in a Dynamic Context: Some Theoretical Considerations." In M. Jussawalla and H. Ebenfield, eds., *Communication and Information Economics: New Perspectives*, pp. 23–49. Amsterdam: North-Holland.
Lawson, A. (1985) "Uncertainty and Economic Analysis." *Economic Journal*, 95, 4 (December):909–27.
———. (1988) "Probability and Uncertainty in Economic Analysis." *Journal of Post Keynesian Economics*, 11, 1 (Fall):38–65.
Leibenstein, H. (1976) *Beyond Economic Man: A New Foundation for Microeconomics*. Cambridge, Mass.: Harvard University Press.
Littler, C. R. and G. Salaman. (1982) "Bravermania and Beyond: Recent Theories of the Labour Process." *Sociology*, 16, 2 (May):251–69.
Loasby, B. J. (1976) *Choice, Complexity and Ignorance: An Enquiry into Economic Theory and the Practice of Decision Making*. Cambridge: Cambridge University Press.
Marx, K. (1969) *Theories of Surplus Value—Part Two*. London: Lawrence and Wishart.
———. (1972) *Theories of Surplus Value—Part Three*. London: Lawrence and Wishart.
———. (1973) *Grundrisse*. Harmondsworth: Penguin.
———. (1976) *Capital*, vol. 1. Harmondsworth: Penguin.
———. (1981) *Capital*, vol. 3. Harmondsworth: Penguin.
Mises, L. von. (1949) *Human Action: A Treatise on Economics*. London: William Hodge.
Nichols, T., ed. (1980) *Capital and Labour: A Marxist Primer*. Glasgow: Fontana.
Nutzinger, H. G. (1976) "The Firm as a Social Institution: The Failure of the Contractarian Viewpoint." *Economic Analysis and Workers' Management*, 10:217–37.
Putterman, L., ed. (1986) *The Economic Nature of the Firm: A Reader*. Cambridge: Cambridge University Press.
Robinson, J. (1942) *An Essay on Marxian Economics*. London: Macmillan.
———. (1960) *Collected Economic Papers*, vol. 2. Oxford: Basil Blackwell.
———. (1965) *Collected Economic Papers*, vol. 3. Oxford: Basil Blackwell.
———. (1969) *The Accumulation of Capital*, 3d ed. London: Macmillan.
———. (1973) *Collected Economic Papers*, vol. 4. Oxford: Basil Blackwell.
———. (1979) *Collected Economic Papers*, vol. 5. Oxford: Basil Blackwell.
Rowthorn, R. E. (1973) "Vulgar Economy: Part I." *Bulletin of the Conference of Socialist Economists* (Spring):1–11. Reprinted in Rowthorn (1980, chap. 1).
———. (1980) *Capitalism, Conflict and Inflation: Essays in Political Economy*. London: Lawrence and Wishart.
Shackle, G. L. S. (1972) *Epistemics and Economics: A Critique of Economic Doctrines*. Cambridge: Cambridge University Press.
Shapiro, C. and J. E. Stiglitz. (1984) "Equilibrium Unemployment as a Worker Discipline Device." *American Economic Review*, 74, 3 (June):433–44.
Simon, H. A. (1951) "A Formal Theory of the Employment Relationship." *Econometrica*, 19 (July):293–305. Reprinted in Simon (1957) and Putterman (1986).
———. (1957) *Models of Man: Social and Rational*. New York: Wiley.
Steedman, I. (1982) "Marx on Ricardo." In I. Bradley and M. Howard, eds., *Classical and Marxian Political Economy: Essays in Honour of Ronald L. Meek*, pp. 115–56. London: Macmillan.
Stewart, I. (1989) *Does God Play Dice? The Mathematics of Chaos*. Oxford: Basil Blackwell.
Stigler, G. J. (1961) "The Economics of Information." *Journal of Political Economy*, 69, 2 (June):213–25.

Stiglitz, J. E. (1987) "The Causes and Consequences of the Dependence of Quality on Price." *Journal of Economic Literature*, 25, 1 (March):1–48.

Thompson, P. (1983) *The Nature of Work: An Introduction to Debates on the Labour Process*. London: Macmillan.

Tomlinson, J. (1986) "Democracy Inside the Black Box? Neo-Classical Theories of the Firm and Industrial Democracy." *Economy and Society*, 15, 2 (May):220–50.

Williamson, O. E. (1975) *Markets and Hierarchies: Analysis and Anti-Trust Implications*. New York: Free Press.

———. (1985) *The Economic Institutions of Capitalism: Firms, Markets, Relational Contracting*. London: Macmillan.

Zimbalist, A., ed. (1979) *Case Studies on the Labor Process*. London: Monthly Review Press.

JR

CHAPTER THIRTEEN

Joan Robinson's Post-Keynesianism

OMAR F. HAMOUDA

Joan Robinson is the scholar who should be most credited for attempting to bring together three strands of economic thinking: (i) the Marshall-Keynes, (ii) the Marx-Ricardo-Sraffa, and (iii) the Marx-Kalecki traditions[1] under the umbrella of post-Keynesian economics. As a former Keynes student who collaborated in the making of the *General Theory*, as well as having been a close friend of Kalecki and Sraffa from the day each arrived in Cambridge until his passing, Joan Robinson was most qualified to pull together contributions from all three to provide a general theoretical premise from which post-Keynesian economists could build.

Joan Robinson was very much aware of the conflicting political implications of the economics of Keynes, Kalecki, Sraffa, and their predecessors. Her attitude toward theory was that, "no economic theory gives us ready-made answers. Any theory that we follow blindly will lead us astray. To make good use of an economic theory we must first sort out the relations of the propagandist and the scientific elements in it, then by checking with experience, see how far the scientific element appears convincing, and finally recombine it with our own political views."[2] She criticized those economists who, in the name of science, abuse symbols and statistics to make their theories more aesthetic than meaningful. She believed that, "Not all economic concepts can be reduced to strictly quantitative terms. To treat something that is in principle unmeasurable as though it were a quantity is a confusion of thought pretending to be scientifically precise."[3]

It has been argued in Hamouda and Harcourt (1988) that there is no unified post-Keynesian general theory acceptable to all, but instead only fragmented pieces that, though each may be coherent on its own, cannot be integrated into a more general framework. This is hardly surprising; post-Keynesians are a heterogeneous group of economists with different ideologies and backgrounds. An eclectic and critical thinker, Joan Robinson has been one of the most vocal and dominant figures among post-Keynesian economists and the one who most actively attempted to provide a fully coherent, synthetic way of thinking in economics.

In the present chapter Joan Robinson's conception of post-Keynesian economics is discussed in the following manner: First, her framework for post-Keynesian economics is presented followed by an account of her assessment of Keynes, Kalecki, and Sraffa, then the issue of short-period and long-period analysis, controversial among post-Keynesians, is discussed.

Joan Robinson's Framework for Post-Keynesian Economics

Joan Robinson did not consider economics as the evolutionary outcome of the thinking of successive authors, but as an ongoing theoretical process that, while focused by the pragmatic issues of the time, draws on writers of different periods to address its timely questions. For her contemporaries, those who postdate Keynes, she felt that the issues at hand demanded that they reach, with Keynes in mind, "back to clasp the hands of Ricardo and Marx, skipping over the sixty years of dominance of neoclassical doctrines from 1870 to the great slump."[4] Many of the first post-Keynesians were to see this as an undesirable and impossible task, although Joan Robinson fought hard to argue that, despite their incompatibilities, differing theories from disparate periods do not preclude a possible synthesis of ideas. For her there was to exist "the paradox that post-Keynesian analysis derives equally from two such apparent incompatible sources as Piero Sraffa's interpretation of Ricardo and Michal Kalecki's interpretation of the theory of employment."[5] She saw such sources as inspiration, able to be improved, and certainly none as the divine truth.

Joan Robinson was to draw from both the theory of effective demand and the classical theories of value and distribution to formulate her pioneering understanding of post-Keynesianism. The aspect of these two theories that most attracted her attention was the exclusive importance each attributed to short-period or long-period analysis. The central aim of classical economists, as argued in Hamouda and Harcourt, was to explain the long-period characteristics of the economy, in the form of natural prices of commodities and natural rates of wages, profits and rents, seen as determined by dominant and persistent forces.[6] The theory of effective demand was, on the other hand, an analysis of the economic short period, introduced by Keynes and Kalecki to explain the mechanism of underemployment equilibrium. Distinguished in Joan Robinson's words, "The theory of short-period fluctuations in effective demand, opened up by Mr. Keynes's *General Theory*, has already made great progress. Marx was mainly concerned with long-run dynamic analysis."[7]

Recognizing the weaknesses in the exclusive use of either type of period analysis, Joan Robinson felt strongly that, "It is therefore necessary to supplement the long-period theory by an analysis of the short-period situation, in which the process of accumulation is going on."[8] She tried to extend Keynes to Ricardo and Marx by arguing that "Keynes was clearing up a particular element in it (effective demand) that Ricardo had ignored and Marx imperfectly understood.

This explains the apparent paradox that the post-Keynesians in Cambridge find an affinity with the classics.''[9] Furthermore, she believed that the affinity between Keynes and Marx was revealed through Kalecki's interpretation of effective demand. Thus, she saw, ''the main lines of the *General Theory* are identical with the analysis that Michal Kalecki erected on the basis of Marx's schema of expanded reproduction.''[10]

To combat the weaknesses of each type of period analysis, Joan Robinson recommended adopting what she perceived to be the particular strengths of each theory: ''The function of the theory of effective demand, in a Marxian setting, is to provide *an account of the realization of surplus value*, which Marx left rather vague. *The theory of prices* in Kalecki's version of the General Theory is more up-to-date than Keynes's. *The monetary aspect* is much more fully developed by Keynes, but there is a weak point in his treatment of it.''[11] Elsewhere, she urged that ''The post-Keynesians must make use of Sraffa to build up a type of long-period analysis which will prevent neoclassical equilibrium from oozing back into the General Theory.''[12]

Selectively critical of all preceding economic theories, Joan Robinson grew to give tremendous emphasis to the role of time in economics, an emphasis that became a trademark of the post-Keynesian school. ''To me,'' she wrote, ''the expression *post-Keynesian* has a definite meaning; it applies to an economic theory or method of analysis which takes account of the difference between the future and the past.''[12] This emphasis on time showed itself in her insistence on the economist's awareness that economic events take place at certain points in time, that they are issues of that time, and that they must be considered within the circumstances in which they occur. For Joan Robinson, economic theories are developed as appropriate to particular situations. She believed that there can be no general economic laws that are true for all time and every place, for while the past is determined and recorded, the future, yet to come, remains undetermined and uncertain.

> The post-Keynesians' system dwells in historical time; it is designed to analyse the consequences that may be expected to follow a change taking place at a particular date in particular circumstances. The system is set up like an artist's mobile. A flick on any point sets everything in motion, but it is possible to see which are the principal interactions and which way causation runs from one to another.

Further, Joan Robinson believed that since the economist is faced with the analysis of dynamic processes of events that are continuously happening and change that is constantly occurring, a theory of equilibrium is inappropriate: ''Short-period theory, showing how utilization of given productive capacity varies with effective demand, is already well developed (in the Cambridge tradition). This can be grafted onto the analysis of development once we have thrown off the incubus of equilibrium and can treat economic theory as an adjunct to the study of history as it unfolds.''[15]

Joan Robinson was aware of the enormous difficulties not only in bringing the contributions of Keynes, Kalecki, Sraffa, and their predecessors together, but also, while maintaining the emphasis on time, in trying to adapt and extend their theories to tackle contemporary economic problems. Thus, she wrote, "Post-Keynesian theory has plenty of problems to work on. We now have a general framework of long- and short-period analysis which will enable us to bring the insights of Marx, Keynes and Kalecki into a coherent form and apply them to the contemporary scene, but there is still a long way to go."[16] Since post-Keynesians draw especially from Keynes, Kalecki, and Sraffa, in the next section follows a discussion of Joan Robinson's perception of the contributions of each.

Joan Robinson on Keynes, Kalecki, and Sraffa

It can hardly be said that all the aspects of the theories of Keynes, Kalecki, and Sraffa are compatible one with another. According to Joan Robinson, however, there are elements in all three theories that can be amalgamated. Even if Joan Robinson's main objective, at least for a considerable part of the postwar period, was to combine Keynes's analysis of effective demand with that of Kalecki in order to provide a short period theory of fluctuations and distribution and to relate this new theory to Sraffa's theory of value, her general interests were nonetheless broad enough to find her critical or accepting of many different parts of Keynes, Kalecki, and Sraffa. In this section an idea of the direction she suggested for a general amalgamation of their contributions is explored. To get an understanding of what Joan Robinson's position was, it is helpful to recall what she thought the essential ideas in Keynes, Kalecki, and Sraffa are, and then to identify such common denominators as she perceived in them.

Keynes's General Theory

Not surprisingly, Keynes's theory plays a crucial role in Joan Robinson's conception of the whole of post-Keynesian economics: "The most obvious application of post-Keynesian analysis (the behaviour of an economy in conditions of uncertainty) is to Keynes's own problems—investment decisions, the determination of the pattern and level of interest rates and the evolution of the general price level—but it is equally necessary to apply it to so-called micro economics and the behaviour of markets."[17] Joan Robinson realized, of course, that earlier theories proposing aspects of either an extremely controlled or an extremely unbridled economy were met with highly conditional appreciation by Keynes. He was, in particular, critical of his predecessor Ricardo for at least two reasons: Keynes rejected a Ricardian mainstay, Say's law, and he objected to the manner in which he thought Ricardo's theory treated money. He came to reject the view that monetary factors and real factors do not interrelate. He was also critical of Marx, not convinced that capitalism either would be, or needed to be, destroyed.

Though not enamoured with "laissez-faire" behavior in the market economy, Keynes nonetheless believed that with the application of rational policies, capitalist economies could be made self-sustaining, tolerable places in which to live. Joan Robinson pointed out that "though Keynes himself rejected Ricardo and disapproved of Marx," his theory often linked up with those classic economists;[18] she argued that there are parallels between Keynes's theory of effective demand and Marx's schema of expanded reproduction as developed by Kalecki.[19] As will be further illustrated below, despite her admiration for Keynes's theory, Joan Robinson found Kalecki's to be the more complete of the two.

From the point of view of macroeconomic analysis, Keynes's monetary theory of production is built around the notion of effective demand, where demand is analyzed in terms of investment and saving behavior and expectations play an important role. According to Keynes, investment and saving are the result of independent decisions. Investment as decided by entrepreneurs is seen to be the driving force. Joan Robinson thought that while Keynes exaggerated the influence of the rate of interest, the principles of a capitalist economy's instability are well described in his *General Theory:*

> Keynes points out that in a developed capitalist economy the two sides of accumulation are not automatically connected. Saving means spending less on consumption and narrowing the market for commodities, so that it reduces the profitability of investment. Investment means employing labour to produce goods which are not available to be consumed and so increases demand relatively to supply. The two sides of the process of accumulation are not linked together in such a way as to keep them in harmony. On the contrary, the very nature of private enterprise causes them to have a chronic tendency to get out of gear.[20]

Keynes attempted to formulate the macroeconomic implications of the fact that it takes *time* to plan, produce, sell, then consume, so that what is desired at one point in time is not necessarily realized at another. That is to say, he was concerned to theorize systematically about the effects of uncertainty on the behavior of the economic system. The element of time is indeed well encapsulated in his theory and as Joan Robinson astutely pointed out:

> "It is generally recognized," he [Keynes] wrote "that the Ricardian analysis was concerned with what we now call long-period equilibrium." It is characteristic of a position of equilibrium that it is fulfilling expectations (as to prices, flows of output, profits, etc.) which were held in the past and is therefore recreating expectations that will be fulfilled in the future. In reality, this situation is never realized. "Thus the fact that our knowledge of the future is fluctuating, vague and uncertain, renders wealth a peculiarly unsuitable subject for the methods of the classical economic theory."[21]

This is in fact the criticism she consistently made as well of Sraffa and the neo-Ricardians.

Joan Robinson saw some particular deficiencies in Keynes's microeconomic theory and she criticised his similarity with aspects of Marshall's microeconomics. Although Keynes's theoretical attacks were often directed against Marshall and Pigou, he had indeed inherited Marshall's method of approach. He used supply and demand curves in his theory of prices and marginal analysis in his theory of investment. Similarly, there are elements of marginal choice and Marshallian reasonable behavior in his analysis of consumption and saving.

Joan Robinson seems, however, not to have recognized an independent, non-Marshallian early contribution that Keynes made to the theory of prices. Kahn (among others) emphasized that, in Keynes, money-wages are indeed an important determinant of the overall price level. More importantly, there is in the *Treatise* a theory of sectorial prices that became one of the great liberating factors for Keynes's own development, as he realized there was no need for the quantity theory of money to determine the overall price level. By the time he came to the *General Theory*, this liberation from the quantity theory allowed Keynes to see how the old-fashioned Marshallian theory of value could be adapted to his theory of how the economy operated as a whole. In the *General Theory* prices are partly governed by "marginal cost" and partly by the "scale of output."[22] Furthermore, as Lerner stated it, "the cost incurred in the production of any commodity constitutes the income out of which comes the demand for all the other commodities."[23] Hence for Keynes, individual prices are related to cost, income, and demand. It is the wage-unit that plays the role of numeraire and measure of value. In the *Treatise*, Keynes seemed to have conceived a hybrid theory of prices. He used the classical idea that the cost of factors of production determines prices, but in addition he managed somehow to introduce demand in a very peculiar way. Any possible link between the theories of prices in his two major works seems to have escaped Joan Robinson's attention. In fact, the subject is yet to be discussed fully. Did Keynes himself feel that his theory in the *General Theory* made his theory in the *Treatise* redundant?

Joan Robinson was primarily preoccupied with Keynes's theory of prices found in the *General Theory* and she insisted that:

> Neither Roy Harrod nor I could get Maynard to take an interest in "marginal revenue." He therefore had to find an explanation of the obvious fact that prices do not immediately fall to the level of average prime cost whenever sales are below full capacity output. This was the point of "user cost." The modern concept of gross profit margins as a mark-up on prime cost would really have suited him much better. Second, following Marshall's notion of "cost at the margin," he took it for granted that there is a tendency for prices to rise somewhat with an upswing in activity and to fall in a recession, when money-wage rates do not change.[24]

In the *General Theory,* Keynes "generally dealt with a rise in incomes overall without much emphasis on distribution."[25] Joan Robinson's objections to

Keynes's theory of prices and his lack of attention to the question of income distribution made her prefer Kalecki's approach to the treatment of effective demand in which both prices and distribution of income were to her mind more adequately considered.

Kalecki's Theory of Effective Demand and Distribution

To develop an analysis of effective demand, Kalecki began with Marx's idea of the class struggle in the dynamic process of a capitalist economy. Marxist schemes of reproduction were his starting idea. While he retained the division, workers-capitalist, his analysis abstracted altogether from the classical and Marxian theory of value. Kalecki provided a relatively simple theory of prices; according to Joan Robinson, "he divided the price system into two parts. In the trade in raw materials, supply and demand rules. In manufacturing industry, prices are set by producer; the profit margin . . . depends upon the 'degree of monopoly' in the market."[26] For Kalecki, individual prices in the manufacturing industry are determined by their corresponding unit cost of production to which a mark-up is added to secure a certain level of profit; prices are expressed in money terms. However, Kalecki's theory of prices is incomplete. While it is easy to compute the unit cost of production of any commodity, the precise determination of the size of the mark-up remains theoretically a puzzle. Kalecki himself admitted that his essential concept of degree of monopoly was vague and that he really succeeded in providing only a workable theory of the degree of monopoly. He illustrated its workability by measuring the mark-up empirically from observed facts.

Satisfied with Kalecki's short-period approach to price theory, Joan Robinson nonetheless had her reservations: "Kalecki at first advanced his theory in strictly short-period terms. . . . I objected that there must be some long-period element in the relation of price to costs. . . . [He admitted some] long-period influence on the formation of prices but it was not well integrated into the short-period analysis."[27] All in all she welcomed Kalecki's theory because, "The importance of Kalecki's line of argument was in integrating the analysis of prices with the analysis of effective demand."[28]

Kalecki regarded Marx's theory of exploitation, whereby the source of profit is surplus labor as reflected in surplus value, as determining the constraints at any moment of time of what the real wage rate and the overall rate of profits could be.[29] Adopting those constraints in his own theory of effective demand, combined with his theory of pricing and distribution (where the different saving behavior of wage earners and profit receivers was crucial), Kalecki could determine the rate of profits, the real wage, and overall activity. As in Keynes, investment spending is the primary cause. In Kalecki's theory, while expected profits provide a major incentive for investment, "actual investment is the principal creator of actual profits, which in turn are a major determinant of the ability to invest. Both equilibrium activity and distribution are determined by the equality of saving and investment.''[30]

Joan Robinson accepted Kalecki's theory of distribution as the post Keynesian theory of relative share. She wrote:

> Kalecki showed that, in a simple two class society in which workers spend all their wages currently as they are received, the flow of gross profit per annum is equal to the value of gross investment plus capitalists' consumption. . . . The short-period level of effective demand is then in balance with the long-period situation when all equipment throughout industry is being utilized at its standard ratio and prices have been set at the level at which the corresponding outputs can be sold. This is not a position of equilibrium, for if effective demand happened to move away, there is nothing to bring it back to the point of balance.[31]

Keynes and Kalecki

Keynes and Kalecki shared many common elements in their short-period analysis of effective demand. Investment is the driving force in both their models. Both conceive production dynamics in a similar way: time to plan, to realize, and to operationalize investment is the major factor in entrepreneurs' decisions to produce and to provide employment; in between decisions, adjustments are continuously taking place. While fond of both Keynes's and Kalecki's theories, Joan Robinson saw Kalecki's as the superior analysis, in which the aspects of Keynes's treatment of effective demand that she identified as defects were avoided. She believed that ''Kalecki gets Keynes back onto the rails where his 'classical' education had led him astray.''[32] For a number of contributions she quite explicitly appreciated the refinements or emphases of Kalecki over Keynes:

• Specifically, in his contribution to the theory of consumption, Kalecki took social relations into consideration while Keynes had not. Keynes simply ''relies upon a psychological law that men are disposed to increase their consumption as their income increases,'' while Kalecki ''separates the 'men' into workers and capitalists and incomes into wages, which will be fully spent as they are received, and profits, of which a proportion will be handed over to rentiers and partly spent by them.''[33]

• A further point of her preference of Kalecki over Keynes relates to the theory of saving and investment: Keynes was concerned about ''the proposition that 'savings equals investment,' over which we made very heavy weather in the early stages of the Keynesian revolution. Kalecki simply asserts that a rise in the rate of investment will increase the flow of wages, which will be spent, and if the accompanying rise in profits causes an increase in spending out of dividends, profits will rise by so much the more.''[34] Joan Robinson felt that the ''distinction between investment and investment decisions enabled Kalecki to clear up the confusion in Keynes's treatment of the inducement to invest.''[35]

• Joan Robinson also appreciated Kalecki's understanding of the role of government and international trade in the theory of effective demand: "Kalecki brings back the budget, the foreign balance and intermediate incomes which combine earning and saving. This provides all the essential elements of the theory of effective demand."[36]

• Kalecki's emphasis on the role of finance in investment also appealed to Joan Robinson: "The monetary aspect of the theory was much more fully elaborated by Keynes, but Kalecki was the first to emphasize that finance has to be available before investment begins, while saving comes afterwards."[37]

• Joan Robinson heralded Kalecki's contribution to the theory of market: While Keynes relied on a kind of Marshallian competition, "Kalecki was able to weave the analysis of imperfect competition and of effective demand together and it was this that opened up the way for what goes under the name of post-Keynesian economic theory."[38]

• All in all she also favored Kalecki's contribution to the trade cycle over Keynes's: "Kalecki did not approach the theory of employment through the multiplier, which makes his version in a way less rich than Keynes's, though no less forceful. On the other hand he went straight to a theory of the trade cycle, on which Keynes was very weak." "Kalecki provided the first coherent model of the mechanism of a self-repeating trade cycle. . . . Kalecki later gave up the search for a 'pure' trade cycle and sought for an analysis combining fluctuations in activity with accumulation over the long run."[39]

It is thus clear that despite the great affinity between Keynes and Kalecki in their short-period effective demand theories and the policy implications, Joan Robinson distinguished sharply between the two and chose Kalecki's theoretical approach to the study of output prices and distribution. To most interpreters, however, Keynes's and Kalecki's theories, on the one hand, and that of Sraffa, on the other, cannot be said to share the same degree of affinity. Joan Robinson herself recalled that Sraffa's "book was not published until 1960. Sraffa had shown a draft to Keynes in 1928. Keynes evidently did not make much of it and Sraffa, in turn, never made much of the *General Theory*. It is the task of post-Keynesians to reconcile the two."[40] Joan Robinson was harshly critical of the equilibrium method that Sraffa used. She nonetheless praised his effectiveness in "knocking down" neoclassical economics and made an effort to make Sraffa appealing to her brand of post-Keynesianism by introducing time into his theory.

Sraffa's "Production of Commodities by Means of Commodities"

Sraffa was Ricardian, without accepting Say's law, and Marxist, while rarely referring explicitly to Marx's theory.[41] Sraffa attempted to reestablish the approach to economic analysis of the concept of the surplus of commodities over the necessities required for their production. This approach was originally to be found both in the classical political economists and in Marx.

Among Sraffa's contributions to the modern rebuilding of classical analysis were the coherence he gave to the core concept of surplus and the correspondence he attributed to share of wages and rate of profits; as Joan Robinson summed it, "Sraffa set up a multi-commodity input-output system and showed that, corresponding to any share of wages, there is a particular pattern of normal prices that yields a particular uniform rate of profit on capital valued at those prices."[42] Further, Sraffa directed his attention to some unsolved problems in Ricardo and Marx, for example, the invariance standard of value and the transformation problem, respectively. As Joan Robinson put it, "Sraffa's argument was largely concerned with the construction of a numeraire in physical terms—the standard commodity."[43]

It is well known that the classical labor theory of value, with regard to the issue of the invariance of the standard, is deficient and that Sraffa provided an alternative way of resolving its deficiencies. In the classical theory of value, the price of a commodity is determined by its cost of production, which in turn is expressed in terms of direct and indirect labor. Relative prices, therefore, reflect the corresponding amount of labor necessary to produce them. Prices in Sraffa's theory are still determined by the cost of production, but now they are to be expressed in terms of a composite commodity standard. Theoretically, the relative prices of any two goods will correspond to their cost of production expressed in terms of the composite commodity standard. The ratio of the cost of production of two goods is then interpreted as the relative prices. Sraffa's theory is self-sufficient, since it does not require the use of the marginal productivity principle or an explicit reference to the demand side. Joan Robinson noted that "A model such as that set up by von Neumann or Sraffa does not need to mention money. All relative prices are determined by technical conditions and the rate of profit. Wages can be expressed in physical terms."[44] Sraffa's model does, however, need the assumption of unique rates of profits and wages to determine a particular level of prices.

According to Joan Robinson, Sraffa was "completely successful in his aim of providing a basis for the critique of neoclassical theory but the model in *Production of Commodities by Means of Commodities* (1960) provides a very narrow basis for constructive analysis."[45] It was Sraffa's equilibrium approach that Joan Robinson found limiting: too abstract or "pure," static, entertaining no notion of causality, no concept of class conflict, and no discussion of the realization of surplus, in sum, having little connection with the dynamics of the capitalist economy. Her frustration is evident in much of her writing about Sraffa, as illustrated in the following selection of quotations:

- "Sraffa's model is too pure to make a direct contribution to formulate answerable questions about reality."[46]
- "All this is a purely logical structure—an elaborate thought experiment."[47]
- "But these models are systems of equations expressing equilibrium relationships. They cannot be used to discuss the behaviour of the human beings who inhabit them."[48]

• "In the formal model there is no causality."[49]

• "There is no room here for short-period 'Keynesian' movements in the level of utilization of stocks of inputs or employment of labour."[50]

• Sraffa follows Ricardo in "the determination of distribution from the technical data, leaving no room for class conflict."[51]

• "There is no discussion of the realization of surplus as profit. It is merely taken for granted whatever is produced is disposed of at such prices as to result in a uniform rate of profits in all lines of production."[52]

• Sraffa left "his logical scheme open-ended with one degree of freedom in the system of equations."[53]

• "[T]he determination of the distribution of net output between wages and net profit is left completely open."[54]

• "Sraffa offers long-period analysis in the sense that the stock of means of production for a particular technique is supposed to be always used at its designed capacity."[55]

• "A long-period model cannot be directly confronted with evidence because any actual situation is affected by short-period influences, such as the state of effective demand and the distribution of money income, which occupy the forefront of the picture."[56]

Despite all the reservations Joan Robinson expressed about Sraffa's approach, including her explicit directive that in regard to assuming "correct foresight," "we must abandon Sraffa and descend from purely logical comparisons into historical time,"[57] she was nonetheless very keen to take Sraffa's model and extend it in such a way as to compensate for all the lacks she identified. In 1980 she began, with the collaboration of Amit Bhaduri, to build "a Sraffaesque model, or rather a family of models, including distribution according to Marx and realization according to Kalecki."[58] She also began to integrate time and changes in technology in the new model. Her analysis tells "something about how the share of wages in the value of net output is affected by monopoly power and the pricing policy of corporations, by particular scarcities, by effective demand, by bargaining power and the social and political climate in which it operates; and about the 'inflation barrier' which drives money wages irresistibly upward when real wages are pushed too low."[59] Unfortunately, Joan Robinson did not live long enough to pursue her ideas of post-Keynesian economics along a Sraffean line.

Of the theories of Keynes, Kalecki, and Sraffa, there are a number of elements that they have in common (or at least that any two out of the three share) that are also shared by Joan Robinson. These include the recognition that:

• Capitalist economies are not self-equilibrating at their full employment of either labor or capital. Competition means that capital flows where investors believe that future returns are highest, with investors often making allowance for differential risks, etc., Keynes's and Kalecki's theories are concerned with the temporal analysis of this dynamic process, whereas Sraffa was more interested at an abstract level in the ultimate result of the competition itself. However, neither Keynes, Kalecki, nor Sraffa was concerned with optimizing problems or with *properties* of equilibrium positions.

• A theory of effective demand depends essentially on investors' decisions and actions. Consumers in the model of Keynes and workers in that of Kalecki simply respond passively to the major constraint on their behavior, namely, their income. Sraffa himself never discussed the realization problem.

• A theory of prices is related, to a large extent, to cost of production. It must be said that even though Keynes (in the *Treatise*), Kalecki, and Sraffa all advanced this relationship, their theories are nonetheless conceptually quite different. Sraffa's theory of prices is an analytical device that portrays the notion of "natural price" or a price of production consistent with the idea of long-run tendencies. Keynes (in the *General Theory*) and Kalecki provided a concept of price associated with short run, a "market price." Keynes included enough ingredients in the *Treatise* to build a hybrid theory in which both market and normal prices could be integrated. All these theories—Keynes's, Kalecki's, and Sraffa's—thus have imbedded in them a time dimension of short and/or long period. Given the alternatives on this point, Joan Robinson seems to have opted for Kalecki's theory.

The Issue of Short Period and Long Period

In the post-Keynesian literature (as is true of all economic literature), the terms short period and long period are often used by different authors to mean different things. Some post-Keynesians understand short period and long period in a temporal sense, while for others these notions are conceptualized as analytical devices. Joan Robinson certainly subscribed to the former and became increasingly critical of theories conceived in an ahistorical framework.

Establishing Definition

Joan Robinson was very much concerned with the temporal dimension of her theory. She conceptualized the short period as a lapse of historical time during which a succession of events takes place. An important property of such a concept is that of the asymmetry between the known past and the unknown future. The known past consists of events that have already occurred and have been recorded as facts. The future consists of unknown expected events that have not yet happened and are subject to speculation because of uncertainty about what is to come. The distinction between past and future in this context is crucial to the understanding of facts, and information based on expected judgment is combined to explain the behavior of economic agents in their decisions to produce, consume, save, invest, etc. Since individuals' decisions are based on limited information, incomplete knowledge, and expectations about future scenarios, and since there are also conflicting interests among various economic groups, the macro outcome of such dynamic behavior is extremely complex to describe and analyze in the short period, let alone in the long period. The long period in the temporal sense is simply understood as a succession of short periods. This explains why post-Keynesians who are concerned with dynamics emphasize short-period analysis and consider the long-period outcome to be simply the consequence of the outcomes of successive short periods. Joan Robinson also came increasingly to argue that this was the correct way forward, though in her *magnum opus*, *The Accumulation of Capital*, she did not give as much emphasis to the short period and its issues as she was later to think appropriate.

Neo-Ricardians in particular (following the classical argument) believe that there are sustained and persistent forces in the capitalist economy that can be studied independently of short-period fluctuations, which are mostly the result of temporary, spasmodic, or once-and-for-all occurrences. These disturbances are considered momentary and of secondary importance. The dynamics of a capitalist economy are primarily generated by the desire to accumulate capital. It is well known, at least since Adam Smith, that capital tends to flow where the expected return is the highest (allowing for differential risk). Competition among suppliers and users of funds and equipment creates a condition in which the various rates of profit tend to equalize. Production and distribution are studied under the assumption that it is "as if" competition has fully worked itself out, which implies unique rates of profit and wages. The long period in this context is the abstract lapse of time required for the system to reach the ultimate position after the economic forces have been allowed to work themselves out fully. This tendency is not understood as an equilibrium state that lasts forever. While economic forces are always tending to drive the economic system towards a state in which the rates of profits are equalized, the fundamental determinants of the overall level of profits are themselves liable to change. This tendency—this gravitation, as it were, of profits—is happily checked at repeated intervals by the improvements in machinery, as well as by discoveries.[60] Neo-Ricardians are primarily concerned with the study of such a tendency. Long-period analysis is, according to them, indispensable if we are to have a meaningful theory of value, output, and distribution.

Defining Priorities

Joan Robinson did not succeed in rallying all post-Keynesians either behind her definitions of short and long period or behind her conception of their roles in economic analysis. Heedless of her, post-Keynesians have set individual priorities and embarked on two distinct research programs. Some are concerned with a study of economic activity that accounts for fluctuations in the level of output and investment, which in turn have an impact on income distribution, growth, and capital accumulation. Others are more interested in analyzing the impact on the level of output and income distribution of fundamental time independent trends inherent in a capitalist economy. The former are satisfied with a period-by-period analysis but this is not satisfactory to the latter group whose aim is to provide a determinate method.

Is post-Keynesian economics in fact amenable to a general theory capable of integrating both short- and long-period analysis? For Joan Robinson the answer is "yes," but her way of answering the question remains controversial among post-Keynesians for two reasons. The first reflects economists' priorities regarding one period over the other, thereby leading to the dominance of short or long period in the analysis. The second reason is due to the tendency among economists to become partisan and to follow the interpreter whose priority is consistent with their own.

The divisions are multiple. For example, Kregel (1983) believes that in Keynes's short-period analysis there is a complete short-period monetary theory of production. Kregel also saw sufficient ingredients in the *General Theory* and in the *Treatise* for a long-period theory of effective demand in which monetary as well as real factors are integrated and expectations and uncertainty have a role to play. Garegnani (1983), rejecting Kregel's approach, illustrates another path. He suggests starting with Sraffa's long-period theory of value and supplementing it with Keynes's short-period theory of output. To do so, he advocates getting rid of all of Keynes's ideas inherited from neoclassical economics, such as the marginal efficiency of capital, Keynes's treatment of the interest rate, and his marginal analysis.

Joan Robinson herself was not above setting priorities or choosing a favorite interpreter. Early in her career she tilted toward long-period analysis, but as time passed she became increasingly and impatiently an advocate of short-period analysis as the starting point in economics. Undeniably for Joan Robinson, Kalecki's theory was the favored interpretation and the catalyst for her own analysis. Her choice was very astute, for switching her emphasis to the short rather than the long period could be accommodated within the framework Kalecki provided.

Concluding Remarks

Even though in the very late period of her life she became extremely disillusioned and skeptical as to whether economic theory can be useful at all, Joan Robinson had nonetheless held during her active years, especially in the 1960s and 1970s, that it is essential that post-Keynesians study the theory of economic dynamics. Further, she added that, "Besides its dynamic approach, the hallmark of post-Keynesian theory is that it takes account of the variety of economic systems and aims to show how the same principles work out differently in different social settings."[61] She repeatedly claimed that this premise for research can be adhered to, "provided that we give up the search for grand general laws and are content to try to enquire how things happen."[62]

In one of her last contributions, Joan Robinson laid down what she thought was to be the primary research concern for post-Keynesians:

> [T]he influence of changes in technology on demand for labour, on accumulation and on effective demand—has been very little discussed. This is a serious defect in our theoretical apparatus, for the evolution of technology is the most important of all aspects of capitalist development. A start on the subject was made in the 1950s [Robinson, 1956], but it was smothered with neoclassical putty, while the anti-neoclassicals were distracting themselves with reswitching. Now it is time to take up the challenge afresh.[63]

Despite the fact that Joan Robinson did not succeed in bringing together all post-Keynesians, she left a legacy whose pieces are proving to inspire one brand of post-Keynesian economics among those who wish to pursue the expansion of economics in the Cambridge tradition.

Notes

I would like to thank Ingrid Rima who encouraged me to write this paper and Betsey Price, Harald Hagemann, and Philip Arestis for their useful and inspiring comments. A fruitful and long discussion with Geoff Harcourt helped me to clarify many issues regarding Joan Robinson's economics.

1. See Hamouda and Harcourt, 1988.
2. Robinson, 1955, rpt. 1979, p. 75. References to works by Joan Robinson list first, the original years of publication, and second, where applicable, the volume listed in the reference section in which the source may be found.
3. Robinson, 1979, rpt. 1980, p. 60.
4. Robinson, 1979, p. 126.
5. Ibid., p. 126.
6. Hamouda and Harcourt, 1988, p. 4.
7. Robinson, 1942, rpt. 1967, p. 95.
8. Ibid., p. 63.
9. Robinson, 1979, rpt. 1980, p. 59.
10. Robinson, 1975, rpt. 1980, p. 121.
11. Ibid., pp. 121–22, emphasis added.
12. Robinson, 1978, rpt. 1980, p. 82.
13. Robinson, 1980, p. 78.
14. Ibid., p. 16.
15. Ibid., p. xiii.
16. Robinson, 1978, rpt. 1980, p. 85.
17. Robinson, 1979, p. 128.
18. Robinson, 1973, vol. 4, p. 64.
19. Robinson, 1975, rpt. 1980, p. 121.
20. Robinson, 1955, rpt. 1979, pp. 62–63.
21. Robinson, 1978, rpt. 1980, p. 78.
22. Keynes, 1936, pp. 292–307.
23. Lerner, 1939, p. 159.
24. Robinson, 1972, rpt. 1979, p. 173.
25. Ibid., p. 174.

26. Robinson, 1977, rpt. 1979, p. 188.
27. Ibid., p. 189.
28. Ibid., p. 190.
29. See Hamouda and Harcourt, 1988, pp. 16–17.
30. Ibid., p. 13.
31. Robinson, 1978, rpt. 1980, p. 82.
32. Robinson, 1977, rpt. 1979, p. 195.
33. Ibid., p. 191.
34. Ibid., p. 191.
35. Ibid., pp. 193–94.
36. Ibid., p. 191.
37. Ibid., 1979, p. 192.
38. Ibid., p. 193.
39. Ibid., p. 193.
40. Robinson, 1978, rpt. 1980, p. 81.
41. See Hamouda and Harcourt, 1988, pp. 12 and 14.
42. Robinson, 1979, rpt. 1980, p. 81.
43. Robinson, 1980, p. 68.
44. Robinson, 1971, rpt. 1973, p. 72, n. 8.
45. Robinson, 1980, p. 64.
46. Ibid., p. xii.
47. Ibid., p. 132.
48. Robinson, 1971, rpt. 1973, p. 72.
49. Robinson, 1980, p. 68.
50. Robinson, 1975, rpt. 1980, p. 132.
51. Robinson, 1980, p. 65.
52. Ibid., p. 64.
53. Ibid., n. 2.
54. Ibid., pp. 64–65.
55. Robinson, 1975, rpt. 1980, p. 131.
56. Robinson, 1979, rpt. 1980, p. 135.
57. Robinson, 1975, rpt. 1980, p. 133.
58. Robinson, 1980, p. 65.
59. Ibid., p. 76.
60. Ricardo, 1951, p. 140.
61. Robinson, 1975, rpt. 1980, p. 106.
62. Robinson, 1980, p. 95.
63. Ibid., 1980, p. 76.

References

Garegnani, P. (1983) "Two Routes to Effective Demand: Comment on Kregel." In J. Kregel, *Value, Distribution and Effective Demand.* Amsterdam: North-Holland.

Hamouda, O. F. and G. C. Harcourt. (1986) *Controversies in Political Economy*, ed. O. F. Hamouda. Brighton: Wheatsheaf Books.

———. (1988) "Post Keynesianism: From Criticism to Coherence?" *Bulletin of Economic Research*, 40, 1:1–33. Reprinted in John Pheby, ed., *New Directions in Post-Keynesian Economics.* Adlershot: Edward Elgar, 1989.

Harcourt, G. C. (1983) "On the Influence of Piero Sraffa on the Contributions of Joan Robinson to Economic Theory." *Economic Journal*, 96:96–108.

Keynes, J. M. (1936) *The General Theory of Employment, Interest and Money.* London: Macmillan.

Lerner, A. (1939) "The Relation of Wage Policies and Price Policies." *American Economic Review*, Supplement, 29 (March):158–68.
Ricardo, D. (1951) *The Principles of Political Economy and Taxation.* Cambridge: Cambridge University Press.
Robinson, Joan. (1937, rpt. 1947) *Essays in the Theory of Employment.* Oxford: Basil Blackwell.
———. (1942, rpt. 1967) *Essays on Marxian Economics.* London: Macmillan.
———. (1959, 1960, 1973, 1979) *Collected Economic Papers*, 5 vols. Oxford: Basil Blackwell.
———. (1971, rpt. 1973) *Economic Heresies.* London: Macmillan.
———. (1978) *Contribution to Modern Economics.* Oxford: Basil Blackwell.
———. (1979) *The Generalisation of the General Theory and Other Essays.* London: Macmillan.
———. (1980) *Further Contributions to Modern Economics.* Oxford: Basil Blackwell.

JR

CHAPTER FOURTEEN

The Quantity Theory and the Mark-up Equation

EDWARD J. NELL

Joan Robinson never thought highly of the Quantity Theory of Money: "The archetypal quantity theory formula MV = PY, like any identity, has to have its terms defined in such a way as to make it hold."[1] She follows with a list of queries as to what the elements of the equation mean, designed to reveal the potential ambiguities. Once we have managed to set it up, however, we are still only halfway to a useful tool of analysis; the next problem is whether causality runs from left to right, as monetarists maintain, or from right to left:

> Suppose that between one year and the next PY rises; either activity has increased—employment and output are higher this year than last, or the general price level has risen because of a rise in costs in money terms; then if the quantity of money has not increased, the velocity of circulation must have risen.[2]

This, Joan says, makes sense. But to read it the other way, to invert the causality, is to take flight from reality: "There is an unearthly, mystical element in Friedman's thought. The mere existence of a stock of money somehow promotes expenditure."[3]

But while she presents a Keynesian case for reading the equation her way, from right to left, Joan never presents specific arguments against reading it the other way. This can be done, however, beginning from some work of Sidney Weintraub, arguing against the monetarist explanation of inflation.

Two Approaches to Inflation

Over the years Weintraub repeatedly contrasted two aggregate equations expressing very different approaches to macroeconomics:

$$\text{The Quantity Equation: } MV = PY \quad (1)$$

$$\text{The Wage-Cost Mark-up: } P = kwN/Y \quad (2)$$

The first holds that, given velocity, V, the supply of money, M, determines the level of nominal income. According to proponents of this approach, real output, Y, will be determined in equilibrium by real forces alone (absolute quantities are determined together with relative prices, which also permits the outputs of different sectors to be aggregated), so the money supply fixes the price level, P, making allowance for temporary exogenous influences.

By contrast, the second equation states that, given labor requirements per unit output, N/Y, the price level, P, stands in a fixed ratio, k, to the money wage rate. Hence, whatever determines money wages—e.g., collective bargaining—fixes the price level.

Both equations explain inflation. Differentiating the first gives:

$$V(dM/dt) = Y(dP/dt) + P(dY/dt)$$

and dividing by Equation 1 yields:

$$dP/P = dM/M - dY/Y \tag{3}$$

Differentiating Equation 2 and dividing yields:

$$dP/P = dw/w - d(Y/N)/(Y/N) \tag{4}$$

Ignoring many obvious qualifications, in the first case, inflation is determined by the excess of the rate of growth of the money supply over the rate of growth of output—the Central Bank is to blame. The policy implication is therefore to control the rate of growth of the money supply, an austerity approach. In the second case, inflation is caused by the pressures that push up money wage rates faster than labor productivity is growing—the trade unions are to blame. The policy called for is one that ties growth in money wages to growth in productivity, an incomes policy.

Of course, causality is a matter of interpretation. Either equation could be true, and yet the causality could run in the opposite direction. For example, the banking system could adapt the money supply to its expectations of the prices leading firms wish to set, so that P or changes in P would determine M or changes in M. Or, in the other case, w, the money wage, might be adjusted to keep up with the expected rises in prices, so the direction of causality would run from P to w. But these are not the ways these equations have normally been understood.

Both equations suffer from faults resulting from aggregation. Neither treats changes in the composition of output or of labor, nor is it always clear what should be included in some of the aggregates, for example, in the money supply, or in the total amount of labor. It is not easy to make unambiguous adjustments to either equation for changes in the degree of utilization. Nevertheless, both equations have been widely used to analyze questions concerning the causes of, and policies toward, inflation.

Weintraub (1959, 1978) has argued for many years that k is a reliable constant over the short and medium term, with only a slight trend in the long run. By contrast, he contended with Joan Robinson that V has shown significant variability. Friedman, and monetarists generally, have held that V is more stable than any competing explanatory parameter, and that, therefore, the quantity equation should be preferred. Kaldor (1970) has argued, however, that V is stable only when and because the money supply itself is adjusting. Friedman (1979) has accepted Kaldor's contention that the money supply is (at least partly) endogenous, but holds that it does not affect the validity of the quantity theory. Recently, Basil Moore (1988) has argued that contemporary economies operate a system of credit money the quantity of which is determined by borrower demand.

An Implication of Endogenous Money

If the money supply is endogenous, however, it can affect the validity of the quantity theory—very dramatically, in fact. To see this, let us take a special but plausible case (Nell, 1983) where banks have agreed to provide lines of credit for business sufficient to cover their working capital needs, up to the full capacity level. (To build a plant a business must negotiate a line of credit to cover working capital needs. Providing its own would mean holding unnecessarily large liquid reserves much of the time, but not to have immediate access to working capital could mean costly delays.) Working capital covers variable costs, the main item of which is the wage bill. So as a first approximation, we can say that the banking system has agreed to advance automatically whatever funds business needs to cover its labor costs. As employment expands and contracts, lines of credit will be activated or reduced, and so bank deposits will fluctuate accordingly. The money supply will vary proportionally with activity. The resulting simple equation is:

$$M = wN \tag{5}$$

But when we combine this with our earlier equations the consequences are striking:

$$\begin{aligned} MV &= PV \\ wNV &= PY \\ P &= V\,(wN/Y) \end{aligned} \qquad\qquad \begin{aligned} P &= k\,(wN/Y) \\ P &= k\,(M/Y) \\ Mk &= PY \end{aligned}$$

Hence it is clear that $V = k$, and that, starting from either equation, the other can be derived. (Notice that this result does not actually depend on the money supply adjusting to demand for working capital. It would follow equally in a situation where banks or holders of wealth sat on a fixed sum, M, which they advanced as a "wages fund," wN, to businesses. Causality would run in the opposite direction, but $V = k$ would still hold.)

When the quantity equation is written in the "Cambridge" or "cash-balances" form,

$$M = (1/V)PY \tag{6}$$

it is clear that $(1/V)$, the proportion of money income the public wishes to hold in money balances, is equal to the share of wages in money income, wN/PY. This follows directly from the fact that business money balances will equal working capital, i.e., the wage bill, and household balances will only rise when business balances fall, that is, when and as wages are paid. When household balances fall as consumer purchases are made, then business balances rise once again, in exactly offsetting measure.

These results do not depend upon an exact equality between the money supply and the wage bill. If, for example, the money supply were *proportional*, rather than equal, to the wage bill:

$$M = xwN \tag{5'}$$

then we would derive

$$P = xV\,(wN/Y) \text{ and } k\,(M/x)Y = P$$

Clearly, $xV = k$. That is, when the money supply is proportional to the wage bill, velocity will be proportional to the mark-up, by the same factor. So the same conclusions follow.

It has to be said that these are surprising results. The velocity of circulation has usually been taken to mean the number of times the stock of money turned over in the course of the transactions making up the period's income, while its reciprocal, the coefficient of the demand for money, has been understood as the average interval of rest between transactions. The length of this interval was held to depend partly on institutional arrangements and partly on decisions determined, in turn, by other economic variables. The connection of such ideas with the mark-up factor is not readily apparent. The average mark-up simply shows the average profit being earned over variable costs, and reflects market pressures interacting with the firms' decisions about their cash flow requirements. But whatever the traditional concept of velocity was supposed to mean, it has always been measured by the ratio of money income to the stock of money. This provides the clue to understanding the connection here. As Joan Robinson repeatedly pointed out, the traditional concept of velocity is little more than a metaphor; no precision has ever been given to it, for no definition has ever been provided to explain just what was to be counted as one round of circulation, that is, when a sum of money should be counted as having returned to its starting point.[4] So what is thought of as a turnover relationship is actually not one: it is simply a proportionality between money income and a sum of money. What it means is undetermined; hence, if we can identify the sum of money with a set of costs—e.g., wage costs—then what we have is the mark-up.

Interest and Prices

Interest must be paid upon lines of credit used to provide working capital. This requires rewriting the matrix equation for prices as a function of the real wage and the rate of profit, to show earnings of profit, equal to interest, upon the wage bill, just as some of the classical economists used to argue.

To illustrate this, let us take a circulating capital system, when the price equation, following Sraffa, will be:

$$p = (1 + r)Ap + \hat{w}L \tag{7}$$

Here p is the relative price vector, r is the rate of profit, A the matrix of circulating inputs, L the labor input vector, and $\hat{w}$ the real wage rate. Assume $\hat{w}$ to be given. To express this equation in money terms, the wage must be paid in money, and then prices must be set at money levels so that the money wage divided by prices will equal the given real wage. This can be seen as follows. First pre-multiply the equation by the relative quantities

$$q'p = (1 + r)q'Ap + \hat{w}q'L \tag{8}$$

Each term of this equation as a real scaler, so we have, in macro terms, $Y = (1 + r)K + \hat{w}N$. Now if we take the wage as paid in money, as above, it can be written in aggregate notation as:

$$PY = (1 + r)PK + wN, \text{ where } \hat{w} = w/p \tag{9}$$

The difference when interest is figured upon the wage bill comes in the last term, which must then be $(1 + r)wN$. The equations are:

$$p = (1 + r)\,[Ap + \hat{w}L] \tag{7'}$$

$$q'p = (1 + r)\,[q'Ap + \hat{w}q'L\,] \tag{8'}$$

$$PY + (1 + r)\,[PK + wN] \tag{9'}$$

Equation 9 enables us to see exactly what k, and therefore V, means. Rearranging, we find:

$$P = Y/(Y - (1 + r)K)\ [wN/Y] \tag{10}$$

from which it follows that:

$$k = Y/(Y - (1 + r)K) = q'p/(q'p - (1 + r)q'Ap) \tag{11}$$

and when interest is earned upon the wage bill, this becomes:

$$k = (1 + r)Y/(Y - (1 + r)K) = (1 + r)q'p/(q'p - (1 + r)q'Ap) \tag{11'}$$

Notice that this last equation, and the earlier ones from which it is derived, imply that endogenous money not only raises the mark-up as compared to a barter world, but also affects relative prices. Endogenous money is not neutral. Even more strikingly, if the average rate of profit and the long-term rate of interest are correlated, Equation 11′ implies that velocity rises with the long-term rate of interest, quite independently of any "economizing" on money balances.

Factors Influencing Velocity and the Mark-up

The preceding equations make it clear that k, and its equivalent V, depend on the rate of profits and relative prices. But money prices do not directly affect k or V if the real wage (the rate of profit) is given, for the money dimension clearly cancels out in Equation 11. But endogenous money raises k and V through the effects of interest in Equation 11′. Further, however, k and so V depend on q', on the quantities of the system. The mark-up depends not only on distribution and prices, but also on the relative sizes of industries and sectors. Thus, for example, a change in the equilibrium rate of growth would be likely to change the velocity of circulation, since it would normally affect q'.

If the money supply is endogenous, any evidence supporting the quantity equation is also *ipso facto* evidence supporting the mark-up equation. Moreover, the reason that velocity is constant is simply that it *is* the mark-up factor, appearing in a different context. Velocity rises with the long-term rate of return because the mark-up does, not as a result of economizing on money holdings. Interpreting the quantity equation as showing the demand for cash balances, we see that household and business balances rise and fall in an exactly offsetting pattern, reflecting the circuit of expenditure. Moreover, the mark-up and therefore velocity reflect not only given distribution, but also the given relative sizes of the different sectors. Hence, neither explanations nor policy conclusions can be derived from the quantity theory, for the quantity equation is simply another way of writing the mark-up equation. Insofar as demand-for-money equations are derived from the quantity theory, they are likewise suspect—even if they are more complex in form, for they may simply be mirroring a more complicated mark-up equation.[5]

But while the mark-up equation used here is valid, though oversimplified, care must be taken in drawing policy conclusions from it, for it *presupposes* both the distribution of income and the pattern of consumption and growth. Policy questions concerning changes in either of these cannot be examined on the basis of a given mark-up, and hence cannot assume a fixed relationship between the real wage and the productivity of labor. As a policy tool, therefore, mark-up theory is more limited than has sometimes been supposed.

The Pattern of Circulation

Now consider the Sraffa model again. Equation 11 gives k for this model, and Equation 11′ gives it for a Marxian variant. A common assumption, actually made by Sraffa, supposes all goods to be traded in an annual market. Let there be a certain stock of money (gold and silver) in such a market, in the hands of merchants. On the first marketing day the entire stock of gold and silver will be swapped for the entire output of goods. Merchants will have goods, and producers money. On the second day, producers will then buy back the goods they need for producing and consuming, thus completing the circuit. Goods will be reallocated for producing and consuming, and the money will be back with the merchants.

Under these conditions the velocity of circulation would clearly be unity, since the stock of money would turn over exactly once. The amount of money would be equal in value to the value of the entire annual output. The value of money would be given by the price of production of gold/silver in marginal mines and the output of mines would be adjusted to keep the quantity of circulating gold/silver equal in value to the aggregate output (given a stable propensity to hoard). Clearly, in this very traditional conception k and V would not have to be equal.

There are at least three good reasons to reject this traditional account. First, it implies a unitary elasticity relationship between output and the price level, unless this were to be mitigated by hoarding and dishoarding. But in such a system, hoarding and dishoarding will tend to exacerbate, rather than mitigate, price movements. (When prices are expected to fall, money will be hoarded; when they are expected to rise, goods will be hoarded.) Second, it requires that all transactions take place at the same time, making it impossible to deal with the fact that some transactions are contingent on others. There is no point in the consumer-goods sector buying replacement means of production until stocks of consumer goods are sold off. This point becomes especially important when we consider systems that produce a surplus. Third, the value of the supply of money must be equal to the total gross output of the system. That is a large investment, and by taking advantage of the fact that some transactions are contingent on others, a significantly smaller supply of money can effectively circulate the entire output.

According to this second conception, the total money supply, initially in the hands of merchants, swaps for the total output of the consumer-goods sector. This leaves consumer goods in the hands of merchants, while firms in the consumer-goods sector have funds. They purchase means of production, keeping back the funds needed to pay wages. Since there is no surplus, *ex hypothesi*, these two transactions add up to total revenue. But the value of the consumer-goods sector's means of production necessarily just equals the wage bill of the capital-goods sector. Hence, the transaction has provided that sector with its wage fund, while the goods not sold to the consumer-goods sector provide it with its own replacements. (Of course, some firms producing means of production may sell only to other such firms, while some sell only to the consumer-goods sector. Call the first subsector IA, and the second subsector IB. The value of the replacement capital goods in IB must necessarily equal the wage bill of subsector IA. This subdivision can be repeated indefinitely; thus there can be an indefinitely extended secondary circulation within the capital-goods sector.) Since both sectors have their replacement means of production and their wage funds on hand, both can hire labor and begin producing. As wages are paid out for work, workers buy and consume consumer goods, returning the money to the merchants. At the end of the period of production, the money will be in the hands of the merchants, the circulation complete, and the process can start all over again.

Clearly, in the second case, the equation $M = wN$ holds, and so the equivalence between k and V also holds. The argument can be readily extended to the case where a surplus is produced[6] by carefully modeling the relationships between speeds of production in relation to consumption (turnover ratios) and sector sizes—which are what the ability to produce a surplus depends on. In the simplest case, speeding up production creates a surplus of consumer goods, since the output of the consumer goods sector is designed to support the population for a given period of time. But just as there is a surplus of consumer goods, there will be unexpended funds, which can now be distributed as profits and circulate the surplus. This distribution will reflect the mark-up; the additional turnover constitutes an exactly proportional increase in the velocity of circulation.[7] Stationary and growing economies must be distinguished, but the more complicated cases follow the basic pattern—with sometimes intricate variations.[8]

Two important points follow. First, changes in productivity, with a given supply of money, do not require changes in prices in the second system, whereas they do in the first. Second, money doesn't drive anything, it adjusts. This is true even though we are talking about commodity money, gold and silver. What drives the system is the ratio between the speed of production and the speed at which money income is spent.[9]

The reason, then, that the quantity equation cannot be treated as a serious explanatory tool of analysis is that when money is endogenously determined (or functions as a wages fund), the quantity equation is not an independent relationship at all. It is simply a disguised form of the mark-up equation, and so is a reflection of whatever forces have determined the mark-up, which itself depends both on distribution and on the relative sizes of the sectors, i.e., on growth.

As Joan pointed out, though for somewhat different reasons, when the definitions are properly chosen, "it is obvious that the formula is correct . . . but then it has no causal significance whatever."[10]

Notes

1. Robinson, 1971, p. 77.
2. Ibid., p. 78.
3. Ibid., p. 87.
4. See Nell, 1968, pp. 157–62.
5. To take an interesting example, Goldfeld's pre-1974 "demand for money equations" over-predict money demand for 1974 and later; after the oil shock "money demand," in real terms, is lower than would be expected from the estimations based on earlier years. But the oil shock set off an inflationary wage-price spiral in which money prices rose faster than money wages, leading to a rise in the average aggregate mark-up. Thus, $1/V$ fell; hence a transactions term derived from $M/P = (1/V)Y$, showing the demand for money based on velocity and the level of current real income, would be reduced compared to earlier periods. It may be too much to suggest that this might account for part of the "missing money," but it opens a wholly unexplored avenue of investigation, particularly in view of the fact that the troubles arose in the demand-deposit equation, rather than the currency equation. It is demand-deposits that we would expect to be endogenous. Cf. Goldfeld, 1976.
6. Nell, 1986, 1988; also Cartelier, 1990.
7. Nell, 1988, pp. 108–9, especially Equation 18′.
8. Nell, 1990, Part III, especially "The Circulation of Commodities by Means of Money."
9. Nell, 1986, 1990.
10. Robinson, 1956, p. 403.

References

Cartelier, Jean. (1990) "Nell's 'Monetary Circulation and Rate of Exploitation': A Comment." Universitie de Picardie.

Friedman, Milton. (1970) "The New Monetarism: Comment." *Lloyd's Bank Review* (October).

Goldfeld, Stephen M. (1976) "The Case of the Missing Money." *Brookings Papers on Economic Activity*, pp. 683–730. Washington, D.C.

Kaldor, Nicholas. (1970) "The New Monetarism." *Lloyd's Bank Review* (July).

Moore, Basil. (1979) "The Endogenous Money Stock." *Journal of Post Keynesian Economics* (Fall):49–70.

———. (1983) "Unpacking the Post Keynesian Black Box: Bank Lending and the Money Supply." *Journal of Post Keynesian Economics* (Summer):537–56.

———. (1988) *Horizontalists and Verticalists. The Macroeconomics of Credit Money.* Cambridge: Cambridge University Press.

Nell, Edward. (1968) "The Advantages of Money over Barter." *Australian Economic Papers* (December):149–65.

———. (1986) "On Monetary Circulation and the Rate of Exploitation." *Thames Papers in Political Economy*. London: Thames Polytechnic. Reprinted in expanded form in P. Arestis, ed., *Post-Keynesian Monetary Economics*, pp. 72–121. London: Edward Elgar.

———. (1991) *Keynes after Sraffa*. London: Unwin Hyman.

Robinson, Joan (1956) *The Accumulation of Capital*. London: Macmillan.

———. (1971) *Economic Heresies: Some Old-Fashioned Questions in Economic Theory*. New York: Basic Books.

Sraffa, Piero (1960) *Production of Commodities by Means of Commodities*. Cambridge: Cambridge University Press.

Weintraub, Sidney. (1959) *A General Theory of the Price Level, Output, Income Distribution and Economic Growth*. Philadelphia: Chilton.

———. (1978) *Capitalism's Inflation and Unemployment Crisis*. Reading, Mass.: Addison-Wesley.

JR

CHAPTER FIFTEEN

Robinson and the "Other Half" of the Keynesian Revolution

INGRID H. RIMA

In her introduction to a collection of essays published under the title *After Keynes* (1973a), Joan Robinson observed that the chief objective of what she termed "the other half of the Keynesian revolution" is to establish that, in an industrial economy, the level of prices is governed by the level of money wage rates:

> This [objective] was a greater shock . . . even than the concept of effective demand governed by volatile expectations. . . . This was such a blow to orthodox ideas that almost all of those who were ready to welcome the Keynesian diagnosis of unemployment somehow refused to take it in until it became too painfully obvious to be ignored any longer.[1]

In point of fact, the profession still resists "taking it in," as Robinson herself later recognized.[2]

The reason for their resistance is not far to seek. The success of the other half of Keynes's revolution will require an entirely different "vision" (to use Schumpeter's indispensable term) of how the world works. The most basic requirement is that economists change their perception of the functioning of the labor market in an industrial economy to recognize that the money wage rate is the "key" price, not simply one price among many. The labor market then emerges as the critical link between microeconomic decision making and the macroeconomic outcome of a "level of prices [that] is governed primarily by the level of wage rates."[3] This wage cost mark-up perception of the determination of the general price level reflects a fundamentally different world view from that held by generations of economic thinkers who have interpreted the general price level as a monetary phenomenon in which sectoral prices are transmuted into an absolute general price level through the role of money serving as a *numeraire*. The contrast with the perception hailed by Robinson as the "other half of Keynes's revolution" is indeed stark!

There is a still further departure from the conventional wisdom about the economy's functioning that is inherent in the wage-cost mark-up view, although it is not part of Robinson's *After Keynes* comment. Specifically, a theory of income distribution is implicit in the wage-cost mark-up equation. Unlike the relatively benign marginal productivity thesis of income sharing, the wage-cost mark-up hypothesis suggests a conflict interpretation of income distribution. As Robinson saw matters:

> Workers, managers and research teams bring about technical progress and accumulation, and the capital falls into the lap of shareholders who are not making the smallest contribution to the process which brings it into being. Income from property is not the reward for waiting; it is the reward of employing a good stockbroker. . . . If this is how the system really works, it is no wonder that the neoclassicals do not want attention drawn to it.[4]

The "other half" of Keynes's revolution is still to be consummated; the object of this paper is to crystallize Robinson's substantially underappreciated contribution to its eventual realization. Her better-known contributions to the "first half" of his revolution were a by-product, so to speak, of "getting Maynard to see what the point of his revolution really was." These contributions were by no means trivial. It was Robinson who pushed Keynes to recognize that the revolution he precipitated stemmed from his abandoning the concept of equilibrium to move toward that of history; analogously, Keynes abandoned the principles of rational choice to explore decisions based on guesswork or convention. Robinson also helped drive home the distinction between the Theory of Money and the Theory of Output, greatly clarified Keynes's convoluted concept of involuntary unemployment, and integrated the foreign trade sector into his analysis of output. These "first half" contributions to Keynes's revolution are major in their own right and require no further elaboration. Our concern is thus with articulating Robinson's contribution to the revolution's "other half."

Although this revolution is yet to be realized, Robinson has been far more instrumental in laying its groundwork than was Keynes himself, who had only a peripheral interest in the problem of inflation and the phenomenon of income distribution, and substantially none in questions related to economic growth and the need to reconsider the conventional basis for free trade. Beginning with her inquiry into the German hyperinflation, a phenomenon that others saw principally through quantity theory glasses, Robinson's analysis went straight to the heart of questions relating to present-day post-Keynesian concerns, among them income distribution, which she considered to be essentially a political phenomenon.[5] Beyond her perception of the untenability of the marginal productivity theory in "Euler's Theorem and the Problem of Distribution" (1934) and her insight into the technical problems inherent in the production function and the measurement of capital controversy arguments, Robinson's particular concern related to the sociological and political aspects of the distribution problem.

Conflict over income shares is a characteristic feature of capitalistic economies. Robinson's growth theory, which implies that advanced economies like Great Britain and the United States are unlikely to experience a succession of "golden ages," portends that these conflicts may well become exacerbated. Indeed, when consideration is given to the implications of her model for import surplus economies like the United States, a more likely scenario is a Robinson-style "leaden age" in which long-run unemployment and underemployment emerge as the most likely counterpart of Keynes's short-run unemployment equilibrium. These themes are explored in the following four sections, each of which undertakes to articulate Robinson's unique contribution to pioneering the "other half" of Keynes's revolution.

I

It is difficult to be precise about the intellectual lineage of Robinson's contribution to the "other half" of Keynes's revolution. It is natural to seek inspiration in her earliest major work, *The Economics of Imperfect Competition* (1933). But this was not a source on which she drew. *Imperfect Competition* relates to the other half of Keynes's revolution only from the standpoint of the concept of demand elasticity which Robinson adopted from Kalecki as the basis for the theory that prices are formed by marking-up prime costs.[6]

Robinson's nontraditional view of the role of labor markets or, more specifically, of the key role of the wage rate is anticipated in her (1938) review of Bresciani Turroni's *The Economics of Inflation.* The translation of Turroni's book into English led her to study the German hyperinflation experience that followed World War I. As an adherent of the quantity theory perspective, Turroni attributed the sequence of the collapsing German exchange rate, rising import, export and home prices and wages to continuous increases in the money supply made available by the Reichsbank to finance the German budget deficit. Robinson, however, did not interpret the German experience in terms of the familiar quantity theory hypothesis, but in terms of the upward thrust of wage rates in response to low rates of unemployment without equivalent increases in labor productivity.

"Something is missing," Robinson wrote, "in Bresciani Turroni's attribution of the hyperinflation that set in July 1921 to the combination of the budget deficits and the increase in the quantity and velocity of circulation of money." Her argument was that

> the missing item is not far to seek; it is the rise in *money wages.* Neither exchange depreciation nor a budget deficit can account for inflation by itself. But if the rise in money wages is brought into the story, the part which each plays can be clearly seen.[7]

The collapse of the Deutschmark increased import and then home prices, which, in the face of low rates of unemployment, generated trade union demands for wage increases. Each wage increase precipitated a further fall in the exchange rate, which called forth a further rise in wages. As Robinson interpreted this experience, an increase in the quantity of money was a *necessary condition*, but it was not the *cause* of the German inflation. Nor was the end of that inflation, in Robinson's view, attributable to the control of the quantity of money. Rather, it was attributable to the halt of trade union wage demands as unemployment reappeared, following the dislocations imposed by the French invasion of the Ruhr. By then the Deutschmark was no longer functioning as a unit of account. Prices and wage rates became tied to the exchange rate so that, in effect, the dollar had become the unit of account. Inflationary forces, Robinson pointed out, became fully spent only as unemployment approached twenty percent, thereby halting worker pressure for further increases in money wage rates. Thus, while most economists interpreted the German inflation as an extreme example of a monetary phenomenon, Robinson's early critique of Turroni's analysis had already conceived of an alternative to the conventional analysis of inflation as a monetary phenomenon.

Robinson's perceptive understanding of the underlying money wage-productivity nexus for explaining the German inflation left her intellectually well poised to make two essential contributions toward paving the way towards the "other half" of Keynes's revolution. While Robinson did not share the fear, so often expressed, that double-digit inflation actually threatens public confidence in the currency, her observations provide perspective about two other aspects of her insight into the problem of inflation: the first relates to the ethics of income distribution in a capitalistic system, which inflation tends to compromise; the second is the revival of the quantity theory of money. She interpreted the reluctance of public service personnel, teachers, police, firefighters, and even hospital nurses and physicians to work without substantial pay increases as reflecting a new awareness, brought about by the differential impact of inflation on the pay structure of their *relative* positions in the income hierarchy. Thus, Robinson interpreted the erosion of their tradition of public service as an expression of their doubt about the equity of the pay system under capitalism. Relative earnings, Robinson recognized, are clearly a *political* outcome; appreciation of this point reflects part of her intellectual debt to Kalecki. This debt is nowhere more clearly in evidence (except, perhaps, in her reliance on his notion of the mark-up with respect to price determination) than in her recognition of the relevance of the political trade cycle with its chronic overlay of a tendency toward rising prices. This led her to surmise that:

> the modern revival of a doctrine so unconvincing as the quantity theory of money can be explained as a refuge from the uncomfortable thought that the general level of price has become a political problem. I believe that the ex-

> traordinary revival of the quantity theory of money in recent years (in an even more hollow form than of old) must be accounted for by the longing to have some kind of theory that provides something to tether the value of money to, some defense against the horrid thought that under laissez faire the private enterprise system does not tend towards equilibrium in any way at all.[8]

The notion that price-level changes distort income distribution patterns, which in turn has implications for the level of aggregate demand, was one of the insights that Robinson derived from Keynes's argument about the relationship between money and real wages. This provided her with the basis for chiding those who advocated cutting money wages during periods of falling demand for failing to understand the adverse effect this would have on aggregate demand. Surprisingly, Robinson noted, even Karl Marx was guilty of this misunderstanding: "Say's Law holds undisputed in Marx's argument," which favored cuts in money wage rates during depression to bring temporary relief.[9]

The critical difference between the orthodox argument for cutting rates during a depression and Marx's similar prescription was that Marx centered on wage cuts as a check on the degree of worker exploitation. Wage cuts, which are necessarily limited by the subsistence requirements of the working man's family, serve to squeeze profits, since in a competitive market price cuts are not similarly limited. Contrariwise, it was Marx's view that capitalists do not resist trade union efforts to raise wages from which, in fact, they benefit since "capitalists could always . . . avail themselves of every rise in wages to raise prices much higher and thus pocket greater profits."[10]

The added insight that Robinson derived from Marx's concern about labor exploitation seems to have directed her analytical attention to the implication of price changes for income distribution; specifically, a rise in prices affects the distribution of profits between rentiers and entrepreneurs.[11] The conflict between rentiers and entrepreneurs becomes especially relevant during inflation and hyperinflation, for fixed-income classes suffer relatively more than others in the community.[12] A loss of rentier income may be harmful to both consumption and investment, since rentier incomes, like wages, are more fully spent than are profits, so that employment in consumer and investment goods industries may decline. On the other hand, a transfer of purchasing power from capitalists to workers via higher wages is likely to stimulate the demand for consumption goods and so tends to increase employment, although a rise in wages at the expense of profits may reduce the incentive to invest. Clearly, Robinson's analysis went considerably beyond Keynes's in her recognition of the employment implications of changes in income distribution. But more than that, her study of Marx led her to recognize that the Keynesian revolution leads back to the concept of the surplus, which is "the core concept of classicism,"[13] and that the "other half" of the Keynesian revolution will require an equally revolutionary theory of income distribution.

II

Robinson's earliest step in the direction of disassociating herself from conventional distribution theory seems to have been related to her discomfort, even before the *General Theory*, with the orthodox theory of wages which "had stuck in my gizzard as a student."[14] As her dissent grew, she was increasingly led in the direction of the historically older classical or surplus view of the distribution phenomenon, into which she incorporated the Kaleckian notion that the residual category of income is *wages* rather than *profits.*[15]

A key feature of this view is that the incomes of the classes of society are determined by principles separate from those that govern the value of commodities or that determine output. Ricardo and his followers conceived of the wage as being determined by the subsistence requirements of the worker and his family, which, from Smith onward, were interpreted broadly enough to make subsistence consistent with a customary or socially established real wage. For Robinson, the level of money wage rates that prevails at any particular time is a historical accident and movements in them are bound up with the competition of different groups of workers to maintain their relative positions.[16] This proposition is central to Robinson's alternative theory of wage share determination, which is articulated with particular clarity in *Essays in the Theory of Economic Growth* (1963). This volume, which she offered "as an introduction rather than as a supplement to my *Accumulation of Capital* [1956]," strongly conveys her perception of labor markets as dominated by conflict. It thus harkens back, in a sense, to her reassessment of trade unions in *Imperfect Competition* in which she concluded that unions reduce imperfections on the demand side of labor markets and bring them closer to the competitive ideal.[17]

Equally anticipatory of the still-to-be-realized "other half" of Keynes's revolution is the proposition, which she attributed to Kalecki, that, with imperfect competition and excess capacity, gross margins are governed by the pricing policies of firms. Subsuming all the influences on gross margins under the umbrella term "degree of monopoly," the share of wages varies inversely with the degree of monopoly.[18] Drawing on the Kalecki/Keynes proposition that relative shares are governed by the rate of investment and the propensity of each class to consume, Robinson was quick to recognize that an autonomous change in the level of investment raises not only the income level (which, in turn, becomes the source of new savings) and the economy's rate of expansion, but also the profit share and the rate of return on investment. Her model of investment, however, is Kaleckian, rather than Keynesian, in the sense that it is an integral part of her theory of income distribution, which is classical in its simplifying assumption that capitalists do not consume the profits they receive as residual income and that workers do not save. Thus, the wage share is the combined wage bill generated by employment in the consumption- and investment-goods sectors. For Robinson, as for Kalecki, the higher the rate of investment that the capitalist class has undertaken, the larger the profit share. With the rate of profit seen as endogenously determined, via the rate of technical progress and the rate of expansion, Robinson was led ultimately to the insight that the remaining distributional variable—namely, the wage rate—must be derived from outside the system, i.e., at any particular time, the wage rate depends on the relative bargaining strength of workers and employers. An increase in the strength of workers reduces the degree of monopoly, which has a positive effect on the relative wage share because it limits the extent of the mark-up, and through it, the profit differential.

The rate of investment simultaneously determines the share of income going to workers in the form of consumption goods; i.e., the latter is the wage share in real terms. For the rate of investment to rise, workers need to be shifted into the investment-goods sector so that a relative decline occurs in the consumption-goods sector. Thus, investment also determines the real wage share; this is the source of the inherent antagonism between workers and capitalists in Robinson's view of income distribution (as in that of many post-Keynesians). The rate of capital accumulation, and thus of growth, has a negative effect on the wage share in the national product that is strongly resisted by workers, especially if a culturally established standard of subsistence is threatened. Analogously, the rate of savings out of profits not only determines the warranted growth rate, it also determines the distribution of income between workers and capitalists.

Along with Kaldor, Keynes, and Klein, Robinson noted the "fact" that relative income shares have historically remained constant.[19] For Robinson this constancy implies that there is a maximum profit share that workers will tolerate. The profits that capitalists receive depend not only on the rate of investment but also on the price level, which tends to rise along with the wage rate increases that accompany an expanding investment sector. Under conditions of full (or nearly full) employment, workers are able to bargain for higher money wage rates to offset the eroding effect of inflation on their real wages. The "inflation barriers" workers have been able to erect have ensured that productivity gains of the U.S. economy in the post–World War II period have accrued to workers, chiefly in the form of higher money wages.

III

Besides inflation, the post–World War II era has been characterized by what Robinson termed *neomercantilism.* The case for free trade, she argued, in her inaugural lecture at the University of Cambridge, emerges in a different light when the chief objective of nations is to earn a surplus from the rest of the world so that they may pursue a policy of "export-led" growth.

Keynes had, of course, already repudiated the doctrine, based on the conventional trade model, that free trade yields gains all around. Thus, Robinson reflected,

> When Keynes attacked the dominant orthodoxy, one of the things that grieved my teachers most was that he should try to rehabilitate the mercantilists, thus damaging the claim of the free-traders to superior benevolence and wisdom. . . . It was the facade of a dogma with solid interests behind it.[20]

Robinson, however, saw that when each country individually pursues its own individual interests, they will pile up tariffs against each other.

> Since the total market does not grow fast enough to make room for all, each government feels it is a worthy and commendable aim to increase its own share in world activity for the benefit of its own people. A chief objective in this pursuit of a surplus on their income account is to gain reserves. The new mercantilists believe it is not necessarily foolish to prefer to acquire sterile money rather than useful goods or profitable assets.[21]

This new reality of international trade objectives is relevant to Robinson's reservations about neoclassical capital theory and also has important implications for the ever-present struggle about income shares. Specifically, she distinguished between capital in the sense of stocks of equipment and materials, and capital in the sense of "command over finance" which permits employers to organize the production of goods which they can sell at a profit.[22] The distinction is not only important for domestic finance; it also relates to foreign investment whose analytical treatment Robinson considered as "the greatest obfuscation of the orthodox theory . . . [whose] concept of capital as a factor of production implied that when one country lends to another, it is transferring real resources to it."[23]

While capital in the sense of capital goods may indeed be moved from one country to another,

> a country which receives an inflow of finance is not receiving a supply of a factor of production called capital; it is enjoying the possibility of running a surplus of imports or amassing monetary reserves; . . . under the old gold standard, net lending for any country was limited to equality with its surplus on its income account. Before the demise of the gold standard but, more particularly, before WWII, small changes in interest rates were adequate to restrain the flow of finance.[24]

Nowadays the pattern has changed both for the newly emerging ex-colonial economies and for older, now mature, industrial economies; all are seeking export-led growth to maintain full or near full employment. Robinson thus viewed neomercantilism as an essentially new phase in the historical development of modern capitalism.

The phenomenon of neomercantilism also has important implications for the determination of the distributive shares and thus for the configuration of an economy's future growth prospects. Robinson herself did not live long enough to study how the capital flows that are the financial counterpart of persistent large trade imbalances are likely to affect individual economies. But the observations she made in her inaugural address about the trade component of aggregate effective demand continue to be relevant:

> The most important benefit of a surplus on income account, which affects the whole economy, is that, provided that there are energetic enterprises and thrifty capitalists to take advantage of it, it permits home investments to go full steam ahead while a deficit country is nervously pulling on the brake for fear of excessive imports.[25]

These observations relate to the trade component of export surplus economies and the implications of the new mercantilism for its trading partners. But the implications of neomercantilism for the theory of income distribution, and thus for the "other half" of Keynes's revolution, remain as uncharted ground.

Robinson herself charted a direction for new inquiry in two later papers on trade: "The Need for a Reconsideration of the Theory of International Trade" (1973d) and "Reflections on the Theory of International Trade" (1974). These reexamined, following Sraffa, the link between Ricardo's theory of foreign trade and his theory of profits. The essence of her argument was that Ricardo's support for free trade, in opposition to the proponents of the Corn Law, was fundamentally linked to his theory of income distribution, for abolition of the Corn Laws would raise the rate of profit by lowering the real cost of wage goods. In Ricardo's thinking, such a policy would enhance the rate of capital accumulation and, through it, the growth of employment, income and wealth. We must therefore credit Robinson with reaffirming the distributional aspects of Ricardo's trade theory that had been swept away, so to speak, with the marginal revolution. A relevant next step, it would seem, is to link Robinson's insights about the "new mercantilism" to her theory of income distribution and, through it, to her theory of growth. The next section suggests not only that the conflict between receivers of wages and non-labor incomes is likely to become exacerbated in an import surplus economy, but also that import surplus nations may become predisposed toward experiencing Robinson's "leaden age" as the long-run counterpart to Keynes's short-run underemployment equilibrium.

IV

It is something of a conundrum that trade theory and the theories of distribution, accumulation, and growth still remain essentially compartmentalized, the theoretical and empirical beginnings of Kaldor (1966), Cornwall (1977), Steedman (1979), Parrinello (1979), and Thirlwall (1979) notwithstanding. Yet Robinson's writings on trade and income distribution, whose Ricardian inspiration is clear, provide the basis for some inferences about the likely impact of large and prolonged import surpluses on the struggle over income shares. International capital movements are capable of generating changes in wage-profit share relationships that are analogous to those associated with inflation. That there has been little interest in linking them analytically is, no doubt, attributable in some measure to the ongoing conventional wisdom about the marginal productivity theory of income distribution—a "wisdom" that appears to have an even more tenacious hold on the economists' minds than Say's Law. Many post-Keynesians, of course, recognize that the "other half" of Keynes's revolution will necessarily include the theory of income distribution. Indeed, something of a consensus appears to be emerging that an analytically compatible theory is to be found in a return to a distribution theory that is "classical" in the sense of viewing the income shares as being determined by principles that are separate from those that govern commodity values or output.

It is axiomatic that maintaining the historical constancy of income shares as an economy evolves depends on the reproduction of its historical employment and income-generating capability. Differently expressed, even in the face of balance-of-payment deficits, an economy must generate the same size wage bill and price its output according to the same mark-up on average wage costs if it is to maintain its employment and output levels and also preserve constant wage-profit share relations.

Prolonged large export surpluses may precipitate changes in income distribution in economies that, like Britain and more recently the United States, have become net borrowers in consequence of their import surpluses. Although income shares are affected in surplus as well as deficit countries, our concern here is with the income distribution implications of import surpluses (and the net borrowing that necessarily accompanies it).

It is not necessary to begin with the often-used simplifying assumption that "capitalists save and workers spend." The ease with which these stringent assumptions and this nineteenth-century terminology can be modified to suit a twentieth-century world in which the relevant distinction is between contractual and residual incomes is generally familiar.[26] So too is there recognition of Pasinetti's insight that if there is saving out of wages, so that workers also become profit receivers, the distribution between wages and profits remains unchanged.[27] The ratio of wages to total income is still determined by the share of investment in total product and the marginal propensity to consume of non-wage earners. Thus, when profits or rentier incomes are spent for consumption, these shares in national income are increased by a factor equal to the reciprocal of their marginal propensity to consume. In effect, receivers of residual income determine their relative share in national income when they decide on their rate of discretionary expenditures.[28] This is the essence also of Keynes's "widow's cruse" and Kalecki's perception that "capitalists get what they spend on capital goods."

While it is not essential to retain the stringent assumption that "capitalists save and workers spend" in order to examine the implications of import surpluses for income distribution, there are other institutional characteristics that are critical to a useful model. In particular, recognition that mark-up pricing is typical in a contemporary capitalist economy is basic to understanding the implications for income distribution that follow when the discretionary aspect of spending takes the form of import spending. The familiar Kaldor-Robinson-Kalecki (K-R-K) model extended to include Sidney Weintraub's consumption-wage bill coefficient offers a convenient vehicle for examining changes in income distribution that may be precipitated in import surplus economies.[29]

Expenditures on imported final goods or production inputs reduce domestic sales, thus causing reductions in the cash flow to firms.[30] Unless the size of their mark-ups can be increased or there are other offsetting factors such as wage "givebacks" and/or layoffs, the substitution of imports for domestic products is likely to compromise the ability of firms to generate funds internally. Firms will have set their mark-ups to finance their planned investment levels; their unexpected need to generate the requisite funds externally implies, as Eichner has shown, a more steeply rising supply curve for investment funds. The marginal supply cost of the funds required to finance planned investment thus becomes inconsistent with the mark-up that the degree of monopoly will support, and the level of investment that firms will undertake is likely to decline. There are a variety of models of the same genre as Eichner's, from which a negative impact on firm's investments deriving from an import surplus can be inferred.[31] This impact is likely to become operative via the effect of a diminished cash flow on the cost of both internal and external finance.

The necessity for firms to resort to higher mark-ups to generate investment funds (which is, of course, limited by the degree of monopoly) has been modified, as Robinson pointed out, by the nature of modern lending. Countries seeking export-led growth have resisted spending their exchange earnings on imports, preferring financial investment instead. This will, no doubt, moderate the increase in the supply price of funds created by the reduced ability of firms to generate finance internally. If the marginal efficiency of capital does not become depressed, domestic investment will not suffer, so that the ratio of profits to wages may well remain constant. However, it is not impossible that the demand for and the supply of investment funds will prove to be interdependent in an economy that is running a large and persistent import surplus in tandem with a large budget deficit, so that investment may become depressed.[32] A depressed level of investment in an import surplus economy is thus not to be ruled out and it can, potentially, divert the economy from its warranted growth rate. This, in turn, all else remaining equal, implies a lower ratio of profits to wages.

The conflict between receivers of wages and non-labor income in an import surplus economy is likely to become exacerbated when the obligation to remit profit and interest payments abroad is eventually confronted. Robinson herself noted that the piling up of obligations on which foreign lenders and investors earn interest and dividends becomes especially burdensome if the capital imports are unrelated to superior profit opportunities in the receiving country and their subsequent enhanced capacity to export. They are even more burdensome when the rest of the world is not inclined to consume its extra income by importing goods from the countries to which it has supplied capital.[33]

It may thus be concluded that when consumers (or business firms) shift the composition of their demand away from domestically produced final goods (or inputs) to imports, it has the effect of raising the supply price of finance, which compromises investment and, through it, the profit share. Even if the degree of monopoly in the import surplus country is compatible with a higher mark-up, or its workers are willing to tolerate measures to reduce the wage share, its international borrowing may become the source of an endogenously generated decumulation and disinvestment process. An import surplus is thus likely ultimately to render a country more recession-prone. Reexamination of the logic of whatever commitment to free trade it has had then seems a likely outcome, along with measures to counter the recessionary tendencies inherent in a weakened incentive to accumulate.

These possibilities make it clear that trade questions cannot be considered apart from their relationship to profit rates and economic growth. Thus, we are back to Ricardo, who so clearly linked trade theory and policy to the rate of profit, and to Joan Robinson, who was surely among the first to appreciate Sraffa's insights into Ricardo's distribution theory. Yet contemporary discussions of trade issues typically abstract from the profit rate and how it relates to the role of trade as a vehicle for the transfer of real resources from one's trading partners. Access to additional real resources facilitates two economic objectives: it can contribute toward an increase in domestic absorption (i.e., $C + I + G + X - M$) via an increased real wage share; it can also increase the profit rate. If the profit rate can be increased without penalizing the wage share, as is the case in a growth economy, the two objectives are not incompatible. But this, as Robinson so clearly understood, may not be the case for an import surplus economy. Indeed, the pursuit of export-led growth by countries like Japan and West Germany may predispose mature import surplus economies, like Britain and possibly even the United States, to experience the scenario of Robinson's "leaden age" as the long-run counterpart to Keynes's underemployment equilibrium.

Notes

1. Robinson, 1973a, pp. 6–7.
2. Robinson, 1973b, pp. 104–5.
3. Robinson, 1973a, pp. 6–7.
4. Robinson, 1973b, p. 66.
5. Robinson, 1966, pp. 52–58.
6. Robinson, 1973b, p. 89.
7. Robinson, 1966, pp. 74–75.

8. Robinson, 1960, pp. 145–58.
9. Ibid., pp. 85–91.
10. Ibid., p. 88.
11. Ibid., p. 90.
12. Ibid., p. 90, n. 2.
13. Cf. Gram and Walsh, 1980, p. 14.
14. Corwin D. Edwards's review (1934) of Robinson's *Imperfect Competition* (and Chamberlin's *Monopolistic Competition*) credited her with developing "a theory of the exploitation of labor by virtue of the imperfection of the market" (pp. 688–90).
15. Robinson, 1973c, p. 100.
16. Robinson, 1973b, p. 99.
17. Although Robinson had become disenchanted with the usefulness of imperfect (and monopolistic) competition theories for addressing questions of entrepreneurial decision making about prices and output, and especially faulted the demand elasticity concept as a useful tool, these self-same reservations led toward her recognition of the unique role of labor markets in capitalistic economies and that wage rates are the link between value theory and the theory of employment.
18. Robinson, 1971, pp. 87–91.
19. Robinson, 1960, p. 94.
20. Robinson, 1973b, p. 1.
21. Ibid., pp. 4–5.
22. Ibid., pp. 21–24.
23. Ibid., p. 21.
24. Ibid., p. 22.
25. Ibid., p. 8.
26. Cf. Eichner and Kregel, 1975, p. 1297.
27. Pasinetti, 1974, p. 113. While worker earnings *qua* wages remain the same, the return on assets acquired with savings out of wages enables workers to obtain a larger share of national income. Analogously, consumption by non-wage earners or "capitalists" out of residual income or "profits" will reduce the share of income going to workers.
28. Cf. Eichner, 1987, pp. 567–73.
29. Weintraub, 1981, pp. 10–24.
30. A shift to imported rather than domestic goods also reduces the capacity utilization rate of the industries affected by the substitution. However, since firms in the industrial sector confront unit labor costs that appear, on the basis of empirical studies, not to be significantly affected by utilization, it may be presumed that the shift to imports does not adversely affect costs of production.
31. Wood, 1975; Kregel, 1976; Shapiro, 1981.
32. While Eichner (1987) doubted that the interdependence of the demand and supply of investment funds is empirically important, his argument was not framed in the context of the effect of a large and persistent import surplus on interest rates (nor one that has occurred in tandem with an equally large budget deficit) in an inflation-prone economy.
33. Robinson, 1973b, pp. 16–19.

References

Cornwall, John. (1983) *Modern Capitalism: Its Growth and Transformation.* Armonk, NY: M. E. Sharpe. First ed. London: Martin Robinson, 1977.

Edwards, Corwin D. (1934) "Review of Imperfect Competition and Monopolistic Competition." *American Economic Review*, pp. 688–90.

Eichner, Alfred S. (1987) *The Macrodynamics of Advanced Market Economies*. Armonk, NY: M. E. Sharpe.

Eichner, Alfred S. and J. A. Kregel. (1975) "An Essay on Post-Keynesian Theory: A New Paradigm in Economics." *Journal of Economic Literature*, 13 (December):1293–1315.

Gram, Harvey and Vivian Walsh. (1983) "Joan Robinson's Economics in Retrospect." *Journal of Economic Literature*, 21 (June):518–50.

Kaldor, Nicholas. (1966) *Causes of the Slow Rate of Economic Growth of the United Kingdom*. Cambridge: Cambridge University Press.

Kregel, Jan. (1976) *Profit, Distribution and Growth: Two Views*. Chicago: Aldine.

Pasinetti, Luigi L. (1974) *Growth and Income Distribution: Essays in Economic Theory*. London: Cambridge University Press.

Robinson, Joan. (1933) *The Economics of Imperfect Competition*. London: Macmillan. 2d ed., 1969.

———. (1934) "Euler's Theorem and the Problem of Distribution." *Economic Journal*, 44 (September):398–414.

———. (1938) "The Economics of Hyper-Inflation." *Economic Journal*, 48 (September):507–13.

———. (1956) *The Accumulation of Capital*. London: Macmillan.

———. (1960) *Collected Economic Papers*, vol. 2. Oxford: Basil Blackwell. 2d ed., 1978. Rpt., Cambridge, MA: MIT Press, 1979.

———. (1963) *Essays in the Theory of Economic Growth*. New York: St. Martin's Press.

———. (1966) *Economics: An Awkward Corner*. London: Allen and Unwin.

———. (1971) "Michal Kalecki." *Cambridge Review* (October).

———, ed. (1973a) *After Keynes*. Papers presented to Section F (Economics Section) at the 1972 annual meeting of the British Association for the Advancement of Science. Oxford: Basil Blackwell.

———. (1973b) *Collected Economic Papers*, vol. 4. Oxford: Basil Blackwell. Rpt., Cambridge, MA: MIT Press, 1980.

———. (1973c) *Economic Heresies: Some Old-Fashioned Questions in Economic Theory*. New York: Basic Books.

———. (1973d) "The Need for a Reconsideration of the Theory of International Trade." [Originally written in 1970.] In M.B. Connolly, ed., *International Trade and Money*. London: Allen and Unwin.

———. (1974) "Reflections on the Theory of International Trade." Lectures given at the University of Manchester. Manchester: University of Manchester Press.

Shapiro, Nina. (1981) "Pricing and the Growth of the Firm." *Journal of Post Keynesian Economics*, 4, 1(Fall):85–100.

Steedman, Ian. (1979) *Fundamental Issues in Trade Theory*. New York: St. Martin's Press.

Thirwall, Anthony P. (1979) "The Balance of Payments Constraint as an Explanation of International Growth Rate Differences." *Banca Nazionale del Lavoro*, 128: 45–53.

Weintraub, Sidney. (1981) "An Eclectic Theory of Income Shares." *Journal of Post-Keynesian Economics* (Fall): 10–24.

Wood, Adrian. (1975) *A Theory of Profits*. New York: Cambridge University Press.

JR

CHAPTER SIXTEEN

Robinson's Dark Room

Investment in Post-Keynesian Growth Theory

CHIDEM KURDAS

> In reality, to find the expected rate of return which governs investment decisions is like the famous difficulty of looking in a dark room for a black cat that probably is not there.[1]

Joan Robinson's writings on growth perplexed and disappointed many of her readers. Even a sympathetic reviewer like Lawrence Klein commented that *The Accumulation of Capital* "does not seem to lead anywhere in particular."[2] The reason for such judgments has not been clearly understood. Is the disappointment attributable to the absence of a central thread in Robinson's arguments on growth? This is not the case, since the "Keynesian" character of her approach does constitute a unifying core. In fact, the cyclical demand-side orientation that unifies post-Keynesian theory also accounts for a weakness in the Robinson version.

Robinson thought the dynamic *consequences* of investment could be studied without exploring the *determination* of investment itself. The quote that introduces this paper is one of her numerous discouraging remarks on the subject. Only a "comparative historical anthropology" can throw light on the rate of capital accumulation. Meanwhile we can study the "proximate causes" and consequences of accumulation.[3] Unfortunately, it turns out that we cannot go ahead without that elusive cat. It is my contention that Robinson's explanation of investment, and the effects attributed to it in post-Keynesian theory, are mutually inconsistent. The inconsistency lies in the secular inertia of income shares versus the cyclical volatility imputed to investment spending. According to Robinson and Kaldor, the rate of capital formation determines income distribution. Furthermore, both economists imply that distributive shares are steady, persistent magnitudes. It is argued below that these two propositions, taken together, can hold only if there is a secular trend rate of accumulation.

In spite of this Achilles' heel, the Robinson model contributes to our understanding of capitalist dynamics. In fact, through its very weakness it teaches a lesson—one that reinforces her methodological admonitions on the need to deal with "historical time."[3] Investment decisions and technological change are messy subjects that cannot be disposed of by a neat and simple formula. Avoiding them is no solution: The critique below demonstrates how dependent a Keynesian growth model is on the representation of such phenomena. Future students of the subject will have to extend Robinson's logical framework with a comprehensive treatment of the determinants of investment spending. In doing so they may have to practice what she preached, namely to forge a historical, in contrast to an equilibrium-based, approach.[4]

Robinson stated that the purpose of her basic accumulation model was to generalize the *General Theory*. This Keynesian perspective, which is the unifying thread of her work, shows itself specifically in the treatment of savings and investment. What distinguishes a Keynesian argument from an alternative approach? Textbook neoclassicism is taken as a convenient, simple alternative in the comparison below.

In the neoclassical view there is simultaneous determination of investment and savings. Since investment and savings are the demand and supply sides, respectively, of one and the same market, there can be no determination of investment independently of savings. The interest rate is both the basis upon which the investment decision is made, and the mechanism that coordinates it with savings. In more formal terms, investment, savings, and the interest rate are the unknowns of a simultaneous equation system that does not partition into independent subsystems.

The Keynesian explanation, by contrast, is not simultaneous but sequential (as Pasinetti has pointed out).[5] Here the investment decision is separate from and logically prior to the determination of the level of savings. In Keynes's original formulation, and following it in the post-Keynesian approach, expectations of future profitability play a dominant role in explaining the level of investment. This grounding in expectations, which were seen as unpredictable and unstable, made investment an independent force and, given the stability of the other components of aggregate demand, the prime mover in cyclical fluctuations. Since the interest rate is not determined by the interaction between investment and savings, Keynes added the notion of liquidity preference to close his model.[6] The "neoclassical synthesis," by stressing the rate of interest as the main explanatory variable in the investment function, blurred the distinction between Keynes's demand-side approach and simultaneous determination models. The distinguishing feature of a demand-side model, then, is the logical priority of autonomous demand in general, and the independence of investment decisions from savings in particular.

Unlike neoclassical theory, in which the description of one market suffices, there are two logically distinct issues in Keynesian analysis: the *determinants* of investment, and the *relationship* between it and savings. A growth theory along these lines has to provide separate answers to these two questions.

Robinson's answers, and the model built around them, are described in the next three sections. The centerpiece is the "desired" rate of capital accumulation at which investment decisions and the amount of savings are in dynamic balance along a growth path. The desired rate of growth is a function only of the relationship between investment and savings. The various other forces that play a role in growth—i.e., labor, natural resources, technological change—do not affect it. Comparison of *feasible* growth with the desired rate defines several different paths, which Robinson calls "ages." The ages constitute a typological framework in which technological change, class relations, and labor availability can be studied, as well as the interaction between them.[7] The last two sections of the paper analyze the basis for the notion of desired growth, and elucidate the inconsistency in its determination.

Capital Accumulation and the Rate of Profit

Nicholas Kaldor suggested that the "Keynesian technique" of exogenous investment decisions (or more generally autonomous demand) "could be alternatively applied to a determination of the relation between prices and wages, if the level of output is taken as given, or to the determination of the level of employment, if distribution (i.e., the relation between prices and wages) is taken as given."[8] But Kaldor acknowledged a serious problem in making the Keynesian proposition do double duty. If the balance of savings and investment is brought about by variations in distribution, we are left without a demand-side mechanism to determine the level of output and employment, and Say's Law seems to come to its own. Nevertheless, Kaldor thought investment (and autonomous demand generally) could play both roles, since the level of output and employment is a short-run variable, explicable in the static setting in which capital stock is assumed constant, while the determination of the real wage takes place in the long-run context.[9] On this basis, Kaldor, Robinson, and Pasinetti developed Cambridge growth theory around the distributional effect of investment.

Cyclical models, by contrast, use the output multiplier. Recently, the dual function imputed to autonomous demand has been criticized and the validity of the Cambridge growth model has been questioned.[10] The critics argue that capitalist economies routinely carry sufficient excess capacity to accommodate fluctuations in the level of investment with changes in output, so that the output multiplier is generally in operation. As an analytical result, there is no reason why autonomous demand should have a permanent impact on the real wage rate.

To demonstrate the possible reactions to a change in investment, consider a two-class, two-sector, closed pure market economy in which all wage income is consumed while a fraction of profit income is saved. National income consists of the wage bill and total profits, and macro balance requires that:

$$I = s.\,(Y - L.\,w) \tag{1}$$

Y is the current level, in real terms, of social product:

$$Y \leq \overline{Y}$$

Where $\overline{Y}$ is real national product at full capacity utilization. It is assumed to be below or at the constraint imposed by full employment of labor. (The employment issue is treated in the "ages" typology described below.)

The question is how the investment-savings equality can be reestablished when there is, say, a rise in the level of investment. In other words, how can the additional profits to underwrite the new investment be generated? If all hypothetical possibilities are to be considered, each of the four variables on the right-hand side of Equation 1—i.e., output, number of workers, savings propensity, and wage rate—represents a mechanism for adjustment. A comparison of these alternatives is useful in understanding the particular mechanism chosen by post-Keynesian growth theorists.

(i) If the economy has sufficient amounts of unused capacity and unemployed labor, i.e., actual output is sufficiently below the full capacity level, increased demand from investment spending results in a higher level of output, which yields the additional profit required to underwrite the additional investment. This was the argument Kalecki used to explain cyclical movements in investment and profits. It differs from the Keynesian multiplier in its explicit consideration of profit income, rather than aggregate output alone.[11]

(ii) The profit share in national product could conceivably be increased by intensifying the work effort so as to produce the same output with less labor, i.e., L may be reduced. In this case the additional profits are at the expense of worker consumption, but without a change in the real wage rate. Barring technological change, a reduction in the per unit labor requirement necessitates either worker cooperation, which would be forthcoming only in extraordinary circumstances such as a war economy, or stepped-up repression of the working class. By its nature, this has to be a temporary and limited response.

(iii) An increase in the proportion of profits saved, that is, a reduction of capitalist consumption, also achieves the same end. This is in fact one part of the neoclassical answer. The disequilibrium between investment and savings is resolved by the rising interest rate and an increased savings propensity. The other part, of course, is the shrinkage in investment due to higher interest rates. Since the motivation for post-Keynesian theory was to provide an alternative to this way of thinking, it is not considered further here.

(iv) Finally, the real wage rate can act as an adjustment mechanism. In the post-Keynesian Cambridge model, the real wage rate adjusts to the growth rate through variations in the price level. A reduction in the money wage is possible but, in view of twentieth-century experience, unlikely. The most likely way that the wage bill can shrink relative to output is through inflation. The higher level of aggregate demand created by increased investment makes it possible for firms to raise prices, while the money wage lags behind. Hence, the real wage falls, and the rise in profitability thus engendered underwrites the faster growth rate. This mechanism, called the "widow's cruse" after an expression used by Keynes in the *Treatise on Money*, constitutes the connection between growth and distribution. Reactions (i) and (ii) increase profits without changing the wage rate, and only (iv) has the potential to affect the secular distribution of income. The wage and profit rates are not the only variables that represent distribution; income shares are also seen as being determined by accumulation.

As noted above, a number of economists have recently concluded that the Cambridge growth model based on mechanism (iv) is not a realistic representation of the capitalist growth process. Garegnani argues that autonomous demand in general and investment demand in particular can only affect the level of national product, not secular income shares.[12] Fluctuations in capital accumulation cause changes in capacity utilization and output; increased savings comes from increased output. In short, according to Garegnani and others,[13] mechanism (i), not (iv), captures the impact of changes in capital formation, since capitalist economies routinely carry excess capacity and can increase output within a wide margin. They further argue that even if a rise in investment is too large to be accommodated by increased capacity utilization and supply bottlenecks develop, any fall in the real wage rate will be temporary. Hence investment has no effect on secular income shares.

There is a distinction to be made between the absolute level of investment on the one hand, and the ratio of investment to capital stock or output on the other. While participants in the debate outlined above do not express the issue in these terms, it will be seen that the validity of a link between growth and income shares actually rests on this distinction. The level of investment is empirically known to be highly volatile. The output multiplier responds to this volatility, giving rise to cyclical movements. The distribution of income between wages and profits tends to be a relatively stable configuration—it changes infrequently and slowly, if at all. It does not have a cyclical character. Kaldor describes this stability as a stylized fact of growth that the Cambridge model is supposed to explain, and Robinson accepts it as such. The rate of accumulation is seen as underlying the historically observed social allocation of income. But this rate of accumulation cannot be the volatile level of investment. It has to be a different variable, the stable ratio of investment to capacity.

A change in the secular distribution of income requires massive economic, social, and political adjustments. For example, one such economic adjustment is the buildup of industries producing capital goods and the relative shrinkage of those producing consumer goods, in order to acquire the sectoral proportion that corresponds to the new shares of consumption and investment in output. The process of achieving this sectoral proportion—the "traverse"—involves reallocation of the labor force as well as of capital stock between industries through a sequence of periods.[14] A more complex kind of adjustment involves the attitudes, customs, and conventions that underlie the living standards of various groups, for a reduction in the real wage provokes resistance and may cause social disruption if it clashes with the population's view of a minimum acceptable level of material welfare. The idea behind the distributional argument is that there is a *rate* of investment, or share of investment in national product, that persists as an average over cyclical ups and downs. It persists for a sufficiently long time so that the sectoral composition of the economy adjusts to it, and social expectations corresponding to that distribution of income come into being. Such persistence is the indispensable condition for a causal relationship between investment and a secular distribution of income. The Garegnani/Vianello criticism of the distributional mechanism is justified in the absence of this condition. In other words, if there is no "long-run" rate of investment, there is no reason for a "long-run" shift in distribution to occur in response to changes in investment. *Cyclical* fluctuations in the level of investment are, of course, accommodated by variations in the level of output.

Robinson notes that the relationship between accumulation and the rate of profit "is not confined to strictly steady growth." She sees it as being applicable even if "The rate of investment is not tethered by a particular ratio to the value of the stock of capital." In this case she still mentions a "long-run average growth." Growth may occur in cycles, but the cycles are around an average that itself remains steady "for a run of years."[15] She makes no attempt to explicate this secular average rate, and it remains a vague possibility that may or may not exist.

The dynamic version of Equation 1 shows the relationship between key proportions of the economy:

$$i = s\,(u - v.\,w) \tag{2}$$

where

$i = I/\overline{Y}$, the share of investment in output
$u = Y/\overline{Y}$, the rate of capacity utilization
$v = L/\overline{Y}$, the reciprocal of technical labor productivity.

This relationship is commonly expressed by the profit rather than wage rate, and divided by capital stock rather than output. With asterisks to indicate the period, it then becomes:

$$r = k^*/s \tag{3}$$

where

$$k^* = I/K.$$

A shift in distribution corresponds to a persistent change in the share of investment in full utilization output (i), and in its ratio to capital stock (k^*), rather than a change in the level of investment. The question is whether this share has any significance apart from the absolute amount of investment actually made each year. Is investment "tethered by a particular ratio to the value of capital stock"? The validity of the widow's cruse mechanism depends on such a secular ratio. Given a change in i, there are two possible Keynesian responses: a change in the utilization rate, u, and in the real wage rate, w. If the change in investment share is temporary, the temporary adjustment of capacity utilization is the appropriate response. If, on the other hand, there is a persistent change in i, a change in utilization is not sufficient. This is so because there will be a rate of capacity use that is technically and economically the most desirable, in the sense that going below it means a sacrifice of profit, while going above it may bring bottlenecks and breakdowns. Actual utilization can diverge from the optimum rate temporarily, but in the long run will tend to gravitate to it. In other words, u is variable only in the short run.

Furthermore, consider that excess capacity $(\bar{Y} - Y)$ is carried to meet unanticipated or cyclical fluctuations in demand. Firms will aim at a utilization rate that allows them this flexibility. If actual utilization is higher than planned, and therefore they are not carrying the excess capacity deemed necessary to meet temporary changes in demand, this in itself would push firms to higher levels of investment. Thus, an increase in investment would lead to further increases in investment if its impact is confined to capacity utilization—precisely the kind of "knife-edge" instability envisaged by Harrod in his concept of warranted growth.

Cyclical instability, on the other hand, is limited by the state of expectations underlying investment decisions. Such expectations are volatile, and once they start to move in the other direction the pressure on capacity eases. There is then no need for a change in distribution to put an end to the centrifugal tendency. But if a persistent drive to accumulate a larger share of social product is the source of the upward pressure on capacity utilization, the most likely outcome is an inflationary spiral that does not cease until there is a fall in the real wage. Thus, distribution emerges as the long-run adjustment mechanism for a persistent discrepancy between the share of investment in output and the savings propensity.

The Desired Rate of Growth

A tenet of the Cambridge approach is that the relationship between investment and profits cuts both ways. "If they have no profit, the entrepreneurs cannot accumulate," writes Robinson, "and if they do not accumulate they have no profit."[16] We have so far discussed only the second proposition. "The question, then, is thrown forward from: what determines the rate of profit? to: What determines the rate of accumulation of capital?"[17] Let us now turn to the first part of her aphorism: no profit, no investment.

Robinson examines various theories of investment and suggests that none, including Keynes's marginal efficiency of capital concept, is capable of explain-

Figure 16.1

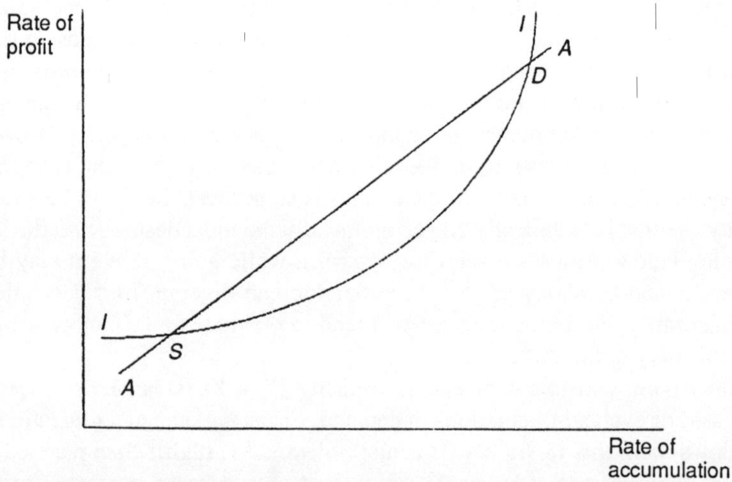

ing the rate of accumulation in the economy as a whole. She concludes that the model should be left open in this respect: "To attempt to account for what makes the propensity to accumulate high or low we must look into historical, political and psychological characteristics of an economy."[18] But leaving the matter at this is also impossible—nothing further can then be inferred about either growth or distribution. So Robinson goes on:

> It seems reasonably plausible, however, to say that, given the general characteristics of an economy, to sustain a higher rate of accumulation requires a higher level of profits, both because it offers more favorable odds in the gamble and because it makes finance more readily available. For purposes of our model, therefore, the "animal spirits" of the firms can be expressed in terms of a function relating the desired rate of growth of the stock of productive capital to the expected level of profits.[19]

In practice, Robinson makes the expected profit rate follow closely in the footsteps of the actual profit rate, and investment plans of period t are based on the realized rate of return in period $t-1$. Robinson does not explicitly account for the formation of expectations regarding the profit rate but, in effect, the investment function would appear to be:

$$k^*_t = f(r_{t-1}) \text{ where } f' > 0 \tag{4}$$

Robinson graphs this relation as the investment schedule (I) in Figure 16.1, which shows the rate of accumulation as a function of the profit rate. However, apart from the positive slope, its exact functional form is not explained. The A schedule maps the widow's cruse relationship described by Equation 3: a higher growth rate generates a higher level of savings by causing a change in distribution in favor of profit income. Between them, the two relationships determine the accumulation rate at which the expectation of profit underlying the decision to accumulate matches the actual profitability resulting from the decision. This is the "desired" rate.

Figure 16.1 shows two such rates, one, "D," stable, the other, "S," not. When the realized profit is higher than expected (the A function is above the investment function), investment plans are revised upward and a higher rate of profit is experienced. Thus, if the economy goes above S, it will grow faster and faster till it reaches point D. Conversely, when the investment function lies above the A function, realized profits are lower than expected and accumulation slows down. Rates above point D are therefore temporary. If the economy were to settle at D, there is a stable and steady growth rate and a distribution of income to match. (Part of Robinson's study is concerned with various barriers to achieving this in a pure market economy.)

The desired rate of growth is notional in the sense that it can be specified even though there is no necessary tendency for the economy to gravitate toward it. If the desired rate is not feasible because of other forces depicted in the Robinsonian typology of growth paths, the particular distribution of income that makes that desired rate possible is also not experienced. Indeed, it may be the social unacceptability of that distribution that renders desired growth unachievable.

The Typology of Growth Paths

Robinson analyzes three other variables that affect accumulation and distribution and complete the picture of capitalist growth (excluding technological change and choice of technique which are not being studied here). These are:

(1) The growth rate of the labor supply.

(2) The initial capital stock.

(3) The bargaining power of workers against capitalists, and the nature of their reaction to changes in distribution; or more simply, how willing and able workers are to resist reductions in the real wage rate.

These define the feasible, in contrast to the desirable, growth rate and may constrain the desire to grow faster. Robinson enumerates several possibilities associated with each of these variables, defining an "age" corresponding to each possibility.

(1) The possibilities with regard to the labor supply are shown in Figure 16.2. If the labor supply happens to grow exactly at the same rate as the stable desired rate of accumulation (at point D), and if there are no other barriers to achieving the desired rate, the "golden" age shines forth. It can only come about by a fluke, since there is no automatic mechanism to bring the labor supply into line with the labor requirements of desired capital accumulation. If the desired rate of growth is too high, in the sense that labor shortages prevent its achievement, the golden age is "restrained." Finally, if accumulation is not keeping up

Figure 16.2

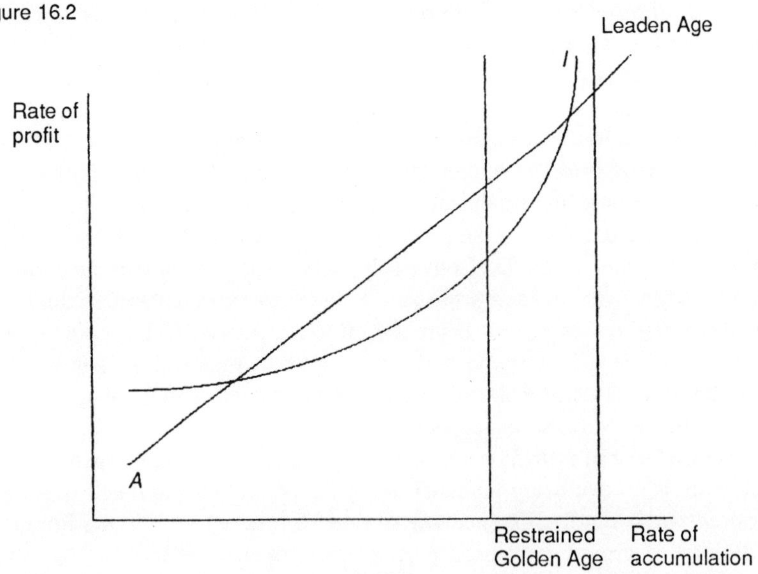

with the labor force, a growing proportion of the population joins the unemployed, and the age is "leaden." (This issue becomes of central importance in the study of technology. The effective growth rate of labor supply, of course, is not just the additional number of workers but also their increased productive power. If there is a shortage of labor, technical change can release this constraint by increasing the effectiveness of labor.)[20]

(2) The desired rate of growth requires a certain proportional relationship between the capital- and the consumer-goods sectors. The incongruously named "platinum" ages describe the process of getting from an initial sectoral composition that is not appropriate for the desired rate of accumulation to one that is. Whereas the golden and leaden classifications denote a path characterized by a steady growth rate, the platinum label actually describes an economy in transition from one growth path to another. The platinum ages are traverses.[21] If the desired growth rate is lower than the one to which the existing capital stock is geared, the capital-goods sector has to shrink relative to the consumer-goods sector—a "creeping platinum" age. On the other hand, "galloping platinum" describes the transition from too small a capital-goods sector—i.e., from a lower rate of growth—to the larger one required by the higher desired rate of growth. In Figure 16.1 the points between S and D are "galloping platinum" traverses, i.e., the investment sector is being built up in order to achieve the higher growth rate at D. Those above D represent "creeping platinum" ages, i.e., the investment sector is being shrunk as the growth rate goes down toward D.[22]

(3) If workers successfully resist the erosion of their purchasing power by hiking up money wages, the profit rate does not go up to the "desired" rate, and

we are in a ''bastard'' golden age. In that situation the price level and the wage rate may chase each other along a spiral; the rising growth rate has then come up against an ''inflation barrier.''

All of Robinson's ''ages'' are defined with respect to the benchmark desired rate. For example, a platinum path is one of building the capacity necessary to achieve a certain desired rate of growth. The various golden ages describe situations of either being at the desired rate, or being inhibited from reaching it due to a lower rate of labor-force growth, or due to labor resistance to the erosion of the real wage. The desired rate itself can be studied independently of the ages, but the ages cannot be defined without the ''desired'' reference point. Without the analysis of the investment function and the distributional adjustment mechanism, the typology of paths has no meaning. Thus, it is relevant to inquire more closely into the determination of the benchmark rate of capital formation.

The Indeterminateness of the Model

The logical structure of the two relations, which between them determine a desired rate of growth, is similar to the general structure of the multiplier-accelerator model. The variables are of course different: levels of output and investment in one type of model, versus the rates of profit and growth in the other. But the relationships are similar. In the multiplier accelerator model, investment determines output, which drives investment. In the Cambridge growth model, accumulation determines the profit rate, which conditions accumulation. The similarity is hardly surprising, as both models are rooted in the original Keynesian conception.

Luigi Pasinetti has provided a particularly lucid critique of the multiplier-accelerator construction, although the basic structure was elucidated by Samuelson.[23] Such models are generally used to explain cyclical fluctuations.[24] Duesenberry, however, utilized a multiplier accelerator model in his exegesis of post–World War II steady growth in the U.S. economy.[25] Pasinetti asked why these theories can explain either cyclical movements or a growth trend, but are unable to explain both phenomena together?[26] The answer is that the same model shows cyclical movements or growth movements depending on the parameters assigned to the investment function. Different writers considered different values for the parameters, and hence arrived at either cycle models or growth models. Thus, Pasinetti pointed out:

> All these theories have the common feature of being based on an endogamous dynamism resulting from the interaction between the multiplier and some form of the acceleration principle. The latter may be framed in a number of ways, but the results are always the same. According to the range of values in which the parameters of the investment function fall, the system produces four main types of behaviour: exponential growth, explosive cycles, damped cycles, steady contraction.[27]

Figure 16.3

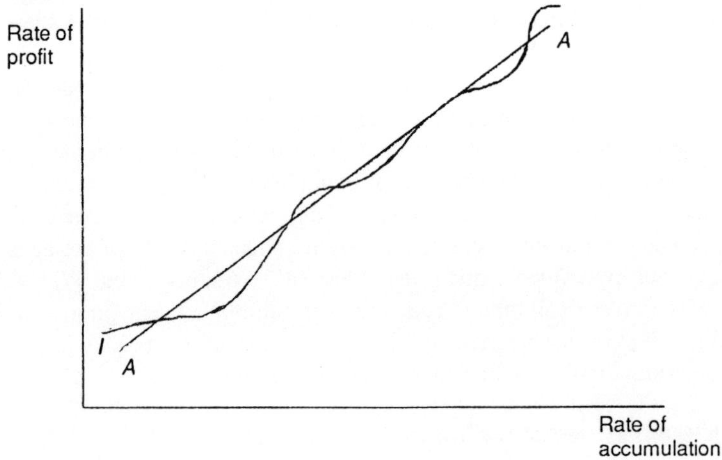

Figure 16.4

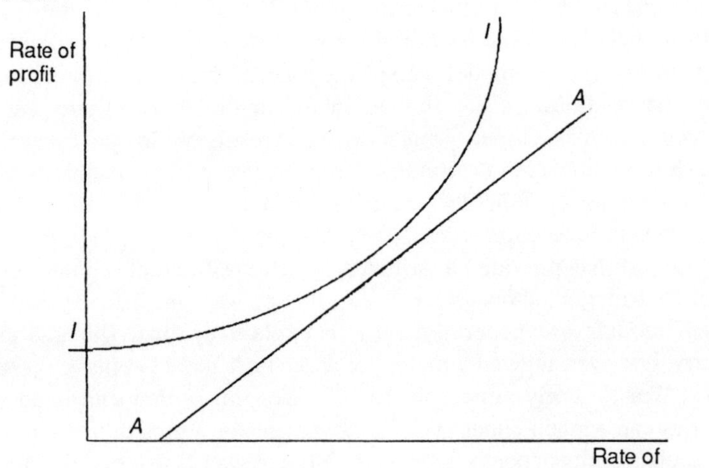

This shows up as a weakness in all the uses to which the multiplier and accelerator principles have been put. The investment function parameters on which the outcome of a given model depends are arbitrarily assumed: "although the various authors have implicitly shown well-defined preferences for some particular values of the parameters of the investment function, they have not developed any explicit discussion to justify their positions."[28] The multiplier and accelerator models are, in this sense, indeterminate.

Reflection shows that these remarks also hold for Robinson's treatment of growth, as one would suspect from the similarity between its structure and that of multiplier accelerator models. There are two points here:

(i) Robinson admitted from the beginning the slim conceptual basis of the investment function. That investment is a positive function of the rate of profit may be plausible, but all this tells us is that the slope of the investment function is generally non-negative, and positive in some range(s). Robinson herself acknowledged, in a footnote, the dependence of the desired growth path on the *assumed* shape of the investment function, pointing out that there is no logical necessity for it to have the shape depicted in Figure 16.1.[29] It is just as possible for the investment function to be such that there are numerous "desired" rates of growth (Figure 16.3), or none at all (Figure 16.4). Depending on how one draws the schedule, capital accumulation may tend to a steady rate, or it may be wildly unsteady with the economy constantly switching from one growth path to another. The point is that the outcome depends on the shape and position of a schedule about which only the vaguest surmise has been made, and that is as indeterminate as the accelerator.

(ii) More importantly, there is no reason for the schedule, whatever its shape, to be stable. The investment function rests on the relation between the *expected* rate of return on investment, on which the decision to invest depends, and the *observed* rate of profit—a highly subjective relationship, and one about which Robinson says very little.[30] Every time the investment schedule shifts, the desired rate of growth also changes. There is nothing in Robinson's analysis to give it any semblance of stability.

This, of course, is in keeping with the view that the "animal spirits" underlying investment decisions are too volatile to be modeled as a determinate relationship. The volatility due to uncertainty is an important feature of the original Keynesian income determination model. It has not been recognized that extending the Keynesian conception of investment, based on volatile expectations, to growth, as Robinson does, leads to an inconsistency. The proposition that free-floating business expectations cause fluctuations in employment, capacity utilization, and output rests on the observed cyclical character of these variables. By contrast, the steadiness of capital and labor shares in income is a stylized fact,[31] one that Cambridge theory takes as its premise.[32] It is contradictory to base these shares on volatile investment spending.

Cyclical versus Secular Changes in Investment

Economists' treatment of time was a central issue for Robinson. She pointed out the confusion between a comparison of equilibrium positions and a historical process taking place in real time.[33] She argued that explicit account should be taken of the time dimension of a movement. The ambiguity of the time dimension of investment is thus ironic. This is no doubt a result of Robinson's need to find a quick and easy way for dealing with the troublesome subject in order to get to questions she considered more amenable to analytical treatment. Other writers, among them Kalecki and Kaldor, were more careful in their handling of the investment question.

Kalecki explicitly distinguished the effect of cyclical forces on investment from secular ones, and tried to formulate a framework that would include both types of influences. We can extract the following general form from the several versions of the Kaleckian investment function contained in his writings:[34]

$$I_t + q = A(T) + B(T)\,[S_t\,;\,dP_t/dt\,] \qquad (5)$$

B(T) is the function that measures business responsiveness to what Kalecki sees as the main cyclical influences on the investment decision: firms' internal savings (S_t) and changes in profits (dP_t/dt). He places some weight on retained earnings both as the direct means of finance and as the indicator of firms' ability to raise funds from outside. He considers changes in profits the main determinant of the expected future rate of return. These two effects show themselves in the amount of investment undertaken with a time lag of *q*.

The function measuring the response to profitability and retained earnings, *B* (*T*), itself changes with time, but is stable in the short period, when changes in retained earnings and profits cause fluctuations in investment. (*T*) indicates a sequence of periods to which *t* belongs. That is, coefficients *A* and *B* evolve over time, but changes in them take longer stretches of time than changes in the variables contained in the square brackets. Hence *T* contains *t*. The term *A* (*T*) reflects factors, whether social, technological, or political, that do not show their effect through profits but nonetheless condition investment. This term looks like an autonomous investment component, but the time tag *T* indicates it is a variable. The Kaleckian investment function has a dual time structure, with the coefficients *A*(*T*) and *B*(*T*) capturing secular changes, but acting as constants in the shorter time span defined by movements in the variables S_t and dP_t/dt. Note that P_t is the absolute amount of profits; it increases regularly with the scale of the economy. Capital formation leads to greater profits and the latter leads to more capital accumulation.

This structure would not seem to be entirely consistent with Kalecki's well-known assertion that "the long-run trend is but a slowly changing component of a chain of short-period situations; it has no independent entity."[35] On the contrary, the coefficient *A*(*T*) embodies institutional determinants that require an explanation independent of short-term variations that are accounted for by the second term of Expression 5.

Needless to say, this distinction between changes in the variables of the relationship versus changes in the coefficients themselves, while interesting, does not amount to a theory of investment on its own. Expression 5 needs further elucidation to go from a listing of components to a real explanation. Kalecki's repeated attempts at formulating slightly different versions of the same idea may be an indication of his own dissatisfaction with the analysis of investment. Small wonder that he described the subject as "the central *pièce de resistance* of economics."

All the same, the Kalecki formula provides the element missing from Robinson's analysis: it includes secular determinants in an explicit way. We have seen that a change in the rate of capital formation can cause a long-run shift in income distribution only if it is itself a relatively "permanent" change. The variable dP_t/dt does *not* embody such a movement; the coefficients $A(T)$ and $B(T)$ do. The justification of the distributional mechanism requires a discussion of such parametric shifts. Robinson does not make this distinction. Her investment function does not deal with secular changes. In effect it does not have the same time dimension as the widow's cruse mechanism. The two relationships, represented by schedules A and I in Figure 16.1, underlying the desired rate have different dimensions and therefore do not belong together.

The distinction between level of investment and the rate of growth of capital stock or share of investment in GNP is relevant here. It is possible to think of a secular relationship between investment and capacity that underlies the rate of growth of capital stock. The relationship itself depends on the specific conditions of the economy under consideration. On the other hand, it is possible to regard the rate of capital formation as having no special significance apart from the absolute amount of investment. In this case the level of investment is not tethered to capital stock and output, and the economy is not characterized by a secular parameter of accumulation. Then, the only changes caused by investment are cyclical ones, and the widow's cruse mechanism does not exist.

Which view is a more accurate description of growth experience can probably only be resolved by empirical research, if at all. The point here is that the widow's cruse mechanism can only be valid if the rate of capital formation does have secular stability. Kaldor's justification of the distributional effect implies that only a persistent change in the ratio of investment to capital stock can cause a persistent change in the distribution of income between wages and profits. For this, the ratio has to reflect a stable relationship between the scale of the economy and investment. It is this dimension that Kaleckian parameters $A(T)$ and $B(T)$ represent.

The point can be further illustrated with Kaldor's own modeling of growth. He derives a secular growth rate by including technological change as an endogenous variable. Kaldor subsumed all increases in productivity under a "technical progress function." He suggests that productivity growth is a function of accumulation:

$$y^* = a + bk^* \tag{6}$$

where y^* and k^* are the growth rates of per worker output and capital input, respectively.

The coefficients a and b represent the degree of "inventiveness" in the economy and the willingness of economic agents to adopt new ideas and methods. The technological progress function involves a given level of technological dynamism. Given a regular flow of invention, Expression 6 shows the impact of investment on the embodiment and therefore *diffusion* of these innovations. Kaldor argues that a high rate of investment means fast diffusion and therefore high productivity growth.[36] Long-term equilibrium is defined as a constant capital to output ratio, which can be expressed as:

$$k^* = y^* \tag{7}$$

Given this condition, the productivity function 6 solves for a unique equilibrium growth rate:

$$k^* = y^* = a/1 - b \tag{8}$$

The growth rate ($a/1 - b$) is determined independently of the other relationships in the model. Savings and investment adjust to bring about this rate.

For reasons that go beyond the scope of this paper,[37] Kaldor's explanation of the technological progress function and the dynamic equilibrium condition is not entirely satisfactory. However, the rate of growth of capital, k^*, derived in this way *does* have the merit of being consistent with the post-Keynesian distribution story. ($a/1 - b$) is based on the "degree of technological dynamism" of the economy, and this dynamism in turn is based on institutional characteristics that are persistent and slow to change. It is plausible that these forces underlie the social distribution of income—they have the same time dimension.

Accumulation fluctuates around and gravitates toward the parametric rate ($a/1 - b$). To complete the story, the absolute amount of investment at any one time period can be seen as fluctuating around the level required by the secular rate of growth. Animal spirits and uncertainty come into play in this latter context. The regular Keynesian multiplier applies to these fluctuations. Whether or not this is a realistic picture of growth, it is a consistent one.

In summary, the argument that the growth rate determines the real wage through its influence on the price level makes sense only if the growth rate can be seen as sufficiently well established. There have to be persistent forces underlying the growth rate that render it a stable parameter of the economy. The view of investment as based on subjective factors that are not amenable to analysis conflicts with the distributional mechanism, which requires that a case be made for a rate of accumulation subject to secular shifts, not to cyclical fluctuations. What is needed is an explanation of what the underlying forces are that may endow accumulation with such a character, and how these forces influence investment decisions.

Future researchers have much to learn from Robinson's mistakes as well as from her insights. Along with Kaldor, Kalecki, and other post-Keynesian thinkers, she asked questions that mainstream economists either ignore or answer superficially, and that remain relevant. It is hoped that an awareness of a weak point in Robinson's trail-blazing work on growth will highlight the nature of capital formation as a critical issue and thus facilitate the task of filling in the gap.

Notes

1. Robinson, 1965, p. 192.
2. Klein, 1958.
3. Robinson, 1965, pp. 55–56.
4. Robinson, 1974.
5. Pasinetti, 1974, pp. 42–48.
6. Garegnani, 1987a.
7. In order to keep the subject matter within the bounds of a paper, I will not deal at all with technological change and natural resources, and only incidentally with the question of labor availability.
8. Kaldor, 1970, pp. 81–82.
9. Ibid., p. 82; in this instance, Kaldor appears to be using the terms "long" versus "short run" synonymously with secular versus cyclical. It is the latter distinction that is being made in this paper.
10. Vianello, 1985; Garegnani, 1987b; Ciccone, 1986.
11. Kalecki, 1971, pp. 28–29.
12. Garegnani, 1987b.
13. Vianello, 1985; Ciccone, 1986.
14. Lowe, 1976.
15. Robinson, 1980, pp. 22–23.
16. Robinson, 1965, p.76.
17. Robinson, 1964, p. 13.
18. Ibid., p. 37.
19. Ibid., pp. 37–38.
20. Ibid., p. 15.
21. Lowe, 1976.
22. For some reason, Robinson does not identify the platinum ages on her diagram (Figure 16.1), although her definition clearly implies that these points are such "ages."
23. Samuelson, 1939.
24. E.g., Hansen, 1964.
25. Duesenberry, 1958.
26. Pasinetti, 1974, p. 55.
27. Ibid., pp. 65–66.
28. Ibid., p. 67.
29. Robinson, 1964, p. 49 n. 1.
30. See pp. 8–9, above.
31. Kaldor, 1970, p. 13.
32. Robinson, 1974.
33. Robinson, 1974.
34. The following discussion is based on the essays "Determinants of Investment" and "Trend and Business Cycle" in Kalecki, 1971 and chaps. 14–15 in Kalecki, 1969.
35. Kalecki, 1971, p. 165.
36. Kaldor, 1957, pp. 595–97.
37. In particular, the notion of firms picking the most desirable capital to output ratio

is troublesome, because Kaldor considers such ratios the outcome of technological change. That is, for him and Robinson, technologies do not exist as blueprints, so each ratio corresponds to a different level of technical development. But Kaldor's model implies that technological *change* exists as a blueprint, which if anything is more implausible a premise than the standard production function.

References

Asimakopulos, A. (1977) "Post-Keynesian Growth Theory." In S. Weintraub, ed., *Modern Economic Thought*. Philadelphia: University of Pennsylvania Press.

Bharadwaj, Krishna. (1986) *Classical Political Economy and Rise to Dominance of Supply and Demand Theories*. London: Sangam Books.

Blaug, Mark. (1985) *Economic Theory in Retrospect*, 4th ed. Cambridge: Cambridge University Press.

Ciccone, Roberto. (1986) "Joan Robinson on Accumulation." *Political Economy: Studies in the Surplus Approach*, 3.

Duesenberry, J. S. (1958) *Business Cycles and Economic Growth*. New York: Norton.

Garegnani, Pierangelo. (1983) "Notes on Consumption, Investment and Effective Demand." In John Eatwell and Murray Milgate, eds., *Keynes' Economics and the Theory of Value and Distribution*. New York: Oxford University Press.

———. (1987a) "Capital and Effective Demand." In A. Barriere, ed., *Keynes Today*. London: Macmillan

———. (1987b) "Two Views of Effective Demand." Unpublished manuscript.

Hansen, Alvin H. (1964) *Business Cycles and National Income*. New York: Norton.

Kaldor, Nicholas. (1954) "The Relation of Economic Growth and Cyclical Fluctuations." *Economic Journal*, pp. 53–71.

———. (1970) "Model of Distribution." In Amartya Sen, ed., *Growth Economics*. Harmondsworth: Penguin.

———. (1985) *Economics without Equilibrium*. Armonk, N.Y.: M. E. Sharpe.

Kalecki, Michal. (1969) *Theory of Economic Dynamics. An Essay on Cyclical and Long-Run Changes in Capitalist Economies*. New York: Augustus Kelley.

———. (1971) *Selected Essays of the Dynamics of the Capitalist Economy. 1933–1970*. Cambridge: Cambridge University Press.

Keynes, John Maynard. (1964) *The General Theory of Employment, Interest, and Money*. New York and London: Harcourt Brace Jovanovich.

Klein, Lawrence R. (1958) Review of *The Accumulation of Capital. Econometrica*, 26.

Lowe, Adolph. (1976) *The Path of Economic Growth*. Cambridge: Cambridge University Press.

Marglin, Stephen A. (1984) *Growth, Distribution, and Prices*. Cambridge, Mass.: Harvard University Press.

Nell, Edward J., ed. (1980) *Growth, Profits and Property*. Cambridge: Cambridge University Press.

———. (1987) "Accumulation of Capital." In John Eatwell, Murray Milgate, and Peter Newman, eds., *The New Palgrave: A Dictionary of Economics*. New York: The Stockton Press.

Pasinetti, Luigi L. (1974) *Growth and Income Distribution. Essays in Economic Theory*. Cambridge: Cambridge University Press.

———. (1981) *Structural Change and Economic Growth. A Theoretical Essay on the Dynamics of the Wealth of Nations*. Cambridge: Cambridge University Press.

Robinson, Joan. (1964) *Essays in the Theory of Economic Growth*. London: Macmillan.

———. (1965) *The Accumulation of Capital*, 2d ed. New York: St. Martin's Press.

———. (1974) *History versus Equilibrium.* London: Thames Papers in Political Economy.

———. (1980) *What Are the Questions? And Other Essays.* Armonk, N.Y.: M. E. Sharpe.

Samuelson, Paul A. (1939) "Interactions between the Multiplier Analysis and the Principle of Acceleration." *The Review of Economic Statistics.*

Thirlwall, Anthony P. (1987) *Nicholas Kaldor.* New York: NewYork University Press.

Vianello, Fernando. (1985) "The Pace of Accumulation." *Political Economy. Studies in the Surplus Approach.*

JR

CHAPTER SEVENTEEN

Technical Change, Profit, and Growth

Immanent Crisis and Rigorous Theory

DAVID LAIBMAN

About ten years ago, at a time when I had no idea that Joan Robinson was aware of my existence, I received in the mail a copy of her manuscript entitled "The Organic Composition of Capital."[1] No covering letter, only this notation at the top of page 1: "See p. 15—J. R." Turning to that page, I found the following marked for my attention (it refers to Professor Samuelson's Surrogate Production Function): "It seems to me to be a great insult to Marx to foist this conception upon him. It is far more honourable to admit that his *value* system is not all-inclusive than to try to make out that he was really a neoclassic at heart."

This admonition was directed toward early versions of my efforts to provide, in a Marxian context, a rigorous theory of the conditions under which technical change that raises the "organic composition of capital" might be expected to occur. Professor Robinson, of course, had long argued that the entire line of reasoning running from technical change to a falling rate of profit was a red herring,[2] and that, whatever might be said about capitalism-specific determinants of technical change, long-run neutrality was all that could be deduced at the level of theory. Now, when a (then!) young Marxist began to propose a formulation in which biased technical change might emerge from capitalist rational choice, subject to a constraint that looked suspiciously like a neoclassical production function (see below), the opportunity presented itself for Professor Robinson to knock off two of her favorite targets with one blast. My deepest regret, in presenting a simple but fully elaborated version of my proposal in this paper, is that I will not have her reaction to it.

Despite the obvious objections, made in a Robinsonian spirit, that the following model suppresses the heterogeneity of the capital stock and all the associated valuation puzzles,[3] and that it ignores the thorny but essential question of the qualitative transformation of goods and production processes through time, I believe it is important to work out a model of capitalist growth with technical change at the same level of abstraction and simplicity as that of the neoclassical models.[4] On this basis, the Marxian immanent critical tendencies, including that of the falling rate of profit, may be reconsidered. I will dispense with the usual literature survey,[5] assuming general familiarity with the issues at hand.

The Composition of Capital

We will work with an aggregative (one-good) model of the utmost simplicity and generality.[6] Production is carried on by homogeneous labor, using a stock of capital to produce output; in obvious notation,

$$K, L \rightarrow X \tag{1}$$

The capital good—the same stuff as output, of course—does not depreciate; there is therefore no material input flow in production, and no distinction between net and gross output. We define, conventionally, two ratios that completely describe the technology in use: $k = K/L$, the capital-labor ratio (Marx's "technical composition of capital"), and $x = X/L$, labor productivity.

Technical Change-Choice

Capitalist accumulation is inherently dynamic. At any moment in time, choices can (and must) be made, but these choices are not choices among statically preexisting alternatives; rather, they are choices of changes. To give expression to the way in which these change-choices are constrained, I have proposed a refurbished version of Kaldor's technical progress function (in its earlier versions, before the retreat from the capital stock to the investment flow).[7] I prefer to call this concept the *mechanization function*; it is illustrated in Figure 17.1.

The mechanization function posits a direct relation (with diminishing returns) between the growth *factors* of x and k, rather than between their growth rates, as in Kaldor. The growth factor of any variable y is $G_y = y_t/y_{t-1}$, the ratio of the value of the variable in a given time period to its value in the period immediately preceding. The growth factor of y can be thought of as "one plus the growth rate of y," but this growth rate is ambiguous in a discrete time model, for which the growth factor seems better suited.[8] We will need a parametric version of the mechanization function, given below. Since the Cobb-Douglas form is by far the most convenient (I have tried others), we will want to represent both positive and negative growth by means of a variable that never takes on negative values. Thus, using G for growth factors and g for growth rates, when y is stationary, $G_y = 1$ ($g_y = 0$); for absolute minimum growth, $G_y = 0$ ($g_y = -100\%$); y is falling (rising) when $G_y < 1$, $G_y > 1$ ($g_y < 0$, $g_y > 0$).

The mechanization function is:

$$G_x = G \cdot Gk^{\alpha} \qquad 0 < \alpha < 1 \tag{2}$$

Figure 17.1

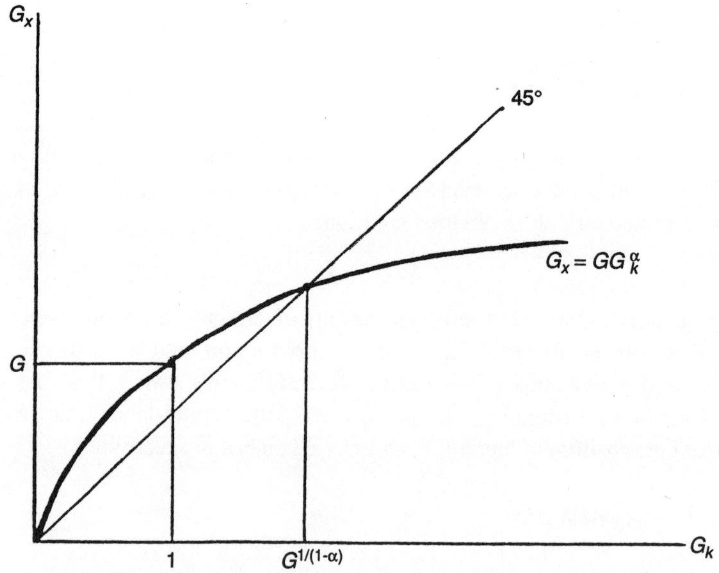

In this expression, G is a parameter reflecting "autonomous" technical progress: organizational and skill improvement raising productivity by some small amount each period independently of increases in the degree of mechanization (G_k); with $G_k = 1$, therefore, $G_x = G$, which should be thought of as lying in the range 1.005–1.01. G is the concentrated indicator of the capitalist society's institutional arrangements surrounding research and development, and dissemination of productivity advances; it is therefore beyond the control of the individual capitalist and not an object of strategic planning, let alone short-period choice. The other parameter, α, expresses the rate at which diminishing returns to mechanization set in within a given short-period scientific-technical horizon: greater increases in productivity can be achieved through raising k, but not in an unbounded manner. As α varies from 0 to 1, it defines a family of curves, bounded by a horizontal straight line at $G_x = G$ (mechanization is completely ineffectual) to a ray from the origin through $(G,1)$ (productivity increases are unbounded). Figure 17.1 illustrates the general case. While α is given exogenously in the short period, it may be thought of as a possible object of strategic planning by capitalists, who are under constant compulsion to find large productivity increases in the short run as a condition for success in the competitive struggle for survival (of which more below). This may be less a matter of conscious policy and more a question of something like natural selection, favoring the survival of capitals that succeed in raising α, thereby planting an α-increasing tendency in the engineering culture of capitalist society which then "operates behind the backs of" individual capitals.[9]

At a moment in time, however, both G and α are given; the mechanization function is the technical-change possibility set for the capitalist, who chooses a position on it in accordance with an objective function. This latter must be specified with some care.

The Conjunctural Profit Rate

Preliminary to doing this, we will need general expressions for the profit rate and for the distribution of income between workers and capitalists. These classes, as always in models whose object is the theory of the abstract capitalist economy, are unambiguously defined and exhaust the economically active population. If W represents aggregate real wages, $W/L = wx$ is the real wage rate, where w is the share of wages in output (W/X). The rate of exploitation is $(1 - w)/w$. The rate of profit, defined conventionally as profits/capital, may be written:

$$r = \frac{X - W}{K} = \frac{x}{k}(1 - w) \tag{3}$$

I have chosen to define the profit rate in terms of the physical capital stock K, ignoring the sense in which the wage represents variable capital, labor power once it has passed into the control of the capitalist in the circuit of productive capital. In classic Marxian terminology, my profit rate is S/C, not $S/(C + V)$. This choice greatly simplifies the workings of the model. More importantly, like the pure fixed capital assumption to which the profit-rate formulation is related, it accurately reflects the conditions of mature, industrialized capitalist economies, in which working financial capital earmarked for payrolls is negligible in size compared to the financial capital tied up in the stock of physical capital goods. Only this latter need be preaccumulated; payrolls for additions to the labor force, if not entirely financed out of new revenue, are financed through short-term borrowing whose interest cost is negligible. It should not be necessary to remark that this definition of r in no way denies or contradicts the distinction between constant and variable capital flows or the importance of this distinction in grasping the inner nature of the capitalist production relation.

We come finally to the maximand. If Kaldor is the progenitor of my constraint, the objective function comes from Okishio: the individual capital seeks to maximize the profit rate that would accrue to it if it were the sole possessor of a new technique, and therefore were able to operate the technique at prices of inputs and outputs appropriate to the old, existing technique. In a multisector world, the capitalist treats prices as constant (thus "failing" to "anticipate" changes in prices consequent upon general adoption of the new technique). In the one-sector case, without relative commodity prices, the relevant constants are the real wage rate wx, *and* the wage share w; the latter follows from the fact that x represents aggregate productivity, which is assumed constant by the individual capitalist.[10] It should be noted that nothing is presumed about the subsequent adjustment of w and wx when the new technique becomes general; any assumption, from Okishio's constant wx to my own constant w, or any other, may be made subsequently in tracing out the movement of the real wage and the profit rate.[11]

The underlying story presumes an intense, competitive struggle for survival among capitals, in which technical change is a major weapon. Each firm must think of itself as an innovator, and must seek to occupy the quasi-monopoly position of sole possessor of a new technique; if it fails to pursue this opportunity, no matter how fleeting the excess return may be, its competitors will do so, and will use the ensuing advantage against it in the race for markets, diversification, and growth.[12] Pursuing the hint in the paragraph directly above, this is a form of capitalism-specific rational expectations: capitalists may "anticipate" the loss of their privileged position; they may even "anticipate" never attaining that position, if they expect other capitals to be able to move to the new technique almost simultaneously; but they cannot take evasive action, in the sense of avoiding the technical change and the ensuing consequences, since that would mean their eventual extinction.

I have chosen the term "conjunctural," rather than the more common "innovator's" or "transitional," to avoid the connotation of a bifurcation into innovators and imitators, as in Schumpeter (1939), and the idea of golden ages with an abnormal period of transition between them. The conjunctural profit rate is the maximand for all capitals, and the struggle for successful accumulation via innovation is a continual process of interruption of equilibrium.

With these conceptual points established, we may define the conjunctural rate of profit:[13]

$$\rho = \frac{XG_X - (wx)LG_L}{KG_K} = \frac{x}{k}\,\frac{G_x - w}{G_k} \tag{4}$$

Optimal Technical Change

The choice problem is now straightforward. The individual capitalist maximizes (4), subject to (2). Since there is nothing unusual or difficult in the workings, we proceed directly to the solution:

$$\overline{G}_x = \frac{w}{1-\alpha} \qquad \overline{G}_k = \left[\frac{w}{G(1-\alpha)}\right]^{1/\alpha} \tag{5}$$

Figure 17.2

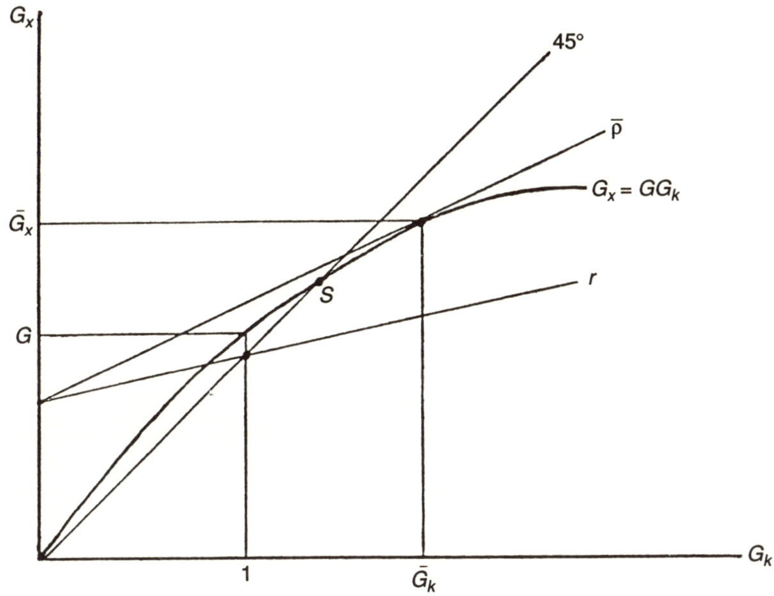

This result is illustrated in Figure 17.2. Solving (4) for G_x, we obtain:

$$G_x = w + \rho\ (k/x)G_k \tag{6}$$

This may be thought of as an iso-ρ line, whose intercept is the wage share coefficient, w, and whose slope is governed by the variable ρ. When $\rho = r$, the iso-ρ line passes through $G_x = G_k = 1$, representing the no-change option. As ρ increases, the line rotates upward; $\bar{\rho}$, the maximum achievable conjunctural profit rate, occurs at the point of tangency between the iso-ρ line and the mechanization function, defining $\overline{G}_x$ and $\overline{G}_k$.

The Organic Composition

We are now ready to pose the question whether micro-rational technical change, as promulgated by capitalists, will result in a rising organic composition of capital. We define the latter as the ratio of the value of the physical capital stock to the flow of current labor [in Marxian notation, $C/(V + S)$], as this appears to be the best way to make the concept a measure of development of the productive forces, independent of the rate of exploitation or w.[14] In our one-sector notation, the composition of capital is:

$$Q = K/X = k/x, \tag{7}$$

the capital-output ratio. Observing that $G_Q = G_k/G_x$, and applying the optimality result (5), we find the growth factor of Q to be:

$$\overline{G}_Q = G^{-1/\alpha}\left(\frac{w}{1-\alpha}\right)^{(1-\alpha)/\alpha} \tag{8}$$

From this, the condition for composition-increasing (composition-decreasing) technical change is easily derived:

$$G_Q \gtrless 1 \text{ as } w \gtrless (1-\alpha)G^{1/(1-\alpha)} \tag{9}$$

Rather than a law of rising organic composition, we have a way to identify the determining factors. $G_Q > 1$ is more likely the higher is w, the higher is α, and the lower is G. First, it should be emphasized that if the required conditions obtain, then the rising composition of capital is established, and is consistent with micro-rational behavior—indeed, it is the outcome of that behavior. Beyond that observation, and in the absence of reliable empirical information, our conclusion must be presumptive (not to say presumptuous!). *If* G is small, owing to the notorious capitalist neglect of fundamental research and the atomistic, wasteful, and secretive duplication of research activities inhibiting dissemination of results; *if* the wage share is kept sufficiently high owing to the increasing size, homogeneity, and political maturity of the working class; *if* the search for short-run ρ-increasing technical change promotes a high and rising α; *then* the accumulation path will reveal a secularly rising composition of capital—as long as the above conditions continue to prevail.

In analyzing these conditions, I was interested in whether capitalist experience would indeed discover a positive association between $\overline{\rho}$ and α. From $\overline{\rho} = (x/k)(\overline{G}_x - w)/\overline{G}_k$, and after considerable manipulation, we obtain:

$$\frac{\partial\overline{\rho}}{\partial\alpha} = \overline{\rho}\,\frac{1}{\alpha^2}\, ln\left(\frac{\overline{G}_X}{G}\right)$$

This derivative is indeed greater than 0, but barely! It suggests the existence of a weak incentive to search for α-increasing innovations; one must, however, remain in doubt as to whether this effect is likely to have a significant impact.

We will return to the issue of the presumption of a rising Q in the context of the growth model below. This section may be concluded with a commonplace but important observation: We have $r = (1 - w)/Q$. It is clear that as a matter of definition, a rising Q entails falling r, or falling w, or both. I believe the emphasis on the issue of the falling rate of profit is misplaced; in so far as our attention is confined to the narrow issue of accumulation reflecting capitalism-specific technical change,[15] the immanent critical tendency *is* the rising composition of capital, since this implies *either* a fall in the profit rate *or* a rise in the rate of exploitation. That these alternatives have not been given equal prominence may be due to Marx's emphasis on the former in volume 3 of *Capital*, or to a predisposition to avoid examining a possibility (rising rate of exploitation) that invokes problems of realization or effective demand, owing to an unreasonable fear of underconsumptionism. Clearly, the theory of the crisis-inducing character of either a falling r or a falling w must be carefully elaborated. It is noteworthy, however, that the Okishio assumption of a constant real wage implies a non-decreasing r but also a rising rate of exploitation, as all productivity gains go to profits. One assumption concerning the response of the real wage to technical change places the capitalist economy on one horn of the falling-r/falling-w dilemma; another assumption places the economy on the other horn. The existence of the dilemma in the first place is the real issue, and this depends on Q-increasing technical change.

Accumulation: The Consistent Path

The issue of critical tendencies may be better examined in the context of a simple, non-steady-state growth model, which brings together many of the distinctively Marxian properties. Two of the three main ingredients are familiar: a constant proportional rate of growth of the labor force,[16] and a classical savings function. The missing link was the theory of optimal technical change-choice, and that is now ready for action.

The growth factor of the demand for labor depends on the chosen rate of mechanization, G_k (we drop the bar for notational convenience), and the growth factor of the capital stock, G_K. New labor can be absorbed into production at a rate given by G_K / G_k. Constancy of the share of unemployed workers (Marx's reserve army) in the total labor force requires that this ratio be equal to the (constant) growth factor of the labor supply, N. Accordingly, we write:

$$G_K = G_k \cdot N \tag{10}$$

remembering that this is a constant unemployment rate condition, not a full employment condition.

All saving/investing is done by capitalists, at a constant rate s, proportional to profits:[17]

$$G_K = \frac{K + \Delta K}{K} = 1 + \frac{s(1-w)X}{K} = 1 + s(1-w)(x/k)$$

$$G_K = 1 + sr \tag{11}$$

Figure 17.3

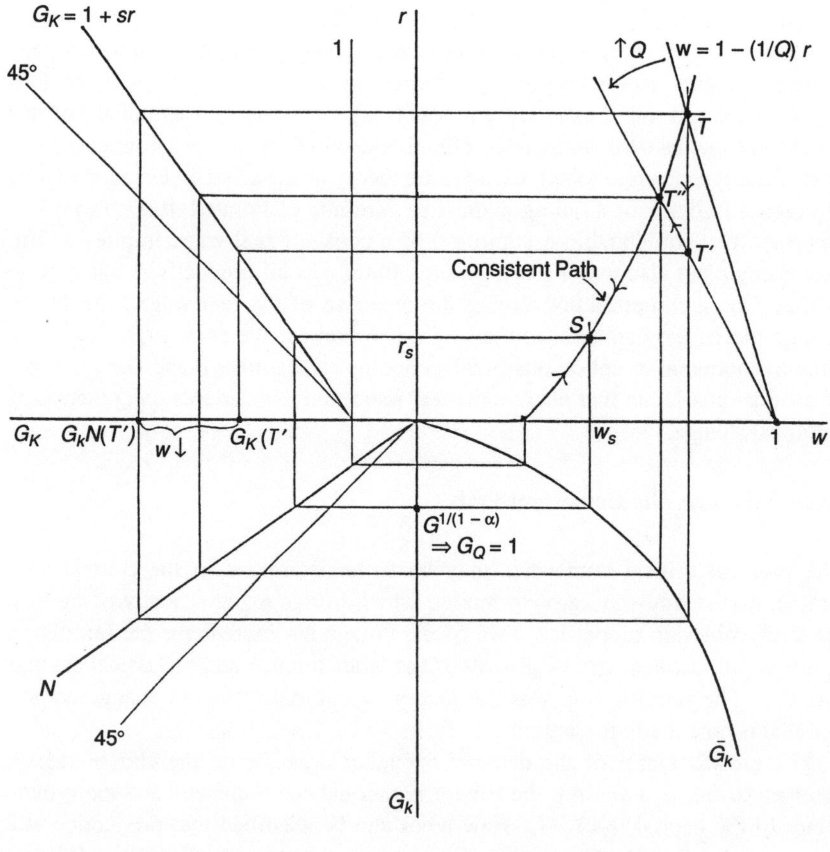

This of course is a variant of the so-called Cambridge Equation.[18]

All the ingredients of the growth path are now in place; the story is told in Figure 17.3. The relation between w and G_k, the desired growth factor of mechanization, is given in the right-hand member of Equation 5, and is shown in the southeast quadrant of Figure 17.3. Equations 10 and 11 are plotted, respectively, in the southwest and northwest quadrants; the rays labeled N and G_K have slopes N and $1/s$. Using all these relationships, a point such as T in (r,w) space can be identified. I call such a point a *consistent point.* It is (in as few words as possible) the conjunction of a profit rate with a wage share such that, given the saving rate, the growth factor of the capital stock is such that, given the growth factor of the labor supply, the rate of mechanization that keeps the rate of unemployment constant is the same as the rate desired for conjunctural profit rate maximization, given the postulated wage share. (One picture is worth a thousand words.)

The locus of consistent points is the *consistent path,* shown in the northeast quadrant of Figure 17.3. Its equation, the solution of Equations 5, 10, and 11, is:

$$r = \frac{1}{s}\,[G\,(1-\alpha)]^{-1/\alpha}\,w^{1/\alpha} - \frac{1}{sN} \tag{12}$$

The point T lies on a profit-rate/wage-share tradeoff (Equation 3), and presupposes a certain level of Q. The key to non-steady-state dynamics lies in the behavior of Q. Referring to Equation 7 and Figure 17.2, it is evident that Q is rising as long as $G_k > G_x$, or, equivalently, $G_k > G^{1/(1-\alpha)}$—i.e., to the right of point S in Figures 17.2 and 17.3. At T, therefore, Q is rising, and the wage-profit curve pencils inward as shown.[19] The resulting movement depends on the social complexities of wage adjustment, of course, but we can analyze cases in which artificial stages given by constancy of w or of r are created. Assume provisionally, for example, that workers initially have the power to preserve their share as productivity rises with Q-increasing technical change. w remains constant, and the profit rate falls, from T to T'. Capital accumulation then falls to $G_K(T')$, and the resulting gap represents rising unemployment.

While many approaches to wage adjustment are possible at this point—either the real wage or w may be considered to depend on the unemployment rate, for example—the most general assumption, and the one required for adjustment to take place, would seem to link unemployment to change in the wage share. As the reserve army grows, it is not necessary for real wages to fall; only for real wages to begin to rise less rapidly than productivity. Thus, we may (conservatively) write:

$$\text{sign}\,\dot{w} = \text{sign}\,(G_K - G_k N). \tag{13}$$

The erosion of the wage share is shown as the subsequent movement from T' to T'' in Figure 17.3. This movement closes the gap between $G_k N$ and G_K from two directions: by increasing the profit rate, thereby restoring G_K, and by reducing the ρ-maximizing G_k. This latter effect is the reason why, when a new consistent point is reached at T'', the profit rate is not restored to its previous level.

The consistent path is thus shown to be a benchmark growth path—one could, with suitable precautions, say "equilibrium" path—for the economy, abstracting from cycles, possible investment catastrophes, etc. Movement along it, from points like T to points like T'', involves "labor-saving" technical change, a falling rate of profit, and a rising rate of exploitation (thought by some to be the essential proposition behind Marx's concept of "relative immiseration"). Against those observations in confirmation of the Marxian vision, however, it must be pointed out that the path has a terminus at point S, when w has fallen to a

Table 17.1

	α = 0.25	α = 0.5	α = 0.75
α = 0.25	0.093 / 0.76	0.05 / 0.76	0.03 / 0.76
α = 0.5	0.12 / 0.51	0.06 / 0.51	0.04 / 0.51
α = 0.75	0.20 / 0.26	0.10 / 0.26	0.067 / 0.26

level—$(1 - \alpha)\, G^{1/(1-\alpha)}$—at which ρ-maximizing technical change implies constancy of Q. If growth proceeds to this point, the economy settles into a steady state, with profit rate r_s, wage share w_s, productivity and the capital-labor ratio growing at the same constant rate, $G^{1/(1-\alpha)}$. Our earlier question concerning the likelihood of Q-increasing technical change may now be reformulated to assess the likelihood of reaching point S.

While no firm conclusions can be drawn from back-of-the-envelope calculations, the following exercise may at least point the way toward a fuller analysis. For $G_Q = 1$, we have $w_s = (1 - \alpha)\, G^{1/(1-\alpha)}$. Substituting this into Equation 12, we find:

$$r_s = \frac{1}{s} G^{1/(1-\alpha)} - \frac{1}{sN} \qquad (14)$$

Table 17.1 shows values of r_s (above the diagonal) and w_s (below the diagonal) for various hypothetical values of α and s, assuming $G = N = 1.001$. Numerous opinions are undoubtedly possible concerning the empirical counterparts of s, w, and r, and α would have to be estimated. Nevertheless, the heavily boxed region in the table, for which both α and s are between 0.5 and 0.75, seems a good guess; if it is, then the steady state would still appear to be out of reach of the advanced capitalist economies, where wage shares are in excess of 50 percent and rates of return in excess of 10 percent.

The connection between consistent-path growth and both cyclical and secular crisis remains to be explored, as does its relation to the conceptualization of stages in capitalist development. I have speculated that an economy evolving along (or close to) its consistent path may encounter barriers—associated with a minimum r entailing financial crisis and a minimum w related to crises of effective demand—before reaching point S.[20] But all this is for another day.

Conclusion

I have proposed a theory of optimal technical change for a capitalist economy, from which conditions for the trend in the composition of capital can be derived.[21] The conclusion seems inescapable: Q-increasing technical change may be carried out by capitalists who are behaving rationally in the pursuit of maximum conjunctural profits. I believe there is, in fact, a presumption that this will be the case, at least for long periods in capitalist development. The Okishio theorem rules out r-decreasing change if the real wage is constant, but it does not rule out the r-decreasing/w-decreasing dilemma. For this reason, the concept of the falling rate of profit, although secondary to the problem of conditions for Q-increasing technical change, is by no means reduced to a mere matter of contingency. With Q-increasing change, if the wage share is constant (one of the benchmark cases for the analysis of the various possibilities), the rate of profit falls. While this case is artificial, in that it requires real wage increases exactly in step with productivity increases, it is no more so than the assumption of a constant real wage.[22] Either assumption points to an immanent critical tendency, and an analysis of capitalism-specific technical change should lead toward a theory of crisis encompassing both falling-r and falling-w crisis potentials. My work on technical change and growth is intended as a contribution toward that theory.

Notes

1. Subsequently published as Robinson, 1978.
2. See Robinson, 1947.
3. See Harcourt, 1972; Laibman and Nell, 1977.
4. E.g., Solow, 1956.
5. See Harris, 1983; Roemer, 1977, 1978, 1979.
6. More complex versions of the model include ones that divide the economy into a capital-goods sector and a consumer-goods sector, entailing both goods-market equilibrium and profit-rate equalization; and productivity embodied in vintages of capital goods, involving a scrapping decision for early vintages. See especially Laibman (1981). Work is in progress on a version with financial relations between "inside" and "outside" capitals; a preliminary result is that the parameters of the financial decision by inside capitals affects the course of technical change.
7. Kaldor, 1957.
8. Discrete time, in turn, has been chosen because it is more amenable to computer

simulation, and this in turn seems to be an invaluable aid in exploring the properties of models such as this one where explicit solutions for the time paths of the variables are unattainable.

9. Empirical estimation of the mechanization function is readily suggested; in a simple linear form, $\log G_x = \log G + \alpha \log G_k$. Since technical change is incorporated in the definition of the variables, the function is not subject to an upward shift over time (although one could break the time series into segments, to test for change over time in the parameters); thus a "straight fit" is all that is required, without any assumptions about distribution, perfect competition, etc. Caution is required, of course; the data are far from reliable. In the vintage version of the model, the mechanization function is specified for the latest vintage capital stock and associated output only. While this is more conceptually satisfying, it makes the prospects of testing even more remote.

10. Okishio (1961) works in terms of arbitrary alternative techniques, rather than with the technical change-choice set proposed in this paper. His criterion for a switch in technique—cost reduction at the given prices—can be shown to be identical to the conjunctural profit rate criterion used here. I stumbled upon this idea independently (Laibman, 1976), only fifteen years late!

11. See Laibman (1982), for detailed argument concerning the relation between the rate of exploitation and the balance of class forces as a rationale for the constant-w assumption.

12. The fact that growth is the key to survival establishes the profit rate, not the amount of profit, as the central strategic variable. See Laibman and Nell (1977); for a contrary view, see Shaikh (1978).

13. Derivation of the right-hand expression in Equation 4 makes use of a feature of growth-factor algebra: $G_x = G_X / G_L$, $G_k = G_K / G_L$.

14. This concept might better be termed the "organic composition of capitalist production." In a multisector model, as was mentioned above, valuation puzzles confound the definition of Q, which puzzles are, of course, blissfully absent here.

15. It may be well to recall the wise agnosticism of Maurice Dobb (1959): "The contradictions of capitalism today on a world scale are so multiform and so complex that the force and extent of them cannot be epitomized in any single curve, like the temperature-chart of a hospital-patient" (p. 103).

16. Relaxation of this assumption is easily accomplished, but little seems to be gained by doing so. Harris (1983) makes the ingenious assumption that capitalists create their own sources of labor supply, if necessary, by raiding noncapitalist sectors at home or abroad. This does not affect the path of accumulation or the rate of profit, however.

17. Note the absence of the usual Keynesian dichotomy between the saving and investment aspects of the accumulation decision; this dichotomy is important in the short run, and in relation to financial mechanisms that we cannot examine here, but it seems inappropriate to carry it over into analysis of long-run growth. The absolute autonomy of the investor in Keynes is an opposite distortion to the disappearance of this autonomy and its replacement by passive maximization in the neoclassics; neither is an adequate representation of the capitalist.

18. There is a slight dimensional problem here. G_K is a pure number; r has reciprocal-time dimensionality. It has not seemed useful to make these concepts consistent by replacing r with some sort of profit factor. Dimensional purists can imagine an additional multiplicative constant with numerical value of unity and the dimension of time.

19. Although the current formulation is more convenient, nothing would be lost if the model were reformulated in terms of a profit rate/real wage tradeoff. In this case, the maximum real wage would rise with productivity, and the w_r-intercept would shift outward to the right.

20. These speculations will be found in Laibman (1983), which also offers some suggestions regarding the incorporation of a state sector into a model of this kind.

21. Capitalist micro-optimality does not imply social optimality. Without launching into the murky waters of "social welfare functions," we may refer to common sense to tell us that raising capital-goods requirements per unit of output is inefficient from a social standpoint.

22. Harris (1983, p. 320n) describes the constant-*w* assumption as "a specific hypothesis concerning the operation of the labour market. Otherwise, one would have to give up the idea of a labour-market determined real wage and resort to some other determination not yet specified. Until such a determination is provided, the mere assumption of a given rate of exploitation would remain without any behavioural content." I have emphasized that constant *w and* constant real wage are analytical devices; neither is likely to occur. But if behavioral content is needed, is it any less behavioral to postulate that workers are concerned with their relative position more than with their absolute level of income? Further, if we assume a nineteenth-century environment of prices falling via competition as a result of productivity increases, then given *money* wages would automatically result in constant relative shares, and constant real wages would require the unlikely occurrence of a fall in money wages exactly equal and opposite in magnitude to the rise in productivity. For further discussion, see Laibman (1982).

References

Dobb, M. (1959) "The Falling Rate of Profit." *Science & Society*, 23, 2 (Spring):97–103.

Harcourt, G. C. (1972) *Some Cambridge Controversies in the Theory of Capital*. New York: Cambridge University Press.

Harris, D. J. (1983) "Accumulation of Capital and the Rate of Profit in Marxian Theory." *Cambridge Journal of Economics*, 7:311–30.

Kaldor, N. (1957) "A Model of Economic Growth." *Economic Journal*, 67:591–624.

Laibman, D. (1976) "The Marxian Labor-Saving Bias: A Formalization." *Quarterly Review of Economics and Business*, 16 (Autumn):25–44.

———. (1981) "Two-Sector Growth with Endogenous Technical Change: A Marxian Simulation Model." *Quarterly Journal of Economics*, 96:47–75.

———. (1982) "Technical Change, the Real Wage and the Rate of Exploitation." *Review of Radical Political Economics*, 14, 2:95–105.

———. (1983) "Capitalism and Immanent Crisis: Broad Strokes for a Theoretical Foundation." *Social Research*, 50, 2 (Summer):359–400.

Laibman, D. and E. J. Nell. (1977) "Reswitching, Wicksell Effects, and the Neoclassical Production Function." *American Economic Review*, 67 (December):878–88.

Okishio, N. (1961) "Technical Change and the Rate of Profit." *Kobe University Economic Review*, 7:86–99.

Robinson, J. (1947) *An Essay on Marxian Economics*. London: Macmillan.

———. (1978) "The Organic Composition of Capital." *Kyklos*, 31, 1:5–20.

Roemer, J. (1977) "The Effect of Technological Change on the Real Wage and Marx's Falling Rate of Profit." *Australian Economic Papers*, 15.

———. (1978) "Marxian Models of Reproduction and Accumulation." *Cambridge Journal of Economics*, 2:37–53.

———. (1979) "Continuing Controversy on the Falling Rate of Profit: Fixed Capital and Other Issues." *Cambridge Journal of Economics*, 3:379–98.

Schumpeter, J. A. (1939) *Business Cycles*. New York: McGraw-Hill.

Shaikh, A. (1978) "Political Economy and Capitalism: Notes on Dobb's Theory of Crisis." *Cambridge Journal of Economics*, 2, 2 (June):233–51.

Solow, R. M. (1956) "A Contribution to the Theory of Economic Growth." *Quarterly Journal of Economics*, 70:65–94.

JR

CHAPTER EIGHTEEN

Joan Robinson

Why Not a Nobel Laureate?

MARJORIE S. TURNER

Joan Robinson was regularly nominated for the Nobel Prize and at least one year she was on what is called the short list of contenders. Presumably, then, hers was one of what Assar Lindbeck has called " 'hot' names."[1] Why was she never honored?

Alfred Nobel left his money for prizes only in five areas: physics, chemistry, physiology and medicine, literature, and Peace. The first prizes were awarded in 1901, and "The basic idea of the original Nobel prizes was to award *specific achievements* rather than 'outstanding persons.' "[2]

Sixty-seven years later, the Central Bank of Sweden at its tercentenary created a "Prize in Economic Sciences in Memory of Alfred Nobel." The bank places an annual amount, equal to a Nobel Prize, at the disposal of the Nobel Foundation. The standard procedures for choice of a Nobel laureate are used and the presentation is made on Nobel Day. The original skepticism of some of the natural scientists in the Royal Swedish Academy of Science toward the proposal was overcome partly through the efforts of Gunnar Myrdal and other economists who were members of the Academy. This memorial prize was first awarded in 1969, so there were fourteen awards made to twenty economists before Joan Robinson's death in 1983. There were twenty female laureates in Robinson's lifetime, though none in economics.[3]

Each field has its own recommending committee. Every fall invitations to nominate candidates are sent out to "statutorily competent" individuals. These include previous Nobel laureates, members of the prize-awarding bodies (the Nobel committees), professors in various prize fields at specifically mentioned universities, presidents of representative authors' organizations, members of certain international parliamentary or legal organizations, and members of parliaments and governments. A person must be nominated to win, but this is no problem, since the Nobel committee members themselves can nominate. About seventy-five departments of economics (not always the same ones) from many

Table 18.1

Table of Reasons, Nobel Awards in Economics 1969–82

	Mathematical/ Statistical	Theory	Other
1969	Frisch, Ragnar Tinbergen, Jan		
1970		Samuelson, Paul	
1971	Kuznets, Simon		
1972		Hicks, John R. Arrow, Kenneth J.	
1973	Leontief, Wassily		
1974			Myrdal, Gunnar von Hayek, Friedrich
1975	Kantorovich, Leonid Koopmans, Tjalling C.		
1976		Friedman, Milton	
1977		Ohlin, Berth Meade, James	
1978		Simon, Herbert A.	
1979		Schultz, T. W. Lewis, Arthur	
1980	Klein, Lawrence R.		
1981		Tobin, James	
1982			Stigler, George

countries are invited to suggest candidates. This nomination process usually produces 150 to 200 proposals yielding between 75 to 125 nominees. "Spontaneous suggestions from persons who have not been asked to submit proposals are not considered."[4] Probably the petition signed by 500 women on behalf of Joan Robinson was thus duly ignored, perhaps not even circulated among the committee. Not all nominators are equal. In the case of economics, Lindbeck says, the important thing is "not how many suggestions each candidate has received but rather *who* the proponents of the various candidates are. Thus very competent nominators, whose judgment the committee ranks highly, may have a strong influence on the committee, particularly if their supporting arguments are convincing."[5]

According to Lindbeck, "A typical feature of the proposals is that the suggestions tend to be concentrated on well-known and highly respected economists, in particular on scholars in the field of 'central' economic theory as traditionally understood. Economists who have been involved in controversies over economic policy issues are often suggested." Lindbeck felt that the nominators often do not appreciate the necessity of awarding for "specific contributions."[6]

Each year, two or more studies are made of each candidate whom the committee regards as particularly meriting attention—that is, between twenty and thirty persons "though usually only a handful of these are regarded as 'hot' names each year." The recommendation of the committee is then presented to the Academy. "So far, the proposals of the prize committee to the Academy have been unanimous."[7] At the awards ceremony a member of the Nobel Committee for Economics makes a presentation, giving primary reasons for the choice. (Each year the full text of the ceremony is published.) On the basis of these published award presentations, I constructed a table that gives the insight of an outsider into the awards in economics during Robinson's lifetime (see Table 18.1).

Of course, many of the recipients might have fallen into more than one column. However, as I read the presentation statements, I noticed that of the twenty recipients, seven made special contributions to mathematics or applied statistical models, ten to theory, and three were difficult to categorize but did not fall under either of the former. For example, in making the 1974 award to Myrdal and Hayek, Erik Lundberg said, "Hitherto the prize in Economic Science . . . has been awarded to researchers who have made pioneering contributions in what may be called 'pure' economics. . . . However there are prominent researchers in the field of the social sciences whose range of interests covers other and wider areas than those embraced by the term 'pure economics.' "[8] George Stigler was thought to have "opened new and important fields for economic research."[9] Lindbeck's reading of the committee's work employs five categories: (1) General ("basic") Economic Theory: Samuelson, Arrow and Hicks; (2) Theoretical Contributions Concerning Specific Aspects of Sectors of the Economy: Meade, Ohlin, Tobin, Lewis, Schultz, Simon, and Stigler; (3) Powerful New Methods of Economic Analysis: Their Development and Application: Frisch, Tinbergen, Leontief, Koopmans, Kantorovich; (4) More Nearly "Pure" Empirical Research: Kuznets, Klein, Friedman; and (5) Nonformalized Innovative Thinking: Hayek and Myrdal.[10]

The Nobel committee responsible for choosing an economist is interesting in itself. Once on the committee, a person may serve many years. Lindbeck does not say how the committee is selected. Of the fourteen committees between 1969 and 1982, R. Bentzel served on all of them; A. Lindbeck and H. Wold on thirteen; E. Lundberg on twelve; B. Ohlin on the first six—he was off two years before being awarded the prize; I. Svennilson on the first three; S. Carlson on nine. Lundberg interrupted his service for two years but returned in 1982 to serve as secretary of the Committee that selected George Stigler. The new blood on the committee is K. G. Maler, I. Stahl, and L. Werin. Lindbeck reports that "a consensus has in fact developed quite 'automatically' within the committee, as if by some kind of invisible hand, after intensive discussions."[11]

The committee has long recognized the existence of a "backlog of 'worthy' candidates." Lindbeck notes that some, like Viner and Kalecki, "missed" awards "due to death not long after the prize was initiated" (both died in 1970). He added to this list Frank Knight (d. 1972) and Roy Harrod (d. 1978), but did not mention Robinson. This mention of Harrod is particularly interesting in that no Keynes-Keynesian has ever been honored and the committee had ten opportunities to name Harrod. The committee had felt some pressure "to speed up the awarding of important contributions that are relatively far back—and perhaps also in some cases of some elderly candidates provided they are regarded as very 'hot names.' "[12] Prize sharing can be a way of taking care of the backlog of worthies. Prizes can be shared by halves, by thirds, or by one-half, one-fourth, etc.[13]

Lindbeck denied that the politics of candidates was ever an issue. Using the prize sharing of Myrdal and Hayek as an illustration, Lindbeck argued that "since the prize is conceived as a purely scientific award," the fact that the recipients are "often regarded as political 'antipoles' did not bother the committee." He also denied that the committee "was positively *attracted* by the idea of combining political antipoles."[14]

We can make a distinction between the politics of economics and politics *per se*. For these purposes, political differences are taken to be ideological differences. The politics of economics is another matter and refers to the definition of the science and the identification of the basic theory. As Lindbeck noted, his view and presumably that of the committee is that the "General ('basic') Economic Theory" is "general equilibrium theory and welfare theory."[15] All could agree that Robinson did not even intend to make a specific contribution to general equilibrium theory.

Whether the politics of economics carries over into politics *per se* is debatable. However, to show how far Robinson's work was from the temper of the Nobel committee in 1982 (her last chance), the speech by Lars Werin presenting the Nobel Prize to George Stigler can be quoted. Werin cites Stigler for:

> reintegrating basic theory with the actual market processes, and for clarifying the role of economic legislation. . . . Stigler . . . has built bridges between theory and facts . . . resolving seeming contradictions between them. In most cases, contradictions disappear if households' and firms' costs of obtaining information on market opportunities and adjusting to them are integrated into the theory. . . . The basic properties of the traditional theory thereby remain intact.[16]

In other words, at least part of Stigler's special contribution was to preserve traditional theory. Werin also mentioned a hypothesis "proposed" by Stigler, "which, to paraphrase bluntly his own wording, reads: what you cannot achieve yourself, let the state do for you." Werin added, "The extent of validity of this hypothesis is still unknown. . . . But reading between the lines of his recent writings, perhaps the hope may be discerned that the research which he has begun so successfully will also stimulate those engaged in politics to become more immune to external pressures."[17] Perhaps a natural scientist would raise an eyebrow over a hypothesis not yet validated but only hoped for. Werin's point

Table 18.2

National Origin for Nobel Laureates in Economics

	Scandinavian	Other European	United Kingdom	United States
1969	Frisch	Tinbergen		
1970				Samuelson
1971		(Kuznets)		Kuznets
1972			Hicks	Arrow
1973		(Leontief)		Leontief
1974	Myrdal	(Hayek)	Hayek	(Hayek)
1975		Kantorovich		
		(Koopmans)		Koopmans
1976				Friedman
1977	Ohlin		Meade	
1978				Simon
1979			Lewis	Schultz
1980				Klein
1981				Tobin
1982				Stigler

was that Stigler had "inspired substantial research on the effects of regulatory legislation and the driving forces behind it." There is more, but the reader can see that here was a reward for a person defending what Robinson was fond of calling "*laisser-faire.*" Robinson persistently questioned whether the free market could contribute very much toward human welfare.

The national origin of the Nobel laureates in economics is also of some interest (see Table 18.2), even though Nobel's will designated that it was to be ignored.

Kantorovich, inventor of linear programming, is a citizen of the Soviet Union. Leontief and Kuznets, although born in Russia, had careers in the United States, and Kuznets was educated in the United States. Hayek, an Austrian by birth and education, taught in both the United States and England. Of the two Dutch economists, Tinbergen and Koopmans, the latter calls the United States his home. Even Sir Arthur Lewis, who was born a British subject on St. Lucia Island, spent time at Princeton University during his long and varied career. In sum, eight of the twenty were American-born and five others spent some important part of their careers in the United States. If any fact can demonstrate the dominance of American economics, this record does. Harvard, MIT, Stanford, and Yale scored, but Chicago came in with three (four, if you count Hayek). (Lindbeck must count Arrow as a Harvard laureate because he scores Harvard three.)

England, once dominant in western economics, could only match Chicago in my count. (Lindbeck must count Hayek for England). None of these was a Keynes-Keynesian.

Lindbeck made the awarding speech for Samuelson in 1970, noting that the fourth area of Samuelson's "specific achievement" was that "Samuelson has made outstanding contributions . . . in the field of *capital theory*. . . . Samuelson . . . showed, partly in cooperation with Robert Solow, that it is possible to develop a logical capital theory—and to speak about a well-defined price of capital—even without adopting such an aggregate concept of capital." Lindbeck also mentioned the "turnpike theorem," but not the reswitching controversy.[18]

As for politics in the ideological sense, Lewis and Myrdal were the only "social democrats." Hayek and Friedman were both founding members of the Mont Pelerin Society. George Stigler has also been a member of the Mont Pelerin Society, as was committee member Erik Lundberg. The one communist to have been honored was Russian mathematical economist Leonid Kantorovich. Certainly there were no Western left-wingers.

Some economists have centered their remarks either on Joan Robinson's sex or her politics to explain her failure to win the prize. Others have raised the question of her own attitude toward her *Imperfect Competition*, which had been her most influential book on mainstream economics. On the one hand, it was written thirty-six years before there was a Nobel prize in economics. On the other, in the second edition in 1969—the year the Nobel was first offered to an economist—she been highly critical of her own method. Although no was was awarded a prize solely on early work, their achievements before World War II were often mentioned in the awarding speeches. In the award to Tinbergen and Frisch, it was noted that since the late twenties and early thirties they had been "working along the same lines." Hicks's *Value and Capital* (1939) was noted as having "breathed fresh life into general equilibrium theory." However, Hicks's *Theory of Wages* (1932) was not mentioned; this is noteworthy, since Hicks's preface to a later edition revealed his puzzlement about the popularity of that book in America. Leontief's dates for his early input-output models were not mentioned, but his *Structure of the American Economy* was published in 1941. Myrdal and Hayek were also cited as having done some pure economic research in the 1920s and 1930s before branching out to "other and wider" areas. Kantorovich invented linear programming in the 1930s, and Ohlin contributed to the development of international trade theory in the 1930s. The rest were younger men. The curiosity is not that Robinson did not win on *Imperfect Competition* but that many Americans continue to think of that as her only "specific achievement."

Robinson's use of the literary as compared to mathematical form must certainly have handicapped her. When Ragnar Bentzel made the awarding speech for Hicks, he said, "Hicks used traditional differential analysis as a mathematical tool. When later more modern mathematical methods began to be introduced into economics, Arrow [who shared the prize with Hicks] used them to study the properties of general equilibrium systems."[19] The fact is that Robinson's *Accumulation of Capital*, coming as it did in the 1950s, still did not employ the "more modern mathematical methods."

Another black mark was possibly Robinson's constant criticism of orthodox theory. Indeed, in a statement that may have referred to Robinson, Lindbeck says:

> It is also clear that the prize awarding authority has tried to favor "constructive" contributions rather than contributions that are "destructive" in the sense of mainly launching criticism that does not lead anywhere. To provide "shoulders" on which other scholars can stand, and thus climb higher, has been favored over attempts to show that "everybody else" is wrong, or that the world is so complex that simple and coherent analytical structures are useless. Skillful polemics that do not seem to push research forward have not been regarded as worthy of being honored.[20]

Reading the record, one can infer Robinson's sins before the committee: she disowned the method in her early contributory work *The Economics of Imperfect Competition*; she worked diligently to undermine the hegemony of the central core of general equilibrium theory in all of her later work; she proposed another path in *The Accumulation of Capital*, but this path led nowhere as far as *mainstream* research programs are concerned (because it did not employ general equilibrium models); she engaged in the capital controversy, which was also destructive of the central core of general equilibrium analysis, its complacency, and its methodology; she failed to use the latest mathematical techniques. Being a leftist, or what members of the Mont Pelerin Society are fond of calling "a Marxo-Keynesian" did not help. Being a nonconventional woman did not ingratiate her. The committee is all-male.

Samuelson has suggested that Robinson would have or should have won a Nobel in 1937, sharing it with Chamberlin, but of course, there was no prize then.[21]

Lindbeck stated that the selection committee had "relied entirely on *qualitative judgement*."[22] Quantitative judgments like the frequency of citations had never been considered. Yet he seemed pleased that the prize winners usually rank very high on citation indices. He conceded that several—Kantorovich, Stone, Meade, and Ohlin—had not. Lindbeck cited Richard Quandt's study of citations in eight leading journals (five American journals, two British journals and one international journal, *Econometrica*). In 1976, Quandt reported that with the exception of Myrdal and Kantorovich, all the prize winners had appeared on his lists of the twenty most frequently cited economists at least once. Quandt added: "If frequency of appearance on the lists is any guide toward predicting Nobel prize winners, the top candidates for a prize in the near future are R. F. Harrod and J. Robinson with three appearances." Then with two appearances each and in alphabetical order, Quandt listed W. J. Baumol, M. Friedman, G. Haberler, H. G. Johnson, L. R. Klein, F. Machlup, R. Solow, and G. Stigler.[23]

That Joan Robinson never won the Nobel Prize is mainly a reflection of the kind of economics that has been dominant in the profession and within the selection committee since the prize was initiated in 1968.

Notes

This chapter is excerpted from *Joan Robinson and the Americans*, by Marjorie S. Turner. Armonk, NY: M. E. Sharpe, Inc., 1989.

1. Lindbeck, 1985, p. 52.
2. Ibid., p. 38.
3. Opfell, 1978, p. xiii.
4. Lindbeck, 1985, p. 46.
5. Ibid., p. 46.
6. Ibid., p. 47.
7. Ibid.
8. Nobel, 1974, p. 240.
9. Nobel, 1982, p. 247.
10. Lindbeck, 1985, pp. 39–45.
11. Ibid., p. 47.
12. Ibid., p. 52.
13. Ibid.
14. Ibid., pp. 53–54.
15. Ibid., p. 39.
16. Nobel, 1982, p. 245.
17. Ibid., p. 246.
18. Nobel, 1970, pp. 255–56.
19. Nobel, 1972, pp. 202–3.
20. Lindbeck, 1985, p. 50.
21. Samuelson, 1985.
22. Lindbeck, 1985, p. 51.
23. Quandt, 1976, p. 752.

References

Lindbeck, Assar. (1985) "The Prize in Economic Science in Memory of Alfred Nobel." *Journal of Economic Literature* 23 (March):37–56.

Nobel Foundation. (1970, 1972, 1974, 1982) "The Prize for Economic Science in Memory of Alfred Nobel." Stockholm: Nobel Foundation.

Opfell, Olga. (1978) *The Lady Laureats*. Metuchen, NJ and London: The Scarecrow Press.

Samuelson, Paul. (1985) Interview by author.

Quandt, Richard E. (1976) "Some Quantitative Aspects of the Economic Journal Literature." *Journal of Economic Literature*, 84 (August):741–45.

JR

CHAPTER NINETEEN

Bibliography

The Writings of Joan Robinson

MARIA CRISTINA MARCUZZO

Foreword

Joan Robinson's extraordinary range of interests encompassed many fields of economics and related subjects. During the more than fifty years that she was active as a writer, she published books, articles in scholarly journals, short papers in newspapers and magazines, and many reviews. Her continued prolific productivity may explain why preparing this bibliography has been such a difficult and time-consuming task.

I realized many years ago while talking to Joan Robinson that she had no record of all her published work and I thought that I could create such a complete bibliography. I produced a first tentative list in 1982, which I published in *Studi Economici*, as the opening piece of a series of bibliographies of great economists. Three years later I produced an updated and revised version, which I decided, however, to leave in the form of a working paper (Modena: Dipartimento di Economia Politica, 1985). It was this manuscript that guided me through the Joan Robinson papers brought to the King's College (Cambridge) Archives after her death in 1983. I worked through these papers with a view toward identifying and dating all her work, and with the intention of doing a more general study of the Cambridge School of Economics.

Meanwhile, my bibliography had circulated among Joan Robinson scholars, and although I think that more work is needed, I was glad to accept Ingrid Rima's invitation to include it in this anthology. By making this bibliography more accessible, I am hoping that it will stimulate further research on one of the great economists of our time.

I wish to thank Geoff Harcourt for facilitating my access to the Joan Robinson papers in the Library of King's College, Cambridge, as well as for his support for this project, and Dr. Michael Halls, the Modern Archivist, for his help. I also wish to thank V. Chick, R. W. Clower, J. Kregel, A. Rosselli, M. Russó,

J. Schor, and F. Wilkinson for encouragement and advice, and I wish especially to express my gratitude to the late R. F. Kahn for all his support.

Underlying the preparation of this bibliography are years of research in many libraries: I would particularly like to mention the following here: the University Library, Cambridge; the Marshall Library, Cambridge; the British Library at the London School of Economics; the Biblioteca della Facoltà di Economia, Università di Modena, Italy; the University Library, Stanford University, Stanford, California; the University Research Library, University of California, Los Angeles; the General Library, University of California, Berkeley; the Dewey Library, Massachusetts Institute of Technology, Cambridge, Massachusetts; the Mugar Library, Boston University, Boston, Massachusetts; and finally, the Widener Library at Harvard University in Cambridge, Massachusetts.

This bibliography was completed while I was a Visitor at the Center for European Studies at Harvard and benefited from a grant from the Italian National Research Council.

Notation and Abbreviations

Each publication listed in this bibliography has been assigned a number, in brackets at the beginning of each entry, that corresponds, as far as I have been able to ascertain, to the chronological order of publication.

Where there is more than one edition of the same text, subsequent editions (2d, 3d eds., etc.) are noted in parentheses at the end of the listing for the first edition. Modifications that appear in later editions are noted separately under the year in which such changes were introduced. Essays that appear in different collections are listed by the number assigned to them for their first appearance in this bibliography. In general, account has not been taken of all the anthologies, essay collections, and the like, in which a particular article may have been republished, except for any edited by Joan Robinson herself. This suits the purpose of the present work, which is to date Joan Robinson's works and establish their order and sequence, rather than to provide a complete inventory of where her various writings may be found. If an article or essay appears in one or more of Robinson's own collections, the corresponding abbreviation appears in brackets, and the year of the article's first publication appears in parentheses. Variations in titles among different sources, indications regarding modifications, and other explanatory details are given in the notes.

The following abbreviations are used for Joan Robinson's collections of essays:

CEP 1:	*Collected Economic Papers*, vol. 1 (1951)
CEP 2:	*Collected Economic Papers*, vol. 2 (1960)
CEP 3:	*Collected Economic Papers*, vol. 3 (1965)
CEP 4:	*Collected Economic Papers*, vol. 4 (1973)

CEP 5:	*Collected Economic Papers*, vol. 5 (1979)
CME:	*Contributions to Modern Economics* (1980)
ETE:	*Essays in the Theory of Employment* (1937)
ETG:	*Essays in the Theory of Economic Growth* (1962)
FCM:	*Further Contributions to Modern Economics* (1980)
GGT:	*The Generalization of the General Theory* (1979)
NFC:	*Notes from China* (1964)
RFC:	*Reports from China* (1977)
RIE:	*The Rate of Interest and Other Essays* (1952)
RRM:	*On Re-reading Marx* (1953)

1930

[1] "Review of H. Clay, *The Problem of Industrial Relations.*" *Political Quarterly*, 1 (April): 293–96.

1932

[2] *Economics Is a Serious Subject. The Apologia of an Economist to the Mathematician, the Scientist, and the Plain Man.* Cambridge: Heffer.
[3] "Review of L. S. S. O'Malley, *Indian Caste Customs.*" *Cambridge Review*, 54 (November 25): 138.
[4] "Imperfect Competition and Falling Supply Price." *Economic Journal*, 42 (December): 544–54.

1933

[5] *The Economics of Imperfect Competition.* London: Macmillan (2d ed., 1969).
[6] "A Parable on Saving and Investment." *Economica*, 13 (February): 75–84.
[7] "The Imperfection of the Market: Comments on G.F. Shove's Note." *Economic Journal*, 43 (March): 124–25.
[8] "Shakespeare and Mr. Looney." *Cambridge Review*, 54 (May 12): 389–90.
[9] "Review of A. Da Empoli, *Theory of Economic Equilibrium.* A Study of Marginal and Ultramarginal Phenomena." *Economic Journal*, 43 (June): 666–69.
[10] "Review of P. H. Wicksteed, *The Coordination of the Laws of Distribution.*" *Economic Journal*, 43 (June): 301–4.
[11] "Decreasing Costs: A Reply to Mr. Harrod." *Economic Journal*, 43 (September): 531–32.
[12] "The Theory of Money and the Analysis of Output." *Review of Economic Studies*, 1 (October): 22–26. [CEP 1; CME]

1934

[13] "Mr. Fraser on Taxation and Returns." *Review of Economic Studies*, 1 (February): 137–40.
[14] "Review of J. E. Meade, *The Rate of Interest in a Progressive State.*" *Economic Journal*, 44 (June): 282–85.

[15] "Euler's Theorem and the Problem of Distribution." *Economic Journal*, 44 (September): 398–414. [CEP 1]
[16] "Review of G. T. Jones, *Increasing Returns*." *Journal of Political Economy*, 42 (October): 694–96.
[17] "What Is Perfect Competition?" *Quarterly Journal of Economics*, 49 (November): 104–20. [CEP 1]

1935

[18] "A Fundamental Objection to *Laissez-faire*."[1] *Economic Journal*, 45 (September): 580–82. [CEP 1]
[19] "Review of H. S. Ellis, *German Monetary Theory*." *Economic Journal*, 45 (December): 729–31.

1936

[20] "Dr. Machlup's Commonsense of the Elasticity of Substitution." *Review of Economic Studies*, 3 (February): 148–50.
[21] "The Long Period Theory of Employment."[2] *Zeitschrift für Nationalokönomie*, 7 (March): 74–93. [ETE]
[22] "Review of P. Einzig, *Bankers, Statesmen and Economists*." *Economic Journal*, 46 (March): 122–23.
[23] "Banking Policies and the Exchanges." *Review of Economic Studies*, 3 (June): 226–29.
[24] "Disguised Unemployment." *Economic Journal*, 46 (June): 225–37. [CEP 4; ETE]
[25] "Review of J. Strachey, *The Nature of the Capitalistic Crisis*."[3] *Economic Journal*, 46 (June): 298–302.
[26] "Review of N. Angell, *The Money Mystery*." *International Affairs*, 15 (July): 598–99.
[27] "Review of R. H. Harrod, *The Trade Cycle*." *Economic Journal*, 46 (December): 691–93. [CEP 1]
[28] "Review of *Britain without Capitalists* by a Group of Economists, Scientists and Technicians." *Economic Journal*, 46 (December): 704–6.
[29] "Review of A. Redford, *Patterns of Economic Activity*." *Economic Journal*, 46 (December): 706–7.
[30] "Disguised Unemployment: A Rejoinder." *Economic Journal*, 46 (December): 759–60.
[31] "Mr. Keynes and Socialism. Review of A. L. Rowse, *Mr. Keynes and the Labour Movement*." *Left Review*, 2 (December): 853.

1937

[32–43, et al.] *Essays in the Theory of Employment*. London: Macmillan (2d ed., 1947).

[32] "Foreword"
[33] "Full Employment" [CEP 4]
[34] "Mobility of Labour"
[35] "Certain Proposed Remedies for Unemployment"
[24] "Disguised Unemployment" (1936)
[21] "The Long Period Theory of Employment"[4] (1936)
[36] "The Concept of Zero Saving"
[37] "Disinvestment"

[38] "Diagrammatic Illustrations"
[39] "The Foreign Exchanges" [CEP 4]
[40] "Beggar-My-Neighbour Remedies for Unemployment" [CEP 4; CME]
[41] "Indeterminacy"
[42] "An Economist's Sermon" [CEP 4]
[43] "Some Reflections on Marxist Economics"[5]

[44] *Introduction to the Theory of Employment.* London: Macmillan (2d ed., 1969).
[45] "Review of R. L. Hall, *The Economic System in a Socialist State.*" *Cambridge Review*, 58 (February 26): 289–90.
[46] "Review of A. W. Knight, *Abolish Slumps.*" *Economic Journal*, 47 (June): 339–40.
[47] "Review of S. E. Harris, *Exchange Depreciation.*" *Economic Journal*, 47 (December): 699–701.

1938

[48] "The Classification of Inventions." *Review of Economic Studies*, 5 (February): 139–42.
[49] "The Concept of Hoarding." *Economic Journal*, 48 (June): 231–36. [CEP 1; CME]
[50] "Review of C. Bresciani Turroni, *The Economics of Inflation.*"[6] *Economic Journal*, 48 (September): 507–13. [CEP 1]

1939

[51] "Review of G. Myrdal, *Monetary Equilibrium.*" *Economic Journal*, 49 (September): 493–95. [CEP 1]

1940

[52] "Review of R. A. Lester, *Monetary Experiments.*" *Economic Journal*, 50 (June): 280–82.
[53] "Review of G. Crowther, *Ways and Means of War* and of J.K. Horsefield, *The Real Cost of the War.*" *Economic Journal*, 50 (December): 505–7.
[54] "Consumption and Prices." *The Times* (London), December 3, p. 5.

1941

[55] "The Financial Problem of 1941." *The Banker*, 57 (January): 8–13.
[56] "Rising Supply Price." *Economica, New Series*, 8 (February): 1–8. [CEP 1]
[57] "Review of R. F. Bretherton, *Public Investment and the Trade Cycle in Great Britain.*" *Economic Journal*, 51 (April): 127–29.
[58] "Marx on Unemployment."[7] *Economic Journal*, 51 (June): 234–48.
[59] "Review of M. Dobb, *Soviet Economy and the War.*" *Economic Journal*, 51 (December): 489.

1942

[60] *An Essay on Marxian Economics.* London: Macmillan (2d ed., 1966).
[61] *Private Enterprise or Public Control.* London: Association for Education in Citizenship, Handbooks for Discussion Groups, no. 11.
[62] "Review of S. E. Harris, *Economics of Social Security.*" *Economic Journal*, 52 (June): 241–43.

[63] "Review of G. H. J. Pierson, *Full Employment.*" *Economic Journal*, 52 (June): 240–41.
[64] "Review of N. H. Borden, *The Economic Effects of Advertising.*" *Economica, New Series*, 9 (August): 294–96. [CEP 1]
[65] "Industry and the State." *Political Quarterly*, 13 (October): 400–406.
[66] "Review of T. Wilson, *Fluctuations in Income and Employment.*" *Economic Journal*, 52 (December): 352–54.

1943

[67] *The Future of Industry*. London: Commonwealth Publication.
[68] *The Problem of Full Employment: An Outline for Study Circles*. London: Workers' Educational Association Study Outlines (2d ed., 1949; 3d ed., 1953).
[69] "Creating Money." *Accountancy*, 54 (January): 64–65.
[70] "Planning." *Fabian Quarterly*, 36 (January): 4–8.
[71a] "Planning Full Employment I: The Need for a Constructive Approach." *The Times* (London), January 22, p. 5. [CEP 1]
[71b] "Planning Full Employment II: Alternative Solutions of a Dilemma." *The Times* (London), January 23, p. 5. [CEP 1]
[72] "Review of T. Ruby-Norris, *The Theory of Consumer's Demand.*" *Economic Journal*, 53 (April): 115–17. [CEP 1]
[73] "The International Currency Proposal." *Economic Journal*, 53 (June): 161–75.
[74] "Review of J. A. Schumpeter, *Capitalism, Socialism, and Democracy.*" *Economic Journal*, 53 (December): 381–83. [CEP 1; FCM]
[75] "Review of G. D. H. Cole, *The Means to Full Employment.*" *New Statesman and Nation*, 26 (December 4): 372–73.

1944

[76] "Abolishing Unnecessary Poverty." In N. Kaldor et al. (eds.), *Planning for Abundance*. London: National Peace Council, Peace Aims Pamphlets, no. 21.
[77] "The Currency Plan." *Socialist Commentary*, 9 (June): 246–50.
[78] "Review of H. B. Larry (ed.), *The United States in the World Economy.*"[8] *Economic Journal*, 54 (December): 430–37. [CEP 1]

1945

[79] "Review of B. Wotton, *Freedom under Planning.*" *Girton Review*, 129 (Michaelmas): 20.
[80] "Review of Oxford Institute of Statistics, *Economics of Full Employment.*" *Economic Journal*, 55 (April): 77–82. [CEP 1]
[81] "Review of League of Nations, *International Currency Experience.*" *Economic Journal*, 55 (December): 405–7.

1946

[82] "Obstacles to Full Employment." *Nationaløkonomisk Tidsskrift*, 84, 5: 169–78. [CEP 1; CME]
[83] "Budget et Inflation." *Bulletin de l'Institute du Science Economique Appliquée* (September), pp. 4–11.

1947

[84] "The Pure Theory of International Trade." *Review of Economic Studies*, 14, 2: 98–112.

[85] "Foreword to the Second Edition." *Essays in the Theory of Employment*, 2d ed. London: Macmillan (1st ed., 1937).

1948

[86] "Case for a Double Price Level." *Listener*, 39 (March 4): 363–64.

[87] "Marx e Keynes."[9] *Critica Economica*, 2 (May): 33–45. [CEP 1]

[88] "Review of E. V. Morgan, *The Conquest of Unemployment*." *New Statesman and Nation*, 35 (May): 359.

[89] "Review of A. P. Lerner and F. D. Graham, *Planning and Paying for Full Employment* and of T. Morgan, *Income and Employment*." *Economic Journal*, 58 (June): 248–50.

[90] "La Théorie Générale de l'Emploi." *Economie Appliquée*, 1 (April–September): 185–96.

1949

[91] "Mr. Harrod's Dynamics." *Economic Journal*, 59 (March): 68–85. [CEP 1]

[92] "Review of M. Dobb, *Soviet Economic Development since 1917*."[10] *Soviet Studies*, 1 (June): 60–64. [CEP 1]

[93] "Review of D. Lynch, *The Concentration of Economic Power*." *Economic Journal*, 59 (December): 580–81.

1950

[94] "Review of R. Schlesinger, *Changing Attitudes in Soviet Russia: The Family*." *Soviet Studies*, 1 (January): 235–37.

[95] "Exchange Equilibrium." *Economia Internazionale*, 3 (May): 396–406. [CEP 1]

[96] "Review of E. Böhm-Bawerk, *Karl Marx and the Close of his System*; R. Hilferding, *Bohm-Bawerk's Criticism of Marx*; L. Bortkiewicz, *On the Correction of Marx's Fundamental Theoretical Construction in the Third Volume of* Capital (ed. by P. M. Sweezy)." *Economic Journal*, 60 (June): 358–63. [CEP 1]

1951

[97–100, et al.] *Collected Economic Papers*, vol. 1. Oxford: Blackwell.

- [97] "Introduction"
- [15] "Euler's Theorem and the Problem of Distribution" (1934)
- [17] "What Is Perfect Competition?" (1934)
- [56] "Rising Supply Price" (1941)
- [72] "*The Theory of Consumer's Demand* by T. R. Norris" (1943)
- [64] "*The Economic Effects of Advertising* by N. H. Borden" (1942)
- [18] "An Inherent Defect in *Laissez-faire*"[11] (1935)
- [12] "The Theory of Money and the Analysis of Output" (1933) [CME]
- [27] "*The Trade Cycle* by R. F. Harrod" (1936)
- [49] "The Concept of Hoarding" (1938) [CME]

[50] "The Economics of Hyper-inflation"[12] (1938)
[51] "*Monetary Equilibrium* by G. Myrdal" (1939)
[71] "Planning Full Employment" (1943)
[98] "War-Time Inflation"
[80] "*The Economics of Full Employment* by Members of the Oxford Institute of Statistics" (1945)
[82] "Obstacles to Full Employment" (1946) [CME]
[99] "Economic Consequences of a Decline in the Population of Great Britain"
[87] "Marx and Keynes"[13] (1948)
[96] "The Labour Theory of Value"[14] (1950)
[74] "*Capitalism, Socialism, and Democracy* by J. Schumpeter" (1943) [FCM]
[91] "Mr. Harrod's Dynamics" (1949)
[92] "The Theory of Planning"[15] (1949)
[84] "The Pure Theory of International Trade" (1947)
[78] "The United States in the World Economy"[16] (1944)
[95] "Exchange Equilibrium" (1950)
[100] "Beauty and the Beast" [CME]

[101] "Introduction" to Rosa Luxemburg, *The Accumulation of Capital.* London: Routledge and Kegan. [CEP 2]
[102] "The Rate of Interest."[17] *Econometrica*, 19 (April): 92–111. [CEP 2; CME; GGT; RIE]

1952

[103–106, et al.] *The Rate of Interest and Other Essays.*[18] London: Macmillan.

[103] "Introduction" [GGT]
[102] "The Rate of Interest"[19] (1951) [CEP 2; CME; GGT]
[104] "Notes on the Economics of Technical Progress" [GGT]
[105] "The Generalization of the General Theory"
[106] "Acknowledgements and Disclaimers"[20] [CEP 2; GGT]

[107] *Conference Sketch Book: Moscow, April 1952.* Cambridge: Heffer and Sons.

[107] "Moscow 1952." *Monthly Review*, 4 (September): 157–72.

[108] "The Model of an Expanding Economy." *Economic Journal*, 62 (March): 42–53. [CEP 2]
[109] " 'Full Cost' and Monopolistic Competition: A Comment." *Economic Journal*, 62 (March): 325.
[110] "Review of C. Bettelheim, *Les Problemes Theoriques et Pratiques de la Planification.*" *Soviet Studies*, 4 (July): 53–58.
[111] "Monetary Policy Again. Comments."[21] *Oxford Bulletin of Economics and Statistics*, 14 (August): 281–84. [CEP 2]
[112] "Review of J. K. Galbraith, *American Capitalism: The Concept of Countervailing Power.*" *Economic Journal*, 62 (December): 925–28.

1953

[113–115] *On Re-reading Marx.* Cambridge: Students' Bookshops Ltd.

[113] "Would You Believe It?" [CEP 4]

[114] "A Lecture Delivered at Oxford by a Cambridge Economist" [CEP 4; CME]
[115] "An Open Letter from a Keynesian to a Marxist" [CEP 4; FCM]

[116] "*Imperfect Competition* Revisited." *Economic Journal*, 63 (September): 579–93. [CEP 2; CME]

[117] "The Production Function and the Theory of Capital."[22] *Review of Economic Studies*, 21, 55 (1953–54): 81–106. [CEP 2; CME]

[118a] "Letters from a Visitor to China, July 1953, Part I." *Monthly Review*, 5 (November): 302–10. [RFC]

[118b] "Letters from a Visitor to China, July 1953, Part II." *Monthly Review*, 5 (December): 397–410. [RFC]

1954

[118c] "Letters from a Visitor to China, July 1953, Part III." *Monthly Review*, 5 (January): 477–80. [RFC]

[118d] "Letters from a Visitor to China, July 1953, Part IV." *Monthly Review*, 5 (February): 536–43. [RFC]

[118] *Letters from a Visitor to China.* Cambridge: Students' Bookshops Ltd. [RFC]

[119] "The Labour Theory of Value: A Discussion." *Science and Society*, 18, 2: 141–51. [CEP 2]

[120] "The Impossibility of Competition." In E. H. Chamberlin (ed.), *Monopoly and Competition and Their Regulation.* Papers and Proceedings of the International Economic Association Conference. London: Macmillan.

1955

[121] "Marx, Marshall and Keynes." Delhi School of Economics, Occasional Paper no. 9, University of Delhi. [CEP 2; CME]

[122] "The Production Function." *Economic Journal*, 64 (March): 67–71.

[123] "A Theory of Long Run Development." *Economic Review* (Tokyo), 6 (October): 382–85.

[124] "The Production Function and the Theory of Capital: A Reply." *Review of Economic Studies*, 23, 3 (1955–56): 247.

1956

[125] *The Accumulation of Capital.* London: Macmillan (2d ed., 1965; 3d ed., 1969).

[126] "Mr. Wiles' Rationality. A Comment." *Soviet Studies*, 7 (January): 269–73.

[127] "Employment and the Plan." *Economic Weekly*, 8 (March 24): 355–56.

[128] "The Industry and the Market." *Economic Journal*, 66 (June): 360–61.

[129] "Review of K. Marx, *The Poverty of Philosophy*." *Economic Journal*, 66 (June): 334–35.

[130] "Review of J. Strachey, *Contemporary Capitalism*." *Economic Journal*, 66 (December): 697–98.

[131] "Unemployment and Planning: India 1955." *Capital* (Calcutta), Annual Supplement, 7–9 (December). [CEP 3]

1957

[132] "What Remains of Marxism?" In *A Contribution to a Symposium*[23] (1957). [CEP 3]

[133] "Notes on the Theory of Economic Development." Annales de la Faculté de Droit de Liège. [CEP 2]

[134] "Une Lettre sur le Capitalism Contemporain." *Cahiers Internationaux*, 82 (January): 27–28.
[135] "The Control of Monopoly in British Industry." *Listener*, 48 (March 21): 459–60, 475.
[136] "Full Employment and After." *Universities and Left Review*, 1 (Spring): 66–68.
[137] "Economic Growth and Capital Accumulation: A Comment." *Economic Record*, 33 (April): 103–8.
[138] "Review of E. E. Nemmers, *Hobson and Underconsumption*." *Economic Journal*, 67 (September): 511–12.
[139] "La Théorie de la Répartition."[24] *Economie Appliquée*, 10 (October): 523–38. [CEP 2]

1958

[140] *China: An Economic Perspective* (with S. Adler). Fabian Tract no. 314. London: Davenport Press.
[141] "Birth Control in China." *New Statesman and Nation*, 55 (January 18): 66–67.
[142] "Plein Emploi et Inflation."[25] *Bulletin de Conjoncture Régionale* (Rennes) 3 (January–March), pp. 26–30. [CEP 2]
[143] "Some Reflections on the Philosophy of Prices."[26] *Manchester School of Economics and Social Studies*, 26 (May): 116–35. [CEP 2; CME]
[144] "The Real Wicksell Effect." *Economic Journal*, 68 (September): 600–605. [CEP 2]
[145] "Il Mito della Concorrenza."[27] *Il Mercurio*, 9 (December): 15–20. [CEP 2]
[146] "Populaciór y Desarollo."[28] *Investigation Economica*, 18: 275–81.

1959

[147] "Economic Possibilities of Ceylon." In *Papers by Visiting Economists*. Colombo: Planning Secretariat.
[148] "The Falling Rate of Profit: A Comment." *Science and Society*, 23, 2: 104–6.
[149] "A Comment on G. D. N. Worswick, 'Mrs. Robinson's Simple Accumulation.' " *Oxford Economic Papers*, 11 (January): 141–42.
[150] "Some Problems of Definition and Measurement of Capital." *Oxford Economic Papers*, 11 (June): 157–66. [CEP 2]
[151] "Review of K. Kurihara, *The Keynesian Theory of Economic Development*." *Economic Journal*, 69 (June): 352–53.
[152] "Letter to the Editor on Capital Theory." *Econometrica*, 27 (July): 490.
[153] "Accumulation and Production Function." *Economic Journal*, 69 (September): 433–42. [CEP 2]
[154] "Depreciation." *Rivista di Politica Economica*, 49 (November): 1703–17. [CEP 2]

1960

[155–157, et al.] *Collected Economic Papers*, vol. 2. Oxford: Blackwell (2d ed., 1975).

[155] "Introduction"
[121] "Marx, Marshall and Keynes" (1955) [CME]
[106] "Notes on Marx and Marshall"[29] (1952) [GGT; RIE]
[143] "The Philosophy of Prices"[30] (1958) [CME]
[119] "The Labour Theory of Value" (1954)
[101] "Rosa Luxemburg's *Accumulation of Capital*" (1951)
[108] "The Model of an Expanding Economy" (1952)

[133] "Notes on the Theory of Economic Development" (1957)
[146] "Population and Development"[31] (1960)
[117] "The Production Function and the Theory of Capital"[32] (1953) [CME]
[153] "Accumulation and the Production Function" (1959)
[139] "The Theory of Distribution"[33] (1957)
[156] "Capital, Technique and Relative Shares"
[144] "The Real Wicksell Effect" (1958)
[157] "Saving without Investment"
[150] "Some Problems of Definition and Measurement of Capital" (1959)
[154] "Depreciation" (1959)
[116] "*Imperfect Competition* Revisited" (1953) [CME]
[145] "*Imperfect Competition* Today"[34] (1958)
[102] "The Rate of Interest"[35] (1951) [CEP 2; CME; GGT; RIE]
[111] "A Note on Bank Rate"[36] (1952)
[142] "Full Employment and Inflation"[37] (1958)

[158] *Exercises in Economic Analysis*. London: Macmillan.
[159] "Teaching Economics." *Economic Weekly*, 12 (January): 173–75. [CEP 3]
[146] "Population and Development."[38] *Pakistan Economic Journal*, 10 (March): 1–7. [CEP 2]
[160] "Review of T. J. Hughes and D. E. Luard, *The Economic Development of Communist China 1949–58*." *Economic Journal*, 70 (June): 409–10.
[161] "Review of B. S. Keirstead, *Capital, Interest and Profits*." *Canadian Journal of Economics*, 26 (August): 488–90.
[162] "General Liquidity." *The Banker*, 110 (December): 790–95. [CEP 3]
[163] "The Present Position of Econometrics, The Choice of Models: A Discussion." *Journal of the Royal Statistic Society*, 123, 3: 274–78.

1961

[164] "Prelude to a Critique of Economic Theory."[39] *Oxford Economic Papers*, 13 (February): 53–58. [CEP 3; FCM]
[165] "Equilibrium Growth Models." *American Economic Review*, 51 (June): 360–69. [CEP 3]
[166] "Beyond Full Employment." *Annals of Collective Economy*, 33 (June): 159–67. [CEP 3]
[167] "From the United States to Cuba." *Listener*, 52 (August 24): 265–67, 280.
[168] "Own Rates of Interest." *Economic Journal*, 71 (September): 596–600. [CEP 3]
[169] "Review of S. Tsuru, *Has Capitalism Changed?*" *Monthly Review*, 13 (October): 265–71. [CEP 3; CME]
[170] "Review of S. Tsuru, *Has Capitalism Changed?*" *Journal of Political Economy*, 69 (October): 504–5.

1962

[171] *Economic Philosophy*. London: Watts and Co. (Reprinted in Pelican Books, 1964)
[172–176] *Essays in the Theory of Economic Growth*. London: Macmillan.

[172] "Foreword"
[173] "Normal Prices" (1962)
[174] "A Model of Accumulation"

[175] "A Model of Technical Progress" (1962)
[176] "A Neoclassical Theorem"[40] (1962)

[173] "The Basic Theory of Normal Prices." *Quarterly Journal of Economics*, 76 (February): 1–19. [ETG]
[175] "A Model of Technical Progress." *Rivista di Politica Economica*, 52 (February): 147–75. [ETG]
[176] "A Neoclassical Theorem."[41] *Review of Economic Studies*, 29 (January): 219–26. [ETG]
[177] "Draft of a Multilateral Trade Clearing Agency" (with R. Frisch). Memorandum from the Institute of Economics, University of Oslo.
[178] "Chinese Agricultural Communes." *Co-existence*, 1 (May): 1–6.
[179] "Latter-Day Capitalism." *New Left Review*, 2 (August): 37–46. [CEP 3; CME]
[180] "Review of H. G. Johnson, *Money, Trade and Economic Growth.*"[42] *Economic Journal*, 72 (September): 690–92. [CEP 3]
[181] "Review of E. S. Kirby (ed.), *Contemporary China. Economic and Social Studies.*" *Economic Journal*, 72 (September): 734.
[182] "Marxism: Religion and Science." *Monthly Review*, 14 (December): 423–35. [CEP 3; FCM]
[183] "Comment on the Production Function Symposium." *Review of Economic Studies*, 29, 1: 258–66.
[184] "Review of R. Frisch, *Planning for India. Selected Explorations in Methodology.*" *Journal of the Royal Statistic Society*, 125, 3: 504–6.

1963

[185] "Review of A. K. Cairncross, *Factors in Economic Development.*" *International Affairs*, 39 (January): 97.
[186] "Review of P. Moussa, *The Underprivileged Nations.*" *International Affairs*, 39 (January): 93–94.
[187] "Public or Private Enterprise." *Applied Economic Papers*, 3 (March): 1–12.
[188] "Review of J. M. Montias, *Central Planning in Poland.*" *Economic Journal*, 73 (March): 124–26.
[189] "Meaning of Alignment." *Seminar*, 45 (May): 27–29.
[190] "Review of J. Maynard, *Economic Development and the Price Level.*" *Economic Journal*, 73 (June): 299–300.
[191] "The Chinese View." *Seminar*, 50 (October): 44–46.
[192] "Learning by Doing: A Further Note." *Review of Economic Studies*, 30 (October): 167–68.
[193] "Findlay's Robinsonian Model of Accumulation."[43] *Economica, New Series*, 30 (November): 408–11.
[194] "Are We Exerting Ourselves Enough? An Interview." *Yojana*, 7, 1: 7–8.
[195] "Foreword to the Second Edition." *Essays in the Theory of Economic Growth*, 2d ed. London: Macmillan (1st ed., 1962).

1964

[196 et al.] *Notes from China*. Oxford: Blackwell.

[196] "Foreword"
[200] "The Chinese Point of View" (1964)

[201] "The People's Communes" (1964)

[197] "Communes in China." *Listener*, 55 (January 30): 177–79.

[198] "Notes from China."[44] *Economic Weekly*, 16 (February): 195–203. [RFC]

[199] "Review of L. Zeitlin, *Life's Value in Cash.*" *Economic Journal*, 74 (March): 219–20.

[200] "The Chinese Point of View." *International Affairs*, 40 (April): 232–44. [RFC; NFC]

[201] "A British Economist on a Chinese Commune."[45] *Eastern Horizon*, 3 (May): 6–11. [RFC; NFC]

[202] "Factor Prices Not Equalized." *Quarterly Journal of Economics*, 78 (May): 202–7. [CEP 3]

[203] "Statement Submitted to Committee on Resale Price Maintenance" (with R. Cohen, R. Kahn, and W. B. Reddaway). *Oxford Bulletin of Economics and Statistics*, 26 (May): 113–21.

[204] "Solow on the Rate of Return." *Economic Journal*, 74 (June): 410–17. [CEP 3]

[205] "Review of H. G. Shaffery (ed.), *The Soviet Economy. A Collection of Western and Soviet Views.*" *Cambridge Review*, 85 (June 6): 491–93.

[206] "China 1963: The Communes." *Political Quarterly*, 35 (July): 285–97. [CEP 3]

[207] "The Final End of *Laissez-faire.*" *New Left Review*, 4 (August): 3–9. [CEP 3]

[208] "Review of S. H. Chou, *The Chinese Inflation.*" *Economic Journal*, 74 (September): 680–81.

[209] "Pre-Keynesian Theory after Keynes." *Australian Economic Papers*, 3 (December): 25–35. [CEP 3; CME]

[210] "India Wake-up." *Economic Weekly*, 16 (December): 1917–20.

[211] "Review of C. Cheng, *Communist China Economy 1949–1962.*" *International Affairs*, 40 (July): 560.

1965

[212–18, et al.] *Collected Economic Papers*, vol. 3. Oxford: Blackwell (2d ed., 1975).

[212] "Introduction"
[159] "Teaching Economics" (1960)
[164] "Prelude to a Critique of Economic Theory"[46] (1961) [FCM]
[165] "Equilibrium Growth Models"(1961)
[202] "Factor Prices Not Equalized" (1964)
[204] "Solow on the Rate of Return" (1964)
[193] "Robinson on Findlay on Robinson"[47] (1963)
[213] "Harrod's Knife-edge"
[209] "Pre-Keynesian Theory after Keynes" (1964) [CME]
[214] "Consumer's Sovereignty in a Planned Economy" (1965)
[218] "Wiles on the Political Economy of Communism"[48]
[215] "Kalecki and Keynes"[49] [CME]
[180] "The General Theory after Twenty-five Years"[50] (1962)
[166] "Beyond Full Employment" (1961)
[179] "Latter-Day Capitalism" (1962) [CME]
[162] "General Liquidity" (1960)
[168] "Own Rates of Interest" (1961)
[207] "The Final End of *Laissez-faire*" (1964)

[182] "Marxism: Religion and Science" (1962) [FCM]
[132] "What Remains of Marxism?" (1957)
[169] "Has Capitalism Changed?" (1961) [CME]
[216] "A Reconsideration of the Theory of Value"[51] (1965)
[131] "India, 1955: Unemployment and Planning" (1956)
[206] "China, 1963: The Communes" (1964)
[217] "Korea, 1964: Economic Miracle" (1965)

[214] "Consumer's Sovereignty in a Planned Economy." In *On Political Economy and Econometrics.* Oxford: Pergamon Press. [CEP 3]
[216] "Piero Sraffa and the Rate of Exploitation."[52] *New Left Review*, 5 (January): 28–34. [CEP 3]
[217] "Korea 1964: Economic Miracle." *Monthly Review*, 16 (January): 541–49. [CEP 3]
[219] "What's New in China." *Eastern Horizon*, 4 (January): 11–15. [RFC]
[220] "Cuba 1965." *Economic Weekly*, 17 (August 28): 1341–45.
[221] "Review of T. C. Liu and K. Hey, *The Economy of the Chinese Mainland, National Income and Economic Development 1933–59.*" *Economic Journal*, 75 (September): 604.
[222] "Review of C. Bettelheim, J. Charrier, and H. Marchisio, *Construction du Socialism in Chine.*" *Co-existence*, 3, 1: 105–7.

1966

[215] "Kalecki and Keynes."[53] In *Problems of Economic Dynamics and Planning. Essays in Honor of M. Kalecki.* Oxford: Pergamon Press. [CEP 3; CME]
[218] "Review of P. J. D. Wiles, *Political Economy of Communism.*"[54] *Indian Economic Review*, 1 (April): 145–52. [CEP 3]
[223] *Economics: An Awkward Corner.* London: Allen and Unwin (2d ed., 1968).
[224] "Introduction."[55] In M. Kalecki, *Studies in the Theory of Business Cycles 1933–39.* Oxford: Blackwell.
[225] *The New Mercantilism.* Cambridge: Cambridge University Press. [CEP 4; CME]
[226] "Review of K. R. Walker, *Planning in Chinese Agriculture: Socialization and the Private Sector 1956–1962.*" *International Affairs*, 42 (January): 159–60.
[227] "The Communes and the Great Leap Forward." *New Left Review*, 6 (May–June): 69–72.
[228] "Comment on D. M. Bensusan Butt, *Pre-Keynesian Theory: A Modest Defence.*" *Australian Economic Papers*, 5 (June): 45–46.
[229] "Review of A. K. DasGupta, *Planning and Economic Growth.*" *Economic Journal*, 76 (June): 397–98.
[230] "Review of C. Chi-Yi, *La Réforme Agraire en Chine Populaire* and of Y. L. Wu, *The Steel Industry in Communist China.*" *International Affairs*, 42 (July): 546–48.
[231] "Comment on Samuelson and Modigliani." *Review of Economic Studies*, 33 (October): 307–8.

1967

[232] "Socialist Affluence." In C. H. Feinstein (ed.), *Socialism, Capitalism and Economic Growth.* Cambridge: Cambridge University Press. [CEP 4; CME]
[233] "Review of R. Lekachman, *The Age of Keynes.*"[56] *New York Review of Books*, 8 (January 26): 20–22. [CEP 5]

[234] "Review of Yuan-Li Wu, *Economy of Communist China: An Introduction*; D. H. Perkins, *Market Control and Planning in Communist China*; J. L. Buck, O. L. Dawson, and Yuan-Li Wu, *Food and Agriculture in Communist China.*" *International Affairs*, 43 (January): 192–93.

[235] "Contribution to Sanity." *Economic and Political Weekly*, 2 (February 28): 111.

[236] "Growth and the Theory of Distribution." *Annals of Collective Economy*, 38 (March): 3–7. [CEP 5]

[237] "The Soviet Collective Farm as a Producer Cooperative: A Comment." *American Economic Review*, 57 (March): 222–23.

[238] "Review of A. N. Young, *China's Wartime Finance and Inflation, 1937–45* and Chi-Ming-Hou, *Foreign Investment and Economic Development in China 1840–1937.*" *International Affairs*, 43 (April): 404–6.

[239] "Marginal Productivity." *Indian Economic Review*, 2 (April): 78–84. [CEP 4]

[240] "Review of H. Portisch, *Eyewitness in China.*" *International Affairs*, 43 (July): 611–12.

[241] "Review of R. Pellisier, *The Awakening of China, 1793–1949.*" *International Affairs*, 43 (October): 797.

[242] "The Badly Behaved Production Function" (with K. A. Naqvi). *Quarterly Journal of Economics*, 81 (November): 579–91. [CEP 4]

[243] "The Economic Reforms." *Monthly Review*, 19 (November): 45–50.

[244] "Review of G. Grossmann, *Economic Systems.*" *Economic Journal*, 67 (December): 871–73.

[245] "Review of M. Wolfson, *Reappraisal of Marxian Economics.*" *Political Science Quarterly*, 82: 627–28.

[246] "China and China Specialists." *Science and Society*, 31 (Summer): 338–41.

1968

[247] "Review of G. Myrdal, *Report from a Chinese Village.*" *International Affairs*, 44 (January): 152–53.

[248] "Review of W. Leontief, *Essays in Economics: Theories and Theorising.*" *Econometrica*, 36 (April): 431–32.

[249] "The Cultural Revolution in China." *International Affairs*, 44 (April): 214–27.

[250] "Review of F. M. Gottheil, *Marx Economic Predictions* and Review of W. Leontief, *Input-Output Economics.*"[57] *Indian Economic Review*, 3 (April): 57–64. [CEP 4]

[251] "Reply to D. Willet, 'A Defence of Adam Smith's Deer and Beaver Model.' " *Journal of Economic Studies*, 3 (July): 33.

[252] "Review of G. Myrdal, *Asian Drama. An Enquiry into the Poverty of Nations.*"[58] *Cambridge Quarterly*, 3 (Autumn): 381–89. [CEP 4]

[253] "Value and Price." *Soviet Studies Information*, 7 (December): 632–72. [CEP 4]

1969

[254] *The Cultural Revolution in China.* Harmondsworth: Penguin (2d ed., 1970).

[255] "A Further Note on Kaldor-Mirrlees's Growth Model Concerning the Degree of Monopoly." *Review of Economic Studies*, 36 (April): 260–62.

[256] "A Model for Accumulation Proposed by J. E. Stiglitz." *Economic Journal*, 79 (June): 412–13.

[257] "The Theory of Value Reconsidered." *Australian Economic Papers*, 8 (June): 13–19. [CEP 4; CME]

[258] "Macroeconomics of Unbalanced Growth: A Belated Comment." *American Economic Review*, 59 (September): 632.
[259] "Review of A. Leijonhufvud, *On Keynesian Economics and the Economics of Keynes.*" *Economic Journal*, 79 (September): 581–83.

1970

[260] *Freedom and Necessity*. London: Allen and Unwin.
[261] "Chinese Economic Policy." *Studium Generale*, 23, 12: 1267–74.
[262] "Economics Today." *Basler Wirtschaftswissenschaftliche Vortrage*, 2, Zurich Polygraphischer Verlag. [CEP 4]
[263] "Foreword." In E. L. Weelwright and B. McFarlane, *The Chinese Road to Socialism*. New York: Monthly Review Press.
[264] "Capital Theory Up-to-Date." *Canadian Journal of Economics, New Series*, 3 (May): 309–17. [CEP 4; CME]
[265] "Review of R. C. Ferguson, *The Neoclassical Theory of Production and Distribution.*" *Economic Journal*, 80 (June): 336–39.
[266] "Harrod after Twenty-one Years." *Economic Journal*, 80 (September): 731–37. [CEP 4]
[267] "Harrod after Twenty-one Years: A Reply." *Economic Journal*, 80 (September): 741.
[268] "Quantity Theories Old and New." *Journal of Money, Credit and Banking*, 2 (November): 504–13.
[269] "Review of C. B. Turner, *Analysis of Soviet Views on John Maynard Keynes.*" *Soviet Studies*, 22 (July): 134–35.

1971

[270] *Economic Heresies*. London: Basic Books.
[271] "The Relevance of Economic Theory." *Monthly Review*, 23 (January): 29–37. [CEP 4]
[272] "Continuity and the 'Rate of Return.' " *Economic Journal*, 81 (March): 120–22. [CEP 4]
[273] "The Existence of Aggregrate Production Functions: Comment." *Econometrica*, 39 (March): 405.
[274] "Capital Theory Up-to-Date: Reply to Ferguson." *Canadian Journal of Economics, New Series*, 4 (May): 254–56. [CEP 4]
[275] "Comment on Going to Europe Again. A Symposium." *Encounter*, 36 (June): 5–6.
[276] "The Measure of Capital: The End of Controversy." *Economic Journal*, 81 (September): 597–602. [CEP 4]
[277] "Michal Kalecki."[59] *Cambridge Review*, 93 (October 22): 1–4. [CEP 4]
[278] "Review of R. Solow, *Growth Theory: An Exposition.*"[60] *Kyklos*, 24: 189–92. [CEP 4]

1972

[279] "Review of T. K. Rymes, *On Concepts of Capital and Technical Change.*" *Kyklos*, 25: 427–29.
[280] "The Second Crisis of Economic Theory." *American Economic Review*, 62 (May): 1–9. [CEP 4; CME]

1973

[281–84, et al.] *Collected Economic Papers*, vol. 4. Oxford: Blackwell.

[281] "Foreword"
[225] "The New Mercantilism" (1966) [CME]
[282] "The Need for a Reconsideration of the Theory of International Trade" (1973)
[250] "Economics versus Political Economy"[61] (1968)
[232] "Socialist Affluence" (1967) [CME]
[253] "Value and Price" (1968)
[257] "The Theory of Value Reconsidered" (1969) [CME]
[266] "Harrod after Twenty-one Years" (1970)
[242] "The Badly Behaved Production Function" (1967)
[278] "Michal Kalecki"[62] (1971)
[280] "The Second Crisis of Economic Theory" (1972) [CME]
[252] "The Poverty of Nations"[63] (1968)
[271] "The Relevance of Economic Theory" (1971)
[262] "Economics Today" (1970)
[239] "Marginal Productivity" (1967)
[278] "Solow Once More"[64] (1971)
[264] "Capital Theory Up-to-Date" (1970) [CME] ("Capital Theory Up-to-Date: A Comment," by C. E. Ferguson)
[274] "A Reply" (1971)
[272] "Continuity and the 'Rate of Return' " (1971)
[276] "The Measure of Capital: The End of the Controversy" (1971)
[283] "Essays 1935: Introduction"
[33] "Full Employment" (1937) [ETG]
[24] "Disguised Unemployment" (1936) [ETG]
[39] "The Foreign Exchanges" (1937) [ETG]
[40] "Beggar-My-Neighbour Remedies for Unemployment" (1937) [CME; ETE]
[42] "An Economist's Sermon" (1937)
[284] "Essays 1953: Introduction"
[113] "Would You Believe It?" (1953) [RRM]
[114] "A Lecture Delivered at Oxford by a Cambridge Economist" (1953) [CME; RRM]
[115] "An Open Letter from a Keynesian to a Marxist" (1953) [FCM; RRM]

[282] "The Need for a Reconsideration of the Theory of International Trade." In M. B. Connolly and A. K. Swoboda (eds.), *International Trade and Money*. London: Allen and Unwin. [CEP 4; CME]

[285] *Introduction to Modern Economics* (with J. Eatwell). Maidenhead: McGraw-Hill (2d ed., 1974).

[286] *Economic Management in China 1972*. London: Anglo-Chinese Educational Institute (2d ed., 1975; 3d ed., 1976).

[286a] "Planning and Management in China Today."[65] *Cambridge Review*, 94 (March 2): 106–20.

[287] "What Has Become of the Keynesian Revolution." In J. Robinson (ed.), *After Keynes*. Oxford: Blackwell. [CEP 5]

[288] "Foreword." In J. Kregel, *An Introduction to Post-Keynesian Economics*. London: Macmillan.

[289] "Ideology and Analysis." A Contribution to the *Festschrift for Eduard Marz*. A. G. Wien: Europa Verlags. [CEP 5]

[290] "Chinese Agricultural Communes." In C. K. Wilber (ed.), *The Political Economy of Development*. New York: Random House.
[291] "Review of T. Brus, *The Market in a Socialist Economy*." *Economic Journal*, 83 (March): 558–60.
[292] "Review of A. Emmanuel, *Unequal Exchange* and of R.G. Wilkinson, *Poverty and Progress*."[66] *Journal of Contemporary Asia*, 3, 4: 457–61. [CEP 5]
[293] "Review of G. Myrdal, *Against the Stream*." *New York Times*, September 23, p. 31. [CEP 5; FCM]
[294] "Samuelson and Marx and Their Latest Critics." *Journal of Economic Literature*, 11 (December): 1367.
[295] "Review of L. S. Reynolds, *World Economics*." *Political Science Quarterly*, 88: 114–15.

1974

[287] "What Has Become of the Keynesian Revolution." *Challenge*, 16 (January): 6–11. [CEP 5]
[296] "History versus Equilibrium." London: Thames Polytechnic. [CEP 5; CME]
[296] "History versus Equilibrium." *Indian Economic Journal*, 21 (March): 202–13. [CEP 5; CME]
[297] *Reflections on the Theory of International Trade*. Manchester: Manchester University Press. [CEP 5]
[298] "The Abdication of Neo-classical Economics." In A. Mitra (ed.), *Economic Theory and Planning: Essays in Honor of A. K. DasGupta*. New Delhi: Oxford Economic Press. [CEP 5]
[299] "Inflation West and East." *Frontier*, October 19. [CEP 5]

1975

[300] "Value before Capitalism." *Kyklos*, 28, 1: 143–48. [CEP 5]
[301] "The Unimportance of Reswitching." *Quarterly Journal of Economics*, 89 (February): 32–39. [CEP 5]
[302] "The Unimportance of Reswitching: A Reply." *Quarterly Journal of Economics*, 89 (February): 53–55. [CEP 5]
[303] "Review of L. L. Pasinetti, *Growth and Income Distribution: Essays in Economic Theory*." *Economic Journal*, 85 (June): 397–99.
[304] "National Minorities in Yunnang." *Eastern Horizon*, 14, 4: 32–43. [RFC]
[305] "Review of L. R. Marchant, *The Phoenix Seat: An Introductory Study of Maoism and the Chinese Quest for a Paradise on Earth*." *History*, 60 (June): 272–73.
[306] "Review of D. McLelland, *Karl Marx: His Life and Thought* and of J. Maguire, *Marx's Paris Writings Analysis*." *Journal of Modern History*, 47, 3: 568–70.
[307] "Introduction 1974: Reflections and Reminiscences."[67] In *Collected Economic Papers*, vol. 2, 2d ed. Oxford: Blackwell (1st ed., 1960). [FCM]
[308] "Introduction 1974: Comments and Explanations."[68] In *Collected Economic Papers*, vol. 3, 2d ed. Oxford: Blackwell (1st ed., 1965). [FCM]

1976

[309] "Introduction." In M. Kalecki, *Essays on Developing Economies*. Atlantic Highland, NJ: Harvester Press.
[310] "Introduzione."[69] In R. F. Kahn, *L'Occupazione e la Crescita*. Torino: Einaudi.

[311] "Planning Models: Two Views. Review of A. Rudra, *Indian Plan Models.*" *Economic and Political Weekly*, 11 (February 28): 361–63.
[312] "Michal Kalecki: A Neglected Prophet." *New York Review of Books*, 23 (March 4): 28–30.
[313] "The Age of Growth." *Challenge*, 19 (May–June): 4–9. [CEP 5; FCM]
[314] "Review of J. Collier and E. Collier, *China's Socialist Revolution.*" *Monthly Review*, 28 (October): 50–51.
[315] "Review of I. G. Shrji, *Class Struggle in Tanzania.*" *Journal of Contemporary Asia*, 6: 344–45.
[316] "Review of J. K. Fairbank, E. O. Reischauer, and A. M. Craig, *East Asia: Tradition and Transformation.*" *Journal of the Royal Asiatic Society*, 102, 1:91–92.

1977

[317–21, et al.] *Reports from China: 1953–1976*. London: Anglo-Chinese Educational Institute.

[317] "Foreword" (1976)
[118] "Letters from a Visitor to China" (1953)
[318] "Reminiscences"[70]
[319] "Economic Recovery"[71] (1964)
[200] "The Chinese Point of View" (1965)
[219] "What's New in China" (1965)
[254] "The Cultural Revolution"[72] (1969)
[320] "Reports and Conversations"
[321] "Retrospect"
[304] "National Minorities in Yunnang" (1975)

[322] "Employment and the Choice of Technique." In K. S. Krishnaswamy, A. Mitra, I. G. Patel, and K. N. Srinivas (eds.), *Society and Change*. Oxford: Oxford University Press. [CEP 5]
[323] "The Labour Theory of Value as an Analytical System." A Contribution to the Conference of the Economic Section of the Academy of Science of Montenegro. [CEP 5]
[324] "Guidelines of Orthodox Economics." *Journal of Contemporary Asia*, 7, 6: 1–22. [CEP 5]
[325] "Michal Kalecki on the Economics of Capitalism."[73] *Oxford Bulletin of Economics and Statistics*, 39 (February): 7–17. [CEP 5]
[326] "What Has Become of Employment Policy?" (with F. Wilkinson). *Cambridge Journal of Economics*, 1 (March): 5–14. [CEP 5; CME]
[327] "Qu'est-ce que le Capital?"[74] *Revue d'Economie Politique*, 87 (March): 165–79. (In French.) [CEP 5; CME]
[328] "Education." *Social Scientist*, 5 (June): 131–37.
[329] "Economics in Dismay." *New York Times*, August 12, p. 21.
[330] "Review of E. Brun and J. Hersch, *Socialist Korea. A Case Study in the Strategy of Economic Development.*" *Monthly Review*, 29 (October): 60–62.
[331] "Review of R. L. Meek, *Studies in the Theory of Value* (2d ed.)."[75] *Monthly Review*, 29 (December): 50–59. [CEP 5; FCM]
[332] "What Are the Questions?" *Journal of Economic Literature*, 15 (December): 1318–39. [CEP 5; FCM]
[333] "M. Kalecki." *Challenge*, 20 (November-December): 67–69.

1978

[334–35, et al.] *Contributions to Modern Economics.*[76] Oxford: Blackwell.

[334] "Preface"
[335] "Reminiscences"
[280] "The Second Crisis of Economic Theory"(1972) [CEP 4]
[12] "The Theory of Money and the Analysis of Output" (1933) [CEP 1]
[82] "Obstacles to Full Employment" (1946) [CEP 1]
[49] "The Concept of Hoarding" (1938) [CEP 1]
[102] "The Rate of Interest"[77] (1951) [CEP 2; GGT; RIE]
[215] "Kalecki and Keynes"[78] (1966) [CEP 3]
[121] "Marx, Marshall and Keynes" (1955) [CEP 2]
[117] "The Production Function and the Theory of Capital"[79] (1953) [CEP 2]
[209] "Pre-Keynesian Theory after Keynes" (1964) [CEP 3]
[264] "Capital Theory Up-to-Date" (1970) [CEP 4]
[327] "The Meaning of Capital"[80] (1977) [CEP 5]
[296] "History versus Equilibrium" (1974) [CEP 5]
[114] "A Lecture Delivered at Oxford by a Cambridge Economist" (1953) [CEP 4; RRM]
[143] "The Philosophy of Prices"[81] (1960) [CEP 2]
[116] "*Imperfect Competition* Revisited" (1953) [CEP 2]
[257] "The Theory of Value Reconsidered" (1969) [CEP 4]
[40] "Beggar-My-Neighbour Remedies for Unemployment" [CEP 4; ETE]
[225] "The New Mercantilism" (1966) [CEP 4]
[282] "The Need for a Reconsideration of the Theory of International Trade" (1973) [CEP 4]
[169] "Has Capitalism Changed?" (1961) [CEP 3]
[179] "Latter-Day Capitalism" (1962) [CEP 3]
[232] "Socialist Affluence" (1967) [CEP 4]
[326] "What Has Become of Employment Policy?" (1977) [CEP 5]
[100] "Beauty and the Beast" (1951) [CEP 1]

[336] "The Organic Composition of Capital." *Kyklos*, 31, 1: 5–20. [CEP 5; FCM]
[337] "Morality and Economics." *Challenge*, 22 (March–April): 62–64. [CEP 5]
[338] "Keynes and Ricardo." *Journal of Post-Keynesian Economics*, 1 (Fall): 12–18. [CEP 5; FCM]
[339] "Review of J. Steedman, *Marx after Sraffa*."[82] *Journal of Contemporary Asia*, 8, 3: 381–84. [CEP 5]
[340] "Understanding the Economic Crises: Review of R. L. Heilbronner, *Beyond Boom and Crash*." *New York Review of Books*, 25 (December): 33–34.
[341] "The Organic Composition of Capital: A Reply." *Kyklos*, 31, 4: 692.

1979

[342–46, et al.] *Collected Economic Papers*, vol. 5. Oxford: Blackwell.

[342] "Preface"
[332] "What Are the Questions?" (1977) [FCM]
[298] "The Abdication of Neo-classical Economics" (1974)

[337] ''Morality and Economics'' (1978)
[296] ''History versus Equilibrium'' (1974) [CME]
[327] ''The Meaning of Capital''[83] (1977) [CME]
[236] ''Growth and the Theory of Distribution'' (1967)
[301] ''The Unimportance of Reswitching'' (1975)
[302] ''The Unimportance of Reswitching. A Reply'' (1975)
[343] ''The Disintegration of Economics'' [FCM]
[300] ''Value before Capitalism'' (1975)
[293] ''Gunnar Myrdal''[84] (1973) [FCM]
[344] ''Thinking about Thinking'' [FCM]
[313] ''The Age of Growth'' (1976) [FCM]
[297] ''Reflections on the Theory of International Trade'' (1974)
[345] ''Markets''[85] (1979)
[287] ''What Has Become of the Keynesian Revolution?'' (1973)
[233] ''Smoothing out Keynes''[86] (1967)
[325] ''Michal Kalecki''[87] (1977)
[326] ''What Has Become of Employment Policy?'' (1977) [CME]
[338] ''Keynes and Ricardo'' (1978) [FCM]
[299] ''Inflation West and East'' (1974)
[325] ''The Guidelines of Orthodox Economics'' (1977)
[322] ''Employment and the Choice of Technique'' (1977)
[292] ''Formalistic Marxism and Ecology without Classes''[88] (1973)
[346] ''Who Is a Marxist?''
[289] ''Ideology and Analysis'' (1973)
[336] ''The Organic Composition of Capital'' (1978) [FCM]
[339] ''Formalism versus Dogma''[89] (1978)
[331] ''The Labour Theory of Value''[90] (1977) [FCM]
[323] ''The Labour Theory of Value as an Analytical System'' (1977)

[345] ''Markets.''[91] In *Encyclopedia Britannica*, vol. 11, 15th ed., pp. 511–15. Chicago: Benton Publisher. [CEP 5]

[347] *Aspects of Development and Underdevelopment*. Cambridge: Cambridge University Press.

[348, et al.] *Generalization of the General Theory and Other Essays*.[92] London: Macmillan.

[348] ''Introduction''
[105] ''The Generalization of the General Theory'' [RIE]
[104] ''Notes on the Economics of Technical Progress'' [RIE]
[106] ''Acknowledgements and Disclaimers''[93] [CEP 2; RIE]
[102] ''The Rate of Interest''[94] [CEP 2; CME; RIE]

[349] ''Foreword.'' In K. Kuhne, *Economics and Marxism*, 2 vols. London: Macmillan.

[350] ''Résumé des Débats.'' In J. Robinson and P. K. M. Tharaka (eds.), *The International Division of Labour and Multinational Companies*. Farnborough, U.K.: European Centre for Study and Information on Multinational Corporations.

[351] ''Foreword.'' In A. S. Eichner (ed.), *Guide to Post-Keynesian Economics*. London: Macmillan.

[352] ''Commento all'Articolo di Garegnani'' (1976).[95] In P. A. Garegnani, *Valore e Domanda Effettiva*. Torino: Einaudi (Appendix A).

[353] ''Un Ulteriore Commento.''[96] In P. A. Garegnani, *Valore e Domanda Effettiva*. Torino: Einaudi (Appendix C).

[354] ''Keynes a-t-il échoué?'' *Annals of Collective Economy*, 50 (March): 27–29.
[355] ''Comment on China since Mao.'' *Monthly Review*, 31 (January): 48–56.
[356] ''Review of D. Patinkin and J. C. Leith, *Keynes, Cambridge and the General Theory*.'' *Canadian Journal of Economics, New Series*, 12 (February): 118–20.
[357] ''Garegnani on Effective Demand.'' *Cambridge Journal of Economics*, 3 (June): 179–80.
[358] ''Misunderstandings in the Theory of Production.'' *Greek Economic Review*, 1 (August): 1–7. [FCM]
[359] ''Review of Mao Tse Tung, *A Critique of Soviet Economics*.'' *Monthly Review*, 30: 52–53.
[360] ''Keynes Today'' (with F. Cripps). *Journal of Post-Keynesian Economics*, 2 (Fall): 139–44.
[361] ''Surplus Value and Profits.'' *Development and Change*, 10 (October): 693–95.
[362] ''Employment and Inflation.''[97] *Quarterly Review of Economics and Business*, 19 (Autumn): 7–16. [FCM]
[362] ''Solving the Stagflation Puzzle.''[98] *Challenge*, 22 (November–December): 40–46. [FCM]

1980

[363–68, et al.] *Further Contributions to Modern Economics*. Oxford: Blackwell.

[363] ''Introduction''
[332] ''What Are the Questions?'' (1977) [CEP 5]
[313] ''The Age of Growth'' (1976) [CEP 5]
[362] ''Stagflation''[99] (1979)
[344] ''Thinking about Thinking'' (1979) [CEP 5]
[364] ''Accumulation and Exploitation: An Analysis in the Tradition of Marx, Sraffa and Kalecki'' (with Amit Badhuri)[100] (1980)
[338] ''Keynes and Ricardo'' (1978) [CEP 5]
[365] ''Time in Economic Theory'' (1980)
[343] ''The Disintegration of Economics''(1979) [CEP 5]
[307] ''Survey: 1950s'' (1975)[101] [CEP 2, 2nd ed.]
[308] ''Survey: 1960s'' (1975)[102] [CEP 3, 2nd ed.]
[366] ''Debate: 1970s''
[367] ''Retrospect: 1980''
[358] ''Misunderstandings in the Theory of Production'' (1979)
[74] ''Joseph Schumpeter: *Capitalism, Socialism and Democracy* (1943) [CEP 1]
[164] ''Piero Sraffa: *Production of Commodities by Means of Commodities*''[103] (1961) [CEP 3]
[293] ''Gunnar Myrdal: *Against the Stream*''[104] (1973) [CEP 5]
[182] ''Marxism: Religion and Science'' (1962) [CEP 3]
[115] ''An Open Letter from a Keynesian to a Marxist'' (1953) [CEP 4; RRM]
[336] ''The Organic Composition of Capital'' (1978) [CEP 3]
[331] ''The Labour Theory of Value''[105] (1977) [CEP 5]
[368] ''Marxism and Modern Economics''

[364] ''Accumulation and Exploitation: An Analysis in the Tradition of Marx, Sraffa and Kalecki'' (with Amit Badhuri).[106] *Cambridge Journal of Economics*, 4 (June): 103–15. [FCM]
[365] ''Time in Economic Theory.'' *Kyklos*, 33, 2: 219–29. [FCM]

[369] "Review of *The Collected Writings of J. M. Keynes, vol. XXIX, The General Theory and After.*" *Economic Journal*, 90 (June): 391–93.
[370] "Review of H. Chenery, *Structural Change and Development Policy.*" *Journal of Developing Asia*, 15: 131–32.
[371] "Review of J. F. Becker, *Marxian Political Economy. An Outline.*" *American Journal of Sociology*, 85 (May): 1474–76.

1982

[372] "The Arms Race." In S. M. McMurrin (ed.), *The Tanner Lectures on Human Values.* Salt Lake City: University of Utah Press.
[373] "The Current State of Economics." *Contributions to Political Economy*, 1 (March): 47–49.
[374] "Shedding Darkness: A Note. Review of A. Leijonhufvud, *Information and Coordination.*" *Cambridge Journal of Economics*, 6 (September): 295–96.

1983

[375] "Garegnani on Effective Demand." In J. Eatwell and M. Milgate (eds.), *Keynes's Economics and the Theory of Value and Distribution.* New York: Oxford University Press.
[376] "Economics of Destruction." *Monthly Review*, 35 (October): 15–17.
[377] "Logica e Ideologica" (with Frank Wilkinson).[107] In F. Vicarelli (ed.), *Rilevanza di Keynes.* Laterza: Bari.

1985

[377] "Ideology and Logic" (with Frank Wilkinson).[108] In F. Vicarelli (ed.), *Keynes's Relevance Today.* Philadelphia: University of Pennsylvania Press and London: Macmillan.
[378] "Spring Cleaning."[109] In G. R. Feiwel, *Issues in Contemporary Microeconomics and Welfare.* London, Macmillan.

Notes

1. Reprinted in CEP 1 as "An Inherent Defect in *Laissez-faire.*"
2. In ETE, section five is omitted.
3. Part of this article is in "Some Reflections on Marxist Economics," in ETE (1937).
4. See note 2.
5. Part 1 in the "Review of J. Strachey . . ." (1936).
6. Reprinted in CEP 1 as "The Economics of Hyper-inflation."
7. Part 1 and Part 2 also in "Marx e Keynes" (1948) [CEP 1].
8. Reprinted in CEP 1 as "The United States in the World Economy."
9. Part 1 and 2 also in "Marx on Unemployment" (1941)
10. Reprinted in CEP 1 as "The Theory of Planning."
11. Previously published as "A Fundamental Objection to *Laissez-faire*" (1935).
12. Previously published as "Review of C. Bresciani Turroni . . ." (1938).
13. See note 9.

14. Previously published as "Review of E. Böhm-Bawerk . . ." (1950).
15. Previously published as "Review of M. Dobb, *Soviet Economic Development* . . ." (1949).
16. Previously published as "Review of H. B. Harry (ed.), *The United States* . . ." (1944).
17. Last section omitted in CEP 2 and CME.
18. Reprinted with a new "Introduction" and the order of essays reverted as GGT (1979).
19. See note 17.
20. Parts 1 and 2 only are reprinted in CEP 2 as "Notes on Marx and Marshall."
21. Reprinted in CEP 2 as "A Note on Bank Rate."
22. Reduced version in CEP 2 and CME.
23. The original publication could not be traced.
24. English version appears in CEP 2 as "The Theory of Distribution."
25. French version of "Full Employment and Inflation" (CEP 2).
26. An amended version of this article is published in CEP 2 and CME.
27. Italian version of "*Imperfect Competition* Today" (CEP 2).
28. Spanish version of "Population and Development" (CEP 2 and *Pakistan Economic Journal* [1960]).
29. Previously published as "Acknowledgements and Disclaimers." Only Parts 1 and 2 are reprinted in CEP 2.
30. See note 26.
31. English version of "Populacion y Desarollo" (1958).
32. Excised version of the article published in *Review of Economic Studies.*
33. English version of "La Théorie de la Répartition" (1957).
34. English version of "Il Mito della Concorrenza" (1958).
35. See note 17.
36. Reprinted in CEP 2 as "Monetary Policy Again. Comments."
37. English version of "Plein Emploi et Inflation" (1958).
38. See note 31.
39. Reprinted in FCM as Piero Sraffa, *Production of Commodities by Means of Commodities.*
40. Shorter version of the article published in *Review of Economic Studies* (1962).
41. Reprinted in ETG as a shorter version.
42. Reprinted in CEP 3 as "The General Theory after Twenty-five Years."
43. Reprinted in CEP 3 as "Robinson on Findlay on Robinson."
44. Reprinted partly in RFC as "Economic Recovery."
45. Reprinted partly in RFC as "Economic Recovery."
46. See note 39.
47. Previously published as "Findlay's Robinsonian Model of Accumulation."
48. In CEP 3, the reference to the original article is given as *Indian Economic Review* 1965 instead of *Indian Economic Review* 1966.
49. In CEP 3, the reference to the original text is given as 1965 instead of 1966. There are two editions of the volume: *Problems of Economic Dynamics and Planning. Essays in Honor of M. Kalecki.* In the first edition (Polish Scientific Publisher, Warsawa, 1964) Joan Robinson's contribution is not included.
50. Previously published as "Review of H. G. Johnson . . ." (1962).
51. Previously published as "Piero Sraffa and the Rate of Exploitation" (1965).
52. Reprinted in CEP 3 as "A Reconsideration of the Theory of Value."
53. See note 49.
54. See note 48.

55. First two pages same as first two pages of "Kalecki and Keynes" (1966).
56. Reprinted in CEP 5 as "Smoothing out Keynes."
57. Reprinted in CEP 4 as "Economics versus Political Economy."
58. Reprinted in CEP 4 as "The Poverty of Nations."
59. Review of M. Kalecki, *Selected Essays in the Dynamics of a Capitalist Economy.*
60. Reprinted in CEP 4 as "Solow Once More."
61. Previously published as "Review of F. M. Gottheil . . ." (1968).
62. See note 60.
63. Previously published as "Review of G. Myrdal . . ." (1968).
64. Previously published as "Review of R. Solow . . ." (1971).
65. Extracted from *Economic Management in China* (1972).
66. Reprinted in CEP 5 as "Formalistic Marxism and Ecology without Classes."
67. An amended version is reprinted in FCM with the title, "Survey 1950s."
68. An amended version is reprinted in FCM with the title, "Survey 1960s."
69. Written for the Italian edition; never published in English.
70. New version of a report written in 1957, which according to Joan Robinson could not be traced.
71. Article taken partly from *Notes from China* (1964) and partly from "A British Economist on a Chinese Commune" (1964).
72. Excerpts from *The Cultural Revolution in China* (1969).
73. Reprinted in CEP 5 as "Michal Kalecki."
74. French version of "The Meaning of Capital" in CEP 5 and CME.
75. Reprinted in CME as "The Labour Theory of Value."
76. There are three reprints of this volume: CME (New York: Academic Press, 1978); *What Are the Questions?* (Armonk, NY: M. E. Sharpe, 1981); and CME (New Dehli: Heritage, 1985).
77. The last section of the 1951 version is omitted in CEP 2 and CME.
78. See note 49.
79. Excised version of the 1953 article.
80. English version of "Qu'est-ce que le Capital?" (1977).
81. See note 26.
82. Reprinted in CEP 5 as "Formalism versus Dogma."
83. See note 75.
84. Previously published as "Review of G. Myrdal . . ." (1973) and reprinted in FCM with the original title.
85. In CEP 5 the reference to the original text is erroneously given as 1974 instead of 1979.
86. Previously published as "Review of R. Lekachman . . ." (1967).
87. Previously published as "Michal Kalecki on the Economics of Capitalism."
88. Previously published as "Review of A. Emmanuel . . ." (1973).
89. Previously published as "Review of J. Steedman . . ." (1978).
90. Previously published as "Review of R. L. Meek . . ." (1977).
91. The version in CEP 5 is an expanded version the article in *Encyclopedia Britannica.*
92. A reprint of RIE (1952) with the order of essays reverted and a new introduction.
93. Only Parts I and II are reprinted in CEP 2 with the title, "Notes on Marx and Marshall."
94. See note 17.
95. Published in English in P. Garegnani, "Some Notes on Capital, Expectations Analysis of Changes" in G. R. Feiwel (ed.), *Joan Robinson and Modern Economic Theory*, London: Macmillan, 1989, pp. 360–61.

96. See note 95.
97. Reprinted in FCM as "Stagflation."
98. Reprinted in FCM as "Stagflation."
99. Previously published as "Employment and Inflation" and "Solving the Stagflation Puzzle" (both 1979).
100. Reprinted in FCM without the mathematical appendix.
101. Previously published as "Introduction 1974: Reflections and Reminiscences."
102. Previously published as "Introduction 1974: Comments and Explanations."
103. Reprinted in CEP 3 as "Prelude to a Critique of Economic Theory."
104. Reprinted in CEP 5 as "Gunnar Myrdal."
105. See note 89.
106. See note 100.
107. Italian version of "Ideology and Logic."
108. Published posthumously.
109. Published posthumously.

JR

INDEX